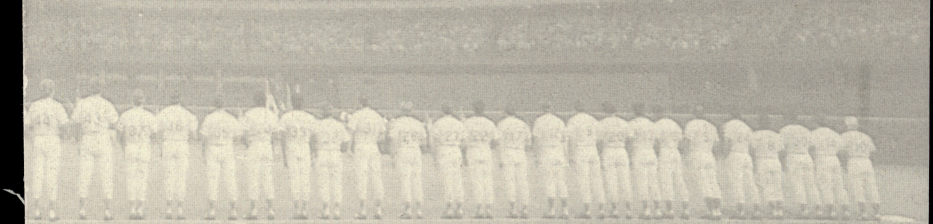

BIG RED dynasty

How Bob Howsam & Sparky Anderson Built the Big Red Machine

How Bob Howsam & Sparky Anderson Built the Big Red Machine

BIG RED dynasty

by
Greg Rhodes and **John Erardi**

Forewords by
Bob Howsam
and
Sparky Anderson

Introduction by
Marty Brennaman

Statistical analysis by **Greg Gajus**

Road West Publishing
Cincinnati, Ohio

Big Red Dynasty
How Bob Howsam & Sparky Anderson Built the Big Red Machine

Copyright © 1997 Gregory L. Rhodes and John G. Erardi

All rights reserved. No part of this book may be reproduced or utilized in any form
or by any means, electronic or mechanical, including photocopying, recording,
or by an information storage and retrieval system, without permission from the publisher.

Major League Baseball trademarks and copyrights used with permission
from Major League Baseball Properties, Inc.

Address all inquiries, including requests for permission to reprint, to:
Road West Publishing
1908 Dexter Avenue
Cincinnati, OH 45206

ISBN: 0-9641402-2-5

Cover design by Lamson Design
Interior design by Northern Connections
Printing by Berman Printing Company
Binding by The C.J. Krehbiel Company

Printed in the United States of America
10 9 8 7 6 5 4 3 2 1

Frontispiece photograph used with permission of *The Cincinnati Enquirer*

*Dedicated to the memory
of Robert I. Westheimer (1916-1997)
He nurtured dynasties.*

GLR

*For Dad, Joanne and Greg who made it to the
1975 World Series in Cincinnati,
and Mom, Nancy and Frank who didn't—
but always had the tea on for Luis.*

JGE

Acknowledgements

Our list is long, but there is no question which two names come first: Bob Howsam and Sparky Anderson. They have been gracious, entertaining and thoughtful with their recollections and observations about the Big Red Machine, and generous with their time. Together, they have blessed baseball with nearly a century of contributions to the sport they love. They have enjoyed such great success that both belong in the Hall of Fame.

Numerous players, club officials, journalists and other baseball men familiar with the Big Red Machine era agreed to interviews over the years, and their memories and unique perspectives provided invaluable contributions. They include (in alphabetical order) Pete Alexis, Marty Appel, Johnny Bench, Chief Bender, Jack Billingham, Pedro Borbon, Rex Bowen, Marty Brennaman, Dave Bristol, Darrel Chaney, Ritter Collett, Dave Concepcion, Pat Darcy, Bill Deane, William DeWitt, Jr., Dan Driessen, Rawly Eastwick, Doug Flynn, George Foster, Cesar Geronimo, George Grande, Ken Griffey, Sr., Don Gullett, David Gunter, Tommy Helms, Bob Hertzel, Reuven Katz, Tommy Lasorda, Jim Maloney, Lee May, Will McEnaney, Joe Morgan, John Murdough, Gary Nolan, Fred Norman, Joe Nuxhall, Tony Pacheco, Pituka Perez, Tony Perez, Bill Plummer, Branch Rickey III, Pete Rose, Roger Ruhl, George Scherger, Dick Wagner, Dick Williams, William J. Williams, Joel Youngblood, Pat Zachry and George Zuraw.

One more man deserves special recognition: the late Ray Shore. Asked to describe how the Big Red Machine came to be, both Bob Howsam and Sparky Anderson said, "Talk to Ray Shore!" Shore served as Howsam's special assignment scout and provided critical information and valued counsel for every trade the Reds made in the late 1960s and 1970s. Ray gave us several hours of interviews, and looked forward to the book. Soon after our last talk, in the summer of 1996, he passed away. As a baseball pioneer—he was the first advance scout—and as influential a scout as the game has ever seen, Shore also deserves induction in the Hall.

The name of Greg Gajus appears on the title page and deservedly so. Gajus researched several questions we raised, and some he initially posed, concerning the Big Red Machine. His findings confirmed and contradicted things we felt we "knew," and we used his data to frame several points in the book. His research on dynasty teams, Dave Concepcion's Hall of Fame candidacy, the starting lineups and batting orders of the Big Red Machine, Anderson's bullpen strategy and the 1977-78 decline of the Reds all contributed to helping us analyze the Big Red Machine era.

The Cincinnati Reds provided support and cooperation, particularly John Allen and Charles Henderson. We would also like to acknowledge Linda Bailey, Chip Baker, Jerry Dowling, Susan DuMond, Barry Federovitch, Harley Frankel, Steve Gietschier, Dennis Gruelle, John Helyar, Bill Hugo, Mike Jesse, John Kiesewetter, Jack Klumpe, Pat Latham, Jan Leach, Rich Levin, Cal Levy, Bob Littlejohn, Roger Love, Bernie Stowe and Gary Waites. Vic Pramaggiore, our Macintosh consultant, earned more than one "save" on this book, as did the ever-supportive gang at Berman Printing (Sue Bass, Jane Cole, Paul Hilvert, Rich Lashbrook, Jenny Meinhardt, Christine Reed and Nancy Roether), and the staff of *The Cincinnati Enquirer* library, including Ray Zwick, Frank Harmon, Chase Clements, Sally Besten, Cheryl Swartz and Juanita Davis, who were prompt and patient with our many requests.

Contents

- **2**   Foreword by Bob Howsam
- **3**   Foreword by Sparky Anderson
- **4**   Introduction by Marty Brennaman
- **6**   1970-1976 / Dynasty
- **16**   Rose, Perez, Bench / The Road to the Reds
- **38**   Howsam / Dynasty Builder
- **62**   Sparky / Who?
- **80**   1970 / First Gear
- **100**   1971 / Big Deal
- **122**   1972 / Near Miss
- **152**   1973-1974 / Dynasty Deferred
- **186**   1975 / Champagne in Boston
- **224**   1976 / Sweep to Greatness
- **260**   1977-78 / End of the Road
- **290**   Appendix: Big Red Machine Scrapbook, 1970–1978
- **292**   References
- **293**   Subject Index
- **294**   About the Authors

Foreword by **Bob Howsam**

I don't know if I can say where the Big Red Machine fits in history. It's not fair to compare teams or players. We know the ballplayer today is faster and stronger, but that doesn't mean he knows the finer points in playing the game of baseball.

But I do know this. We were the best at that period. I was proud that my club won more games in the '70s than any other club, and there were other fine teams—the Orioles, the Dodgers, the Pirates, the A's. I'm just happy you had a ballclub like the Big Red Machine; you can be so proud of it. And that goes for our entire organization. We had some fine baseball men, fellows who knew the game and were a pleasure to work with. Our organization became the best in baseball. We had many clubs send their people in to see how we operated.

One memory I will always have is standing on Fountain Square with 30,000 people cheering you as the World Champs. In 1976, it was the finest hour I ever had, having won seven post-season games in a row, back-to-back championships. I was thrilled by what had happened.

But there are so many other rewards in baseball. It's quite a feeling to take a young man, put him in the minor leagues, and watch him give his all to make it to the big leagues. With those who do, there is a very special sense of achievement. With those who don't, but try so very hard, and better themselves along the way, well, there's a great sense of achievement in that, too.

Maybe I identify with that player who never made it. I always did want to be a ballplayer. Then the service came along. Then I married and had two sons, and I was 26 and knew I couldn't develop into a major league ballplayer. Even as a general manager, the one thing I missed was to be around the batting cage and hit. But as I told my managers, you must have the respect of the players. You may want to be one of the boys, but it is tough to do that. If I have had any success in baseball, it's because I tried to look at it on the basis of sound business.

The other principle I always tried to follow was to put the fans first. Everything we did in Cincinnati was aimed at the fans. I think baseball has meant a lot to this country. We have a great game, but we can never take the fans for granted. Sometimes I would walk through the Riverfront Stadium crowd and see parents with their young children. Whatever problems you were having with the press or the players, you knew it was all worthwhile when you saw the happiness the game brings. Yes, we have a great game, but we can never forget the fans.

Bob Howsam
Glenwood Springs, CO

Foreword by Sparky Anderson

I'm not going to sit here and tell you that the starting eight of the Big Red Machine in 1975-76 is the greatest of all time. But if somebody else has a better one, I want to sit and watch it. If they're better than the starting eight in '76, oh my goodness!

When I'm out speaking, I try to explain to people how good these guys were. In 1976, they played 162 games, then swept the playoffs—that's 165 games—then swept the World Series—that's 169 games. They won 115 games, and the eight guys played together only 53 times!

Somebody asked me in 1975: "Would you take Freddie Lynn in center field over Cesar Geronimo?" I said, "No." Because on our ballclub, Geronimo fit perfectly. He'd go get the ball and he could throw it. We didn't need power from Geronimo.

I have to give credit to Bob Howsam. He fit that team together like a checkerboard. Nowadays, they fit clubs together with "name" players. So-and-so makes $5 million a year. Bob didn't go out and buy that ballclub; he built it. There were others who helped him, and he listened to them. He had great baseball people. But then Bob made the decision. The Morgan-Billingham-Geronimo deal is the one people remember, but Bob got us Denis Menke, George Foster, Tommy Hall, Clay Carroll, Wayne Granger and Bobby Tolan. The list goes on and on.

And it wasn't just the guys Bob acquired, or the superstars that we had. Every one of the guys made it a great experience. Tommy Carroll, Jimmy Stewart, Bob Bailey, Bill Plummer, Pat Corrales, they were all a part of it. I'll never forget Donny Gullett asking me if he could have a day off to go to his wife's graduation. I thought to myself, "Donny's 19, he married a girl a couple of years older, he wants to go to her college graduation." I said, "Sure, what school's she graduating from?" He said, "High school." I thought to myself, "Holy Geez, I managed in the minors for five years and never heard *this*." We worked it out so he could get the time off. My memories of all these guys are so strong.

I was 35 years old when I went into Cincinnati. When I came out nine years later, the guys had made me a star. Over those nine years, they averaged 96 victories a season. I tell people, "Just think what I could've done if I had some players!" Bench, Rose, Morgan, Perez, Concepcion, Foster, Griffey, Geronimo. A better starting eight? I'd have to see it with my own eyes. And if I saw it, I'd just have to say, "Oh my goodness!"

Sparky Anderson
Thousand Oaks, CA

Introduction by Marty Brennaman

When I first arrived in Cincinnati in 1974, I knew the names Rose, Bench, Morgan and Perez, but not Griffey, Concepcion, Geronimo and Foster. But it didn't take me long to find out. The next thing I know, the Reds are roaring from 12½ games back, coming out of nowhere, and almost catching the Dodgers in September.

One July night in 1974, in the first game of a twi-night doubleheader against the Giants at Riverfront Stadium after the All-Star break, the Reds were trailing, 13-9, going into the bottom of the ninth. Johnny Bench beat out an infield hit to cut it to 13-12, and Tony Perez hit a two-run home run to straightaway center field off Randy Moffitt to win it. The fans went nuts.

It was a harbinger. The fans who came to Riverfront Stadium in '75 and '76 came with the expectation that something special was going to happen every night. I've never seen that sense of anticipation, that electricity, on an ongoing basis. You could feel it. People *expected* the Reds to win, even in the late innings when they were behind. They *expected* to be sent home happy. I'm not talking about a run or two; I'm talking about five or six runs back. The attitude was that some way, somehow, somebody was going to erase the deficit and win the game.

When Joe Morgan got on first base with second base open, or on second base with third base open, the buzz would start. When he'd take that lead at first base, with "one foot on the carpet," it forced us in the broadcast media to use that as a descriptive phrase to convey to people what a tremendous lead he had. Nobody else could consistently take the lead he took. For two seasons, he was the best all-around player I have ever seen—and I'm including Ken Griffey, Jr. and Barry Bonds in that.

I'll never forget the night John Candelaria was mowing down the Reds hitters in Game Three of the 1975 playoffs against the Pirates in Three Rivers Stadium. He struck out 14 guys. But here comes Pete Rose in the top of the eighth of a 2-1 game and he hits a two-run bomb off Candelaria to put the Reds up, 3-2. The Pirates scored one run in the ninth to tie it back up, and the Reds scored two in the tenth to win, 5-3.

The Big Red Machine specialized in that kind of late-inning thunder. In Game Three of the 1976 playoffs against the Phillies, the Reds trailed, 6-4, going into the bottom of the ninth at Riverfront. George Foster and Johnny Bench hit back-to-back homers and Ken Griffey legged out an infield hit that scored Davey Concepcion, and the Reds won it, 7-6. Talk about electricity! The fans were unconscious, absolutely out of their minds.

The Big Red Machine was so good, they wouldn't just beat you. They'd spot you two or three runs going into the ninth and *then* beat you. The Reds' speed, power and experience made other teams nervous. But the Reds had class; they never rubbed a victory in anybody's face.

In '75 and '76, I got World Championship rings. I just figured, "This is the way it's supposed to be." I didn't realize how good these guys were. But now I know. It was one of the greatest teams in the history of baseball and arguably the greatest starting eight ever. They had three of the greatest players ever (Bench, Morgan and Rose) who were either in their prime or very close to it, another guy in his prime who should be in the Hall (Perez), one of the greatest shortstops to ever play the game (Concepcion) and the best outfield in baseball at the time (Griffey, Geronimo and Foster). The pitching staff didn't get the credit it deserved; the starting pitching was better than we thought, and I haven't seen a bullpen that could match the Big Red Machine's for interchangeable parts. They had three or four guys who could close, and three or four guys who could set up. Clay Carroll and Pedro Borbon could literally go out there every day.

I also took it for granted that the Reds were supposed to draw 2.5 million or 2.6 million fans every year. But the front office was marketing the heck out of the club. The marketing director, Roger Ruhl, was absolutely immersed in various and sundry ways to get people to come to the ballpark. Other clubs would come in here during the winter months for two or three or four days and would leave with a blueprint for their own franchises. It made me realize there is a certain formula for success in sports. "The fans are always first." That was Bob Howsam's formula and it is just as important today as it was in the 1970s.

Bob was right when he said we would never again see a team like the Big Red Machine. They're baseball's "last great team." Any "great" team that comes along now is going to have to be measured against them.

No matter how long I'm here, no matter what else happens, I will never be associated professionally with anything as great as that club. If my signature phrase is going to be my legacy—if it's what I'm going to be remembered for—then I'm thrilled. Because I owe it all to the Big Red Machine. They are the ones who inspired it. To the fans, to the players, to Bob Howsam and Sparky Anderson, to the entire organization, I say, with deepest appreciation…

And this one belongs to the Reds!

And it always will.

Now, fasten your seat belts for a wonderful ride with the Big Red Machine and the people who made it go.

Marty Brennaman
Cincinnati, OH

The most honored starting eight of all time, the Big Red Machine of the Cincinnati Reds, posed at Riverfront Stadium in 1975. Pitcher Don Gullett (third from left) joined (from left to right) Ken Griffey, Pete Rose, Johnny Bench, George Foster, Joe Morgan, Cesar Geronimo, Dave Concepcion and Tony Perez. The "Great Eight" included four MVPs, five Gold Glove winners, and seven All-Stars.

4 World Series • 2 World Championships • 5 MVP Awards

Chapter 1

1970-76 Dynasty

5 Western Division Crowns • Record 683–443 (.607)

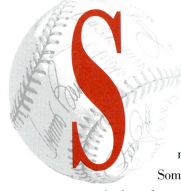

SINCE THE MODERN ERA OF baseball began in 1901, nearly 1,500 National and American League teams have marched to the playing fields to compete for recognition as the best in baseball. Some played on green grass in the shadow of wooden stands, some on plastic turf dwarfed by steel and concrete. Many came in flannels, some in double knits, others in pinstripes. Some brought small mitts and heavy lumber, others sported large gloves and skinny-handled bats.

All carried hopes of greatness, but as the seasons have faded only a handful of those teams have earned history's verdict as being among the truly great.

The Big Red Machine of the Cincinnati Reds earned its place in the pantheon of great teams with its dominating performance from 1970 through 1976. In those seven seasons, the Reds won five division titles, four league pennants and back-to-back World Series. The club averaged 98 wins for a winning percentage of .607. Apart from the Yankee juggernaut that dominated baseball for 44 years from 1920 to 1964, the Reds became one of only 12 other teams to average over .600 for five years or more.

In the peak years of the dynasty, from 1972 to 1976, the Reds' winning percentage was .626, an average of 100 wins a season.

The 1975-76 Reds won a total of 210 games. Only five teams have ever won more in a two-year span.

After the history-making seven-game sweep of the Phillies and the Yankees in the League Championship Series and the World Series in 1976 (a feat never duplicated since league divisions were formed in 1969), *Sports Illustrated* wondered "How Good Are The Reds?" and compared them to the 1927 Yankees, then considered the greatest team of all time.

In the book, *Baseball's Ten Greatest Teams*, baseball historian Donald Honig rates the 1976 Reds over the 1927 Yankees at four positions (catcher, shortstop, second base and third base), and probably better at a fifth (left field). Ultimately, Honig gives the edge to the Yankees as the greatest baseball team of all-time because of their "depth of superb pitching."

But the point is made: the 1976 Reds had the greatest *starting eight* of all time.

"The Big Red Machine teams will never be forgotten," declares Johnny Bench. "They'll be remembered because of the professionals they had, the character they had, the skill they had. Those teams were a symbol of what baseball should be."

Twenty years have passed. And yet the Big Red Machine just keeps getting better. Time has added luster to the legacy.

Comparing teams of different eras is always difficult because strategy and equipment have radically changed over the years. But it is possible to compare to what degree teams have dominated the game in their eras, and no team has ever been more dominating than the 1975-76 Reds.

Take batting average. The 1976 Reds batted .280, compared to the .307 for the 1927 Yankees. But league batting averages were much higher in that era. The rest of the American League averaged a robust .282 in 1927. The rest of the N.L. hit only .253 in 1976, making the Reds' average more impressive than the Yankees' when compared to the league averages.

Most of the teams on the "all-time great" lists, including the 1927 Yankees, the 1955 Dodgers, the 1938 Yankees and the 1976 Reds led the majors in runs scored. But the Reds' total of 857 runs outperformed the National League average of 626 by 37 percent, which is the second best performance of all-time (second to the 41 percent of the 1931 Yankees).

The 1927 Yankees were led by (from left to right) Lou Gehrig, Tony Lazzeri, Earle Combs and Babe Ruth. All are in the Hall of Fame.

The 1976 Reds led the major leagues in 10 major offensive and defensive categories: runs, hits, doubles, triples, home runs, walks, batting average, on-base percentage, slugging percentage and fielding average.

No other team has ever led all these categories in their own league in one season, let alone all of baseball.

In addition, the Big Red Machine led the National League in stolen bases, demonstrating a combination of speed and power that has seldom been matched. The Dodgers of the early 1950s are the only other club since the 1920s to lead in the speed, power and hitting categories of stolen bases, home runs, slugging average and batting average.

The superior offensive and defensive statistics forged by the Big Red Machine of the 1970s were largely the achievement of the legendary starting eight.

"Johnny Bench, Pete Rose, Joe Morgan, Tony Perez, Dave Concepcion, George Foster, Ken Griffey, Cesar Geronimo," recites the manager of the Big Red Machine, Sparky Anderson.

"I was 35 years old when I went into Cincinnati in 1970. When I came out nine years later, the guys had made me a star. Over those nine years, they averaged 96 wins. I tell people, 'Just think what I could have done if had some players!'"

When Anderson wrote all eight names in the starting lineup, victory was nearly automatic. The "Great Eight" played only 87 games together as a starting lineup in 1975-76 (including regular and post-season games). *They went 69-18, a winning percentage of .793.*

"We didn't think we could get beat," remembered Joe Morgan, "because we almost never did get beat."

Baseball's 21 Greatest Dynasties

Which were baseball's greatest dynasties?

To make the list, a team had to win at least 60 percent of its games for a minimum of five years, and/or won at least two world championships in five years. The amazing 45-year dynasty of the New York Yankees (from 1920 to 1964) posed a challenge: the Yankees won 62 percent of their games and 20 World Series during that stretch. For this list, the dynasty was partitioned into five different groups, each representing the best of different eras in the Yankee reign.

In chronological order, here are baseball's greatest dynasties:

Chicago Cubs 1906-10 The Cubs of Tinkers to Evers to Chance should also be remembered for the rotation of Three Finger Brown, Ed Ruelbach, Jack Pfiester and Orval Overall. The team averaged a 1.98 ERA over five years and set the regular-season win record with 116 in 1906.

Philadelphia Athletics 1910-14 Connie Mack's first great team featured the $100,000 infield, two Hall of Fame pitchers and three World Series titles in five years.

Boston Red Sox 1912-18 This team was a perfect four-for-four in World Series competition. A pitching-dominated team, the Sox led the league five times in fewest runs allowed (helped by a young left-hander named Babe Ruth).

New York Giants 1921-25 John McGraw's team won four straight N.L. titles, hit .296 over the five years and led the league in runs scored three times.

New York Yankees 1921-28 Murderer's Row featured Babe Ruth in his prime and Lou Gehrig beginning in 1926, and won six pennants in eight years.

St. Louis Cardinals 1926-31 Branch Rickey's first great team beat two of the greatest teams ever in the World Series, knocking off the Ruth/Gehrig Yankees in 1926 and the A's in 1931.

Philadelphia Athletics 1928-32 Connie Mack's second dynasty was good enough to beat the Yankees from 1929-31, and included Hall of Famers Lefty Grove, Al Simmons, Jimmy Foxx and Mickey Cochrane.

New York Yankees 1936-43 The Joe McCarthy Yankees featured Joe DiMaggio; the 1936 and 1939 squads are often cited among the greatest teams of all time. These Yankees led the league in runs scored and fewest runs allowed six times, and four years in a row from 1936 to 1939.

St. Louis Cardinals 1941-46 The Cardinals of Stan Musial were obscured by World War II, but one cannot ignore their .655 winning percentage over six years (including three straight years with 105 or more wins).

New York Yankees 1949-53 Casey Stengel's Yankees posted a record five straight World Series titles with the team that made the transition from DiMaggio to Mickey Mantle.

Brooklyn Dodgers 1949-56 The "Boys of Summer" won only one World Series, but took five league titles, finished second three times and boasted Hall of Famers Jackie Robinson, Roy Campanella, Duke Snider and Pee Wee Reese.

New York Yankees 1954-58 Led by Hall of Famers Mickey Mantle, Whitey Ford and Yogi Berra, the mid-'50s Yanks appeared in four straight World Series, winning two.

New York Yankees 1960-64 Roger Maris arrived in 1960, and Ralph Houk took over in 1961 to keep the Yankees on top until the decline of Mantle, Ford and Berra.

Los Angeles Dodgers 1962-66 They played under .600 ball in the regular season, but Sandy Koufax and Don Drysdale led this weak-hitting team to three pennants and two World Championships in five years.

Baltimore Orioles 1969-74 Earl Weaver's great club averaged 99 wins a year, and played in three straight World Series, winning one.

Cincinnati Reds 1970-76 The Big Red Machine won four pennants and back-to-back World Series. Bench, Rose and Morgan won five MVP awards in seven years. Top to bottom, this team had the greatest starting eight of all-time.

Oakland A's 1971-75 Although the A's played under .600 ball, Reggie Jackson, Catfish Hunter and Rollie Fingers led the team to five straight division titles and three straight World Championships.

New York Yankees 1976-81 The first dynasty of the free agency years, Steinbrenner's Yankees won two straight World Series and led the league in fewest runs allowed four times in six years.

Oakland A's 1988-92 The A's of Tony LaRussa won four division titles over five years, but only one World Series. They make the dynasty list on the strength of their .600 regular-season winning percentage.

Toronto Blue Jays 1989-93 The Blue Jays have the lowest winning percentage of any of the dynasty teams (.564) but their consecutive World Series victories in 1992 and 1993 earn them a ranking.

Atlanta Braves 1991-96 The pitching-rich Braves dominated baseball with a .607 winning percentage, but won only one World Series.

The 1975-76 starting eight of the Reds was a perfect blend of power, speed and defense—and panache.

This was a great team, and the players knew it. They reveled in it. Broadcaster Marty Brennaman remembered that the often outrageous fashion styles of the 1970s meshed perfectly with the flair of the Reds.

"I can remember getting off the plane at Logan Airport (in Boston for the 1975 World Series)," said Brennaman, "and impressed as people were with how they could play the game, they were equally impressed with the way they dressed. It was like *Gentlemen's Quarterly*."

In Rose, Bench and Morgan, the Reds had not just three of the best players in the game, but three of the most flamboyant, confident and provocative players in all of sport. They relished the media attention; they became icons of baseball in the 1970s.

They were not always loved. The press and fans labeled Rose a "hot dog." Morgan was conceited. Bench was arrogant and aloof. But there was a heroic quality that endured and finally triumphed: Rose hitting the winning home run before 40,000 hostile Mets fans in Game Four of the 1973 playoffs in New York; Bench overcoming the fear of lung cancer to hit his epic home run in the 1972 playoffs; Morgan's back-to-back MVP awards in 1975 and 1976.

With Rose, Bench and Morgan leading the charge, and a masterful front office banging the promotions drum, the Big Red Machine not only set attendance records in Cincinnati, it became the best drawing team on the road as well.

The Reds' record-breaking performance of 1976, and the recognition the starting lineup received in the award voting of the 1970s, makes this was the most talented starting eight to ever take the field. The Big Red Machine featured four Most Valuable

Five Greatest Starting Eights

(Honorable mention: 1906 Cubs, 1912 Red Sox, 1931 and 1942 Cardinals, 1936 and 1961 Yankees, and 1970 Orioles)

Dennis Gruelle

Team	Starters	Hall of Fame	MVPs in Lineup	All-Stars	Gold Gloves	Career Games •	Major League Ranking	
1976 Reds	Bench, Perez, Morgan, Concepcion, Rose, Foster, Geronimo, Griffey	Bench, Morgan, Perez, • Rose •	Bench, (2) Foster, Morgan, (2) Rose	Bench, Perez, Morgan, Concepcion, Rose, Foster, Griffey	Bench, Concepcion, Geronimo, Morgan	19,230	Runs scored Home runs Batting avg. Stolen bases Fielding avg.	1 1 1 2 1
1955 Dodgers	Campanella, Hodges, Gilliam, Reese, Robinson, Amoros, Snider, Furillo	Campanella, Reese, Robinson, Snider, Hodges •	Campanella, (3) Robinson	Campanella, Hodges, Reese, Robinson, Furillo, Snider	No Gold Gloves awarded before 1957	13,797	Runs scored Home runs Batting avg. Stolen bases Fielding avg.	1 1 1 2 4 (tied)
1938 Yankees	Dickey, Gehrig, Gordon, Crosetti, Rolfe, Henrich, DiMaggio, Selkirk	Dickey, Gehrig, DiMaggio	Dickey, Gehrig, (2) Gordon, DiMaggio (3)	Dickey, Gehrig, Gordon, Crosetti, Rolfe, DiMaggio, Selkirk		12,243	Runs scored Home runs Batting avg. Stolen bases Fielding avg.	1 1 9 1 6 (tied)
1929 Athletics	Cochrane, Foxx, Bishop, Boley, Hale, Simmons, Haas, Miller	Cochrane, Foxx, Simmons	Cochrane, (2) Foxx (2)	No All-Star Games before 1933		11,761	Runs scored Home runs Batting avg. Stolen bases Fielding avg.	4 5 5 (tied) 13 1
1927 Yankees	Collins, Gehrig, Lazzeri, Koenig, Dugan, Meusel, Combs, Ruth	Combs, Gehrig, Lazzeri, Ruth • Likely to be inducted	Gehrig, (2) Ruth			12,421 • Games played by starters in their careers	Runs scored Home runs Batting avg. Stolen bases Fielding avg.	1 1 1 7 6 (tied)

Players in its starting lineup (Bench, Morgan, Rose and Foster).

The starting lineup of the Dodgers of the 1950s featured two MVPs: Roy Campanella and Jackie Robinson. The 1927 Yankees included two: Babe Ruth and Lou Gehrig. The Yankees of the late 1930s included three: Joe DiMaggio, Joe Gordon and Gehrig. The Yankees of the late 1950s-early 1960s featured four: Mickey Mantle, Yogi Berra, Roger Maris and Elston Howard.

The Big Red Machine featured six perennial All-Stars who were selected five or more times (Bench, Rose, Morgan, Perez, Foster and Concepcion), and in 1976, the Reds placed seven of their eight starters on the All-Star team. The only absent starter was the Gold Glove center fielder Geronimo (who hit .307 in 1976). The 1939 Yankees were the only other team to have seven of their eight starters in one All-Star Game (Bill Dickey, DiMaggio, Gordon, Frank Crosetti, Red Rolfe, George Selkirk and Gehrig).

The Reds of the mid-1970s consistently led the National League in fielding average, a statistic largely determined by the skills of the starting eight. From 1970 to 1976, the Reds led the league five of the seven years. Much of the Reds' defensive success came "up the middle" in the key positions of catcher, shortstop, second base and center field. Bench, Concepcion, Morgan and Geronimo each won Gold Gloves from 1974 to 1977. Since the Gold Glove award was begun in the mid-1950s, only one other team, the Baltimore Orioles dynasty of late 1960s-early 1970s, featured four Gold Glove winners in the same lineup.

How the starting eight of the Big Red Machine will fare in baseball's ultimate honor, enshrinement in the Hall of Fame, is still to be determined. Two players, Bench and Morgan, have been elected to the Hall (and Sparky Anderson will certainly join them.)

Two others, Rose and Perez, will likely be chosen. Clearly, the Reds of the 1970s featured four Hall of Fame caliber players in their everyday lineup, plus Concepcion who ranks among the top 20 shortstops of all time and is a legitimate Hall of Fame candidate. Only the 1950s Dodgers, the Yankees of the late 1920s and mid-1930s, and the New York Giants of the early 1920s also featured four or more Hall of Famers among their starting eight.

Taken together, the recognition in MVP balloting, All-Star selections, Gold Glove awards and Hall of Fame voting makes the starting eight of the Big Red Machine the most honored of all time.

The Big Red Machine's rush to the history books has been led by its unsurpassed starting lineup, but any great team must also feature superior pitching. The Reds of the 1970s never produced a Cy Young contender, never enjoyed a consistent 20-game winner. On a team whose nickname glorified offense and lacked a dominant pitching performer or personality, the pitching staff was often overlooked. But the team ERA was better than the league average in six of the seven seasons from 1970-1976.

The serious injuries to Gary Nolan and Don Gullett, and the frequent arm problems that plagued the staff created an impression that the Reds won in spite of their pitching. Yet, Nolan and Gullett won nearly two of every three of their pitching decisions, and when the two were healthy, they were as dominating as any pair of starters in the league. They won 65 percent of their games from 1970 to 1976, better than Tom Seaver and Jerry Koosman of the Mets, and better than Don Sutton and the number two starter for the Dodgers (Claude Osteen, Andy Messersmith and Doug Rau).

The Reds' most consistent pitcher, Jack Billingham, twice won 19 games, and one more victory each year would have given the staff the cachet of a 20-game winner. As it was, only Jim Merritt in 1970 won 20 games during the Reds' reign.

But while the Reds pitching staff won't be enshrined in the Hall of Fame, it will be remembered for helping launch a baseball revolution. When Sparky Anderson assumed control of the Reds in 1970, complete games were still expected of starters and bullpens were not yet dominant in pitching strategy. But Anderson inherited a deep bullpen led by Wayne Granger and Clay Carroll. Over the next seven seasons, Anderson added Pedro Borbon, Tom Hall, Will McEnaney and Rawly Eastwick, and earned the reputation of "Captain Hook." Anderson's tactics shaped the modern bullpen. His relief corps led the league in saves five of the seven seasons from 1970 to 1976, and Granger (1970), Carroll (1972) and Eastwick (1976) each led the league in saves.

The Cincinnati Enquirer

Four of the "Boys of Summer" Dodgers posed at Crosley Field in 1953. From left to right were Jackie Robinson, Duke Snider, Roy Campanella and Gil Hodges. All but Hodges are in the Hall of Fame.

The pitching staff lacked stars, but not depth, and the workhorses of the bullpen helped pull the Big Red Machine into the history books.

"People always felt our pitching was suspect," recalled Joe Morgan. "But you have to remember, when a guy goes to the mound, his job is to pitch to win. Our guys knew how to win. We got five runs for them, maybe they gave up three. If we got two runs for them, they gave up one. When Don Gullett was healthy, he was as good a pitcher as anyone in the major leagues. Jack Billingham kept us in the ballgame; he kept the runs down. Gary Nolan, Freddie Norman, all these guys knew how to win."

Dynasties are among the most difficult achievements in all of sports, for they require not only continued success on the field, but sustained excellence throughout all facets of the organization. The Big Red Machine was Rose, Bench, Perez and Morgan. But first, it was Bob Howsam.

Howsam came to the Reds in 1967 as the executive vice-president and general manager. He inherited the best offensive club in the National League and some fine young talent in the farm system. But he also inherited a perennial disappointment, a club that had won but one pennant in 27 years.

Howsam cleaned house and launched a new era. He ran an efficient machine, though not without controversy. He bemoaned the changes in player relations and baseball's failure to protect the interests of the fan. He was criticized as being too unyielding on everything from hair to salaries, an arch-conservative who could not adapt. Yet it was Howsam who took a gamble on a young manager named George Anderson, and it was Howsam who first capitalized on the advantages of Astroturf. Howsam balanced his power-hitting club with speed and thus terrorized the league. By the time he retired in 1978, he had developed one of the most successful teams of all time and had built the Reds into the number one organization in all of baseball.

The secret of Howsam's dynasty-building was his scouting and player development network that continued to fuel the Big Red Machine. The glory years of the Reds were dominated by the great starting lineup that coalesced in 1975-76. But the "Great Eight" started together in only 70 regular-season games of a dynasty that stretched over seven years and 1,127 games. The story of the Big Red Machine is also that of the Hal Kings and Bobby Tolans, the Tom Halls and Denis Menkes, the Doug Flynns and Pat Darcys, and the leaders of the front office: Dick Wagner, Chief Bender, Rex and Joe Bowen, and Ray Shore.

Howsam's years with the Reds catapulted him into the ranks of the great organizational geniuses of the game, and when his team is favorably compared to the Dodgers of the 1950s, the Yankees of the 1920s, or the Yankees of the 1930s, Howsam stands well in comparison to the men who led those dynasties: Branch Rickey, Ed Barrow and George Weiss. Rickey, Barrow and Weiss are in the Hall of Fame, and Howsam should follow.

Hallowed names of baseball.

"Murderer's Row:" Babe Ruth, Lou Gehrig, Ed Barrow, manager Miller Huggins.

The "Bronx Bombers:" Joe DiMaggio, Bill Dickey, George Weiss, manager Joe McCarthy.

The "Boys of Summer" Dodgers: Jackie Robinson, Roy Campanella, Duke Snider, Branch Rickey, manager Walter Alston.

The "Big Red Machine:" Pete Rose, Johnny Bench, Joe Morgan, Tony Perez, Bob Howsam, manager Sparky Anderson.

DYNASTY RANKING

All 21 clubs that either played a minimum of .600 ball for five or more seasons or won two or more World Series in five years are ranked below, by regular-season winning percentage.

Team	Yrs.	WS	W	L	PCT.	Avg./162 Games W	L
Cubs 06-10	5	2	530	235	.693	112	50
A's 28-32	5	2	505	258	.662	107	55
Cardinals 41-46	6	3	606	319	.655	106	56
Yankees 36-43	8	6	799	427	.652	106	56
A's 10-14	5	3	488	270	.644	104	58
Yankees 49-53	5	5	487	280	.635	103	59
Yankees 54-58	5	2	486	284	.631	102	60
Yankees 60-64	5	2	505	296	.630	102	60
Reds 72-76	**5**	**2**	**502**	**300**	**.626**	**101**	**61**
Dodgers 49-56	8	1	767	466	.622	101	61
Yankees 21-28	8	3	750	477	.611	99	63
Orioles 69-74	6	1	586	374	.610	99	63
Red Sox 12-18	7	4	632	406	.609	99	63
Braves 91-96	6	1	550	356	.607	98	64
Giants 21-25	5	2	461	304	.603	98	64
Yankees 76-81	6	2	548	365	.600	97	65
A's 88-92	5	1	486	324	.600	97	65
Cardinals 26-31	6	2	547	374	.594	96	66
A's 71-75	5	3	476	326	.594	96	66
Dodgers 62-66	5	2	473	340	.582	94	68
Blue Jays 89-93	5	2	457	353	.564	91	71

The humble beginnings of the Big Red Machine and baseball's all-time hit leader, Pete Rose, originated in the summer leagues on the west side of Cincinnati in the early 1950s. Rose (bottom row, left) was eventually signed by the Reds out of high school at age 19 in 1960.

Chapter 2

Rose Perez Bench
The Road to the Reds

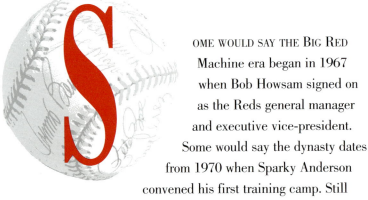

SOME WOULD SAY THE BIG RED Machine era began in 1967 when Bob Howsam signed on as the Reds general manager and executive vice-president. Some would say the dynasty dates from 1970 when Sparky Anderson convened his first training camp. Still others claim that day in 1971 when the Reds announced the trade that brought Joe Morgan to the Cincinnati Reds.

In fact, the dynasty was born years before, along the banks of the Ohio, in the cane fields of Cuba and on the plains of Oklahoma.

PETER EDWARD ROSE: APRIL 14, 1941, CINCINNATI

He was a river rat. When Pete Rose and his buddies weren't playing in tunnels they had built along the river, or playing ball along side it, they were swimming across it to the Kentucky shore. They swam back, or paid a nickel for a ride aboard the ferryboat Boone No. 7. When rain made the river too wide to swim, flooding their tunnels and sending the real rats to higher ground, the river rats scurried after them with baseball bats in their hands.

The boys spent hours dodging the trains that rambled by on River Road, and in the winter, rode sleds from Hillside Avenue down toward the river. In the summer, they played Wiffleball in their backyards and "rubberball" at Schulte's Fish Garden; the eye of the giant walleye mural was their strike zone. They raided the gardens along the river for watermelons and the nearby orchard for apples. In the early evening, they boarded a bus driven by Harry Hackman. He liked the boys and chauffeured them downtown for free, sometimes to Crosley Field where the Reds played under the lights. The boys yelled out the windows to the fans headed to the game. Pete Rose loved to watch Enos Slaughter of the St. Louis Cardinals and Jackie Robinson of the Brooklyn Dodgers run the bases.

On weekends, Pete was a waterboy for his dad's semipro football team; afterward, Pete and his buddies gathered beer bottles and redeemed them for a few cents apiece. As 15- and 16-year-olds, Rose and his buddy, Walt Harmon, ran in the same backfield for an older men's semipro football team, and played Friday night softball with a group of older men. The team was sponsored by a local tavern.

There was plenty for boys to do in the working class neighborhood of Anderson Ferry, located only five miles west of downtown Cincinnati. Pete lived at 4404 Braddock Avenue, hard on a hillside about a quarter mile from the river. Dad's real first name was Harry, but everybody called him by his nickname, "Pete." He became "Big Pete" after little Pete came along. In the summertime, Big Pete took his kids camping on the banks of the Ohio. On Saturday mornings when the ponies were running, Big Pete took the family to River Downs. Big Pete would bet two bucks, four bucks tops. Terry Boyle—son of the scout, Buzz, who would ultimately sign little Pete to a Reds contract—frequently saw little Pete at the track when he was in junior high school.

"Pete was in the eighth grade," said Terry. "He had the Racing Form in his back pocket. I worked at the pass gate. Pete reminded me of one of the Dead End Kids. I can still see him coming through the gate with that horse thing in his pocket." Pete was two when his dad bought him his first baseball glove; four when he smacked a baseball off an outside window and cracked the glass.

"We're not fixing that window," Big Pete told his wife. "That's

Pete's first hit."

Pete played Knothole baseball at Boldface Park. He was a catcher. Pete loved to wave the ball in the batter's face.

"Hey, batter, batter, batter," Pete would say after a strike.

Pete's dad was an excellent athlete. He played baseball, but football was more his game. Pete's mom, LaVerne, whom her friends call "Rosie," provided the baseball genes in the family. Her brother, Buddy Bloebaum, had been a top amateur player in Cincinnati and later a bird-dog scout for the Reds.

Little Pete was, by far, the smallest of the river rats. He hung from tree limbs and chin-up bars and asked, "Do you think I'm gonna grow?"

To and from ball games, from the Knothole level through high school, Big Pete counseled his son about looking, acting and playing like a ballplayer.

"Play hard, but not dirty, and always within the rules. Run hard right from the get-go. That's how singles become doubles, and doubles become triples."

When Pete was eight, Toot Fox, who worked at Schulte's Fish Garden, introduced the boy to the Reds slugger, Joe Adcock.

"Pete, maybe Mr. Adcock can give you some tips on hitting," said Toot.

Pete gazed up at the 6-foot-3 Adcock like Jack eyeing the beanstalk and said, "My dad tells me how to hit."

Uncle Buddy Bloebaum, a top-flight pool hustler who now operated a pool hall, told Big Pete to make little Pete a switch-hitter. Big Pete told his son's Knothole coach that Pete must switch-hit or he'd join another team.

Toot Fox managed a softball team that played weekends in Kentucky. Little Pete said to Fox, "We've got the best outfield in

Jackie Schwier Collection

A slow-to-grow Pete Rose looked up to most of his boyhood friends, including Bernie Wrublewski. Wrublewski's T-shirt advertised Cincinnati's Hudepohl brewery, a sponsor of Reds baseball.

the city." Fox told him to "just get up there and do it with the stick." Little Pete hit a bad-ball pitch down the left-field line, exploding from the batter's box with no intent of stopping. He up-ended the second baseman, kicked the ball loose at third and made a headlong slide into home. *Safe!*

When he reached Fox in the on-deck circle, Pete said, "Is that what you mean, you S.B?" Fox shot back, "That's exactly what I mean. And it's Mr. S.B. to you."

When he was three days shy of his 16th birthday, Pete climbed into the boxing ring at the Findlay Street Neighborhood House for a bout with a youngster named Virgil Cole. The bout—the opener for that evening's amateur card—was arranged by Big Pete, who had been an excellent amateur fighter himself. Both boys weighed 112 pounds. The eager but wild-swinging Rose was no match for the experienced Cole, who slammed punch after punch into the river rat's face and body. The bout is recalled in Rose's biography, *Pete Rose: My Story*, by Roger Kahn.

During the second round, Rose's sister, Caryl, cried out: "Dad, can't you stop it? They're beating his brains out. They're killing him."

Answered Big Pete: "He's all right. He's not getting hurt. He knows how to defend himself."

Pete stayed on his feet, but lost by a lopsided margin. When he got home that night, black and blue with bruises, he proudly told his mother: "Look at me. But he couldn't knock me out."

When Pete went out for the baseball team at Western Hills, he asked to play catcher. But the team already had a good one, so coach Paul Nohr tried Rose at second. Rose was little but scrappy. Nohr knew that Big Pete's son would hang in there on double plays and attempted steals. Pete had decent speed, but wasn't the fastest guy on the team. Nobody ran harder.

When he didn't make the Western Hills football team as a sophomore, Pete felt disgraced and aimless. He turned off to school and failed. Had he gone to summer school, he could have moved on with his class, but his father said, "No; no summer school. You'll miss summer baseball." By the time he was a senior, Pete had used up his eligibility. So he joined the Lebanon Merchants in the Dayton League and played 6 p.m. games with full-grown men.

Buddy Bloebaum tried to convince Reds scout Buzz Boyle of Rose's worth. Boyle got interested when Pete hit a home run over

Jackie Schwier Collection

Harry "Pete" Rose not only passed along his nickname to his son but also a fierce competitive spirit. At age 47, "Big Pete" dove and tackled a folding chair during a TV interview to prove he still had the skills to play football.

the lights in Cheviot. Boyle understood that Rose—5-foot-10 and 150 pounds—might be a late bloomer like Uncle Buddy.

Buzz and other scouts occasionally sent prospects to Crosley Field to work out. Manager Fred Hutchinson would check them out. One day, Hutch said to Boyle, "How many times are you gonna bring that Rose kid in?"

Boyle answered that he wasn't bringing him in. Pete had talked his way by the security guards. His uncle, Curly Smart, was a Reds clubhouse helper. When one of Boyle's assistants told Phil Seghi, then the Reds farm director, that Pete was a prospect, Seghi said, "We've got enough little shits in our organization as it is. We need someone who can really play ball."

But it wouldn't hurt to give a local kid a shot. Hadn't the Reds taken a pass on a pint-sized graduate of Western Hills several years earlier and come to regret it? Don Zimmer was now the Cubs second baseman.

Much has been made over the years of how the Reds signed Rose merely as favor to Boyle and Bloebaum. That is largely true. But the $7,000 bonus that Pete has always claimed the Reds paid him showed more faith than that. Maybe it was the Baltimore Orioles' interest in Pete that did it. The Reds didn't want to kick themselves later for not taking a chance on a kid who had his Uncle Buddy's genes and Harry's persistence. The Reds thought he might have a chance if his size were to catch up with his desire.

"I remember the last game I played for Lebanon before signing with the Reds," recalled Rose.

"I went five-for-five off a guy who was a minor league pitcher. Uncle Buddy was there. He said, 'Go home and wake up your dad and when he asks how many hits you got, just go like this.'"

Bloebaum placed his hand with five fingers spread out on his face and dragged it downward.

"I did that," said Pete. "I woke Dad up. That was on a Wednesday night. I graduated from West High on Friday, signed with the Reds on Saturday and left for Geneva on Sunday."

Geneva, New York, in the New York-Penn League, was Rose's first minor league stop. Wearing a Cincinnati Reds cap pulled down low on his forehead, Pete walked into McDonough Park, introduced himself to manager Reno DeBenedetti, and said: "I'm your new second baseman." Actually, Geneva already had a second baseman. His name was Tony Perez.

In his first game, Rose went 2-for-5. *The Geneva Times* liked what it saw: "Rose is an aggressive and eager ballplayer at second, and gives promise that he could be a good hitter." But in 85 games, he made 36 errors—three times worse than what an adequate second baseman should make.

The fans appreciated his hustle. At year's end, they voted him the most popular player. He was awarded two Samsonite suitcases. They figured he'd be moving on. But when Big Pete asked a Reds scout for an insider's opinion, the scout shared one of the reports filed on little Pete: "Pete Rose can't make a double play, can't throw, can't hit left-handed and can't run. He also has limited range on balls hit to his right."

But Pete had gotten his taste.

He traded his '37 jalopy for a '57 Plymouth.

In the offseason, true to his late-blooming genes, Rose grew two inches and added 20 pounds. He worked at Railway Express unloading boxcars. He reported to spring training at nearly 6 feet tall and 175 pounds.

"I didn't even recognize him," said Ron Flender, a Geneva teammate and Elder High School graduate. "Pete had just sprouted. You looked at him and thought, 'What the heck has *he* been doing?' He was unbelievable. Everything he hit was a basehit. He sprinted to first base, even on a routine out. I don't remember him running to first base on a walk that way in high school. But he did in Tampa. When you're hot, you're hot. He was having a tremendous year."

"You run like that to first base all the time?" Tampa manager Johnny Vander Meer asked Rose during spring training.

"I'm looking for a job," answered Rose.

"Keep running like that and you might get one," said Vander Meer.

Rose hit .330 with 30 triples—a Florida State League record.

"Every time I looked up," said Vander Meer, "he was driving one into the alleys and running like a scalded dog and sliding headfirst into third."

In Tampa, Rose patented his headfirst slide.

"Those headfirst slides were kind of a joke with the other players," said Flender. "Nobody was sliding headfirst. He wound up hurting his wrist one time. A hairline fracture. It didn't stop him long. I think he was out about three days."

At Rose's next stop, Macon, Georgia, in 1962, he hooked up with Tommy Helms. The team's manager was Dave Bristol.

Rose was his typical fun-loving self.

"We traveled in station wagons in those days," said Art Shamsky, a future big-leaguer. "Pete and I were in the back talking baseball one night, like we always did, and all of a sudden he gets this idea. 'Let's do something crazy,' he says. So, he crawls out the back window, onto the top of the car. Imagine this, now, it's pitch black and the car is speeding along and the driver is trying to stay awake, and Pete puts his hand on the windshield. He scared the shit out of the guy."

Later, Shamsky would tell biographers that he was the driver. But, in every version, Rose is atop the car. Shamsky also remembers the night that he, Rose and a pitcher climbed on top of an awning outside their hotel room in Augusta, Georgia, to "look in" on a party next door. Problem was, the pitcher fell through the awning and was suspended only by his shoulders.

"When we stopped laughing, we pulled him out," said Shamsky.

In Macon, Rose began to see himself as a future major leaguer. His parents drove a new mint-green Corvette to Nashville that Pete had just ordered. He and Helms drove it back to Macon, but not before they were stopped for speeding, hauled before a justice of the peace and told to empty their pockets. The justice counted the take (just shy of $200), and left Rose and Helms $8 to cover the cost of gas from the courtroom to Macon.

"Have a safe trip and good luck in the game tonight," said the justice of the peace.

Early in spring training, 1963, the sportswriters asked Reds manager Fred Hutchinson whether there were any phenoms on the premises.

"There are three I'm going to take a look at," said Hutch. "Pete Rose, Bobby Klaus and George McWilliams. I saw Rose in the rookie league this winter, and the kid really showed me something."

One of the writers, Earl Lawson, already knew of Hutch's interest in Rose. During the annual winter meetings, Hutch told Lawson: "If I had any guts, I'd put the kid (Rose) on second base and forget about him."

Hutch figured his veteran ballclub could use a little shake-up. If Rose could provide that by displacing a complacent veteran with rookie hustle, so much the better.

Bristol was on hand during the second game of the Grapefruit League season when Rose made a huge impression on Hutch.

"It was (late) in a game at Al Lopez Field," said Bristol. "We were sittin' together in the bullpen and Pete said, 'I think I'll go in (the clubhouse).'"

Mike Ryba, one of the Reds scouts who was in camp as an instructor, told Rose he'd better not. "You might get in the game."

Rose entered the game in the ninth inning as pinch-runner for Wally Post, doubled in the 11th inning, doubled again in the 14th and scored the winning run.

"Pete Rose has more bounce to the ounce than a hot golf ball on concrete," wrote one sportswriter. "He runs out bases on balls as though pursued by the devil."

New York Yankees slugger Mickey Mantle, who was catching some sun one day on the visiting dugout steps in Tampa, saw Rose run to first base on a walk. Mantle turned to his buddy, pitcher Whitey Ford, and said, "Look at that. There goes Charlie Hustle."

Rose didn't hustle only on the field. He hustled home from the ballpark, too. He hadn't been able to arrange to have his car brought down from Cincinnati. He couldn't afford to rent a car and his veteran teammates weren't inclined to help out a kid going for one of their jobs. Rose knew that hitch-hiking was bush for a big-leaguer.

"So I'd get out of my uniform and into sneakers and jeans and I'd jog the whole five miles back to the hotel," he said. "No big deal. Besides, it strengthened my legs."

On March 21, when Rose stretched a single into a headfirst double, Hutch said: "As of now Pete Rose is on the roster."

But Rose went into a 2-for-25 nosedive, and *The Cincinnati Enquirer's* Lou Smith wrote that Rose's chances of making the club were 50-50. Reds general manager Bill DeWitt said a decision would be made within five days. Hutch wanted his phenom to see some more big-league pitching. Rose went 2-for-4 against the Dodgers, both doubles. On April 2, Rose went 3-for-4 against the White Sox; on April 3, he went 2-for-3 against the Mets.

In his book, *Cincinnati Seasons*, Lawson tells of sitting in the cocktail lounge of Tampa's Causeway Inn with seven or eight Reds players shortly before the team broke camp.

"Handing each a piece of paper, I asked them to jot down the names of the 25 players they thought would open the season with the Reds," said Lawson. "Only one player (second baseman Don), Blasingame, listed Rose's name."

"Blazer" knew the kid was after his job.

In his second year in professional ball, Rose played for the Tampa Tarpons, a Single A club in the Reds farm system. Rose had numerous opportunities to use his new headfirst slide: he hit a record-setting 30 triples.

Jackie Schwier Collection

The club headed north with the Chicago White Sox for four exhibition games. On April 5, in Macon, Rose went 2-for-5. He didn't know how good that was. Before the game, Reds third baseman Gene Freese, formerly a White Sox player, had called aside his buddy, the Sox's Nellie Fox.

"See this little fellow we have playing second base?" Freese said. "See if you can get your guys to throw him nothing but high fastballs. He ain't been gettin' around on them too good, and I want to see if he can hit them."

Freese was trying to save Blazer's job.

For four days, Rose saw almost nothing but high fastballs.

"Hell, he hit nothing but rockets all over the place," recalled Freese, years later. "To all fields, batting left- and right-handed. It didn't matter who we wanted as our second baseman. It was gonna be Rose because the kid could hit."

On Saturday in Charleston, West Virginia, two days before the opener at Crosley Field, Rose had a double in four at-bats. After the game, Hutch told Rose, "We've booked you into a hotel room (in downtown Cincinnati). I don't want you going home."

"Why not?" asked Rose.

"You're our starting second baseman," answered Hutch. "The word is going out and I don't want the neighbors bothering you."

On the train ride from Charleston to Cincinnati, Blasingame wandered by Rose's seat.

"Well, Rook, you got big-league pants now," said Blazer. "Let's see if you can wear them."

Rose, not quite 22 years old, 6 feet tall and 192 pounds, didn't hesitate: "You're a little guy to be talking to me that way," he shot back.

On Opening Day in Cincinnati, Rose walked to the plate to the cheers of the hometown crowd. He was the first local player in nine years (Herm Wehmeier) to start for the Reds.

The first pitch from Pittsburgh Pirate Earl Francis was on its way. Rose, as was his custom from his playground days when he would watch the ball from the pitcher's hand all the way back to the eye of the giant walleye mural that served as the strike zone at Schulte's Fish Garden, followed Francis' pitch into the catcher's glove. He looked veteran umpire Jocko Conlan directly in the eye.

Conlan stepped out in front of the plate and dusted it off.

"What are you looking at, kid?" Conlan asked Rose.

"What? What?" asked Rose.

"Why are you turning around like that?" asked Conlan. "If you want to know if it's a strike or ball, look out at the scoreboard."

"I always look back," Rose answered.

"Well, don't do it anymore," said Conlan. "I don't need that."

Rose took three more balls and sprinted for first base.

The fans howled with delight.

The river rat, the scalded dog, was headed for home.

A<small>TANASIO</small> R<small>IGAL</small> P<small>EREZ</small>: M<small>AY</small> 14, 1942, C<small>AMAGUEY</small>, C<small>UBA</small>. While Pete Rose roamed the banks of the Ohio River and played Knothole baseball in Cincinnati in the 1950s, Atanasio Rigal Perez worked next to his father and grandfather in the sugar factory in Central de Violeta in Camaguey Province. Like Rose, Perez dreamed of baseball. Four hundred miles away, in wide-open Havana, the best *beisbol* was played with real baseballs on manicured grass beneath bright lights.

"Tani" Perez wanted to play baseball under those lights someday. He didn't want to work the rest of his life in a sugar factory.

In the 1950s, the best team in Cuba was the Havana Sugar Kings. They were the Triple A farm club of the Cincinnati Reds. Their director of scouting was a young man named Tony Pacheco. He had taken the job in 1956, after he was hit in the head by a pitch. His playing days were over. Three years later, Pacheco laid eyes on Perez. For 50 years, scouts like Pacheco had been sending young Cubans like Tani Perez across the Straits of Florida to play baseball.

Pacheco had hundreds of bird-dog scouts in Cuba, one in every town. The bird-dog in Central de Violeta wrote Pacheco a letter every week with the names of 15 prospects in it. Pretty soon, Pacheco had 100 prospects from Camaguey province. So, Pacheco had the bird-dog set up a tryout. One "tool"—speed or arm or glove or bat—would be enough to get a player invited. The bird-dog assembled his 15 best prospects. One was a 140-pound string bean with brown eyes, a long neck and a wonderful smile.

His name was Tani Perez. He had just turned 17.

"His strength was his bat," Pacheco recalled years later. "He was a very poor defensive player, very erratic. He was a shortstop. But he could hit. I didn't sign anybody out of that tryout, not even

Perez continued to live in the Caribbean after joining the Reds, and regularly conducted clinics for island youngsters. This session was held in the U.S. Virgin Islands.

Tony. But I remember I liked him."

Pacheco invited Perez to the Havana Sugar Kings baseball school. The Sugar Kings' 15 best prospects lived together in a boarding house. The club paid all their expenses. Tani progressed steadily. But he had trouble pulling the ball. He hit the ball between right-center and right. "His hands were rolled in too much on the bat," recalled Pacheco. "That brought his elbow into his body. It stopped his hands. But he still hit the ball hard."

The instructors worked with Perez on changing his grip, so that he could follow through on every swing. At first it was awkward, but Perez stuck with it.

"Every Saturday, we'd send the team into the interior of the country, where one of our scouts was the manager of the team," said Pacheco. "Games were played on Sunday. On Monday morning, I'd find out how Tony did. Tony was very quiet. I remember one Monday morning I asked Tony how he did in yesterday's game. He said, 'I got two hits.' I asked him what kind of hits. 'Two home runs,' he said. I asked to where he hit them. 'Left field,' he said. Well, that did it. Soon after that, I signed him."

That was in March 1960, three months before the Reds signed Rose.

Perez's "bonus" was $2.50—the cost of a visa to the United States.

Pacheco had the power to sign Cuban players on behalf of the Reds, but it was the Reds who decided whether the player was ready to play ball in the States. The Reds wanted Pacheco to keep Perez in "COO-bah" for another year.

"No, he is ready now," Pacheco insisted.

The Reds relented. But there was somebody even closer to Tani who had to be convinced. Tani's mother did not want him to leave.

"I told her, 'Don't worry, Mama,'" remembered Perez. "'You see Minnie Minoso? I am going to be better than him.'"

Havana-born Minoso had his best years for the Chicago White Sox in the 1950s, and Perez loved the way the effervescent Minoso played the game.

"My mother said, 'You love to dream, Tani. You cannot dream that way. You will see,'" Perez recalled. But she let him go.

When Perez arrived in Tampa in 1960, he was given an old baseball uniform. It was for an 180-pound player, way too big for the 147-pound Perez.

"It was one of those sleeveless uniforms," Pacheco recalled. "It looked bad on him. The holes where the sleeves had been went all the way to his waist."

"I looked ridiculous in it," recalled Perez, smiling. "I think it was (Ted) Kluszewski's uniform. But what was I going to say? It doesn't fit me?"

His Latin teammates called him *Flaco*, Spanish for Skinny.

During an intrasquad game, Flaco made some errors and struck out a couple of times. At a post-game evaluation, farm director Phil Seghi asked the scouts if anybody should be sent back home.

Pacheco suggested a 17-year-old catcher named Miller.

"I didn't know Seghi had signed Miller," recalled Pacheco. "The other scouts, they signaled me to shut up. But I had already started, so I figured I'd finish. Seghi was getting angrier by the minute. Finally he said, 'Well, your guy (Perez) looked so bad, I felt like going out there and taking the uniform off him and sending him back to Havana on the next plane!'"

Pacheco laughed at the memory.

"By then, I knew I was in an argument with the boss and didn't want to carry on. I just said, 'Phil, maybe he's better than you think.'"

Even Dave Bristol, who would later become Perez's manager in the minors and in Cincinnati, had his doubts when he first saw Perez.

"He was so skinny that when somebody slid into him at second base on the double play, it took him five minutes to fall down," said Bristol.

In Tampa in 1960, Perez knew only two words of English—"yes," and "no." He couldn't even distinguish the items listed on the menu. He'd point to some unknown gibberish and hope for a decent main meal. One time, he was especially disappointed when the waitress brought him his entree: apple pie.

Perez made $250 a month that summer in Geneva. Every pay day, he sent home all that he could afford—usually $30 to $50.

He hit only six home runs that first year. The Reds wanted him to improve his production—and his English. He did both. The following season, he hit .348 with 27 home runs and 132 RBI.

Between 1960 and 1962, Perez's first three seasons in the minors, he returned to Cuba each winter to see his family. But in 1963, his father counseled against it.

"In 1963, I stayed in the States, and I stayed in the States every year after that, too," said Perez. "My father told me if baseball was going to be my life, I should do it that way. Besides, things were getting bad in Cuba."

Tony had seen the decision coming. The governments of Cuba and the United States were at loggerheads. In 1961, Castro's forces had repelled the U.S.-sponsored Bay of Pigs invasion and used this bloody defeat of Cuban exiles to solidify support for the Castro

Perez and his wife, Pituka, applied for U.S. citizenship in 1971. Their witnesses were teammate Lee May and his wife, Terrye.

regime. In October 1962, U.S.-Cuba tensions peaked when President John F. Kennedy squared off with Soviet premier Nikita Khrushchev over Soviet missiles in Cuba.

Because Perez couldn't go home, he lived with minor league teammate Lee May in Tampa. May helped Perez with his English and also bestowed the nickname "Doggie" on Perez.

"You could always depend on Doggie to drive in the big run," May explained. "He's the big dog, the top dog, the king of the hill."

After the 1964 season, the Reds requested Perez to play winter ball in Venezuela. But with Perez having trouble securing a passport, Seghi told him to head for Puerto Rico. Manager Preston Gomez was believed to be a perfect fit for Perez, who needed only some refinement before he was ready for the big leagues.

When Perez arrived in San Juan, he hooked up with another Cuban player, Jose Martinez, who also had been assigned to Gomez's team. One day, Martinez took Perez to meet the de la Cantera family of San Juan. The family was from Martinez's hometown, Cardenas. The de la Cantera family had fled from Cuba in 1961 after Castro came to power.

The oldest of the family's daughters—Pituka, age 20—was not at home when the ballplayers got there. When she finally arrived, the strapping Perez, no longer the 147-pound string bean, respectfully stood up from his chair.

Pituka's reaction was immediate. Years later, she could still recall it.

"I said to myself, 'Oh my lord!' Tani was tall, quiet and smiling. He was looking straight into my eyes. I went into the kitchen and said to my cousin, 'Come here. I will give you a quarter if you find out if he is married or single.' After two minutes, I was still in the kitchen when I felt a tapping on my shoulder. I turned around and it was Tani. He said, 'Are you the one who wants to know about my status?'"

Four months after the chance meeting, she and "Tani" were married. Pituka and her two sisters had been educated at the Catholic school in Cardenas, where they had learned English and grammar. Their father, a contractor, played baseball as a boy. As a man, he flew to the U.S. three times to watch the World Series.

"Pituka immediately became a huge factor in Tony's career," said Pacheco. "She helped him with his English, made sure he ate the right foods, took great care of him. She knew the importance of

The Cincinnati Enquirer

Perez (right) and Gordy Coleman platooned at first base in 1965 and 1966. Perez, originally a middle infielder, was a first-base candidate by the time he made the major leagues. Coleman eventually became director of the Reds' speakers bureau in the Big Red Machine years.

baseball in their lives. She knew it from the start."

Although only a year younger than Rose, Perez didn't make it to Crosley Field until almost two years after Pete.

Like Rose, Perez vividly remembers his debut.

"The Reds called me up (from Triple A San Diego) and I flew all night. My team was playing in Denver. The Reds had a twi-night doubleheader against the Pirates at Crosley Field. I played both games. Bob Veale pitched one game, Joe Gibbon the other, both left-handers."

The first time up, Perez lined out to shortstop.

He hit the ball well that day, but he was 0-for-8.

Nevertheless, he smiled.

He was a Great Leaguer. Just like his idol, Minnie Minoso.

JOHNNY LEE BENCH: DECEMBER 7, 1947, OKLAHOMA CITY. Far from islands in the Caribbean and rivers in Ohio, Johnny Lee Bench grew up in the dry plains of the southwest, in central Oklahoma. He was three years old when his father, Ted, began playing catch with him in Lindsay, Oklahoma. When Johnny was five, his family moved to Binger, population 500.

"When my dad hit balls to me in the cornfield as I was growing up, it was like in the movie (*Field of Dreams*)," Johnny said.

Once, in a pickup game, Johnny and his dad squared off against Johnny's two older brothers, Teddy and William.

"Dad hit one, God, I thought about a million feet," said Johnny. "He hit it clear into the cornfield and we lost the ball, never could find that ball. In my mind, nobody has ever hit a ball further."

Ted Bench, a truck driver for a gas distribution company, died in 1991, two years after Johnny was elected to the Hall of Fame. To truly know Johnny, you had to know Ted. And to know Ted, you had to know Ted's parents.

Johnny Bench's grandparents came to Oklahoma when Ted was five years old—in a covered wagon. Ted's father, a Frenchman, and his mother, a full-blooded Choctaw Indian, were traveling to Oklahoma because she had a land grant of 160 acres from the U.S. government. The grant had its genesis in her Choctaw heritage. The federal government was making reparations to the displaced "five civilized tribes."

In his genes, Ted carried the DNA of the Choctaw tribe. The Choctaws were the most athletic of the five civilized tribes. Their game was lacrosse. Ted's game was baseball; he was a catcher.

He played ball in the Army, taking over behind the plate when he was 18 years old after the regular catcher broke his thumb. Nobody was able to break Ted's hold on the job in his next three years at Ft. Sill in Lawton, Oklahoma, during which his team won three championships. Ted was known for his great arm and daring pickoff throws. He also played catcher while stationed in Italy in the 1940s. But bone chips in his shoulder ended Ted's career behind the plate. He gave up catching for good in 1949, at age 31. Just about the time Johnny came along.

As soon as Ted organized a PeeWee team in Binger in 1955— the Binger Bobcats—he put seven-year-old Johnny behind the plate.

"He was a natural from the start," said Ted.

Ted told Johnny to throw to a target, even during warmups.

"Even if you're lobbing the ball, pick out a target—the ankles, the knees, something," Ted told Johnny. "There's going to be times in the game when you're going to have to throw. If you've always picked out a target, it's automatic for you."

Johnny couldn't get enough of baseball.

"We had a gravel driveway," recalled Katy, Johnny's mom. "He hit every piece of gravel out of it. He'd throw up the pieces of gravel, one-by-one, and smack it until it was all gone."

Every Saturday morning, the young J.B. would buy a half-gallon of Neapolitan ice cream at Helms' grocery and bring it home to eat. Johnny and his dad watched Pee Wee Reese and Dizzy Dean on NBC-TV's broadcast of the "Game of the Week."

Johnny also couldn't get enough of hunting. Some of his fondest childhood memories were of hunting quail with his dad, two older brothers and their pointer dogs. Johnny's best shots, though, came with his BB gun. When, as a four-year-old, he intentionally plugged Teddy in the back from eight feet, and later plugged William in the leg as William sprinted toward the mailbox, the gig was up. Mama Katy locked up Johnny's BB gun on top of the closet for a month. The gunslinging Durango Kid was BB-less in Binger.

There were other dangers in Binger.

Binger sits in the Sugar Creek Valley at the bottom of a shallow basin, five miles across. The ridge that runs on the the high side of the basin protects Binger from the worst of the tornadoes. They generally skip over the top of Binger, but not always.

"Went to the basement 11 times in two weeks once," said Johnny.

He also earned some pretty good spending money around Binger. Johnny picked cotton for two cents a pound. Pull 300 pounds and you got six bucks. Johnny worked in the peanut fields, too. He worked on the combines, sometimes until two in the morning, then put on a pair of goggles to work on the trucks "because when the dirt comes off the vines you just choke on the dust."

By age 14, he was playing American Legion ball in Anadarko, 20 miles from Binger, with boys three years older. Mostly, he pitched and played first and third—the team already had a catcher. But he still loved catching. His first catcher's mitt originally belonged to Jeff Torborg of the Dodgers, handed down to Johnny from Anadarko's Gary Griffith, whose brother, Derrell, played for the Dodgers. When Johnny was 16, he threw a no-hitter for the Legion team.

"That's when I realized I had a ballplayer on my hands," said Ted. "It bothered me that he wasn't catching, but he was playing with good players."

Johnny didn't catch much at Binger High, either. There were

The Cincinnati Enquirer

The Binger High School senior class of 1965 had 21 students, but the school fielded a baseball and basketball team, and Bench starred on both.

only 10 players on the team. Their "field" was just that—a sandy pit whose only relationship to a diamond was the geometric form it took once the bases were plopped down.

The backstop was made of chicken wire.

Still, Johnny was blessed. He'd been born into almost the perfect baseball environment. His two older brothers were good high school players, and Binger was full of young kids eager to play ball. David Gunter, who had moved to Binger when he was 11 years old, became a fast friend of Bench's. Baseball was their bond.

"There's only one way to get good as a baseball player, and that's to play," said Gunter. "For as long as I know, Johnny always wanted to be a ballplayer. As soon as he saw Mickey Mantle (a fellow Oklahoman) on the 'Game of the Week,' he said: 'That's what I'm going to be.' When John and I were kids, by noon Saturday we had been playing home run derby for three hours. Our parents would be down at the ballpark chewing us out for being late for lunch."

As Bench's baseball ability grew, so did his intense desire to play professionally.

"In high school, he was the first one on the field and the last one off it," said Gunter. "He didn't drink, didn't smoke, didn't stay up all hours of the night chasing girls. He knew—the way the rest of us didn't—that what he wanted to be was a major league ballplayer. He left Binger very good and became very great in a very short time. He went from a sand pit with nine other guys on his baseball team to the game's greatest catcher within five years."

But first came an event that was to change Johnny forever.

On April 1, 1965, a school bus carrying Johnny and the Binger baseball team was on its way back home from a game against an Indian school on the reservation in Riverside.

The brakes failed.

At a "T" intersection at the bottom of a hill, the vehicle's front bumper caught the railing. The bus flipped three times on its way down a 50-foot slope into a ravine. Two of the boys were thrown through the windows. One was hit by the bus bumper, the other run over. They were lying on the side of the hill, dead, when Johnny and his buddies saw them.

"I have never developed many close friends," wrote Johnny in

The Cincinnati Enquirer

Ted and Katy Bench became familiar sights at Riverfront Stadium in the 1970s, after moving to Cincinnati.

his autobiography, *Catch You Later*, "and maybe it's because that accident changed me to the point where I have denied friendships."

Bench finished his senior year at Binger as the best catcher and pitcher on the team, and his play in regional tournaments drew plenty of attention. Scouts say sagebrush can't hide talent; neither could the obscurity of tiny Binger. Word of the Oklahoma phenom soon spread throughout the scouting fraternity.

"One day the scouts were there, and I was pitching the finals of the county tournament," recalled Bench. "I took infield (practice) as a catcher because they all wanted to see me throw."

Several teams were ahead of the Reds in scouting Bench, but once tipped off, the organization moved fast. An Orioles scout had asked Jim McLaughlin, who was then the Reds director of player personnel, what he thought of a prospect named Johnny Bench.

"Oh, we're not too high on him," McLaughlin told the scout.

After the scout walked out the door, McLaughlin turned to an associate and said, "Who is this (Bench) guy? We better get some scouts down there."

Tony Robello and Bob Thurmond were dispatched to Binger. They liked what they saw, but immediately understood why previous Reds reconnaissance had overlooked Bench. He was doing a lot more pitching and playing of third base than he was catching. But his arm was better noticed behind the plate.

Robello almost missed Bench. On one of Robello's first visits to Oklahoma, Bench was pitching. Robello was not that impressed with Bench's potential as a pitcher. Most of the other scouts left after several innings. But Robello stayed, and when Bench moved behind the plate to catch the last innings, Robello immediately recognized a prospect.

"A lot of teams rated (Ray) Fosse and (Gene) LaMont higher than John," Robello recalled. "Obviously, we didn't. (Bench) had the great arm, the great power. We liked everything about him more than those other guys. You couldn't project at that time that he would end up being such a great player, but you knew the potential was there."

Robello liked Bench so much that he argued with McLaughlin that Bench should be the Reds' top pick. But the Reds needed a third baseman and drafted Bernie Carbo first instead.

Twenty clubs passed on Bench in the first round. Fifteen additional opportunities were there to take Bench before the Reds made him their second-round pick—the 36th player chosen in baseball's first-ever draft. Seven catchers were drafted ahead of Bench, of whom only two, Ray Fosse and Ken Rudolph, played in the majors. Of the 35 players chosen ahead of Bench, only 16 reached the majors.

The Reds low-balled Bench with a $5,000 offer. He and Ted negotiated it up to $6,000, plus $1,000 a semester (for eight semesters) if he chose to attend school during the offseason. As soon as Johnny arrived in Tampa in 1965—the city that Pete Rose had set afire four years earlier with 30 triples—the club brass immediately realized it had been blessed again.

"Bernie Carbo was an impressive ballplayer, wonderful with the bat," recalled Mike Moore, who was the Tarpons assistant general manager. "But when you'd look at the two of them together, Bench was such a tremendous prospect that you just had to wonder how anybody was drafted ahead of him."

And, to at least one person, it appeared Bench had something to prove.

"He was a proud, proud man," Carbo would later recall. "I think (Johnny) was a little resentful of me being the number one (draft choice) and him being the number two. But that just made him more determined."

Bench, however, said he didn't feel that way.

"Hell, I was glad to be second," he said. "I had always looked at Bernie and said, 'Why is he first?' But I didn't look at myself and say, 'Why wasn't I first?' I just didn't know who was supposed to be good and who wasn't supposed to be good."

The Cincinnati Enquirer

Bench signed his professional contract the summer he graduated from high school and immediately started play with Tampa in Single A ball. He then moved on to Peninsula (Virginia) and Buffalo before joining the Reds late in 1967.

His powerful, quick throwing arm, his startling footwork and graceful catching of foul pop-ups and relay throws quickly set Bench apart from the other prospects. Even among his fellow pros, Johnny Bench commanded attention. What also stood out in Tampa to teammates and club brass was Bench's confidence.

"The thing I was most taken with was his ability to handle pitchers," said Moore. "I mean, here was this 17-year-old kid walking right in here like he had handled them forever."

Larry Gable, the first professional pitcher that Bench caught, was mesmerized.

"He didn't play like a 17-year-old, that's for sure," said Gable. "He had that tremendous arm. I used to tell people I gave up base hits just so I could watch Johnny cut 'em down at second."

Bench had some adapting to do at the plate to hit professional pitching, however. In 68 games that year with Tampa, he hit .248 with two homers and 35 RBIs. But he had little to learn behind the plate. Observers were absolutely agog.

"But he wasn't one of those guys who thought he knew it all," said his second-year pro manager, Pinky May. "He had an open mind, took it all in and then put it into practice."

The Reds promoted Bench to Double A ball in 1966 to Hampton, Virginia, where he played for the Peninsula Grays.

Bench, who roomed with Carbo in a Hampton apartment, was a Peninsula Gray for only 98 games before being called up to Triple A Buffalo. He had shown himself to be a quick study with the bat (.294, 22 home runs and 68 RBIs) and there was nothing left to learn in Virginia. In the Carolina League All-Star game, Bench had thrown out three runners in one inning. Of his 22 home runs, he hit nine in his last nine games as a Gray.

"If you hit the ball over this one sign (in the outfield), you would get a suit," recalled Bench. "I think I hit nine homers (in Hampton) and seven of them went over that sign."

Actually, it was 12 home runs with 10 of them hit over the sign.

"It made for a quick, free wardrobe," Bench remembered.

His incredible season also earned him a very unusual tribute dreamed up by the Peninsula general manager, Marshall Fox. The promotions-minded Fox knew the popular Bench was too good to play for Peninsula for long and he planned to make the most of it. As soon as Bench was called up to Buffalo, Fox retired Bench's number (19) in a public ceremony.

"It was a little out of the ordinary," said Pinky May, "but Johnny wasn't an ordinary player."

Bench, who would be named Most Valuable Player of the Carolina League at season's end, shuffled off to Buffalo accompanied by a parade that stretched all the way to the airport. In Buffalo, more than 20,000 fans jammed old War Memorial Stadium for Bench's Triple A debut. The stadium was filled because a local meat cutter's union had bought up all the tickets and given them away free.

Three batters into the game, Bench suffered a broken thumb and was out for the year.

"I wasn't even on the bench for a total of four hours," Bench remembered. "I came in, signed my contract, took batting practice, and then in the first inning, I took a foul tip off my thumb. I caught the rest of the inning, then I went back to the dugout and told the manager, 'I think I broke my thumb.'"

He never even got to hit.

After Bench was hurt, he hustled off to Cincinnati to watch some games at Crosley Field. Sammy Ellis, then a Reds pitcher, recalls the day Bench yelled out to the Reds bullpen from the stands.

"If any of you guys are catchers, you'd better remember me," Bench said. "I'm going to take one of your jobs."

Ellis said he and the other pitchers laughed.

"But he wasn't kidding," said Ellis.

Bench opened the 1967 season in Buffalo, and struggled early in the season in part because his reputation had preceded him. The Bisons rolled into Rochester to play the Red Wings, the Baltimore Orioles Triple A affiliate. Cy Kritzer, who covered the Bisons for *The Buffalo Evening News*, recalled that Red Wings manager Earl Weaver told him, "You're going to see your phenom stopped."

And Weaver was right.

The phenom was stopped.

But Bench learned a great deal on that trip into Rochester.

"Some of the veteran (Bisons) pitchers took me out to the ballpark and said, 'Hey, you're going to learn how to hit the curveball,'" Bench recalled. "All of a sudden, my hitting turned around."

Later in the season, when the Red Wings visited western New York, they sent Jim Palmer to the mound. Palmer, who had won 15 games with the Orioles the previous season, was rehabbing from back and shoulder ailments.

"(The Red Wings) had a big lead and Palmer was cruising along real easy," recalled Kritzer. "Eventually, Buffalo loads the bases and out to the mound comes Weaver. He tells Palmer, 'Don't let up this guy; he's got something.' But Palmer hangs a curveball, and Johnny knocks it onto the adjoining golf course, about 430 feet away."

Bench had 23 home runs and 68 RBIs and a .259 batting average by the time the Reds called him up in late August. He was later named the 1967 Minor League Player of the Year.

When Johnny walked into the Reds clubhouse in August 1967, the team's backup catcher, Don Pavletich, said to Bench, "I guess you're here to take my job, huh?"

Bench shook his head to indicate "no" and then pointed to the first-string catcher, John Edwards.

"I'm here to get his job," said Bench.

It didn't take long. Although Bench hit only .163 in 25 games (14-for-86) for the Reds in late 1967, his defense was outstanding. Edwards was traded in the offseason, and the Reds had a new starting catcher.

"He was by far the best catching prospect I'd ever seen," said Cincinnati native Don Zimmer, who managed Buffalo the second half of that '67 season. "I had this friend in Florida who was a big baseball fan. He'd read *The Sporting News* to try to get a line on the top rookies. I said I'd give him 100 picks for the 1968 Rookie of the Year, knowing he'd break out *Sporting News* and pick all these guys hitting .338."

Zimmer had somebody else in mind.

He eyed his sheet of paper with the title, "1968 N.L. Rookie of the Year."

"Johnny Bench," Zimmer scribbled.

Shortly after coming to the Reds, Johnny Bench (center) joined the Army Reserves. He and Pete Rose (left) served one stint together in Ft. Thomas, Kentucky.

The Cincinnati Enquirer

DESTINATION: BIG RED MACHINE

Player	DOB	1960	1961	1962	1963	1964	1965	1966	1967	1968
Menke	1940	*Yakima*	*Vancouver*	Milwaukee	Milwaukee	Milwaukee	Milwaukee	Atlanta	Atlanta	Houston
C. Carroll	1941		*Quad City*	*Boise*	*Denver*	Milwaukee	Milwaukee	Atlanta	Atlanta	Atlanta/CIN
Helms	1941	*Palatka*	*Topeka*	*Macon*	*San Diego*	*San Diego*	SD/CINCY	CINCINNATI	CINCINNATI	CINCINNATI
Rose	1941	*Geneva*	*Tampa*	*Macon*	CINCINNATI	CINCINNATI	CINCINNATI	CINCINNATI	CINCINNATI	CINCINNATI
Norman	1942		*Shreveport*	*Lewiston/KC*	*Bghmtn/KC*	*S.Lke/Cubs*	*Wenatchee*	*Dallas/Cubs*	*Spokane/Cubs*	*Albuquerque*
Woodward	1942				Milwaukee	Milwaukee	Milwaukee	Atlanta	Atlanta	Atlanta/CIN
Bailey	1942		*Asheville*	*Clmbs/Pitts.*	Pittsburgh	Pittsburgh	Pittsburgh	Pittsburgh	Los Angeles	Los Angeles
Perez	1942	*Geneva*	*Geneva*	*Rocky Mt.*	*Macon*	*San Diego*	CINCINNATI	CINCINNATI	CINCINNATI	CINCINNATI
Merritt	1943			*Erie*	*Charlotte*	Atlanta	Minnesota	Minnesota	Minnesota	Minnesota
May	1943		*Tampa*	*Tampa*	*Rocky Mt*	*Macon*	*San Diego*	*Buffalo*/CIN	CINCINNATI	CINCINNATI
McGlothlin	1943			*Quad City*	*Hawaii*	*Hawaii*	California	California	California	California
Morgan	1943				*Modesto*	*San Antonio*	Houston	Houston	Houston	Houston
Billingham	1943		*Orlando*	*St. Pete.*	*Salisbury*	*St. Pete.*	*Albuquerque*	*Spokane*	*Spokane*	L.A.
Rettenmund	1943						*Stockton*	*Stockton*	*Elmira*	Baltimore
Nelson	1944				*Middlesboro*	*Sarasota*	*Tidewater*	*Evansville*	*Indy*/W.Sox	Baltimore
Granger	1944						*Raleigh*	*Arkansas*	*Tulsa*	St. Louis
Tolan	1945				*Reno*	*Tulsa*	St. Louis	St. Louis	St. Louis	St. Louis
Lum	1945				*Waycross*	*Binghamton*	*Yakima*	*Austin*	*Rchmnd*/Atl	Atlanta
Borbon	1946							*Cedar Rapids*	*St. Pete.*	*Modesto*
Plummer	1947						*Saratoga*	*Eugene*	*Modesto*	Chic. (NL)
Hall	1947							*Sarasota*	*Wisc. Rapids*	Minnesota
Carbo	1947						*Tampa*	*Peninsula*	*Knoxville*	*Asheville*
Crowley	1947							*Miami*	*Miami*	*Rochester*
Bench	1947						*Tampa*	*Peninsula*	*Buffalo*/CIN	CINCINNATI
Armbrister	1948								*Cocoa*	*Cocoa*
Concepcion	1948									*Tampa*
Kirby	1948							*Sarasota*	*Modesto*	*Tulsa*
Chaney	1948							*Sioux Falls*	*Knoxville*	*Asheville*
Simpson	1948								*Sioux Falls*	*Asheville*
Nolan	1948							*Sioux Falls*	CINCINNATI	CINCINNATI
Geronimo	1948								*Johnson City*	*Ft. Lauderdale*
Foster	1948									*Medford*
Griffey	1950									
Darcy	1950									
Grimsley	1950									
Eastwick	1950									
Gullet	1951									
Driessen	1951									
Flynn	1951									
Zachry	1952									
Alcala	1952									
McEnaney	1952									
Sarmiento	1956									

This chart traces the careers of 42 prominent Cincinnati players during the Big Red Machine era. Nearly every player on the 1975-76 team is included, as well as several others who played in the 1970-74 period. Both minor and major league clubs are represented. If a player left the Reds, the chart notes the player's affiliation for one additional season.

Players listed in red were drafted by the Reds, or originally signed with the Reds. *Italics* indicate minor league clubs.

1969	1970	1971	1972	1973	1974	1975	1976	1977	1978
Houston	Houston	Houston	CINCINNATI	CINCINNATI	Houston				
CINCINNATI	CINCINNATI	CINCINNATI	CINCINNATI	CINCINNATI	CINCINNATI	CINCINNATI	White Sox		
CINCINNATI	CINCINNATI	CINCINNATI	Houston						
CINCINNATI	CINCINNATI	CINCINNATI	CINCINNATI	CINCINNATI	CINCINNATI	CINCINNATI	CINCINNATI	CINCINNATI	CINCINNATI
Spokane	LA/St. Louis	St. L./S. Diego	S. Diego/CINCY	CINCINNATI	CINCINNATI	CINCINNATI	CINCINNATI	CINCINNATI	CINCINNATI
CINCINNATI	CINCINNATI	CINCINNATI	Retired						
Montreal	Montreal	Montreal	Montreal	Montreal	Montreal	Montreal	CINCINNATI	CINCY/Boston	
CINCINNATI	CINCINNATI	CINCINNATI	CINCINNATI	CINCINNATI	CINCINNATI	CINCINNATI	CINCINNATI	Montreal	
CINCINNATI	CINCINNATI	CINCINNATI	CINCINNATI	Texas					
CINCINNATI	CINCINNATI	CINCINNATI	Houston						
California	CINCINNATI	CINCINNATI	CINCINNATI	CINCY/Chi (AL)					
Houston	Houston	Houston	CINCINNATI	CINCINNATI	CINCINNATI	CINCINNATI	CINCINNATI	CINCINNATI	CINCINNATI
Houston	Houston	Houston	CINCINNATI	CINCINNATI	CINCINNATI	CINCINNATI	CINCINNATI	CINCINNATI	Detroit
Baltimore	Baltimore	Baltimore	Baltimore	Baltimore	CINCINNATI	CINCINNATI	San Diego		
Kansas City	Kansas City	Omaha/KC	Kansas City	CINCINNATI	CINCINNATI	Injury	Kansas City		
CINCINNATI	CINCINNATI	CINCINNATI	Minnesota						
CINCINNATI	CINCINNATI	Injury	CINCINNATI	CINCINNATI	San Diego				
Atlanta	Atlanta	Atlanta	Atlanta	Atlanta	Atlanta	Atlanta	CINCINNATI	CINCINNATI	CINCINNATI
California	CINCINNATI	Indianapolis	CINCINNATI	CINCINNATI	CINCINNATI	CINCINNATI	CINCINNATI	CINCINNATI	CINCINNATI
Indianapolis	Indy/CINCY	Indy/CINCY	CINCINNATI	CINCINNATI	CINCINNATI	CINCINNATI	CINCINNATI	CINCINNATI	Seattle
Minnesota	Minnesota	Minnesota	CINCINNATI	CINCINNATI	CINCINNATI	CINCY/Mets			
Indianapolis	CINCINNATI	CINCINNATI	CIN/St. Louis	St. Louis	Boston	Boston			
Rchstr/Balt.	Baltimore	Baltimore	Baltimore	Baltimore	CINCINNATI	CINCINNATI	Atlanta/Balt.		
CINCINNATI	CINCINNATI	CINCINNATI	CINCINNATI	CINCINNATI	CINCINNATI	CINCINNATI	CINCINNATI	CINCINNATI	CINCINNATI
Nwprt News	Columbus	Columbus	Indianapolis	Indy/CINCY	Indy/CINCY	CINCINNATI	CINCINNATI	CINCINNATI	retired
Asheville	Indianapolis	CINCINNATI	CINCINNATI	CINCINNATI	CINCINNATI	CINCINNATI	CINCINNATI	CINCINNATI	CINCINNATI
San Diego	San Diego	San Diego	San Diego	San Diego	CINCINNATI	CINCINNATI	Montreal		
CINCINNATI	CINCINNATI	CINCINNATI	CINCINNATI	CINCINNATI	CINCINNATI	CINCINNATI	Atlanta		
Indianapolis	CINCINNATI	CINCINNATI	CINCINNATI	Kansas City					
CINCINNATI	CINCINNATI	CINCINNATI	CINCINNATI	Injury	Injury	CINCINNATI	CINCINNATI	CINCY/Calif.	
Houston	Houston	Houston	CINCINNATI	CINCINNATI	CINCINNATI	CINCINNATI	CINCINNATI	CINCINNATI	CINCINNATI
Fresno/SF	Phoenix/SF	SF/Cincy	CINCINNATI	Indy/CINCY	CINCINNATI	CINCINNATI	CINCINNATI	CINCINNATI	CINCINNATI
Bradenton	Sioux Falls	Tampa	3 Rivers	Indy/CINCY	CINCINNATI	CINCINNATI	CINCINNATI	CINCINNATI	CINCINNATI
Covington	Williamsport	Columbus	Columbus	Denver	Indy/CINCY	CINCINNATI	Indy/CINCY	Retired	
Sioux Falls	Indianapolis	Indy/CINCY	CINCINNATI	CINCINNATI	Baltimore				
Bradenton	Tampa	Raleigh/3 Rvrs	3 Rivers	Indianapolis	Indy/Cincy	Indy/Cincy	CINCINNATI	CINCY/St L.	
Sioux Falls	CINCINNATI	CINCINNATI	CINCINNATI	CINCINNATI	CINCINNATI	CINCINNATI	CINCINNATI	N.Y. (AL)	
	Tampa	Tampa	3 Rivers	Indy/CINCY	CINCINNATI	CINCINNATI	CINCINNATI	CINCINNATI	CINCINNATI
			Tampa	3 Rivers	Indianapolis	CINCINNATI	CINCINNATI	CINCY/Mets	
	Brdtn/S. Fls	Tampa	3 Rivers	3 Rivers	Indianapolis	Indianapolis	CINCINNATI	CINCY/Mets	
	Bradenton	Sioux Falls	Key Wst/3 Rv	3 Rivers	Indianapolis	Indianapolis	CINCINNATI	CINCY/Mont	
	Sioux Falls	Tampa	3 Rivers	Indianapolis	Indy/CINCY	CINCINNATI	CINCINNATI	Montreal	
			Bradenton	Seattle	Tampa	Indianapolis	Indy/CINCY	CINCINNATI	CINCINNATI

Bob Howsam arrived in Cincinnati in 1967. Backed by a generous Board of Directors and his own savvy management team, he began building a first-class baseball operation that culminated in consecutive World Championships and league attendance records.

Minor League Executive of the Year, 1951 and 1956

Chapter 3

Howsam
Dynasty Builder

Major League Executive of the Year, 1973

By the summer of 1964, the main cogs in the Big Red Machine were all on the road to careers in baseball. Pete Rose was in his second season with the Reds, Tony Perez was playing his final year of minor league ball in San Diego, and Johnny Bench was drawing the interests of scouts as he played high school ball in Oklahoma.

A young infielder named Joe Morgan was impressing the Houston Colt 45's with his speed and power at their Double A club in San Antonio. In Toronto, a journeyman ball player named George "Sparky" Anderson was struggling in his first year as manager in the International League.

And, in Denver, 46-year-old Robert Lee Howsam, the man who would eventually pull all this baseball talent together in Cincinnati, sat in the office of his new investment company and pondered a return to baseball.

Howsam, who had been involved in professional sports in the Denver area since 1947, had retired from the sports business the year before and formed a new company, Howsam and Brown, an investment firm specializing in mutual funds. Howsam regretted leaving sports, but his baseball, football and stadium-building ventures had accumulated a sizeable debt. With his family's future foremost in mind, he had chosen the prudent path of retiring his obligations and launching a safer although less-satisfying business.

In Denver, which had been over-looked in baseball's expansion of the early 1960s, Howsam felt that he had little chance of ever again being involved in major league baseball. But a call from the St. Louis Cardinals and his former mentor, Branch Rickey, re-opened the issue of Howsam's professional future. Would Howsam be interested in returning to baseball in a front-office position with the Cardinals? Historically one of baseball's best franchises, the Cardinals had gone 17 years without a pennant and were now struggling in the '64 season, 10 games out of first.

For Howsam, any inquiry coming from Branch Rickey was flattering. Howsam's administrative apprenticeship in baseball in the late 1940s and early 1950s had been directed in large part by Rickey, and Howsam had enormous respect for this most innovative and influential of all baseball executives. But returning to professional baseball would mean abandoning his new business and uprooting his family from its native Colorado. He drove home to talk to Janet, his wife of 25 years.

There had been no mention between them of Bob's regretting his decision to leave the sports business in 1963, nor of his longing to return, but such feelings need not be spoken to be well understood.

Janet listened to her husband speak of Rickey's call.

"Do it, Bob," she said. "Go see what he has to say. You miss baseball."

Bob Howsam's memories of baseball begin in La Jara, Colorado, an eye-blink of a town on US 285, just 25 miles north of the New Mexico border. La Jara is one of several small towns scattered throughout the fertile San Luis Valley, an agricultural haven that attracted the Howsam family in 1927. To the east rises the Sangre de Cristo range (with four 14,000-foot peaks just 30 miles from the Howsam home); to the west looms the San Juan Mountains and the Continental Divide. The Rio Grande River trickles out of the San Juans just northwest of La Jara and flows through the farmlands of the valley south to Mexico. The historic valley boasts the oldest settlement in the state, as well as a rich Hispanic heritage. But it wasn't history that attracted the Howsam family. It was sweet clover and alfalfa.

Lee Howsam, Bob's father, operated a honey business just outside Denver, where Bob was born in 1918. Nine years later, Lee moved the operation to La Jara, population 900, to take advantage of cheaper land and the bountiful green fields with their bee-enticing blossoms. La Jara supported three other major honey producers, and Howsam and Sons was a successful fourth. The young Howsam spent his summers learning the bee business from his father, driving the narrow roads around La Jara checking the hives, and working in the nearby vegetable packing sheds.

But the valley's short hot summers offered opportunities other than work for an industrious teenager; there was plenty of time for baseball, too. La Jara High School did not have enough students to field a baseball squad—there were only 12 graduates in Howsam's class—so Bob joined a La Jara team assembled with boys from surrounding farm communities. He played in the semiprofessional State League as a big left-handed first baseman with much enthusiasm and a fair amount of skill.

Playing was his passion, not watching or listening to the game. In the 1930s in southern Colorado, the nearest big league club was over 800 miles away in St. Louis. The Howsams' honey business was successful—even in the depression, honey sales remained strong at three cents a pound—but there were no long vacations that included baseball. And there were few chances to gather around the radio to listen to the Cardinals or the St. Louis Browns or any other club. Most teams broadcast only a handful of games, and pulling them in across the Rockies during the daylight hours was nearly impossible. But the airwaves in southern Colorado hummed with the World Series that was broadcast nationally over network affiliates. On October afternoons, young Bob would come in from the honey shop with his dad and lie down in front of the radio. Together, they followed the heroics of the Cardinals, Yankees, Giants and Tigers, the top clubs of the mid-1930s.

Howsam, who in later years would develop one of the best scouting systems in major league baseball, never saw a scout in La Jara, nor was he aware of any in Denver, where his La Jara team played in the state tournament.

"I always did want to be a ballplayer," Howsam recalled. "But I never got the chance. As I try to go back and evaluate how good a ballplayer I would have been, I think I would have been a pretty good one. I try to break it down. I could run—I was a sprinter and had success at it—I had good power and I didn't strike out much."

The closest Howsam came to the major leagues as a player was facing the barnstorming House of David All-Stars and the Kansas City Monarchs of the Negro Leagues. Both clubs toured Colorado, playing against the top local talent, and in La Jara, Howsam's semipro club offered the opposition. One of his fondest memories was a strikeout against the legendary Satchel Paige. "One for the scrapbooks," recalled Howsam.

As much as Howsam loved playing the game, he understood his future was in catching bees, not flies. Howsam and Sons honey business beckoned much more insistently than baseball. After high school, Howsam headed for the University of Colorado at Boulder. As Howsam planned for a future without baseball, he met the person who would eventually lead him back to the game: Janet Johnson, the daughter of Governor and soon-to-be United States Senator Ed Johnson, one of the most popular politicians in

Colorado history.

With marriage plans in his future, Howsam left the University of Colorado and enrolled in a more practical venture, a business college in Denver. He graduated in 1939, at the age of 21, married 19-year-old Janet and headed back to La Jara to help run the honey business.

In the next two years, as world events thrust the United States ever closer to war, Howsam enrolled in the Civil Pilot Training program in nearby Alamosa, Colorado. He finished the program in Parkersburg, West Virginia, and along the way, made his first contact with Cincinnati, flying into Lunken Airport on the far east side of the city, about eight miles upriver from where Riverfront Stadium and his Cincinnati Reds would play some 30 years later. He joined the Navy and was assigned to a test and delivery squadron that checked out fighter planes for aircraft carrier duty. He spent most of the war in Brooklyn and saw his first major league games at Yankee Stadium and Ebbetts Field. When the war ended, Howsam headed back to La Jara to his wife and two young sons and what appeared to be a long future in the family business.

Then, in 1947, his father-in-law, Senator Johnson, asked his affable son-in-law to move to Washington to become his administrative assistant and perhaps flourish in the world of politics. "We all agreed it was a wonderful opportunity," remembered Howsam. He liked the political whirl, but a few months after he arrived, his career detoured again.

Senator Johnson, a great baseball fan, had become involved with efforts to revive minor league baseball in Colorado. Before the war, the Western League had prospered with teams in Colorado, Iowa, Nebraska and South Dakota. In 1947, as baseball regained its pre-war prominence, a Denver sportswriter organized a new Western League and prevailed upon Senator Johnson to serve as the league's non-paid president. After attending organizational meetings in Denver in the spring, the Senator returned to Washington and summoned his son-in-law.

"They elected me as the unpaid president of the league and I've got to have an executive vice-president," said Johnson, looking at Bob. *"And you are it."*

Howsam negotiated a six-month leave of absence from his

The Sporting News

Senator Ed Johnson (right) sent his son-in-law, Bob Howsam (left) into the baseball business in 1946 when he anointed him director of the Western League. In 1951, the senator presented Howsam *The Sporting News* award as Outstanding Minor League Executive.

Washington job, assuming he would be back after the season was over, and headed for Denver.

The former first baseman knew the intricacies of the game on the field, but now he had to learn the business side: everything from making up schedules to stadium construction and repair (only two of the teams had established fields), to hiring umpires. The job included helping complete an outfield fence before an opening game, and writing checks to the umpires from his own account when the League's revenues were insufficient. All on a salary of $500 a month.

"I was the only one in the front office," Howsam recalled. "The funny part of it was the senator wanted me to travel every day to the other cities (Pueblo, Omaha, Lincoln, Council Bluffs and Des Moines) and I had to cover that out of the $500, too."

Despite some attendance problems with the Denver club, the Western League was on its way to becoming the top draw in A baseball (the highest minor league level at that time) after one season. But when the Denver owners announced they wanted to sell the club, the league was thrown into a crisis, just when Howsam thought he would return to Washington.

"The Denver owners thought you just opened the gates and people would come in," remembered Howsam. "Well, you didn't. So I talked my Dad and my brother into coming in with me and we formed Rocky Mountain Empire Sports, Inc. and bought controlling interest in the club."

Howsam never returned to Washington.

Years later, at the major league level, Howsam would be linked to the opening of new parks, overseeing the debut of Busch Stadium in St. Louis and Riverfront in Cincinnati. But his baptism in ballpark construction began much earlier when the Howsams decided that the Denver Bears attendance problem was due in part to Merchants Park, an aging wooden facility that had already been condemned once. Howsam himself had played at Merchants Park in state tournaments in the 1930s; Babe Ruth, Lou Gehrig and Josh Gibson were among the legends to have appeared there. But nostalgia was not enough to save the old park. The Howsams bought a former dump site on the west side of Denver for $33,000, raised another $250,000 and built Bears Stadium, the first modern ballpark in the history of Denver.

There was barely a blade of grass on the site when the Howsam family bought it. But vision and a fierce determination to succeed pushed the project forward.

"He (Bob Howsam) thinks things through very carefully," said Jim Burris, a former general manager of the Denver Broncos. "When he decides on a course of action, nothing but nothing is going to swerve him from that course."

Bob Howsam's vision and his belief in running a first-class operation for the fans were evident on August 14, 1948, at the opening of Bears Stadium when 11,000 people filled the park. As one fan recalled, "The fans went from the wooden benches of the old park to theater-style seats at Bears."

At age 30, only two years removed from the honey business, Bob Howsam now owned a baseball team and a ballpark.

In the next decade, the Denver Bears and the Western League became the model for successful minor league operations. In Howsam's first three seasons, the Bears drew 463,000, 380,000 and 424,000, outdrawing at least one major league team each year, and earning for Howsam *The Sporting News* award as Outstanding Minor League Executive in 1951.

"The Bears president-general manager can be found almost every night between seasons holding a session with some [organization], talking baseball and showing baseball films," observed *The Sporting News*. "He staged special nights for surrounding towns and organizations throughout the season." The paper also remarked on the "neat and clean" park that was by now a trademark of a Howsam operation.

Howsam shied away from outlandish promotions, focusing his special event nights on family-oriented entertainment. He also tried a couple of "All-American" innovations that didn't work out.

"I came up with two ideas back then," Howsam remembered. "One was I wanted to get the best hot dog possible. So I went to Wilson in Chicago and they put together an all-beef hot dog. But you know the funny part—people aren't used to eating all-beef hot dogs. They thought they were tough. So I had to go back to the old kind. Then I went out to Denver University and I tried to have them come up with a spray. I wanted something I could spray around the stadium early in the game and make it smell like a bakery. People would want to eat. But they couldn't do it."

Despite these culinary setbacks, the Bears profited. Howsam credited a part of his success to the fact that his family owned the Bears outright.

"So many of the clubs in those days were owned by a major league club. Every time they needed money to operate, they asked the big club for it. But we had to reach into our own pockets. You learn a lot in a hurry."

Howsam also displayed a horse-trader's knack for swinging a good deal. For years, the Bears were the only team in A ball to have their own plane. Maintenance free.

"We bought our own DC-3," said Howsam. "We put it in the Frontier fleet, which was an airline out of Denver. They needed extra planes. They agreed to meet our schedules and then use it the rest of the time for their own flights. So they got an extra plane and kept it up and it didn't cost us a dime. That's how you end up with your own plane in A ball."

The young general manager had shown he knew how to solve two of the front office's biggest challenges: fiscal management and attracting people to the ballpark. But Howsam also discovered that he excelled in confronting the most enduring of all baseball's enigmas: how do you recognize major league talent in a young prospect?

Successful general managers either become good judges of talent or good judges of scouts. The most successful do both, and Howsam learned early that nothing was more important or satisfying than scouting, developing and evaluating players, and forming a network of skilled baseball men whose decisions he could trust.

Howsam had never worked as a scout, nor even seen many major league baseball games before he began his front office work in 1947. However, his years of playing amateur and semipro ball had given him a firm grounding in the skills of the game. Now, on a daily basis, he watched as young players came into the league and were tested and rated by the big clubs. He sat with the scouts, attended organizational meetings, quizzed his managers and coaches and measured his evaluations against the old-time baseball men.

In 1953, the Denver Bears' working agreement with the Boston Braves ended and Howsam signed on with the Pittsburgh Pirates and to a lifetime devotion to the Pirates general manager, the man who had practically invented the art of developing players, the legendary Branch Rickey.

In the early 1920s, when Rickey was president of the Cardinals, he invented the farm system; by 1939 the Cards had 32 minor league teams and about 650 players. The Cardinals did not purchase one player between 1920 and 1945, harvesting them all from within their own farm system. Rickey was eloquent, persuasive and intimidating, with a mesmerizing voice and a preacher's passion for the game. This was a man who had spent his honeymoon running a tryout camp.

Rickey was over 70 when Howsam met him, his stature as baseball's wise man unquestioned. He commanded respect and demanded excellence. He was "Mr. Rickey" to the baseball world; that is, to all but an unsuspecting general manager out of Denver.

Soon after the Pirates and Bears signed their working agreement, Howsam flew to Columbus, Ohio, for an organizational meeting with his new bosses to review the rosters.

"I walked in and I was going to make the right impression," recalled Howsam.

He knew *The Sporting News* referred to Rickey as "Branch" and to his son (who also worked for the Pirates) as "Twig." Howsam walked up to the legend and his son.

"Hi Branch, Hi Twig," he said.

The scouts in the room could barely conceal their astonishment. At the first opportunity, one dragged Howsam aside and whispered urgently, "Don't you ever call Mr. Rickey, 'Branch'!"

Despite the *faux pas*, Rickey did not say anything to Howsam.

"He didn't embarrass me at all," recalled Howsam. "In fact, the first thing I know, Mr. Rickey says, 'Bob, tell me about this ballplayer. We're interested in him. Have you seen him play much?' I told him I had and that I liked him. And he says, 'OK, we'll draft him.' Now if you don't think that wasn't something. Here's a man who's probably the best observer of talent who's ever been in the game of baseball. And he shows that kind of confidence in you."

The next two years Howsam spent spring training with Rickey and the Pirates.

"I would watch him work out pitchers, listen to him lecture the players," said Howsam. "I was like a puppy dog. He allowed me to

The Cincinnati Enquirer

Pittsburgh general manager Branch Rickey took a young Bob Howsam under his tutelage in the mid-'50s when Howsam's Denver Bears became the Pirates' Triple A farm club. Howsam modeled his career in large part on the strategy, wisdom and philosophy of the legendary Rickey.

be right at his elbow."

Rickey's maxims became Howsam's guiding principles. When you look for pitchers, the big man is better than the small man. Look first for power in a hitter. The overstriding hitter cannot be corrected. It is better to trade a player a year too early than a year too late. Stock your farm system with many players: quality out of quantity.

Above all, Rickey preached the gospel of speed. He felt speed was the best indicator of major league ability and the only asset that helped a club both on offense and defense. Rickey believed you could teach a boy to hit, you could teach a boy to field, but if he was slow at 18, he would always be slow. Rickey developed the 60-yard dash as the defining test of speed. His grandson, Branch Rickey III, a career baseball man, remembered his grandfather's reasoning.

"Not 30 yards or 90 feet," said the grandson. "Not 45 yards. But 60 yards. After 40 yards or so, a lot of kids who looked good would start to break down; their agility, coordination would fall apart. You couldn't see that at 30 yards."

In the 1970s, Branch Rickey III scouted for the Pirates. Some 50 years after his grandfather had set the standard, the 60-yard dash still prevailed.

"And nobody did more running of the 60-yard dash than Howsam's scouts," said Rickey. "I can't think of another organization that better epitomized my grandfather's approach to the game."

In 1955, the Denver Bears switched their working agreement from the Pirates to the New York Yankees, and Howsam joined forces with George Weiss. Howsam had gone from Rickey, the most influential front office executive in baseball history, to Weiss, the most successful. In Rickey's words, "Weiss couldn't tell a bull from a cow" when it came to judging players, but Weiss learned to judge scouts.

"He could read his scouts," said Howsam. "When one scout said a player was 'fair,' he knew that meant poor. When another scout called a man 'fair,' he knew that meant he'd better check him out right away. You have to be able to read scouts to understand their ratings."

The Sporting News

Some of the winning tradition of the New York Yankees was imparted to Bob Howsam by Yankee general manager George Weiss (above) when the Yankees and the Denver Bears were affiliated in the 1950s.

Like most minor league general managers, Howsam yearned for a shot at the big leagues, a chance to take a team to the World Series. Now he was working with a man who had been behind the great teams of the Yankees of the 1940s and 1950s.

"I wanted to win a World Series someday," said Howsam, "I was going to be like Weiss. One time at his home in Connecticut, I asked him how many World Series rings he had. I thought maybe he would say eight or ten. He said, '19.' Nobody in the history of the game will ever win 19 World Series rings again."

Although he wasn't winning World Series, Howsam earned another *Sporting News* executive of the year award in 1956. The paper complimented the Bears boss not only on his attendance marks but also for developing a perennial contender. The Bears had finished first twice and second five times since the family took control in 1948.

In the late 1950s, after a decade in the minor leagues, Howsam began to chase a dream that would put him not only in the major leagues but would also allow him to remain in his native Colorado. Baseball had expanded west in 1958 when the Dodgers and Giants moved to California. Denver, on the basis of the attendance marks that Howsam's Bears had set in the 1950s, appeared to be the next serious candidate. But the major leagues showed no interest in expansion, and in 1959, encouraged by his father-in-law, Senator Johnson, Howsam decided to join Branch Rickey's efforts at forming a third major league, the Continental League.

To head off the threat, Major League baseball agreed to expansion, and in 1961 added two of the Continental League's prospective franchises, the Houston Colt 45s and the New York Mets. Denver—to the disappointment of the Howsams and city leaders who saw their city as "major league"—was again on the sidelines.

The Howsams were immediately presented with another opportunity, however, when Lamar Hunt contacted them about joining him as founders of a second professional football league, the American Football League. Rocky Mountain Empire Sports bought the Denver franchise rights, and in 1961, the A.F.L. began its inaugural season, with the Denver Broncos playing in an expanded Bears stadium. The Howsams built a new grandstand and added portable seats to reach the league's minimum of 35,000 seats. (After the addition of more seats in the 1960s, the park, then owned by the city, was re-named Mile High Stadium.)

In time, the A.F.L. became a great success. But the costs of the aborted Continental League start-up, the development of the Broncos and the expansion of the stadium had left the Howsams with a significant debt.

"It was not fair to my family," said Howsam, "to keep a debt that was considerably more than I could handle. We had spent so much enlarging the stands and it just didn't pay off as quickly as I thought. That first season of football, we lost two home dates to snow-outs. It was sad to leave sports."

By 1963, Howsam had formed his new investment firm and turned his back, or so he thought, on professional sports. George Weiss' rings were safe.

Then came the call from Rickey in the summer of 1964 that would return Howsam to baseball—and eventually to the Reds and the Big Red Machine. Rickey had joined the Cardinals in 1962 as a special consultant to owner August Busch, Jr., and immediately developed an adversarial relationship with general manager Bing Devine. Over the next two seasons, despite Devine's trade with the Cubs that brought Lou Brock to the Cardinals for pitcher Ernie Broglio, and the development of such talents as Bob Gibson, Ken Boyer and Tim McCarver, the Cardinals did not challenge for the pennant. In the middle of the 1964 season, owner Busch, prodded by Rickey, fired Devine. Rickey phoned Howsam and invited him to St. Louis for an interview; he didn't mention which position, but Howsam knew it had to be of substance to warrant a call from Rickey. He discussed the opportunity with his family, and with Janet's blessing, flew to Missouri.

"Mr. Rickey picked me up and took me to meet with Mr. Busch," Howsam recalled. "I was with them about 15 minutes and Busch said, 'I'd like you to be our general manager.'"

Seventeen years after he joined minor league baseball, Bob Howsam had finally made the majors.

Howsam's arrival in St. Louis coincided with an unbelievable two-month surge on the part of the Cardinals that catapulted them into a three-way pennant race with the Phillies and Reds. On the final day of the season, the Reds lost a 10-0 game to Jim Bunning and the Phillies; the Cardinals, needing a win, blasted the Mets 11-5 and popped the champagne corks. In a tough World Series, the Bob Gibson-led Cardinals beat the Yankees, four games to three. Howsam was thrilled at the club's good fortune, but he knew the credit would rightly go to Devine, manager Johnny Keane and the players.

But as Howsam assessed the organization, he realized he would soon have the opportunity to put his own stamp on the club.

"I'd been brought up with Rickey's philosophy," said Howsam. "Young players were very important. The Cardinals didn't have many; they had older players in Triple A. I immediately started building a bigger scouting force, and a more extensive farm system."

Unwilling to tinker with the lineup that had won in '64, Howsam basically kept the club intact, but under new manager Red Schoendienst (Johnny Keane had resigned after the series to manage the Yankees), the Cardinals won 13 fewer games, fell to 80-81, and slipped all the way to seventh place. Over the next two seasons, Howsam traded the popular but aging infield of Bill White (31), Dick Groat (35) and Ken Boyer (34) for several players who made little immediate impact. Howsam was roasted in the press and hung in effigy.

In more successful deals, he traded pitcher Ray Sadecki, who had won 20 games in 1964, for Orlando Cepeda, and he picked up Roger Maris from the Yankees. That acquisition allowed the club to move outfielder Mike Shannon to third base. With the addition of Del Maxvill at short, and holdovers McCarver, Brock, Stan Javier and Curt Flood, Howsam had solidified a starting lineup that would capture the 1967 and 1968 National League pennants.

But Howsam was not in St. Louis to enjoy those victories. His mentor Rickey had been fired by the Cardinals in 1965 (he died later that year), and Howsam increasingly clashed with Dick Meyer, who worked for Busch in brewery operations and also participated in baseball decisions.

"Dick Meyer was one of the smartest businessmen I know, but he was always interfering," recalled Howsam. "Like on the Cepeda trade. Meyer said he was a one-legged player. I said, 'Dick, I've looked at the X-rays, I've talked to the doctors. He's OK!' The delay almost cost us the deal. Finally, I told him, 'I know you're a smart fellow, but I'm going to run this ballclub.' You know, you get tired of this."

In early January 1967, Gussie Busch informed Howsam he had heard from the new president of the Cincinnati Reds, Frank Dale.

"He wants permission to talk to you about running the Reds," said Busch. "What do you think of that?"

Frustrated at the lack of complete control he had with the Cardinals, Howsam was intrigued by the possibility.

"As much as I would like to stay here, I think I should talk to them," replied Howsam, setting in motion the deal that would bring him to Cincinnati.

Frank Dale, the publisher of *The Cincinnati Enquirer*, had purchased the Reds in early 1967 with an investment group known as 617, Inc. (617 Vine was then the address of *The Enquirer*).

Dale's group had bought the club from Bill DeWitt, who had come to the Reds in November 1960 as general manager under Powel Crosley. When Crosley died in early 1961, DeWitt assumed control of the business affairs and eventually purchased the club.

Like Bob Howsam, Bill DeWitt had learned the game and business of baseball from Branch Rickey. DeWitt's apprenticeship began in 1916 as Rickey's office boy with the Cardinals. He advanced through the Cardinal system until the 1930s, when he bought the St. Louis Browns, and led them to their first and only pennant in 1944. When DeWitt arrived in Cincinnati in 1960, he inherited a whirlwind of a manager, Fred Hutchinson, but a so-so club that had finished under .500 three straight seasons.

DeWitt and Hutchinson set out to rebuild the Reds for the 1961

Reds president Frank Dale (left), former owner Bill DeWitt (center) and Pete Rose were all members of the Reds "family" when Bob Howsam joined the organization in 1967.

season, and in a series of trades secured Gene Freese, Don Blasingame and Joey Jay for Roy McMillan, Ed Bailey and Cal McLish. They installed Gordy Coleman at first base, returned Frank Robinson to his natural outfield position, and brought up Johnny Edwards to catch. The chemistry clicked; several players had "career" years, and the Reds won their first pennant in 21 years. Every general manager dreams of taking over a mediocre club, making a few deals and winning the pennant. DeWitt, more successfully than any GM before him, had done just that.

The changes DeWitt wrought were not just short-term. The Reds nearly won pennants again in 1962 and 1964, and they were developing some of the best young talent in the league. Then, on December 9, 1965, DeWitt, ever mindful of the dictums of his mentor Rickey, traded a player a year too soon rather than a year too late. Calling Frank Robinson "an old 30," DeWitt sent him to Baltimore for pitchers Milt Pappas and Jack Baldschun, and outfielder Dick Simpson. DeWitt knew the deal was risky; he even called 10 or 12 of his top assistants together before the deal and had them "vote" on the trade by secret ballot. They overwhelmingly supported the deal. Here was a chance to improve what had been a chronically weak pitching staff with two proven pitchers in Pappas and Baldschun. Deron Johnson, who had a league-leading 130 RBIs for the Reds in 1965, appeared to be a capable RBI replacement for Robinson.

But the deal backfired. Robinson won a Triple Crown and the American League's Most Valuable Player award, led the Orioles to four World Series, and eventually made baseball's Hall of Fame, wearing an Orioles cap on his plaque even though he played more seasons with the Reds. Pappas, Baldschun and Simpson were all gone from the Reds by 1968, and without Robinson in the lineup, Johnson failed to hit. DeWitt's 1961 magic was forgotten in the aftermath of the trade—he suffered heavy criticism from the fans and sportswriters for what came to be regarded as the worst trade in the history of the Reds.

But more pertinent to DeWitt's long-range future with the Reds was his opposition to another trade that was brewing: Crosley Field for Riverfront Stadium.

By the mid-1960s, the deteriorating neighborhood near Crosley Field, the traffic and parking tangles and the park's low seating capacity had convinced the Reds and the city that the club needed a new and bigger ballpark.

City officials favored a site on the bank of the Ohio River as a catalyst for helping rejuvenate downtown. DeWitt disagreed. Fearful of flooding and traffic congestion, he commissioned studies of several potential sites, including what was to become Kings Island amusement park 20 miles north of Cincinnati, and a site in the northern suburb of Blue Ash.

The birth of the Cincinnati Bengals also complicated the stadium dilemma for DeWitt. Architects proposed a round, multi-purpose facility to house both the Reds and the new Bengals.

"The architects tried to convince him that the round stadiums were state of the art, but he disagreed with them," recalled his son, William DeWitt, Jr. "He felt baseball fans were going to get the short end on the design."

Sensing problems in Cincinnati, other cities began to court DeWitt and the Reds. San Diego was particularly aggressive; DeWitt and business manager John Murdough flew to Southern California to meet with Jack Kent Cooke, who wanted to bring major league baseball to the San Diego area.

Dick Wagner, later the president of the Reds, worked for Cooke as the manager of the Forum in Los Angeles. Wagner recalled that Cooke told him he had a "handshake" deal with DeWitt to move the Reds west.

Murdough denies the discussion ever went that far, but it was apparent that DeWitt was besieged with offers. Warren Giles, then president of the National League, and a former Cincinnati general manager under Powel Crosley, told DeWitt that he would not approve any out-of-town sale unless DeWitt was unable to find a local group willing to keep the Reds in Cincinnati.

With an out-of-town sale precluded, and with civic momentum building towards a riverfront site, DeWitt grudgingly accepted the inevitability of a downtown stadium. Lease issues then followed, with the city demanding a 40-year commitment. But DeWitt, who still had serious reservations about the site, would not commit himself or his heirs to 40 years with a possible white elephant. If DeWitt had been able to negotiate a shorter lease from the city, he might have remained the Reds owner and led the Reds into the '70s. But with progress at a standstill and civic leaders anxious to move forward, he finally agreed to sell the club to any group that would keep it in Cincinnati and agree to the city's terms.

In January of 1967, the 617, Inc. investor group, headed by *Enquirer* publisher Dale, agreed to buy the Reds for seven million dollars and sign a 40-year commitment to a new stadium.

Murdough accompanied DeWitt to a downtown bank for the formal closing.

"We exchanged papers, signed documents and when it was over, we walked back to our offices at the Central Trust Tower," recalled Murdough. "There were tears running down his cheeks. He had that big check in his briefcase, but all he could say was, 'I just lost my ballclub.'"

Later, DeWitt would admit that the riverfront site was a wise choice. The interstate system and pedestrian walkways moved crowds quickly in and out of the stadium, making it one of the most accessible parks in the United States. And while DeWitt was not an official member of the regime that ushered in the Riverfront era in 1970, he left a legacy of talent that would launch the Big Red Machine dynasty: Pete Rose, Tony Perez, Tommy Helms, Lee May, Gary Nolan, and a catching prospect named Bench.

The 617, Inc. group had the money to buy the Reds, but they were not baseball men, and their first task was to find a new general manager. They wanted someone with major league experience, who was promotions-minded and committed to a vigorous farm system. Board member William J. Williams headed up a search committee and quickly turned to DeWitt and two other former general managers of the Reds, Gabe Paul and Warren Giles, for recommendations. Two names topped the list: Buzzy Bavasi with the Dodgers and Bob Howsam at St. Louis.

"I called Gussie Busch in St. Louis for permission to talk to Howsam," recalled Williams. "He said he wouldn't stand in his way. I also called Walter O'Malley, but he was very reluctant to let me talk to Bavasi."

Williams and fellow board member Barry Buse flew to St. Louis to meet with Howsam.

"We talked and outlined what we wanted," remembered Williams. "We wanted a GM who would be on his own; we wouldn't second-guess him. Then we got on compensation and settled that. Once we got to know him, we almost stopped right there. I did finally talk to Bavasi, but he was hoping for the (GM) job with the Dodgers and he said he doubted he wanted to come to Cincinnati."

Within a week, the board voted to hire Howsam as the Reds' new general manager.

On January 22, 1967, Frank Dale introduced Bob Howsam to the Cincinnati community at a press conference. Howsam proclaimed himself happy with the Reds' "good young talent" and said he had no plans to replace manager Dave Bristol. As part of his duties at St. Louis, Howsam had regularly evaluated the other managers in the league and Bristol had impressed him. Supportive of his manager and given the luxury of a three-year contract, Howsam made few changes on the eve of the 1967 season. Off the field, Howsam came to different conclusions.

DeWitt had left Howsam with a solid foundation of young players and veteran talent, and there were some excellent prospects in the farm system. However, Howsam's vision of a first-class operation extended to the front office as well.

"DeWitt was a very good baseball man, but he didn't spend his money," Howsam recalled. DeWitt, who never had significant financial backers, ran a lean operation, all the way down to a minimum of furniture.

"I had more office equipment in class A baseball in Denver than DeWitt had in the major leagues," recalled Howsam. "I was used to running a more top-notch organization."

With the new ownership group supporting his expanded budget, Howsam upgraded the office, including adding several new positions devoted to marketing, public relations and expanding the Reds fan base.

"I believe that you have to spend money to make money," said Howsam, "but I also believe in making the dollars you spend

The Bob Howsam regime began on January 22, 1967, when Frank Dale (left), chairman of the Reds' new ownership group, introduced the new vice-president and general manager. Joining Howsam (center) and Dale were Mrs. Janet Howsam, William J. Williams (second from right) and Bill DeWitt (right).

count." Howsam doubled the front-office staff, adding a speakers bureau, an advertising director, a group sales department and a bigger promotions staff.

Howsam also brought in two trusted associates from St. Louis—Dick Wagner, who was named assistant to Howsam and who ran the business side of the club, and Sheldon "Chief" Bender, who became director of player personnel with responsibility for the minor league system. Wagner, who would eventually succeed Howsam as president of the Reds and become the man Cincinnati fans loved to hate for dismantling the Big Red Machine, was among Howsam's most dedicated and loyal lieutenants at St. Louis. Howsam had known Wagner since the Western League days when Wagner was president of the Lincoln, Nebraska team. Howsam thought him particularly adept at promoting baseball and in developing programs aimed at bringing young people and families to the ballpark. Wagner would also become infamous as Howsam's "hatchet" man. If a part of the Howsam persona was the unflappable, avuncular boss, it was possible in part because Wagner carried out the more onerous chores.

Wagner also set the tone for the front office in terms of work style: long hours, loyalty to Howsam and total dedication to the Reds and the game of baseball. Roger Ruhl, who was hired as publicity director in 1971, was working for the Cincinnati Royals (now the Sacramento Kings) of the National Basketball Association before joining the Reds. On Christmas Eve, 1970, he had attended a Royals party with Bob Cousy, then coach of the team, and returned home to find a message from Wagner. Could he meet Ruhl the next day to discuss a job with the Reds?

Rather than express shock at the audacity of a meeting on Christmas, Ruhl had the perfect response for Wagner. The Royals

BASEBALL MEN: DICK WAGNER

Not many baseball executives began their careers as vice presidents, but Dick Wagner did. Fresh out of the Navy in 1946, Wagner, only 19, was hired by the Detroit Tigers to be the vice president and general manager of their class D club in Thomasville, Georgia. It wasn't as glamorous as it seemed.

"I washed the uniforms, painted the bases, ran all the promotions," recalled Wagner. Over the next five years, he held front office jobs in Michigan, Florida and Texas.

When he re-entered the Navy for the Korean War, a sergeant looked at his resume and said, "Son, we don't have any ballclubs here for you to run."

Wagner returned to baseball after the Korean War, but left the game in the early 1960s to work for the Ice Capades and manage a radio station. He joined Howsam in 1964 in St. Louis and after a brief stint as manager of the Forum in Los Angeles, he returned to baseball for good when Howsam lured him to Cincinnati in 1967.

The Cincinnati Enquirer

Dick Wagner oversaw the business side of the operation as Howsam's executive assistant.

played on Christmas, and Ruhl had to be in at the office early to get out the game "stat" sheets. Certainly he would meet with Wagner, Ruhl said. But it would have to be for breakfast since he was already going to work. They met at 7:30 Christmas morning and Ruhl was hired. Later, the joke was that Ruhl didn't even have to show up for the interview once he said he was working Christmas. That was the kind of commitment Wagner expected.

Howsam may not have expected his staff to work Christmas Day, but he did expect them to outwork everybody.

"Our people worked and that was our success," Howsam said. "Nothing was going to interfere with my people building a baseball club. Time, effort, seven days a week. If it took scouts to drive 200 miles a day to look at two different games, they did it."

Sheldon "Chief" Bender, nicknamed after the Hall of Fame pitcher Charles "Chief" Bender, typified the dedication Howsam demanded. Bender was a career baseball man, having played for years in the minor leagues before moving into scouting and front office work with St. Louis in the early 1950s. He was the assistant farm director of the Cardinals when Howsam arrived in 1964, and although Bender was part of Devine's team, Howsam soon grew to appreciate Chief's organizational abilities.

Howsam and Bender were both "Rickey men" and they shared strong beliefs in the virtue of developing young talent. Bender could run a farm system, spot young talent and bring it along. To Howsam, there were no greater skills.

One thing that impressed Howsam was Bender's total commitment to the profession. During the season, Bender felt he had to see a game every day.

"I'd see the Reds at home, then when the team was on the road, I'd pack up my family—even the dog—in the car and head off to see one of our minor league clubs. Anywhere within 500 miles or so. The longer trips, I'd get there just about game time. I'd hurry up to the stands, and my wife would drop off the dog in the general manager's office."

Although Howsam brought several front-office people with him from St. Louis, he didn't "clean house" initially in Cincinnati, In retrospect, he felt it would have been easier if he had. There were some unpleasant situations as the transition from the DeWitt regime unfolded.

"I always said if I ever go to run another organization, I would fire everybody no matter what, and then hire everybody back that I wanted," Howsam now says. "So they understood one thing: they are there because of me. Otherwise your loyalties are not very good. Fellows, thinking, 'Well, he didn't bring me in.'"

By 1969, the front office had a decidedly Howsam orientation. Loyalty to the general manager and total dedication to the Reds were essential in the new regime, but Howsam was not looking for blind devotion. Everyone on Howsam's staff could expect to have his opinion solicited. In fact, Howsam's method of operation was always to ask for opinions before giving his. He realized his perspective, given too early, could shade an argument. Howsam respected the different perspectives among the staff, and there was plenty of good-natured haggling back and forth as these veteran baseball men disagreed on the value of a player. But once a decision was made, there would be no dissension.

"'Yes' men do you no good," said Howsam. "The rule I had was say what you want, I may not agree with you, but say it. But when you go out that door, don't you ever talk about how that isn't the way you would have done it. We're a team and once we decide what we want to do, nobody's going to second-guess it, or you won't be around long."

Perhaps nowhere within the organization was the impact of the new general manager felt more rapidly than in scouting and player development. It was too late to alter the team's strategy for the winter draft in January of 1967, but Howsam wanted to recast the club's philosophy before the big June draft. DeWitt's Reds had been built on an efficient farm system that emphasized quality. Howsam, ever the Rickey disciple, wanted as many young players as he could afford. In 1965 and 1966, the Reds had drafted 69 players; Howsam's Cardinals had selected 115. *Quality out of quantity.* But quantity required more scouts, a new farm club—and additional expenses. The board of directors approved the plan, increased their investment, and Howsam immediately added a fifth club to the Reds minor league system in the rookie league to open 25 new player slots. It was an investment that would eventually yield impressive dividends.

At first, Howsam elected to retain the scouting director, Jim McLaughlin. But it soon became apparent Howsam would need his own person in this job. The telling moment came in the final preparations for the June draft. After months of intense review, the Reds were prepared to draft Wayne Simpson, who would make the major leagues in 1970. But, at the last moment, McLaughlin suggested another pitcher from northern Ohio.

"I just couldn't believe it," Howsam recalled. "Here was Simpson recommended so highly. And here was McLaughlin asking about a player he had seen only in a couple of games at a tournament."

Howsam was astonished that his scouting director would jeopardize Simpson's selection with such a haphazard recommendation. The issue was not so much which pitcher was the

BASEBALL MEN: CHIEF BENDER

When he was in high school in the mid-1930s in St. Louis, Sheldon Bender attended a tryout camp for the Cardinals. The Cards didn't draft him, but they needed a couple of kids to practice with the team.

So, on summer afternoons when St. Louis was home, the high-school senior would hop a streetcar to Sportsman's Park and take fielding practice with Pepper Martin, Johnny Mize, Joe Medwick and Enos Slaughter.

"I was on cloud nine," recalled Bender.

In 1937, Bill DeWitt signed Bender to a minor league contract with the St. Louis Browns. Bender never made it to the major leagues, but after World War II he joined the coaching ranks with Branch Rickey's Cardinals.

Bender proved adept at judging talent, and after working as a scout in the Caribbean, he graduated to director of Cardinals' farm teams. Howsam discovered him there in 1964 and brought him to the Reds in 1967.

During the Big Red Machine era, Bender served as director of player personnel and brought up many young players, including Ken Griffey, Don Gullett and Rawly Eastwick.

© Cincinnati Reds

best prospect. (Simpson made it to the major leagues; the other player never made it above A ball.) Howsam was a man who demanded thorough research and preparation. The impropriety of the McLaughlin's maneuver galled him. By the fall of 1967, McLaughlin was gone and Howsam hired brothers Joe and Rex Bowen from Pittsburgh, both Rickey-trained men, to head up scouting.

When Howsam was hired in January 1967, the Reds hoped to be in their new stadium within two years. But Howsam, who had always stressed the philosophy of putting the fan first, would not allow Crosley Field to deteriorate. He continued to keep it in top-notch condition.

"We cleaned up the concessions, put in new counters, made sure things were painted and cleaned," he recalled.

Prior to the 1968 season, the promotions-conscious regime installed a 35-foot-long sign on the back of the scoreboard to keep I-75 drivers informed of coming games and attractions ("Willie and the Giants Here This Weekend!").

Howsam expected anyone associated with the Reds, from fans to sportswriters, to feel that the Cincinnati operation was first-class. Ruhl, Howsam's publicity director, recalled that the only time Howsam dressed him down was for a paltry spread at a buffet

Janet Howsam (left) contributed to the family atmosphere her husband was trying to foster in the Cincinnati organization. She attended nearly every home game, entertaining friends of the club in the Reds private box. She also hosted luncheons, including this 1967 affair for the wives of the Reds players. From left to right were Karolyn Rose, Margie Abernathy and Terrye May.

The Cincinnati Enquirer

at the Reds spring training facility in Tampa. A frugal clubhouse man simply could not bring himself to buy the quality of food Howsam wanted, and Ruhl himself ended up at the supermarket shopping for ham and beef that met the boss's standards. A small thing, but it typified Howsam's style, in both the quality he wanted and his attention to detail.

While Howsam demanded a first-class operation, it did not include pretentious behavior on his part. In St. Louis, when he took over Devine's job, he discovered that along with the company car came a chauffeur. Interestingly, the chauffeur was the same one Branch Rickey had used in his St. Louis days. While Howsam learned much from the old master, he didn't remember any lessons on chauffeurs. "He made me feel awkward," Howsam recalled. Howsam hardly knew what to do. He sat in the front seat instead of the rear and further confused the driver when he opened doors himself.

There would be no chauffeurs in Cincinnati. Howsam, an old-fashioned family man himself, wanted to instill feelings of family within the whole organization. His staff naturally called him "Mr." Howsam, not because he was a cold, distant boss, but rather as a sign of respect for the head of this extended household.

"He was in no way a dictator," recalled Sparky Anderson. "He ran it, but he ran it softly. Everybody knew he was going to run it, but he was very gentle. To Bob, it was family."

Although the Reds had finished seventh in 1966, the starting lineup included Pete Rose (age 25), Tony Perez (24), Tommy Helms (25), Leo Cardenas (28), Vada Pinson (28), Deron Johnson (27), Johnny Edwards (28) and Tommy Harper (26). Among the 1967 prospects, were Lee May, a good-looking power hitter, Gary Nolan, a polished young pitcher, outfielder Bernie Carbo and Johnny Bench.

This was the nucleus of the team Howsam carefully evaluated over the next three seasons. He realized he had inherited some fine players, but not all would fit into his plans.

The experts picked the Reds to finish fifth in 1967, but Cincinnati led the N.L. through May. Then, injuries knocked several starters from the lineup, and Howsam's old club, the Cardinals, slowly began to pull away. The Reds remained in contention for second place until the final weeks of the season, but ultimately faded to fourth. However, there were several significant developments that provided Howsam some room to maneuver. One was the injury to Deron Johnson early in the season that allowed Lee May to play every day. May split time between the outfield and first base and won *The Sporting News* Rookie of the Year award. Another was the success of Perez at third base and his emergence as a power hitter. Rose, who moved to the outfield for the first time, handled the new position well, and the rookie catcher Bench appeared to be ready for a starting job.

After a season of observing and evaluating his talent, Howsam determined that three of the veterans on the club had to be moved: Pinson, Cardenas and pitcher Milt Pappas.

"Pinson was quite a player, but he was not a player I wanted on my club," recalled Howsam. "I had always heard that Cardenas was an outstanding shortstop. But he had to play in so close, his arm was weak, that he couldn't go in the hole and throw anybody out."

Pappas had never met the expectations of the club after the Frank Robinson deal and Howsam also thought Pappas was something of a "clubhouse lawyer." Pappas was the Reds player representative and became involved in a nasty, public exchange

Draft Choices

The success of the Big Red Machine rested in part on excellent draft choices made by the Cincinnati organization in the late 1960s. In baseball's first draft in 1965, in the Bill DeWitt era, the Reds selections included Johnny Bench, Bernie Carbo and Hal McRae.

In 1967, Bob Howsam's first year in Cincinnati, the club drafted 98 players, 51 more than had been chosen by DeWitt's organization in 1966. Howsam believed strongly in Branch Rickey's theory: *quality out of quantity.*

Howsam's first draft brought Wayne Simpson and shortstop Frank Duffy to the Reds. The next year, the Reds had a weak draft, with only Milt Wilcox seeing action with the Big Red Machine. But Reds scouts made one important find in Venezuela: Davey Concepcion.

In 1969, the Reds picked Don Gullett, Ross Grimsley, Rawly Eastwick and Ken Griffey, and scouts found Dan Driessen who had been overlooked in the draft. The '69 draft was rated number one by *Baseball America*.

Year	Draft Choice	Residence	Round
1965	Bernie Carbo	Michigan	1
1965	Johnny Bench	Oklahoma	2
1965	Hal McRae	Florida	6
1966	Gary Nolan	California	1
1966	Darrel Chaney	Indiana	2
1967	Wayne Simpson	California	1
1967	Frank Duffy	California	1
1968	Milt Wilcox	Oklahoma	2
1968	Dave Concepcion	Venezuela	Free Agent
1969	Ross Grimsley	Tennessee	1
1969	Don Gullett	Kentucky	1
1969	Rawly Eastwick	New Jersey	3
1969	Ken Griffey	Pennsylvania	29
1969	Dan Driessen	South Carolina	Free Agent

with the club in June 1968, when the team voted, against his wishes, to play on the evening of Senator Robert F. Kennedy's funeral.

Angered that politics was intruding on his beloved sport of baseball, Howsam marched down to the clubhouse to address the players. So infuriated was Howsam, he literally could not speak.

Howsam could not swing a satisfactory trade for Pappas, Cardenas or Pinson in the winter of 1967-68, but he did trade three other starters: Tommy Harper, Deron Johnson and Johnny Edwards. The only significant player he received in return was Alex Johnson from St. Louis.

On paper, by position, the starting lineup (Rose, RF; Helms, 2B; Pinson, CF; Perez, 3B; May, 1B; Bench, C; Johnson, LF; Cardenas, SS) matched up well with all the contenders in 1968, and Cincinnati was among the pre-season favorites. But pitching problems plagued the team all season and the Reds finished fourth, 14 games behind St. Louis. Cincinnati's record of 83-79 failed to improve on their 87-75 mark of the year before.

But during and after the 1968 season, Howsam made three significant trades, bringing in players who would make a substantial contribution to the Big Red Machine. On June 11, 1968, a few days after the Kennedy tribute incident, the Reds and the Braves pulled off a three-for-three swap that sent pitchers Pappas and Ted Davidson and utility infielder Bob Johnson to Atlanta for Tony Cloninger, Clay Carroll and Woody Woodward. Although Cloninger was the big name associated with the deal, Carroll and Woodward were the real finds for the Reds.

Scout Ray Shore had pushed for Carroll. Shore thought that Carroll, unlike a lot of relievers who relied on just one pitch, had "starter's stuff." He was "no trick-pitch pitcher." Most significantly, he had a resilient arm and a bulldog personality that snarled, *Give me the ball!* He would be a key member of the Reds bullpen for the next seven seasons. In Woodward, Howsam hoped he had the shortstop to replace Cardenas. Woodward, 25, started several games in the second half of the season under the careful scrutiny of the Cincinnati brass. He made the plays, so in November, Howsam shipped Cardenas to Minnesota for 25-year-old left-hander Jim Merritt. The benefits of the Pappas trade kept accruing.

Howsam's third deal was another trade with the Cardinals: Pinson for Bobby Tolan and Wayne Granger. Again, Howsam turned to his former club, and again, he significantly improved the Reds. The Cardinals started Roger Maris instead of Tolan in '68 and Tolan had sulked. He came to the Reds as a question mark, but Howsam had watched Tolan come up to the major leagues in 1966 and had always been impressed with his blend of speed and power. Essentially, Howsam had "traded-in" Vada Pinson for a newer model; Pinson was 33, Tolan, 23.

The off-season deals left Howsam, Bristol and the prognosticators confident of the Reds chances in 1969. It would be the first season of divisional play, made necessary by the addition of franchises in Montreal and San Diego. The Reds were favored not only to win their division, but to capture the pennant as well.

Mindful of the club's pitching troubles in the previous seasons, Howsam stacked the team with eight experienced starters in spring training: Jim Maloney, Gary Nolan, Jim Merritt, George Culver, Tony Cloninger, Mel Queen, Jerry Arrigo and Jack Fisher. Clay Carroll and Wayne Granger were expected to handle the bullpen duties. And when pitching problems did surface, Howsam added two war-horses, Camilo Pascual and Pedro Ramos, both at the end of long careers.

The Reds began slowly, and by May 19, they were nine games back of Atlanta. But at the All-Star break, the Reds were only 3½ behind the Braves, with Los Angeles and San Francisco also in the race. On August 3, at Philadelphia, the Reds slugged it out with the Phillies, winning 19-17, and took first place. By August 11, their record stood at 17 games over .500 and their lead was three games.

As late as September 11, the Reds held the lead, but on an 11-game road trip to Los Angeles, San Francisco, San Diego and Houston, the Reds dropped seven games, and fell four behind the streaking Braves. After a private team meeting called by Merritt, the Reds regrouped, winning four in row from the Dodgers at Crosley Field, but the Reds could not gain ground on the Braves or the Giants and finished third at 89-73, four games behind Atlanta.

In the offseason, Howsam made another move of considerable significance for the development of the Big Red Machine. He traded Chico Ruiz and the talented but unpopular Alex Johnson to the Angels for pitchers Jim McGlothlin, Pedro Borbon and Vern Geishert. Howsam knew that Johnson's abilities would bring value, and in McGlothlin and Borbon he got it.

"We decided there were only 20 pitchers in the American League that interested us," said Howsam. "McGlothlin made the list based on his ability, temperament, poise, attitude and behavior on and off the field." But it was Borbon who would make the most impact. Scout Ray Shore had managed Borbon in winter ball in the Dominican Republic in 1967.

"I always liked him," remembered Shore. "He could throw every day and he was tough in relief. I always brought Borbon's

The Reds and Dodgers, Opening Day opponents in 1969, joined in the traditional ceremonies at Crosley Field. This edition of the Reds was the first to be nicknamed the "Big Red Machine." They challenged for the pennant until the final ten days of the season.

name up when we were talking trades; the Angels just didn't hold him up that high."

Borbon would become a regular in the Reds bullpen for the next 10 seasons.

But this trade caused little attention compared to the biggest off-season move, announced on October 8. Immediately after the season ended, Howsam's comments suggested a managerial change was imminent.

"I think we should have won it," he said. "After I reviewed all the clubs in contention, I concluded that we had the ballclub to win it all."

Howsam liked Bristol. "I respected him as a baseball man. He could work for me. But I had come to the conclusion that Dave Bristol was not going to take me where I wanted to go."

Ray Shore felt that Howsam based the Bristol decision on much more than the 1969 results.

"He got fired because he learned under Gene Mauch and did a lot of things on his own," claimed Shore. "He wasn't used to having a whole lot of communication with his general manager. There was a disagreement in philosophy; Bob expected Dave to come to him more and he didn't."

On October 8, Howsam informed the popular Bristol that his contract would not be renewed. Had the Reds won four more games in 1969 and captured the division title, it is likely Bristol would have been re-hired. But four games made Bristol expendable and changed the history of the franchise forever.

One day later, Howsam plucked from obscurity a prematurely gray, no-name coach from the California Angels to lead the Big Red Machine into the next decade.

BUILDING A MACHINE

In his first three years in Cincinnati, Bob Howsam pulled off 10 trades, bringing 18 new players to the Reds. The most critical acquisitions for the Big Red Machine era were Clay Carroll and Pedro Borbon, who anchored Sparky Anderson's bullpen during the dynasty years.

Howsam also brought in Bobby Tolan, Jim Merritt, Woody Woodward and Jim McGlothlin, who helped the Reds to pennant victories in 1970 and 1972, and catchers Pat Corrales and Bill Plummer who backed up Johnny Bench.

Year	Reds Players	Traded to	In Exchange for
1967	Tommy Harper	Cleveland	George Culver
			Fred Whitfield
			Bob Raudman
1968	Dick Simpson	St. Louis	Alex Johnson
1968	John Edwards	St. Louis	Pat Corrales
			Jimmy Williams
1968	Milt Pappas	Atlanta	Tony Cloninger
	Ted Davidson		Clay Carroll
	Bob Johnson		W. Woodward
1968	Vada Pinson	St. Louis	Bobby Tolan
			Wayne Granger
1968	Leo Cardenas	Minnesota	Jim Merritt
1969	Ted Abernathy	Chicago (NL)	Bill Plummer
1969	George Culver	St. Louis	Ray Washburn
1969	Alex Johnson	California	Jim McGlothlin
	Chico Ruiz		Pedro Borbon
			Vern Geishert
1969	Gerry Arrigo	Chicago (AL)	Angel Bravo

The Cincinnati Enquirer

When he was hired by Bob Howsam in the fall of 1969, the unknown George "Sparky" Anderson was "Sparky Who?" in the newspaper headlines. But Howsam knew him well. Howsam had hired Anderson to manage minor league clubs for the St. Louis and Cincinnati organizations. Anderson came to the Reds having won four minor-league pennant races between 1965 and 1968.

National League Manager of the Year, 1972 and 1975

Chapter 4

Sparky Who?

Cincinnati record, 1970-1978: 863-586 (.596)

THE MEDIA WAS APOPLECTIC. THE fans were mystified. Had Bob Howsam flipped? What had possessed the Reds general manager to hire 35-year-old unknown George "Sparky" Anderson to manage the Cincinnati Reds, a team that, by many accounts, had the best talent in the National League?

This wasn't a team that needed to be developed. It was a team that appeared ready to win. Why couldn't Howsam have chosen a proven commodity? How about Dick Williams or Bill Rigney or Bob Scheffing or Charlie Metro? Why not hire one of them?

The Cincinnati Enquirer had even run a headline that morning that asked incredulously, "Sparky Who?"

The press conference scheduled to introduce the Reds' new manager was standing room only. As Anderson looked out upon the gathered media at the Netherland Hilton Hotel, he could sense what the writers and broadcasters were thinking.

In a way, they were right. But they didn't know the whole story.

Anderson had been in Cincinnati many times before. He had been the San Diego Padres third base coach in 1969. Ten years before that, he had played a full season at second base for the Philadelphia Phillies. But his was a forgettable presence.

Howsam, however, knew Anderson. Sparky had managed minor league clubs from 1965 to 1967 in the St. Louis Cardinals organization when Howsam was the Cardinals general manager. After Howsam came to Cincinnati, he hired Anderson to manage the Reds minor league club in Asheville, North Carolina.

Howsam made a habit of personally visiting all of the Reds minor league clubs during the season. He also talked at length with the managers over the telephone at least once a month. "Character" was something he had always strived to decipher—whether it be in players, coaches or front-office hires.

In Anderson, Howsam knew he was getting a man who cared deeply for the correct playing of the game, and would brook no nonsense from anyone who got in the way of that philosophy.

Although Anderson seemed like a gamble for Howsam, it was a calculated gamble.

"I'll always gamble—if I believe in the man I'm gambling on," said Howsam. "I knew Sparky was honest and forthright. I needed a leader, somebody to get all that ability out of our players."

One thing was for certain. In Sparky Anderson, Howsam had a man who had always gotten the most of *himself*.

George Anderson was born in Bridgewater, South Dakota, population 632, on February 22, 1934, in the heart of the Great Depression.

His grandfather, Oscar Anderson, had emigrated to America from Norway as a boy. Oscar's family had originally settled in Iowa, but moved to South Dakota when he was still young. Oscar grew up to be a house painter, as did his son, Leroy, who, besides painting silos and barns, worked part-time for the post office in Bridgewater.

It didn't make for a luxurious existence.

"But I ain't lying when I say we were rich in love," recalled Sparky Anderson. "We lived together and we stuck together."

Crammed into the same house were Anderson, his four siblings, their parents and paternal grandparents.

"We lived in a two-story house," remembered Anderson. "In the summer, it was beautiful. The winters were brutal. We slept upstairs and I swear there were icicles inside the house. All we had was a potbelly stove on the first floor. When it came time for bed, we had to pile on all the blankets we had."

On Halloween night, Bridgewater youngsters pilfered as many outhouses as they could and then lined them up on Main Street.

"My grandfather used to sit in ours with a shotgun," Anderson recalled. "We didn't have much, but nobody was going to get our outhouse."

In the book, *Sparky!*, by Anderson and Dan Ewald, Anderson remembered he and his dad, Leroy, played catch every day that Leroy could.

"My daddy was the toughest man I ever saw in my life," Anderson said. "He wasn't mean. He was just lead-pipe tough. He taught me never to run scared. If you start running scared, you'll be running your whole life. Daddy kept to himself. He didn't bother anybody. But he didn't want anybody bothering him. If someone said the word 'fight,' they'd hit the ground before the 't' got out. Daddy didn't want us fighting, but he made the message clear. Don't let anybody push you around. If you have to fight, make that first punch count. If you hit someone hard the first time, you ain't got no fight. It's history."

It was a lesson that stood Anderson in good stead when his family moved to Los Angeles in November 1942; "Georgie" was 8 years old. His father and grandfather were seeking better jobs in the civilian war-supply plants. The Andersons relocated in the neighborhood now known as Watts, close to the University of Southern California campus.

"We moved into a house at 1087 West 35th Street, off Vermont," said Anderson. "It was a rough neighborhood. It had two bedrooms so my parents could divide us up as best they could. My brother and I shared a bedroom with my grandparents. My two baby sisters slept in the other one with my parents. My oldest sister slept on a pull-out couch. We had one bathroom, but at least it was indoors. My mother kept her washing machine on the back porch. Eventually, we put a bed back there so my brother and I could move out of my grandparents' room."

He played kickball and sockball—like baseball, except that players hit the ball with their fists and put out baserunners by

Courtesy of George Anderson

Young George Anderson and his father, Leroy, paused during a game of catch outside their house in Los Angeles in the mid-1940s. Leroy Anderson moved his family west from South Dakota in 1942.

hitting them with the ball. And he scrapped.

The family's famous fighting spirit had migrated westward, too.

"One day I slipped in front of a bigger kid to catch the sockball," said Anderson. "He got mad and pushed me to the ground. I got up and knocked him down with my fist. That established me. No one messed around with Georgie Anderson after that."

But the most fortuitous event in Anderson's young life occurred on his way home from the Third Street Grammar School one afternoon. A baseball came flying over U.S.C.'s outfield fence and landed in the bushes. Keen-eyed George knew exactly where. The student manager couldn't find it, but Anderson did. He offered to take it back to the ballpark—that was one sure way to get inside the place—but the student-manager told him to keep it.

"It's not mine," countered Anderson, again displaying his midwestern roots.

He walked the ball inside the park and asked where he could find the boss.

"Son, what's your name?" asked U.S.C. baseball coach Ron Dedeaux.

"Georgie Anderson."

"Georgie, would you like to be our batboy?"

"I sure would."

"You're it then. But there's one rule: I have to check your report card. As long as your grades are good enough, Georgie, you're the Trojans' batboy."

"Georgie" shagged baseballs for Dedeaux's team, shotputs for Olympian Parry O'Brien, footballs for the punter and free throws for future N.B.A. All-Star Bill Sharman. For six years, Anderson never missed a day at U.S.C. unless he was sick.

"Coach Dedeaux took me under his arm and became my second father," said Anderson. "He taught me more than baseball; he helped me become a man. I always was intense about baseball. Coach Dedeaux taught me another dimension. He taught me enthusiasm. There's a difference. Intensity is fine, but he taught me it's also good to smile."

That advice dovetailed with something Anderson's father had said when George was 11 years old.

"Everything in life will cost you something except one thing," Leroy told his son. "And that's to be nice to people. That's the only thing in life that's free. It'll never cost you a dime to be nice. And you'll feel good."

Leroy's son would later recall those words as "the greatest lesson of my life."

In L.A., Anderson began playing organized ball for the first time.

"We played on Saturdays at Rancho Playground, near Dorsey High School," recalled Sparky. "Getting there wasn't easy, and it took time. I'd board the 'J' streetcar, get a transfer and take a bus to the park."

Among the boys he met: Billy Consolo, who later received $65,000 to sign with the Boston Red Sox, and Ed Palmquist, who pitched with the Dodgers and Twins.

If there was one characteristic that defined Anderson, it was that he could not stand to lose. He even tried to "manage" the school games so the kids who were weaker athletically wound up on the other side. One of his teachers called his mother to school to talk about her son's aggressiveness.

"Their solution was that I would spend time every day teaching those who couldn't do it, how to catch the baseball," said Anderson.

"That didn't last long. I simply didn't have any use, or any time, for losers."

Anderson had a competitive fire that drew everyone's attention. It was West Coast scout Lefty Phillips who helped him channel his enthusiasm.

Anderson met Phillips at Rancho Playground, where Phillips was bird-dogging for Bobby Mattick, the Reds' top scout on the Coast. Phillips' job was to flush the talent out of the sandlots and bring in Mattick for "the kill." Mattick's credits were impressive: Frank Robinson, Vada Pinson, Curt Flood and Jim Maloney, all of whom he signed to Reds contracts.

"Lefty liked me and frequently drove me home," remembered Anderson. "We'd talk baseball, nothing else. He always told me, 'Nothing you do in baseball will come easy. Your only chance is to become an Eddie Stanky type-player.'"

Sparky played three years of varsity baseball at Dorsey High. His team won 42 straight games in an area where some of the best high school baseball in America was being played. Consolo was Dorsey's third baseman, Anderson its shortstop.

"Billy could play," said Anderson. "Me, I had a terrible arm."

By the time Anderson was a senior in high school, Phillips had become a scout for the Brooklyn Dodgers. Even though a Pittsburgh Pirates scout offered shortstop George Anderson a $3,000 bonus, Leroy Anderson told the scout, "No, I'm sorry. Lefty Phillips will sign my son. He has been good to him."

Loyalty to Lefty made Anderson a Dodger—for $2,400, which included $1,200 as a signing bonus and $1,200 for the season, and a promise from Lefty to Leroy Anderson that George would be assigned to Class C Ball in nearby Santa Barbara.

The year was 1953, and the second baseman in Santa Barbara was player-manager George Scherger, who was 13 years older than his fresh-faced double-play mate.

"I admired 'Shugs' because he wanted to win so bad," said Anderson.

Courtesy of George Anderson

Georgie Anderson played baseball at Dorsey High School in Los Angeles. His spirited play and dedication to the game drew the attention of Dodger scouts, who signed him in 1953.

BASEBALL MEN: GEORGE SCHERGER

"I'll tell you what kind of player I was," remembered George Scherger. "I was managing at age 26!"

Scherger, who was Anderson's first hire in Cincinnati, began his baseball career in 1940. After he returned from World War II in 1946, his baseball supervisors judged his arm so weak they recommended he become a player-manager if he wanted to stay in baseball.

In 1953, Scherger was playing second base and managing the Dodgers Santa Barbara club when George Anderson made his professional debut.

"Sparky was the shortstop, I was the second baseman. He was about 18, I was 33. He was more than your typical kid. He didn't hit that much, but he hustled like hell, and I liked guys like that."

Scherger served as bench coach, outfield coach and base coach for the Reds during Anderson's tenure.

Scherger coached third base for the Reds in 1976. The Phillies' Mike Schmidt awaited the throw.

It was a mutual admiration society.

"Anderson was fearless," recalled Scherger. "On a double play, he'd kneel in front of the bag and risk getting spiked. He risked his life on the bases. I remember a game one night when he knocked down a big catcher blocking the plate. He did to that guy what Pete Rose did to Ray Fosse to win the 1970 All-Star game at Cincinnati. It meant the ballgame."

Also on the 1953 Santa Barbara squad was Larry Sherry, a right-handed pitcher who became a World Series hero with the Dodgers in the 1959 Series.

"One night, Fresco Thompson, the Dodgers minor league boss, drove to Santa Barbara to see us play," said Anderson. "He saw me go in the hole for a ground ball and ricochet a throw off the mound to first base."

In spring training of 1954, Thompson reminded Anderson of it.

"You're no shortstop," Thompson said. "We'll make you a second baseman."

With the switch in positions, Anderson progressed up the Dodger chain: Class A Pueblo, Colorado, in the Western League in 1954; Class AA Ft. Worth in the Texas League in 1955 (where his teammates included future managers Dick Williams, Danny Ozark, Norm Sherry and Maury Wills, and where Anderson got the nickname "Sparky" from a radio announcer who noticed he was such a feisty player) and Class AAA Montreal in the International League in 1956.

It was in Montreal where Anderson achieved his greatest fame as a player.

"In 1956, my rookie year in the International League, I had 81 hits in my first 167 at-bats," he said. "I was hitting .485! Believe it or not, I beat out 16 consecutive push bunts. We played Buffalo and you could put me down for two bunt hits before we took the field. Big Luke Easter was at first base.

"People couldn't believe it. No one could be hitting .485 with a stroke like that. But everything I hit fell in. It was impossible. I remember one game I got jammed and it hit right off the fists. The ball blooped over the pitcher's mound. The shortstop came in to make a play, but the ball had so much backspin that it started rolling back toward the mound."

Anderson, who had never been anything more than a Punch 'n Judy hitter, regularly took batting practice like a poor man's Ted Williams in front of an astonished crowd of players.

"Players from other clubs were actually watching me take batting practice—like maybe they could learn something from my swing," said Anderson. "Learning from me, chronic minor-league infielder, as if I'd be something to see, swinging a bat. How could they know I was over my head, operating from outer space?"

Baseball is a game of percentages, and they finally caught up with George Lee Anderson, temporary superstar.

It started with a bunt.

"Spook Jacobs was at first base and he came in, fell flat on his face, reached out and tagged me," Anderson recalled. "After that, I couldn't even get a bunt hit. I went so bad that I was benched for three games and my average was still .360. I can remember games against Rochester. A guy named Dick Rand was catching. Every time I'd walk up to the plate, he'd say, 'The elevator's going down,' and I'd get all ticked off. I was a hothead."

Over the final weeks of the season, Anderson went 8-for-150. He still entered the final game of the season with a chance to finish at .300. However, unlike Ted Williams, who 15 years earlier had gone 6-for-8 in a final-day doubleheader to raise his average from .399 to .406, Anderson went 0-for-3 and finished at .298.

"Believe it or not, through that entire hot streak, I never moved out of the No. 8 spot in the order," said Anderson. "What really bothered me, though, was that they called up Chico Fernandez and Rocky Nelson to the big leagues. I was leading the team in hitting and didn't get called up."

In 1957, Anderson hit a more typical .260. In 1958, he had his best overall season, batting .269, stealing 21 bases, hitting two home runs and knocking in 56 runs. He finished second in the

The Sporting News

In 1957, the last year the Dodgers played in Brooklyn, Anderson played for the Dodgers minor league club in Los Angeles.

MVP race, albeit a distant second to winner Rocky Nelson.

The Philadelphia Phillies were impressed and traded for Anderson. They were *too* impressed. Dodger general manager Buzzy Bavasi had flat-out picked the pocket of Phillies general manager Roy Hamey. The Dodgers gave up Anderson and in return got three players—outfielder Rip Repulski, right-handed pitcher Jim Golden and left-handed pitcher Jim Snyder —and some cash.

Anderson played just one season with Philadelphia, hitting .217. A year later, Bavasi sold Repulski on waivers to the Boston Red Sox for $25,000; the year after that, he sold Golden to the Houston Colt 45s in the expansion draft for $75,000. Snyder pitched for the Dodgers for three seasons.

"The way things turned out," figured Sparky, "the Dodgers got a hundred thousand dollars cash and a pretty good pitcher for a guy they originally signed for $3,000. That guy was me."

If there was anything beyond Anderson's bedrock upbringing that confirmed for him there was a right way to do things and a wrong way—and that the wrong way would invariably lead to disaster—his experience with the Phillies in 1959 was it.

This experience had as much to do with his later success as a manager as did the way his father raised him, the way Lefty Phillips tutored him and the way the Brooklyn Dodgers nurtured him.

In Anderson's six years in the Dodgers chain, the big club had won three pennants and a World Championship, and finished second once and third once. Over the same six-year period, the Phillies had finished over .500 only once.

"To a guy who grew up in the Dodger system, the difference was painful—not only in skills, but also in attitudes," said Anderson.

The Dodgers camp emphasized a routine schedule. Players were out of bed by 7:30, finished with breakfast by 8:30 and on the field for calisthenics by 9:30 sharp.

"Every half hour, you were scheduled to be somewhere, doing a specific thing. This was for everybody. Nothing was left to chance," said Anderson.

But in the Philadelphia camp, chaos ruled.

"You were due to report at 9 o'clock. Well, *around* 9," Anderson said. "Sometimes practice began at 10 in the morning; sometimes at 11; sometimes at 10:30. When you went to the practice field after calisthenics, there was no set program. Nobody told you when to start hitting, or how to go about it when you did. Nobody ever put you to work on some specific phase of the game."

The Dodgers emphasized running, with coaches overseeing every lap. But with the Phillies, players were on the honor system.

"When practice was over, you did your running on your own. Nobody was there to tell this guy he would do 20 laps, or another guy 10 or 15. Guys would run five laps, six laps, then quit and go to the clubhouse. Naturally, since it was my first year and I wanted to make the club, I kept running until the last guy was in."

Anderson made the club and headed north. By the time the Phillies arrived at their stadium for the home opener, the fans were ready for them.

"As we ran out on the field, I heard this thunderous sound from the stands," recalled Anderson. "Cheers? Are you kidding? About 35,000 people were booing us before a ball had been pitched."

The fans expected a long season—and got it.

"I was raised in an organization where all anybody ever talked about was winning," said Anderson. "That was all anybody cared about. When you lost, you didn't talk in the clubhouse. You didn't talk on the bus. Here it made no difference.

"One day in Chicago, we were down by two, maybe three, runs in the ninth. I was psyching myself up, like, 'We've got a chance to get the Cubbies in the ninth.' But the Phils couldn't wait to go out one, two, three, so they could run to the clubhouse, take a shower and get to their favorite restaurant."

The Phillies finished in last place, but not before making a trip to Los Angeles that proved personally embarrassing to Anderson.

"We played the Dodgers at the Coliseum, and I'm the big shot, coming home with a major league team," said Anderson. "It was my daddy's first major league game, and, of course, we got slaughtered. Afterward he came up to me and asks, 'Son, is that really a big-league team you're on?' I had to admit, it didn't look much like one."

But that one season with the Phillies helped Anderson develop his managing philosophy.

"I realized you can't be in a game as a professional unless winning and losing are everything, your whole life. You have to suffer when you lose—for that day. The next day, you start all over again. You have to like to win; you have to want to win—not by killing or cheating, but by anything short of that."

The 1959 season was Anderson's last in the major leagues. An hour before the Phillies were to break camp in 1960 and head north, Anderson was told he had been sold to Toronto of the International League. He was miserable. He had to admit he didn't belong in the majors, but he spent most of the season in Toronto feeling sorry for himself. Still, he was able to take a bad situation and learn from it.

"I can pinpoint the end of that season as the most important in my baseball career," he said. "I made up my mind to start observing the inside strategy of baseball closer. I wanted to learn more about it. I realized I wanted eventually to manage a ballclub."

His manager in Toronto, Charlie Dressen, realized it, too. One day in 1962, Dressen called Anderson over.

"He'd always whistle at you," recalled Sparky. "So this one day he whistled for me and I ran over. 'Little Man,' he said, 'you ain't never missed a sign. Someday you'll be a manager.' Coming from him, that was quite a compliment. The man had six eyes."

Dressen saw some of himself in Anderson: a hustler, a fighter, instinctively competitive, a student of the game. In 1964, Dressen's vision proved to be 20-20: 30-year-old Sparky Anderson was named manager of the Toronto club.

"I thought I was ready, but dammit, I wasn't," said Anderson. "I was aggressive—in fact, my aggressiveness became a problem. I overdid it, but I didn't know it then. I wanted every decision on the field to go my way. Man, I battled those umpires. I fought them too often and too hard. After I was canned, I discovered that jobs weren't easily available for a manager with a short fuse."

Toronto let him go at the end of the 1964 season and an uncertain Anderson headed home to California.

Like most young ballplayers in the 1950s and 1960s, Anderson had always worked regular jobs during the offseasons. After his first pro season in 1953, he found a job making dinette sets.

"I didn't even own one," said Anderson. "But I got the job of fastening legs onto tables. I worked on the line opposite a young man from Utah. He put on one set of legs. I put on the other. We worked six days a week with 14 hours overtime."

The next offseason, Anderson worked in a factory making TV antennas for 90 cents an hour. Later, he packed boxes for Sears and waxed floors. He packed donuts for Ralph's Bakery, but quit after gaining 20 pounds. Selling cars was his longest-running, off-season job. In the winter of 1964, with no baseball job in sight, Anderson was working for Milt Blish at a GM dealership.

"I was excellent until it came to closing a sale," said Anderson. "Then I'd end up saying to somebody without much money, 'Hey, you can't afford one of our cars.' That would drive 'Uncle Miltie' crazy. 'George,' he'd say to me, 'you know damn well those people are gonna walk out of here and go right down the street and buy a car they can't afford from someone else.' And he'd laugh."

Anderson would always remain appreciative to Blish for sticking with him, and in the winter of 1964-65, Anderson was beginning to consider that Blish might be his boss for quite a while. Without a baseball job to report to, selling cars was likely to become Anderson's full-time job.

Then, in early 1965, with the baseball league season about to begin, the St. Louis Cardinals suddenly lost one of their minor league managers when he resigned to take over a family business for his ailing father-in-law. The manager's job at Rockville, South Carolina, in the Western Carolina League, was available.

Bob Howsam was running the Cardinals at the time, and his farm director, Chief Bender, approached him and asked who was available at this late date. Howsam called Dick Walsh of the Los Angeles Dodgers, who recommended Sparky Anderson.

"Oh no, not that hothead," shot back Bender.

Bender had caught Sparky's managerial "act" in Jacksonville in 1964 and came away unimpressed. "Sparky got on his older players. He fought the umpires on every decision that went against him."

Howsam, who preferred too much fire to too little, realized Anderson was still young. He suggested Bender call Sparky anyway.

Bender did his best to talk Anderson out of the job.

"Sparky, we have an opening. I don't know if you'd be interested."

"I'll take it," said Sparky.

"Sparky, it's only a Class D ballclub in South Carolina."

"It don't matter. I'll take it."

"Sparky, I haven't even mentioned salary to you."

"I don't care; pay me what you want. I'll take it."

He took it. No more selling cars.

The Sporting News

Sparky's one season in the majors came as a Philadelphia Phillie in 1959. Anderson hit only .218, and was cut the next spring.

When Anderson arrived in spring training, full of vinegar, Bender was taken aback.

"Here comes Sparky with all that white hair," said Bender. "I told one of our field coordinators that the young kids at Rock Hill would ride him—call him 'grandpa'. So this guy says he would urge Sparky to touch up his hair. Sparky stayed that way (tinted hair) for several years until he had success at the big-league level and then he quit using the tint."

Anderson mastered his hair problem, but hadn't yet fully absorbed the lesson of Toronto. He was in a new job—a job he had feared he wasn't even going to get. He didn't want to let up on the gas pedal. Managing was too important to him not to give it his all. His intensity often roared out of control, just as Bender had feared.

On one occasion after a loss, Anderson became so upset during a clubhouse tirade, he didn't realize he had picked up a television set. He was about to throw it against it a wall when he caught himself. He didn't stop himself after another loss when he saw a player enjoying some watermelon.

"Boy, this is good," said the youngster.

"Good is it?" Anderson shouted. "I'll show you what good is!"

Watermelon slices flew around the clubhouse. The lockers dripped red juice.

"I was wild," Anderson admitted.

Once in Toronto after a loss, he heard one of his players ordering hamburgers from the clubhouse man.

"I jumped up like I was hit by a bolt of lightning," Anderson recalled. When the hamburgers were delivered, Anderson summoned his players.

"Who ordered these?" screamed Anderson, holding the offending burgers aloft.

No one replied.

"The least you could do is admit it!" he ranted. "Since you won't, I guess you don't want 'em."

Anderson took one of the burgers and started squeezing it in his hand. He mangled all five before one of his wide-eyed players finally spoke up.

"Skip, my folks just drove in from Detroit and were hungry. I ordered them for my folks."

A chastened Anderson ordered five new sandwiches.

"He was really tough on these kids," recalled Bender. "I said, 'Sparky, you got to take it easy.' He finished last in the first half of the season, but then took the group and won the pennant in the second half."

But Anderson might not have won anything that year had it not been for a decision by a friendly umpire.

"There was an argument on the field one night," recalled Sparky. "I was very hot-tempered. Used to really get into it. Well, I go out onto the field and start arguin' with the ump. And he bumps me. This big guy bumps me. He didn't mean to do it. It was an accident. But I was so wound up, I grabbed him with both my hands up around his chest and I tried to throw him to the ground. They tore me off of him and got me inside the locker room.

"I knew I was done. Done for at least the rest of the year, and maybe done for good. Heck, I had just been rescued from the scrap heap and given the job in Rock Hill at the last minute. And now look what I'd gone and done. So I'm sitting there, feeling bad, feeling terrible, and I hear this voice, 'Sparky…'

"I look up. It's the umpire. 'Sparky, can we talk?' I said, 'Oh, gosh, yes.' I didn't know what he was gonna say or do. He said,

'You know, I didn't mean to bump you. And I won't deny that I did. But here's what we're gonna do. You got run for bad language. That's the truth of it, and that's how I'm going to report it. Everything else came after I bumped you. You don't deserve a long suspension, and I'm not going to report it in such a way that you get one.'"

George Lee Anderson had just had a life sentence commuted.

"I never forgot it," remembered Sparky, years later. "That man, in his own way, saved my career. What I had done to him on the field had put the fear of God in me. It woke me up. I had gone too far; I had crossed over the line. I vowed that I would never, ever, let something like that happen again. I won't say I didn't have arguments after that. But from that day forward, I started putting my hands in my back pockets."

Anderson was learning. He knew the game. He thought he knew people. But what he had come to realize was that his intensity in Toronto and Rock Hill had worn out his players. He personally had responded well to his managers' intensity as a player, but most players weren't like that. Anderson began to let the "Uncle Sparky" side of him come out, the gregarious side, the fun-loving midwestern side. In the back of his mind, he had known that some players needed a pat on the back, some a kick in the butt and some you just let them be themselves. But now he began to put it into practice.

"In 1966, we sent him to St. Pete and he wins the pennant there," remembered Bender. "In 1967, we sent him to Modesto and he wins there."

George Anderson was turning into Sparky Anderson.

When Howsam and Bender left their positions with the Cardinals to join the Reds, they hired Sparky in 1968 to manage the Reds Double A club at Asheville.

In the spring training of 1968, Sparky and George Scherger—Sparky's rookie league manager of 15 years earlier—roomed together. Scherger was managing Cincinnati's Tampa club.

"All Sparky wanted to do was talk baseball, which, of course, was good enough for me," recalled Scherger. "He'd tell me, again and again, 'Shugs, I'm gonna manage in the big leagues. I know I am. And when I get my job, you're gonna be the first coach I sign.'"

Sparky led the Asheville team to the pennant. That gave him his fourth pennant in four years, and at the end of the 1968 season, Sparky was offered a job as a coach on the San Diego Padres, with his friend, Padre manager Preston Gomez. Bender was upset at losing his very successful young manager and he approached Reds manager Dave Bristol about finding a job for Sparky on the big club.

"I said to Dave, 'Can't you work Sparky onto your staff?' But Bristol had his buddies, nice guys, and he couldn't work him in. I told Sparky we'd 'option him out' for a year to get some big-league experience. But I didn't know if we'd ever get him back."

Anderson coached third base for the Padres in 1969. At the end of the season, Sparky's old baseball mentor from high school days, Lefty Phillips, who was now the manager of the California Angels, offered Anderson a job as an Angels coach for the 1970 season. On October 8, Sparky drove to Lefty's house, and together they drove to the office of Dick Walsh, who was now the Angels GM.

"I picked up Lefty at his home in Eagle Rock," said Sparky. "He had just heard a news flash on the radio that the Reds had dropped Dave Bristol as their manager. I said that was too bad. I didn't even remotely associate Bristol's dismissal with my own immediate future. What reason would I have to think in terms of managing a big-league club at this stage?"

After lunch with Walsh, Sparky and Phillips joined him in his Angels office. Walsh pulled a contract out of his desk drawer and handed it to Sparky. The figure on the contract read $17,000.

"I tried to keep my composure," said Sparky, whose top pay as a player was $10,000 in Triple A Toronto in 1960. "As far as I was concerned, I had just hit the jackpot."

He signed the contract at 2:45 p.m. on October 8, 1969.

Only a few minutes after Sparky signed it, Walsh's phone rang. His secretary advised him it was Bob Howsam calling from Cincinnati.

"Yes, Bob?" asked Walsh, taking the call. "By the way, two people you know, Lefty Phillips and Sparky Anderson, are sitting across from me."

"That's a funny coincidence," Howsam said to Phillips. "You may not want to talk now, but we're changing managers. What I'm calling you about is permission to discuss the managing job here with Anderson."

Walsh asked Sparky and Phillips to leave the room.

"Damn you, Bob—I thought we just signed a good man, and now you want him," said Walsh, who was quick to add he wouldn't stand in any man's way for such an opportunity.

Walsh called Sparky and Phillips back into the room. Looking directly at Sparky, Walsh said: "Well, George, how would you like to manage the Cincinnati Reds?"

Sparky moved forward to the edge of his chair.

"Look, Dick, you and I have known each other a long time. This isn't the kind of thing you kid about."

"I'm not kidding," said Walsh. "Bob Howsam wants you to call him in Cincinnati as soon as you get back to your house in Thousand Oaks. He's looking for a manager for the Reds. And you're the man he wants!"

Howsam wanted to name a manager before the 1969 World Series began. He had fired Dave Bristol as soon as the Mets-Braves National League playoffs had concluded. He then convened a summit meeting in his office: Bender; Dick Wagner; Rex Bowen, a special assistant; Joe Bowen (Rex's brother), director of scouting; Ray Shore, special assignment scout; and Tom Seeberg, the Reds publicity director.

Various names were bandied about. Dick Williams was among them. Shore felt Howsam's first choice was Charlie Metro, but just the day before, Metro had taken the job of managing the Kansas City Royals. Seeberg piped up with a new name. He and George Anderson had been in the same class at Dorsey High School. They'd known each other since they were kids, and Seeberg knew of Anderson's minor league success.

"Has anyone given any thought," said Seeberg, "to hiring a guy like Georgie Anderson?"

Not George, or Sparky, but *Georgie*, which is what Anderson was called back in the old neighborhood.

Everybody in the room knew Anderson, but envisioned him as a not-quite-ready-for-prime-time manager. The highest level he'd ever been in the Reds organization was Double A in 1968. They all knew what he had accomplished in the minor leagues, but he was only 35 years old.

Howsam asked Seeberg what he felt Anderson would contribute as the Cincinnati skipper.

"He knows the system," said Seeberg. "He pays close attention to details and fundamentals. He's good with young players."

Howsam nodded. He immediately liked the boldness of the choice. Anderson was fresh blood, and of good bloodlines. He was sure of himself, and yet he was a good listener. Howsam liked that combination. But he didn't yet say so. He asked what the others thought.

Bender was a dissenter—a milder one than he had been back in 1965 when the Cardinals were looking for a manager for their Rockville club. But a dissenter, nonetheless.

"Naming an unknown like Sparky is not going to play well here in Cincinnati," Bender told Howsam. "We all know who he is, but nobody else does. We've got a lot riding on this."

Bender had Howsam's neck to consider. Howsam had taken over the general manager's job only two years ago. He'd be sticking his neck out too far with this sort of a hire, Bender believed.

But, as is Bender's style, he deferred to the boss.

"If you're willing to do it, then it's worth the gamble," Bender said.

In Howsam's mind, it wasn't that much of a gamble.

"I had seen Sparky many times over the years," recalled Howsam. "He liked young ballplayers; he was willing to work with them. We had some very good players, but they needed to know how to do certain things. We thought they needed work in fundamentals. Sparky was extremely capable of that. Sparky was a good family man. He was willing to work and wouldn't be thinking about other things."

But "focused" isn't the word one would use to describe Anderson on October 8, 1969, sitting in the office of Dick Walsh in Anaheim. Anderson was ecstatic. He had always felt he would manage in the big leagues someday. But manage the Cincinnati Reds, widely regarded as a "comer" in baseball? Anderson sat back in his chair and gazed up at the ceiling and closed his eyes. The smile was still on his face.

"George, I want you to sit here in this office for a while," said Walsh. "They'll wait a little longer in Cincinnati for your call. You're driving Lefty home to Eagle Rock, and I'll be damned if I'll

The Cincinnati Enquirer

Tom Seeberg (right), the Reds publicity director, and former high-school classmate of "Georgie" Anderson, was the first to recommend Anderson to Bob Howsam in a free-wheeling discussion among Howsam's staff about managerial candidates.

let you out on that freeway and get my manager killed."

"How do you know this job's really mine?" asked Anderson.

"I'm telling you, you've got it, George," said Walsh. "If I were you, I'd start thinking about how much money to ask for."

"You tell me what to ask for," said Anderson, who couldn't have cared less about the money, but cared everything about the job.

Walsh suggested $35,000—shaking up Anderson one more time.

Eventually, Anderson regained his equilibrium, and headed for Eagle Rock with Phillips. Once there, Phillips couldn't bear the suspense. He knew Anderson couldn't either. He told Anderson to call Howsam from his Eagle Rock home.

"I can't wait to find out if this whole thing's for real," said Phillips.

As soon as Anderson reached Howsam, he began to have doubts the job was really his.

"Sparky," began Howsam, in his soft-spoken manner. "I want you to come to Cincinnati as soon as you can get out of Los Angeles, so we can chat. I want to listen to some of your ideas. I had a chance to watch you for several years, when you worked for us before. And I must say I always liked the way you handled our young players. But what I'd like to hear are some of your ideas about the game of baseball and managing."

"That's pretty hard to say on the telephone," said Anderson, adding that he'd rather sit down with Howsam to talk about specifics. But Howsam pushed ahead.

"If you had a star pitcher who was supposed to do his running after a workout, but walked off the field to the clubhouse without doing it, what would you do about that?"

"I'd go right in and get him," answered Sparky. "But let me say this, Mr. Howsam. I've got enough confidence in myself to know that I'll be able to handle any situation that comes up. But until that happens, I can't really tell you how I'd handle anything."

"If the job was offered to you," Howsam said, "would you be interested in managing the Cincinnati Reds?"

"I'd very much like to," said Anderson.

"How much money do you want?"

Anderson took a deep breath.

"Thirty-five thousand dollars."

"I think that may be a little high for any manager in his first year, Sparky," said Howsam. "But you're not way out of line. You've seen our club. What do you think of it?"

"It's as good as anything in the league."

"How many of our players do you know personally?"

"Only Darrel Chaney," replied Anderson. "He played shortstop for me at Asheville. I've talked to Pete Rose and Johnny Bench, but that's about all."

"All right, Sparky, I think we've talked enough," said Howsam. "Would you manage the Reds for $28,500?"

"Yes, I would," said Anderson, trying to sound calm.

"OK, then. You know Chief Bender. He'll be in touch with you within an hour. We want you out of California tonight and in here tomorrow morning."

Howsam hesitated for a second. "Do we have a deal?" he asked.

"It's a deal, Mr. Howsam."

Anderson could hardly believe it. Years later, he'd explain why.

"I'd seen (the Reds club) the year before," he said. "I didn't think they could miss winning. Still, I was just a 35-year-old guy with no real major league experience. Nobody knew me from nothing. I thought Bob Howsam was taking a terrible gamble."

Anderson showed off his new uniform for the press at the news conference on October 9, 1969.

The Cincinnati Enquirer

Bender was waiting in Cincinnati when the jet carrying the Reds' new manager touched down a little before 9:00 a.m., October 9. Sparky had barely slept, his mind already plotting his first big-league moves. And number one was to keep a promise.

From Bender's home, Sparky called George Scherger—his first professional manager in Santa Barbara 17 years earlier—and talked him into being his bench coach in Cincinnati. Sparky then called Pete Rose.

"Pete, I think you deserve to be the captain," said Anderson. "With the career you've had here, the way you've dedicated yourself to the Cincinnati Reds, I have to make you captain."

Besides the obvious leadership Rose could provide, Anderson likened Rose's captaincy to Willie Mays' in San Francisco. Mays brought the lineup card to home plate every night. Anderson knew the fans of Cincinnati would rather see Rose than the Reds manager.

"Sparky, anything you want done, let me know," answered Rose. "I'll go along with anything that's reasonable, and so will the other guys."

Sparky said he wanted his players to wear suit jackets on the road. He wanted them to have relatively closely cropped hair. He wanted them to portray a big-league image.

"Done," Rose told Anderson. "If you've got me and Johnny Bench on your side, you're fine."

"Thanks, Pete."

Sparky and Bender drove downtown to the Reds offices to speak with Howsam. From there, they all went to the Netherland Hilton hotel for the press conference. When they reached the Netherland, Anderson checked his watch.

11:50 a.m. Cincinnati time, 8:50 a.m. on the West Coast.

Only 48 hours had elapsed since Sparky had officially resigned as a Padres coach, and not even 24 hours had passed since he had taken the Angels coaching job.

"Ladies and gentleman," announced Bob Howsam, "I want to present the new manager of the Cincinnati Reds—George 'Sparky' Anderson."

Anderson looked out at the sea of microphones and TV cameras, and plunged into the news conference with all the enthusiasm he genuinely felt.

"I was very brash, free-wheelin'," recalled Sparky, years later. "There was nothing out there that could stop me or scare me. I never had any fears of any kind. Now, I know what could happen. But I didn't know it then."

SPARKY'S APPRENTICESHIP

Sparky Anderson was an unknown name to the fans of the Cincinnati Reds, but he had been in professional baseball for 17 years when Howsam hired him in 1970. Fifteen of those seasons had been spent playing and managing in the obscurity of the minor leagues. As a manager, he had a 395-295 minor league record.

Here was the record the Reds considered:

Playing Career

Year	Club	Ave.	HR	RBI	SB
1953	Santa Barbara	.263	5	55	13
1954	Pueblo	.296	0	62	14
1955	Ft. Worth	.266	0	42	6
1956	Montreal	.298	0	47	4
1957	Los Angeles	.260	2	35	8
1958	Montreal	.269	2	56	21
1959	Philadelphia •	.218	0	34	6
1960	Toronto	.227	5	21	12
1961	Toronto	.240	0	22	5
1962	Toronto	.257	2	38	2
1963	Toronto	.249	3	25	3

• Major leagues

Managing Career

Year	Club	League	W	L	Finish
1964	Toronto	International	80	72	5th
1965	Rock Hill	Western Carolina	24	40	8th (1st half)
			35	23	1st (2nd half) •
1966	St. Pete.	Florida State	42	24	2nd (1st half)
			49	21	1st (2nd half) ••
1967	Modesto	California	38	32	2nd (1st half)
			41	29	1st (2nd half) ••
1968	Asheville	Southern	86	54	1st
1969	Third base coach, San Diego Padres

• Won Playoff   •• Lost Playoff

The Cincinnati Reds defeated the Pittsburgh Pirates to win the National League pennant on October 5, 1970, at Riverfront Stadium. Rookie Don Gullett retired the final batter and the celebration began. *"The Reds mob Don Gullett. They are all over him. They pick up Sparky Anderson. Up in the air goes Sparky on the shoulders of the Reds players, as the Reds win the National League flag,"* reported Reds announcer Jim McIntyre. Anderson (10) and Gullett (35) were congratulated by coach Alex Grammas (right center), Jim McGlothlin (center in cap), Wayne Granger (behind Grammas) and Mel Behney (33).

National League Champions • 102 wins-60 losses

Chapter 5

1970
First Gear

Johnny Bench, MVP • Lost to Baltimore in World Series, 4-1

THE BIG RED MACHINE ERA dawned with the opening of spring training on February 20, 1970, at the Reds' facilities in Tampa. And from day one, the players realized a new regime was in place. Sparky Anderson's training camp was brutal. Anderson and the players laughed about it afterwards, but not in the hot Florida sunshine.

"I look back at that training camp and I think, 'How did I ever think I could get away with it?!'" Anderson recalled. "Lee May and Tony Perez joke about it all the time now. But they called me the minor-league so-and-so. I just came in wild."

The Reds of the '60s had a reputation for looking impressive in spring training, but then fading during the season, often due to sore pitching arms. Anderson hit that problem hard. Sparky's theory about healthy arms began with the legs.

"When I pitch batting practice, I get tired in the legs before the arms or the rest of my body," said Sparky. "A pitcher's legs get weak and he changes his style of throwing, so he hurts his arm."

Day after day, pitching coach Larry Shepard led his staff through sprints and other conditioning exercises. Howsam noticed. "This is the best conditioned club I've ever been associated with in the majors or minors," he said. Dave Bristol had stressed conditioning, but Anderson's camp was, in Johnny Bench's words, "Stalag 17."

Another reason for the tough camp was that Anderson, a first-year big-league manager, just didn't know to do it any other way.

"I didn't know the 'major league rules,' handle the 'delicate players' and all that," he said. "To me they were ballplayers. 'Let's go!' That was the greatest gift I had. I didn't know."

But Anderson did know that he had only a one-year contract. He had never forgotten the emptiness he had felt six years before when he had been out of baseball. He knew that Bristol had been fired the year before for failing to win a division title with essentially the same team. Howsam's expectations were clear, and Sparky was going to leave no excuses behind in the Florida sun.

The pre-season polls picked the Reds to finish anywhere from first to fifth. Part of the uncertainty rested on the outcome of several young players the Reds planned to feature in 1970. Six regular positions were set: Bench catching, May at first, Helms at second, Perez at third, Tolan in center and Rose in right. But in left field, the Reds were relying on rookies Bernie Carbo and Hal McRae, and, at shortstop, the competition was between rookie Dave Concepcion and Woody Woodward.

The pitching staff had veteran leadership in Jim Merritt, Jim Maloney, Jim McGlothlin and Gary Nolan. Two rookies—21-year-old Wayne Simpson and 19-year-old Don Gullett—earned roster spots with outstanding springs. Both had big-league arms, but their maturity and control put them on the club. Simpson, the number one draft choice in 1967, had progressed rapidly to Triple A at Indianapolis in 1969, but struggled to a 4.89 ERA and the team sent him to winter ball. He led the Puerto Rican league in wins, strikeouts and ERA, and continued his impressive work in spring training. Gullett, the club's number one pick in 1969, had dominated the Northern League at Sioux Falls in A ball in his first pro season, and was a long shot to make the club. But his performance in Tampa won him the left-hander's slot in the bullpen and Anderson hailed him as the next Sandy Koufax.

The Reds would open the season with five rookies in key

positions, all 23 or younger. Rose expressed confidence in the kids and in management's decision to bring them along.

"The thing I like about having all these rookies is that it shows what a job is being done with the Cincinnati organization," said Rose. "It all goes back to Bob Howsam and the job he's done trying to build a dynasty here in Cincinnati."

Young talent and an early opportunity to break into the major leagues were to become trademarks of the Howsam-Anderson years. Howsam felt the ideal mix was to introduce three new young players every year, which would help overcome the tendency to let a successful club grow too old. He didn't always reach the goal, but the stream of talent flowing into the Reds farm system in the late '60s produced a remarkable rookie crop in 1970.

In the final week of spring training, the Reds played Indianapolis, their Triple A farm club, before heading home for the start of the 1970 season. Although many of the regulars sat out these games, Rose did not. His 1970 contract made him the first Red to reach $100,000, but Rose was never the prima donna. He never ducked a game or disappointed the fans.

In an exhibition game a few years later, Rose made an out in his first at-bat. Anderson took all the regulars out after the third inning, except Rose who asked to bat one more time. He lined a hit over the infield and never stopped at first. He dove headfirst into second under the tag. The fans yelled their appreciation; Rose signaled Sparky to bring in a pinch-runner.

"That's what they came to see," Rose told Sparky. "Now they got their money's worth."

In Tampa, in this final exhibition game of 1970, Rose attempted to score on a hit by Johnny Bench. Pete rounded third as the relay came in from the outfield and he crashed full speed into catcher Jim Hibbs. Hibbs flew backward as Rose tumbled across the plate with the tying run. In a meaningless exhibition game, Rose had risked serious injury to score. It proved to be just a warmup for a similar, but far more famous collision three months later in the 1970 All-Star Game.

The Cincinnati Enquirer

Sparky Anderson admired the rigorous, disciplined style of the Dodger training camps when he was a player. He brought the same intensity to the Reds in 1970. Johnny Bench (foreground) called Anderson's camp "Stalag 17."

A Machine By Any Other Name

"Murderer's Row." "The Gashouse Gang." "The Boys of Summer." "The Big Red Machine." The road to baseball immortality is paved with great nicknames, and the Reds were blessed with one of the best.

The name surfaced in 1969, but its origins are murky. Bob Hunter, a Los Angeles writer, hung the name on the Reds after they outslugged the Phillies, 19-17. But Pete Rose claimed he used the name to distinguish the Reds from his red antique Ford. "That was the Little Red Machine," said Pete, "and the team was the Big Red Machine."

The name first appeared in the Reds yearbook in 1970. Out-of-town sports editors began putting it in headlines and the club eventually trademarked the name. Nobody popularized the nickname more than *Cincinnati Enquirer* cartoonist Jerry Dowling. Dowling's first Big Red Machine cartoon appeared in 1969, and he returned to the theme throughout the 1970s.

This Dowling cartoon became the Reds' official "Big Red Machine."

Baseball entered the new decade on April 6 with Opening Day ceremonies in Cincinnati and Washington, and with Commissioner Bowie Kuhn hoping two prominent off-season problems would fade in the spring sunshine. Denny McLain, the star pitcher of the Detroit Tigers, had been suspended for an association with alleged bookmakers. And St. Louis outfielder, Curt Flood, had announced his intention to challenge baseball's hallowed reserve clause, which bound a player to a team for life. Although McLain's transgressions were shocking and damaging to the image of the game, Flood's litigation would ultimately shake the foundation of baseball by opening the door to free agency. Eventually, the free agency issue would contribute to the dismantling of the very dynasty that Bob Howsam was carefully nurturing in Cincinnati.

But such outcomes were impossible to foresee in April of 1970, and a confident group of Reds took the field for the final Opening Day at Crosley Field. Jim Merritt started and pitched a complete game, 5-1 victory over Montreal. Nolan followed the next day with a shutout. In the eighth inning of the third game, Anderson finally made his first trip to the mound as a big league manager when he relieved a tiring Jim McGlothlin. But McGlothlin got the win and so did rookie Wayne Simpson the next day in his first start, an impressive 3-0 shutout of the Dodgers. By April 15, the Reds were 8-3, in first place by two games, and had held their opponents to fewer than four runs in 10 of the 11 games.

The pitchers credited Shepard for the intense conditioning in spring training and for emphasizing the changeup. When McGlothlin threw a good change in his first start, the pitchers on the bench jumped up and waved towels at Shepard out in the bullpen.

Sparky appreciated the camaraderie and the sense of unity; he and Shepard nurtured it.

"I have not met with my pitchers since the spring," revealed Anderson. "I've turned them all over to Larry. Larry's got the pitchers thinking like they're a separate team. The pitchers want very badly to hold their end up. Then, it's up to the hitters to get the runs."

The first challenge to the pitching staff came on April 16, when Jim Maloney ruptured an Achilles tendon against the Dodgers at Crosley Field. The 29-year-old Maloney had carried the Reds' pitching through most of the 1960s, and he retired as the club's career leader in several pitching categories. He attempted a comeback at the end of the year, but Howsam traded him in the offseason.

Anderson called on rookie Gullett to relieve Maloney, and the left-hander picked up his first major league win, signaling the transition from the Reds' best pitcher of the '60s to its most dominant hurler of the '70s.

In an earlier season, Maloney's injury would have ruined whatever hopes the Reds had of remaining in first place. But the starting rotation of Merritt, McGlothlin, Nolan and the surprising Simpson was deep enough to offset Maloney's loss. Fueled by the pitching and the hot start of Perez, Bench and Bobby Tolan, the Big Red Machine won 70 of its first 100 games, a mark unmatched in its dynasty era. They won 10 of their first 13 games, and then in early May ran off eight in a row. Simpson was in the middle of his own 11-game winning streak that would stretch until July 12. By mid-June, Perez and Bench had hit 43 home runs and were on a pace to match the all-time teammate homer mark set by Roger Maris (61) and Mickey Mantle (54) in 1961. At the All-Star break, Perez was the early favorite for the Most Valuable Player award with 29 home runs, 90 RBIs and a .356 average. Bench, close behind with 28 home runs and 79 RBIs at the break, would ultimately take the award with a strong second-half showing.

Even Anderson's short-lived experiment to drop Rose to third in the batting order and hit Tolan leadoff did not hurt the Reds. Sparky abandoned the idea shortly after the season began, to Pete's delight. Tolan hit well anywhere Sparky put him and finished the year hitting .316 with 16 homers, 80 RBIs and 57 stolen bases.

The Reds even survived the debut of Pedro Borbon, the reliever Howsam acquired in 1969 from the Angels. Borbon opened the 1970 season at Indianapolis and spent most of the season there, but he was called up to start the second game of a doubleheader against San Diego on May 26. The Reds had lost the first game and Borbon fell behind, 3-0, on a Clarence Gaston homer in the first inning before anyone was out. Nate Colbert followed him to the plate and Borbon nailed him with an inside fastball. Colbert headed to the mound to discuss Borbon's intentions, but his teammates held him back and players returned to the dugouts.

Afterwards, Anderson declared that Borbon was under no orders to throw at Colbert and that he was worried about his young pitcher.

"Imagine, his first game in the National League and people think he's gonna go out there and pop someone," lamented Anderson.

But Sparky need not have worried about Borbon. He developed into one of the Reds' all-time great relievers and clubhouse characters, a hard-headed, hard-throwing pitcher who certainly had a fitting start.

As the summer approached, Cincinnati baseball fans enjoyed a burst of civic pride not felt since the Reds had won the 1940 World Series. The Reds were the talk of baseball with their .700

1970 Monthly Standings

National League West

April 30

	W	L	GB
Cincinnati	16	6	–
Los Angeles	10	10	5
Atlanta	10	11	5½
San Francisco	10	12	6
Houston	7	14	8½
San Diego	7	14	8½

May 31

	W	L	GB
Cincinnati	31	14	–
Atlanta	27	19	7
Los Angeles	28	20	7
San Francisco	24	26	12½
Houston	21	29	15
San Diego	22	31	15½

June 30

	W	L	GB
Cincinnati	52	22	–
Los Angeles	43	32	9½
Atlanta	37	35	14
San Francisco	36	38	16
Houston	33	43	20
San Diego	31	47	23

July 31

	W	L	GB
Cincinnati	72	34	–
Los Angeles	59	42	10
Atlanta	50	53	20½
San Francisco	49	52	20½
Houston	46	57	24½
San Diego	40	64	31

August 31

	W	L	GB
Cincinnati	86	49	–
Los Angeles	72	58	11½
San Francisco	69	63	15½
Atlanta	65	67	19½
Houston	62	70	22½
San Diego	50	82	34½

Final Standings

	W	L	GB
Cincinnati	102	60	–
Los Angeles	87	74	14½
San Francisco	86	76	16
Houston	79	83	23
Atlanta	76	86	26
San Diego	63	99	39

winning percentage and 10-game lead. They would host the All-Star Game, the city's first since 1953, on July 14. And the new park, recently christened "Riverfront Stadium," was set to open June 30.

Construction had begun on Riverfront in 1968, and although the stadium later came under intense criticism for its drab design, circular shape and artificial surface, Riverfront was a state-of-the-art, multi-purpose facility when it opened. The circular design and the turf were necessary so the Reds and the Bengals could enjoy maximum use of the facility. Similar stadiums were under construction in Philadelphia and Pittsburgh. Circular Busch Stadium (with natural grass) and the Astrodome had opened in the mid-'60s, and Riverfront was in the vanguard of what appeared to be the shape of the future. With the boost the stadium was expected to give downtown, the opening of Riverfront loomed as a significant sporting and cultural event for Cincinnati.

Bob Howsam, who believed with great conviction in the power of baseball to entertain and unite a community, could not have planned his future in Cincinnati any better than to be running a baseball team as it gained in civic prominence. With his experience in opening new parks in Denver and St. Louis, his instincts for promotion and marketing, and his demand for excellence, Howsam brought unrivaled experience and enthusiasm to the unfolding of Riverfront. He was not involved in the initial plan of the facility, but he oversaw the design of the stadium's baseball features as they evolved.

Howsam envisioned the park as the "stage" for the performance of his team. Over the next seven seasons, Riverfront would host the star-studded revue known as the Big Red Machine.

"People sit there for three hours watching a show," Howsam explained. He was going to have the best baseball theater he could devise.

The initial plans called for a plexiglas barrier behind home plate similar to the backstop at Crosley Field. Howsam eliminated it. "It blocks out the sound which is a big part of fan enjoyment." Sound barriers were retained, however, in the private boxes and the press box area. Many fans and reporters who watched the games from those spots later complained they felt removed from the game.

Howsam also appreciated that baseball fans, like theater goers, are at heart critics who enjoy a good dispute now and then. At Crosley Field, he had drawn a yellow line across the scoreboard to match the height of the center field wall; any ball hit above the yellow line was a home run. Howsam admitted that if an occasional rhubarb arose over where the ball hit on the scoreboard, so much the better. For the new stadium, Howsam placed the bullpens in view so that the fans could follow the manager's thinking and engage in some critiquing.

"We made a mistake in St. Louis by putting the bullpens out of sight," Howsam recalled. "As soon as the fans see a pitcher warming up, they all become instant managers."

Howsam's most discussed feature of the new park, however, was the introduction of the all-Astroturf field, leaving only the sliding pits, the mound and the home plate area in dirt. Riverfront was the first to have this design, and while the National League office approved the concept, it was reluctant to part with tradition. Howsam was ordered to paint what would have been the dirt portion of the infield brown. But the manufacturer of Astroturf, Monsanto, could not guarantee a paint. The decorating plans were scrapped, thus sparing fans the pretense of artificial grass posing as artificial dirt.

Howsam, a dogged defender of many of baseball's traditions,

1970 Monthly Standings
National League East

April 30

	W	L	GB
Chicago	13	5	—
Pittsburgh	11	8	2½
St. Louis	9	7	3
New York	10	9	3½
Philadelphia	10	9	3½
Montreal	5	13	8

May 31

	W	L	GB
Chicago	25	19	—
New York	25	23	2
Pittsburgh	23	26	4½
St. Louis	21	24	4½
Philadelphia	20	27	6½
Montreal	16	30	10

June 30

	W	L	GB
New York	40	33	—
Pittsburgh	40	37	2
St. Louis	37	37	3½
Chicago	35	37	4½
Philadelphia	12	40	7½
Montreal	29	44	11

July 31

	W	L	GB
New York	55	46	—
Pittsburgh	56	48	½
Chicago	54	49	2
Philadelphia	46	54	8½
St. Louis	45	58	11
Montreal	44	59	12

August 31

	W	L	GB
Pittsburgh	70	63	—
Chicago	69	64	1
New York	68	64	1
St. Louis	64	69	6
Philadelphia	62	70	7½
Montreal	57	75	12½

Final Standings

	W	L	GB
Pittsburgh	89	73	—
Chicago	84	78	5
New York	83	79	6
St. Louis	76	86	13
Philadelphia	73	88	15½
Montreal	73	89	16

Riverfront Stadium opened on June 30, 1970. The stadium was the first to feature Astroturf over the entire field, including the "skin" part of the infield. The National League asked the Reds to paint this portion of the infield brown to simulate dirt, but the plan was dropped.

especially those involving player-management relations and the personal appearance of players, nonetheless supported artificial surface. Granted, he was forced to use it because the field had to host both baseball and football, but Howsam *liked* turf: it was pleasing to the eye, prevented rainouts and rewarded speed, one of the most exciting attributes of the game.

By covering the infield with carpet, Howsam had performed the ultimate in baseball's nefarious tradition of doctoring fields. He had created a permanent surface that would benefit the type of players he coveted most: those with speed.

The Reds closed Crosley Field with a flourish, winning the final game in storybook fashion when Bench and May hit back-to-back home runs in the eighth inning to beat the Giants, 5-4. Crosley proved to be a most hospitable field in its final season. The Reds finished 28-8, but there was some worry the Reds might not dominate offensively at Riverfront as they had at Crosley. Riverfront measured 130,000 square feet to Crosley's 119,000, and the home-run distances were longer in every direction, except down the right-field line.

Defense was also a question. The Reds' only experience on an outdoor carpet was at Candlestick Park in San Francisco where the Giants experimented with it in 1970. On a road trip into Houston preceding opening night at Riverfront, Anderson drilled the infielders on groundballs—in the Astrodome outfield. He was trying to emulate the all-Astroturf surface of Riverfront.

The concerns about defense and offensive production in Riverfront would proved valid over time. As the Reds coaches and front office people watched closely over the remainder of the 1970 season, they saw that the big, quick Astroturf field dramatically favored certain players and skills. The demands of Astroturf became the dominating factor in judging talent and fashioning trades, culminating in the dramatic Houston–Cincinnati trade of 1971 that brought Joe Morgan to the Reds. But with few exceptions, the 1970 Big Red Machine adapted well to Riverfront. Although the club did not match its fantastic start at Crosley, the Reds won 29 of their 45 games at Riverfront.

The June 30th opener drew 51,050, the largest crowd ever to attend a sporting event in Cincinnati. The fans endured many inconveniences—the escalators, parking garage and concession stands were only partially completed—and the Reds played one of their worst games of the year, losing to the Braves, 8-2.

Two weeks later, the new home of the Big Red Machine entertained its first national television audience, and President Richard Nixon, with the 1970 All-Star Game. The Reds placed Rose, Perez, Bench, Merritt and Simpson on the All-Star squad. Going into the ninth inning, the hometown heroes had contributed little, and the game was anything but memorable, with the American League leading, 4-1. But a rare ninth-inning rally (only the third time in All-Star history a ninth-inning rally had tied or won the game) evened the score and set the stage for the thunderous 12th-inning collision between Rose and Ray Fosse, a 23-year-old catcher for the Cleveland Indians.

Rose and Fosse, who had not known each other before the All-Star festivities, had coincidentally met the evening before, shared dinner and then talked baseball into the late hours at Rose's house. Now, in the 12th inning of the game, their names were to become forever linked.

Rose first had a chance to win the game with two out in the ninth-inning rally, but with all 51,000 fans yelling for the hometown kid to get a hit, Pete struck out. Rose, who loved the spotlight of such a glamour game, longed for another at-bat. With two out in the 12th, he stepped into the box against Angels pitcher Clyde Wright, adjusted his batting helmet with that familiar tap on the head and lined a single to center field.

Dodger infielder Bill Grabarkewitz followed with another single and then Jim Hickman of the Cubs hit a low line drive up the middle that bounced into the outfield. With two out, Rose was running on contact and as he swung around third, center fielder Amos Otis charged the ball, fielded it cleanly and launched his throw to Fosse.

A couple of steps past third, at full speed, Rose took a quick glance back at Otis to assess the situation and recognized immediately there would be a play at the plate.

The videotape of the play shows that two-thirds of the way home, Rose started to lean forward, preparing for his trademark headfirst slide, but Fosse had the baseline blocked. Fosse later admitted he could have moved a step inside the line, taken the throw and swiped at the Rose as he slid by. But to Fosse, that was the wrong play.

"I wasn't going to look like a fool and get out the way," Fosse recalled. "I was the Cleveland catcher not the San Diego chicken."

Ray Fosse blocked the plate as he waited for the ball and Pete Rose in the 12th inning of the 1970 All-Star Game at Riverfront Stadium. An instant later, Rose crashed into Fosse, scoring the winning run.

"I started to slide and I saw I couldn't make it," said Rose. "Headfirst, it would have been worse. No way. I just had to run and hit him. I thought I hit a mountain."

The collision sent Fosse tumbling backward, and Rose fell over him to the plate. Fosse never caught the throw, Rose was safe and Riverfront exploded in cheers. Fosse would go on to play eight more seasons in baseball, but the damage to his shoulder would bother him throughout his career. Rose was criticized for being pitiless, but Fosse never blamed Pete.

"We both made the plays we thought we had to make. A couple of aggressive ballplayers doing their jobs," said Fosse.

The replay of the collision made for great television and quickly became the signature moment of the 1970 All-Star Game—and in time one of the most recognizable events in the video era of baseball. It propelled Rose and his team into the national spotlight as never before. Here was a defining moment for a team on the edge of greatness, an aggressive baseball machine that would steamroll the opposition. Enshrinement in baseball history requires such highlights, and the Rose-Fosse collision became the first link in a seven-year chain of memorable events that eventually placed the Big Red Machine among baseball's epic teams.

On July 26, the Red played their 100th game of the season. Their 70-30 start was the best since the 1944 Cardinals had gone 73-27. The Reds had a chance to win every major award: the MVP, Cy Young, Rookie of the Year and Manager of the Year. Bench, Perez, Rose and Tolan all were subject of MVP talk, Wayne Simpson and Jim Merritt looked like Cy Young candidates, rookie Carbo was hitting over .300 with 17 home runs and Anderson appeared to be a sure bet for Manager of the Year. There was speculation that the Reds might top the 1954 Indians mark of 111 victories, or even challenge the all-time record of 116 held by the 1906 Cubs.

But beginning July 31, the Reds encountered a string of injuries to their pitching staff that ended all thoughts of a record-setting winning mark and eventually crippled their chances against Baltimore in the World Series.

Wayne Simpson was the first to fall. He remembered the moment: "I threw a fastball to Billy Williams and the whole shoulder seemed to give way. I finished the inning, but couldn't raise my arm before the next inning started." He made only two more appearances in 1970, totalling five innings.

No one can say for certain what caused the 22-year-old's shoulder to blow apart on that July day in Chicago, but there is no doubting the record: in the year and a half before his injury, Simpson pitched 508 innings, an unusually high number. He pitched 162 innings at Indianapolis in the 1969 season in 27 starts, which was not excessive. But then, with less than two months rest, he started winter ball in Puerto Rico. Simpson pitched 151 innings in the 69-game season that ended January 20. He then pitched in the playoffs, and one month later was in spring training with the Reds. He logged 24 innings at Tampa, tops on the squad, and threw many more unofficial innings as he worked to make the club. By July 31, 1970, Simpson had pitched another 171 innings, and his shoulder finally collapsed.

On September 9, in Los Angeles, 20-game winner Jim Merritt, the first Cincinnati left-hander since Eppa Rixey to win 20, left the game in the first inning with a sore elbow. He pitched only three more innings after the injury and his playoff effectiveness was uncertain. McGlothlin had won 11 games before the All-Star break, but then missed two months when he was struck twice by batted balls—in the knee and in the face—and never regained his form.

After reaching the .700 plateau after 100 games, the Reds were barely .500 the rest of the way, going 32-30 in their final 62 games. The offense floundered as well, especially Perez. After hitting 29 home runs and driving in 90 RBIs before the All-Star game, he had only 11 homers and 39 RBIs in the second half. Despite this August and September swoon, Bench, Perez and May finished the season with 129 home runs, second only to the 1961 threesome of Maris, Mantle and Bill "Moose" Skowron.

As early as mid-August, Howsam turned his attention to the postseason. He had always admired George Weiss for his ability to pick up a late-season player to fine-tune a squad entering the World Series. As Howsam evaluated his team, he saw a glaring lack of post-season experience.

"I was trying to get a fellow like Ron Fairly, who had experience in a World Series, to try to provide leadership," recalled Howsam. "But I couldn't get the deal made, not for the type of player we wanted. I didn't want to upset the club."

The Reds clinched the West on September 18, when they beat the Braves in Atlanta and the second-place Dodgers lost to Houston in Los Angeles. The news reached the clubhouse at two in the morning. The few players who were still there spilled a little champagne, but others learned about it the next morning. Clay Carroll heard the news in the coffee shop of the Marriott Motor Hotel, which did not lend itself to a champagne shower. "I don't know what to do," complained Carroll. "You just can't stand up in a restaurant and shout, but that's what I feel like doing."

In the playoffs, the Reds faced the Pirates, another young team at the beginning of an impressive run that would see them win the

Jim Merritt (left) and Johnny Bench accepted Cincinnati Baseball Writers Association awards from *Cincinnati Enquirer* sportswriter Bill Ford as the Reds' top pitcher and club MVP. Merritt was the only 20-game winner during the Big Red Machine era.

Eastern Division five of the next six seasons, and capture the World Series in 1971. They featured several fine players, but at 89-73 the Pirates would have been 13 games behind the Big Red Machine. Ray Shore had scouted Pittsburgh in September. He returned with with an optimistic report. Although their lineup included Roberto Clemente, Matty Alou, Manny Sanguillen, Al Oliver and Willie Stargell, Shore believed the Reds had the edge despite their pitching problems.

The best-of-five series, the first ever played entirely on artificial surface and in round stadiums, opened at the new Three Rivers Stadium in Pittsburgh. The series went against form, with two of the league's top offensive clubs stymied by excellent pitching. The Reds scored only nine runs in the three games and the Pirates only three. Although the Reds swept the series, 3-0, the Pirates had a shot at winning every game. Nolan tossed a shutout in Game One, but the Reds couldn't score until the tenth. Pinch-hitter Ty Cline tripled and Rose singled him home. In the second game, Merritt, Carroll and Gullett held the Pirates to one run and Tolan scored all three Cincinnati runs to put the Reds up, two games to none.

The playoffs moved to Riverfront for the third game on Monday, October 5, and perhaps Pirate management realized its chances were slim. They advanced the players only one day's worth of meal money. The game was tied, 2-2, in the bottom of the eighth when Cline again started a rally. He walked and Rose followed with a single. Tolan then pushed a soft single to left. Cline, who possessed average speed at best, was no sure bet to score on the shallow ball. Stargell rushed it and threw hard to home, but Sanguillen had to reach toward first base to catch it and then lunge back to tag the sliding Cline. Umpire Paul Pryor called him safe and the replay confirmed it. Gullett came on in the ninth and faced Oliver with

WAYNE SIMPSON

In high school in Los Angeles, he could throw a football 90 yards in the air. His arm had baseball scouts drooling. The Reds made young Wayne Simpson their number one pick in the 1967 draft. Three years later he was in the major leagues. No rookie pitcher ever opened with more success. By the All-Star Game, Simpson was 13-1 with a 2.69 ERA, and a candidate for the Cy Young award.

But in the previous 15 months, Simpson had pitched more than 500 innings. He tore his rotator cuff on July 31, and never fully recovered. The Reds traded him to Kansas City in 1972. After several operations and failed comebacks, he retired with a career record of 34-31.

With pitching coach Larry Shephard monitoring his recovery, Simpson attempted a comeback in 1971. He started 21 games, but never approached the success of his 1970 season.

the tying run on second. From the Reds broadcast booth, Jim McIntyre called the pennant-winning moment.

Swung on and a groundball to Helms. He has it. He'll flip it to May. The Reds win the National League flag! And the celebration breaks loose…and the Reds mob Don Gullett. They are all over him. They pick up Sparky Anderson. Up in the air goes Sparky on the shoulders of the Reds players, as the Reds win the National League flag. They're mobbing each other in front of the Reds dugout…as the Reds wrap up the National League pennant, as Don Gullett and Wayne Granger do the job in the ninth inning. They beat the Pirates, 3-2!

The clubhouse celebration began immediately, although someone forgot the champagne.

"Wait a minute. Something's missing!" shouted Clay Carroll. "Where the (bleep) is that (bleep-bleep) champagne?!" It turned up, and with the showers turned on, no one was safe.

"Give me your wallet, give me your watch," said equipment manager Bernie Stowe to the players and front-office personnel as they were carried to the showers. Seconds later, the players descended on Howsam and dragged the suit-clad GM to the shower.

Howsam had celebrated his first major league pennant with the Cardinals in 1964, but this one was much sweeter; this was *his* club. Anderson gave his boss the credit; he pointed at the drenched Howsam across the clubhouse and said to an interviewer, "This was an organizational victory."

Privately, both Howsam and Anderson were somewhat surprised the Reds had won the pennant. Although Howsam believed the club would contend for the pennant, he had thought the team was still a year away, with five rookies playing such a big role. Sparky had believed the club could win the division, but wasn't sure the crippled pitching staff could get by the Pirates. But the pitching had been brilliant, with an ERA of 1.29. If the staff could hold together for another week, if Merritt's arm would rebound, if McGlothlin or Cloninger could come up with one more good game, if Nolan continued to pitch well, then the Reds just might win the World Series.

Position by position, discounting the experience factor, the Reds matched up well against the Orioles. Baltimore had future Hall of Famers Brooks and Frank Robinson, as well as Jim Palmer, but the

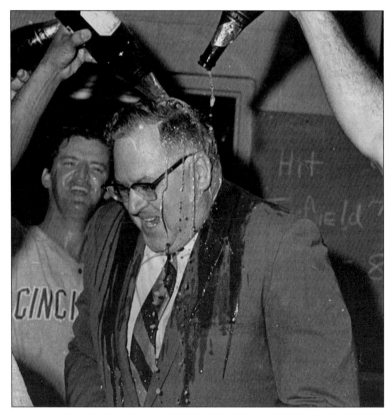

© Cincinnati Reds

Clay Carroll helped douse Bob Howsam with champagne after the Reds defeated the Pirates to win the pennant.

1970 SCRAPBOOK

THE OPPOSITION

WESTERN DIVISION

Against	Won	Lost
Atlanta	13	5
Houston	15	3
Los Angeles	13	5
San Diego	8	10
San Fran.	9	9

EASTERN DIVISION

Against	Won	Lost
Chicago	5	7
Montreal	7	5
New York	8	4
Philadelphia	7	5
Pittsburgh	8	4
St. Louis	9	3

The pitcher the Reds didn't want to face – **Bill Hands** of the Cubs was 4-0 against the Reds, including 3 complete-game wins.

The pitcher they loved to see – **Steve Carlton** of the Cardinals was 0-4 against the Reds.

The batter who loved the Reds – **Hank Aaron** of Atlanta hit .400 (22-for-55) with 4 HRs and 10 RBIs.

The batter who should have stayed home – **Joe Morgan** of the Astros hit .233 (14-for-60) with 1 HR and 1 RBI.

CLUB LEADERS

Batting Average	Tony Perez	.317
Home runs	Johnny Bench	45 •
RBIs	Johnny Bench	148 •
Stolen bases	Bobby Tolan	57
Runs	Pete Rose	120
ERA	Wayne Simpson	3.02
Wins	Jim Merritt	20
Saves	Clay Carroll	35 •
Games	Wayne Granger	67

• League leader

AWARDS

National League MVP	**Johnny Bench**
Sporting News Rookie of the Year	**Bernie Carbo**
Gold Glove	**Johnny Bench**
	Pete Rose
	Tommy Helms
Cincinnati Reds MVP •	**Johnny Bench**
Outstanding Reds Pitcher •	**Jim Merritt**
Reds Newcomer of the Year •	**Bernie Carbo**

• Awarded by Cincinnati Chapter of Baseball Writers Association

TRADES

Jun 15	**Ty Cline** acquired from Montreal for **Clyde Mashore**	
Dec 15	**Greg Garrett** acquired from California for **Jim Maloney**	

THE DRAFT

Cincinnati drafted 65 players; eight played in the major leagues.

Joel Youngblood	Houston, TX	C-SS
Tom Carroll	Pittsburgh, PA	P
Will McEnaney	Springfield, OH	P
Ray Knight	Albany, GA	P-3B
Pat Zachry	Waco, TX	P
Pat Osborn	Florida State Univ.	P
Jim Norris •	Univ. of Maryland	OF
Duane Kuiper •	Indian Hills (Iowa) CC	SS

• Drafted by Reds, but signed with another club

Reds countered with three Hall of Fame caliber players themselves: Bench, Rose and Perez. These were two of the great teams in baseball history: the Reds on the edge of a dynasty and Baltimore in the middle of its impressive run. From 1969 to 1974, the Orioles averaged 99 wins a year, a .610 winning percentage. They won pennants in 1969, '70 and '71, and division titles in '73 and '74.

The Series opened at Riverfront, with Palmer and Nolan pitching. In what would prove to be a theme in the Series, the Reds jumped on Palmer early, building a 3-0 lead. Tolan ignited two rallies, capped by an RBI single by Bench and a two-run homer by May. The Orioles tied it at 3-3, setting the stage for the infamous sixth inning.

The inning started spectacularly when Brooks Robinson made a great play on May. Robinson played all the big Cincinnati right-handers to pull. He was in perfect position to stab May's shot over third. He leaped and "pivoted" in mid-air, then threw a long one-hopper to Boog Powell that beat May by a half-step. Of all the plays Robinson would make in this Series, this became the video granddaddy. Even the Reds were awed.

"He was going toward the bullpen when he threw," said Carroll. "His arm went one way, his body another and his shoes another."

It proved to be a run-saving play, as Carbo walked and Helms singled, moving Carbo to third. Anderson then sent pinch-hitter Cline to bat for shortstop Woodward.

Cline swung and chopped the ball into the ground in front of the plate. The ball bounced straight up. Catcher Elrod Hendricks threw off his mask and moved a couple of feet up the first-base line to make the catch. Umpire Ken Burkhart, considered one of the better umpires in the league, took two steps up the third-base line so he could call the ball fair or foul. Focused on the ball, facing first base, Burkhart didn't see Carbo streaking for the plate.

"I was a little surprised when Carbo came in," admitted Burkhart. In fact, Carbo's decision surprised *everyone*.

"He's not supposed to go on a ball right in front of the plate," said Grammas.

"A foolish move," Sparky said.

"Instinct, that's why I went," explained Carbo.

Hendricks also failed to see Carbo. But Palmer yelled at Hendricks, who caught the ball, turned and dove for Carbo, who had started to slide behind Burkhart. Caught between the two players, Burkhart ducked under the diving Hendricks, and fell forward toward the mound.

As Burkhart was falling to his knees, he turned toward home plate, but too late to see the tag. He immediately signaled out, making the call on experience. He knew that Hendricks had the runner beat, but he never saw the tag, and that was the problem. As Hendricks had lunged and tagged Carbo with his glove hand, he had kept the ball in his right hand.

Unbelievably, this was the second time in the 1970 season Burkhart had victimized the Reds with the same mistake. On July 12, Atlanta catcher Hal King had tagged May with his glove while holding the ball in his other hand. Burkhart called May out, and Sparky was tossed after arguing the call.

Now, Carbo jumped in front of Burkhart and Anderson joined him, hands in his back pockets. Anderson and Carbo hadn't seen the ball in the wrong hand; they were arguing that Hendricks missed the tag or that Burkhart couldn't make the call because he couldn't see the play. Carbo, who insisted he was safe, didn't realize he had missed home plate on his slide. As he argued, he stomped on the plate and, at that moment, was actually safe.

All of this was made clear by the replays afterward. Although Burkhart endured a great deal of criticism, the Reds did not use the call as an alibi.

"Bernie Carbo would have been out easy if Burkhart wasn't in the way," said Anderson. "That's why he (Burkhart) can't be blamed for anything."

Baltimore manager Earl Weaver got the last word. "The umpire did a tremendous job," he said to an amused crowd of reporters.

When the game resumed, the Reds rally died. In the top of the seventh, Brooks Robinson hit what proved to be the game-winning home run.

The Game Two starters were Mike Cuellar and McGlothlin. The left-handed Cuellar was originally signed by the Reds out of Cuba in the late 1950s. He appeared briefly with the Reds in 1959, eventually wound up in Baltimore, and won 24 games in 1970. But the Big Red Machine was 17-3 against left-handers at Riverfront and confidently jumped on Cuellar early to take a 4-0 lead. In the fourth, with the Reds again threatening to score, Brooks Robinson pulled off another miracle, spearing May's shot and starting a 5-4-3 double play.

Robinson's defense ignited the offense as Powell hit a home run in the fourth. In the fifth, the Orioles bunched five singles and a double to score five runs. Bench hit a home run in the sixth to close the lead to 6-5, but veteran relief pitcher Dick Hall retired the final

In the pivotal play of Game One of the 1970 World Series, Elrod Hendricks tagged Bernie Carbo with his glove, but not the ball. Umpire Ken Burkhart, caught out of position, missed the call.

The Cincinnati Enquirer

seven hitters, and the Series moved to Baltimore.

Facing a mountain no team had ever climbed—coming back to win the Series after losing the first two games at home—Anderson hoped to start his 20-game winner Merritt in the third game. But Merritt's elbow was still sore and Anderson named Tony Cloninger to pitch Game Three. Cloninger gave up just five hits through the first five innings, but two were home runs and the Orioles led, 4-1. Brooks Robinson made two more highlight plays at third base, including robbing Bench of extra bases in the fifth. Once again, the Orioles seemed to feed off Robinson's defense. With the bases loaded and two out in the sixth, and Wayne Granger on in relief of Cloninger, pitcher Dave McNally hit a grand slam.

Anderson could only shake his head. "Every mistake we've made, they've hit out of the park. They told us McNally would hit the high fastball out of there, and that's exactly what we gave him to hit."

Nolan got the start in Game Four, and the Reds again jumped out to an early lead. But the Orioles rallied and led, 5-3, heading into the eighth inning. The Reds put the first two on against Palmer. Eddie Watt, the Orioles top relief pitcher, came on to face the hot Lee May. During Watt's warmup, May ambled over to the Reds dugout for a scouting report. Back came the advice: look for sinkers. Hendricks called for a sinker on the first pitch, but it didn't sink until it cleared the left field wall, a 440-foot monster home run. Clay Carroll worked the final three and two-thirds innings, giving up just one hit, to pick up the 6-5 win.

Optimism filled the Reds clubhouse after the victory, but the ugly reality of two sore arms doomed whatever hopes the team might have entertained. The Reds had no healthy pitchers to throw in Game Five. It was McGlothlin's turn, but he had injured his arm in

Brooks Robinson turned in a highlight reel's worth of great plays in the 1970 World Series. He robbed Bench, May and Perez of hits, thwarted several Cincinnati rallies and won the Series' MVP award.

Game Two and it was so swollen he couldn't pitch. Anderson might have used Carroll or Gullett as emergency starters, but both had pitched in the fourth game when Nolan was shelled early. Merritt's elbow was still sore, but he told Anderson he could go. Short of any other options, Anderson started Merritt against Cuellar.

The Reds again started fast, taking a 3-0 lead on hits by Rose, Bench, May and McRae. But in the bottom of the first, Frank Robinson hit a two-run home run. Another two-run rally in the second knocked out Merritt and put the Orioles ahead for good. Two more runs in the third off Granger gave Baltimore a 6-3 lead and the Reds never recovered. Cuellar gave up only two singles after the first inning.

To no one's surprise, Brooks Robinson was the MVP. Rose, co-owner of a car dealership with Bench, wrote in his "Rose Prose" column for *The Cincinnati Enquirer*, "If I had known Brooks Robinson wanted a car that badly (it came with the MVP award), Johnny Bench and I would have given him one. Every year the Lord picks out a guy who's the best player in the World Series and this year, it was him."

The Orioles had shown tremendous character in the Series, being down 3-0 twice and 4-0 once and coming back to win all three games. But even though Anderson didn't make any alibis for his beleaguered pitching staff, it was obvious the Reds had not been at their best for the Series.

Sparky said later, "Their top starters, we beat up on them. We just didn't have any pitching, no pitching at all. That Series, people look at it and say, 'Oh, five games,' but no, no, no. Sometimes what the outcome is, isn't what the whole picture is."

Howsam chalked it up to experience. "I came away from that Series thinking we had better players than they did. But we didn't have the experience." The World Series defeat figured to teach some hard lessons to Howsam's young team.

Although the Reds had lost the Series, they had set a club record by winning 102 regular-season games. Several of the younger players had established themselves. In particular, 22-year-old Bench had one of the best seasons ever by a catcher: 45 home runs, 148 RBIs—and the MVP award. Carbo won *The Sporting News* Rookie of the Year award. Concepcion hit a surprising .260 in his first year. The biggest question mark heading into 1971 was the pitching staff, with Simpson, Merritt and McGlothlin all facing comebacks.

The other significant success story in 1970 was Riverfront Stadium. In 43 dates in the new facility, the Reds drew 1.2 million fans (an average of 28,736 per game) with 10 sellouts. The Reds shattered all previous club attendance records by drawing a total of 1.8 million fans. With a full season at Riverfront ahead for the defending National League Champions, Howsam and Wagner expected the Reds to break the two million mark.

In the fall of 1970, despite the loss to the Orioles, the prevailing mood in the Riverfront offices was one of optimism. The future had a rosy Red glow. But over the next few months, a series of misfortunes would disable the Big Red Machine, bringing the dynasty talk to a halt. The enduring story of 1971 would come not from the team's performance on the field, but from the brilliant moves Howsam would engineer from the adversity.

(© Jerry Dowling & *The Cincinnati Enquirer*, 1971)

After the glory of 1970, the Reds stumbled badly in 1971. Off-season injuries and spring-training mishaps led to a slow start. They fell 16 games out of first place after only 50 games and never pushed their record over .500. Their fourth-place finish was the lowest in the Howsam-Anderson years, and set the stage for an overhaul of the Big Red Machine.

Fourth Place • 79 wins-83 losses

Chapter **6**

1971
The Big Deal

All-Stars: Johnny Bench • Clay Carroll • Lee May • Pete Rose

DESPITE THE WORLD SERIES LOSS to the Orioles, the Cincinnati organization exuded great confidence. Yes, the Reds had been beaten, but the lack of healthy pitching explained much of the collapse, and Howsam was optimistic as he looked to 1971.

"We could go into next year without making any changes and still be better than we were," he said in the fall of 1970.

Most baseball people agreed. "The Reds may have the brightest future of any ball club in the majors," wrote *New York Times* baseball columnist Arthur Daley.

But Howsam was still concerned about his crippled pitching staff. Immediately after the Series, the Reds began talking to Cleveland about 28-year-old Sam McDowell, a big left-hander who had won 20 games in 1970 and had led the American League in strikeouts five of the preceding six seasons.

At the winter meetings in Los Angeles in December, the Reds offered the Indians Lee May, shortstop prospect Frank Duffy and Tony Cloninger for McDowell. The Indians asked for Milt Wilcox or Ross Grimsley rather than Cloninger. Unwilling to part with one of his young pitchers, Howsam nixed the deal. This was one of the best trades Howsam never made. Nineteen-seventy was McDowell's last dominating season, and Duffy and May were key figures in two trades later in 1971 that brought Joe Morgan and George Foster to the Big Red Machine.

The organization's high hopes for 1971 began to collapse in early January. Bobby Tolan suffered a rupture of his Achilles tendon in a Reds basketball game in Frankfort, Kentucky. In the late 1960s, Pete Rose had organized a team to appear in charity events and keep the players in shape. At first, Howsam supported the team, buying uniforms and warm-up suits. Then he changed his mind, partly because Anderson saw the team play in the 1969-70 offseason and watched Rose wind up in a brawl with an opposing player. Concerned about the risk of injuries, Howsam asked Rose to cancel the games for the 1970-71 offseason. Tickets had already been sold, Rose countered. Because Howsam had no official power to stop the activity, the games continued until Tolan went down.

Tolan's injury was a disaster. Sparky Anderson would have to fashion an outfield out of Bernie Carbo, Hal McRae, Jimmy Stewart and Rose. None was a legitimate center fielder. Certainly none had the speed required for the vast expanse of Astroturf in Riverfront Stadium. Tolan was also the Reds only stolen base threat. Defensively and offensively, the Reds had no replacement for Tolan, and the doctors said he would not return before June.

The calm of the 1971 preseason was also interrupted by the usual holdouts, with several players asking for large raises based on their individual performances and the overall success of the team. Howsam offered salary increases to several players, although not nearly what they had hoped. The players had received $13,000 World Series checks, and for some of the younger players, this had nearly doubled their salaries. The team payroll would approach $1 million, and Howsam, a frugal negotiator who had learned his baseball from one of the tightest of all executives, Branch Rickey, was not going to upset the delicate balance of the salary schedule for even his star players.

The early 1970s were still in an era when most players were paid according to the performance of the preceding year. Players

The Cincinnati Enquirer

Pete Rose and several of his baseball teammates played charity basketball games in the off-season. Bobby Tolan suffered his Achilles injury at such a game in early 1971. The mishap doomed the '71 season—and ultimately led to the trade for Joe Morgan.

typically received modest increases or modest decreases. Even one great year early in a career was not enough to move a player into the higher salary brackets. Young players had to put two or three good years together before they could jump to $50,000. And a veteran who slumped might be asked to take a cut or to sign at the same salary as the year before.

The most expensive part in the Big Red Machine was Rose at $105,000. He began his negotiations by asking for $250,000 over two years. Bench, who had made $40,000 in 1970, also floated the idea of a multi-year deal, asking for $500,000 over three years. Bench had recently appeared on the TV show "Mission: Impossible" and Chief Bender said of his salary request, "You can say that's what he is embarking on here…'Mission: Impossible.'"

The Reds had never given a multi-year contract and Howsam had no intention of considering it, even for Bench and Rose. "We're not going to be pushed into an unsound position by any player with regard to his contract," said Howsam. "After all, we have a whole organization to think of."

Bench, who was less combative in contract talks than Rose, signed for an estimated $85,000, but Pete remained a holdout. Rose had "slumped" to .316 in 1970, down from his back-to-back batting title seasons of .335 and .348, and the club used this as ammunition. A quarter of a century later, Rose still remembered the bitter negotiations.

"I led the league (in 1970) in hits. Third in the league in doubles and runs. And I won a Gold Glove. And we went to the World Series," recalled Pete. "What do you think the first thing is they said? 'Well, you dropped 32 points on your batting average.' Next thing they say is, 'You didn't even lead the team in hitting.' I'm telling you, this is the God's honest truth, strike my mom dead.

1971 MONTHLY STANDINGS
NATIONAL LEAGUE WEST

April 30
	W	L	GB
San Francisco	18	5	—
Los Angeles	13	11	5½
Houston	11	12	7
Atlanta	10	11	7
Cincinnati	8	12	8½
San Diego	5	16	12

May 31
	W	L	GB
San Francisco	37	14	—
Los Angeles	26	24	10½
Houston	25	24	11
Atlanta	22	28	14½
Cincinnati	20	29	16
San Diego	15	35	21½

June 30
	W	L	GB
San Francisco	50	29	—
Los Angeles	43	35	6½
Houston	37	39	11½
Atlanta	38	45	14
Cincinnati	36	44	14½
San Diego	28	51	22

July 31
	W	L	GB
San Francisco	66	43	—
Los Angeles	55	51	9
Atlanta	56	53	9½
Houston	63	53	11
Cincinnati	49	59	16
San Diego	38	69	26

August 31
	W	L	GB
San Francisco	79	56	—
Los Angeles	71	64	8
Atlanta	70	68	10½
Cincinnati	68	70	12½
Houston	64	71	15
San Diego	51	85	28½

Final Standings
	W	L	GB
San Francisco	90	72	—
Los Angeles	89	73	1
Atlanta	82	80	8
Cincinnati	79	83	11
Houston	79	83	11
San Diego	61	100	28½

I led the team in hitting 161 games. I led the team in hitting every fuckin' day of the year, every fuckin' at-bat until the last at-bat. I made an out and Perez made a hit and he hit .317. That's how tough they were in negotiating. And you wonder why we held out?"

Rose's representative in the contract talks was Hy Ullner, a discount furniture store owner. In a move that angered the Reds, Ullner took the talks public. The Reds were making plenty of money, Ullner claimed, and Rose was among the club's most valuable players. How could he not deserve a raise when the club had won the pennant?

"We're not in the Branch Rickey era anymore. Howsam was Rickey's man and sometimes he thinks like Rickey did," Ullner charged.

Such talk from a furniture salesman was tough for a baseball man to take and Howsam refused to budge, even when Rose lowered his demands to $115,000. Howsam, who could not bring himself to offer Rose an increase based on merit, finally broke the logjam when he agreed to consider Rose's request for a cost-of-living increase. But even that was not without rancor.

Bender recalled the negotiations: "Pete comes back in and says he at least needs a cost of living increase. So I go to Bob again and Bob says, 'You know, he doesn't live on $105,000, he only lives on half that much. Offer him the cost of living on half his salary. Just explain to him that he doesn't live on $105,000.' So now Pete comes back in and he can't believe it. 'You're kidding me!' he says. and he storms out of the office."

Rose finally signed for a modest increase. The next season Ullner was replaced by Reuven Katz, who would represent Rose and Bench during the rest of the 1970s.

Sparky now had a full camp, but old and new problems continued to create uncertainty. He tried McRae and Rose in center field and even had Concepcion taking fly balls, but none looked comfortable. Merritt and Simpson still reported sore arms, and Lee May, Tony Perez and Concepcion all suffered injuries.

"In spring training, Tony strained all the tendons on the back of his hand," Sparky recalled. "He played with it, but he couldn't reach the fence during batting practice. Lee May tore up his knee in a collision at first base. David was in the hospital. He dove into third and jammed himself under the bag and broke his finger. If I had known that things like this could happen, I would have been scared to death to ever take a managing job."

The Reds faced Atlanta on Opening Day before a full house of 51,000. With May out, Perez played first and Woody Woodward started at third. Woodward made three errors and the Reds lost, 7-4. They went on to lose the first four games and by the end of April they were in fifth place, eight back of the streaking Giants.

May and Concepcion both returned to the lineup, but the offense continued to falter. The starting rotation was unsettled most of the season. Simpson and Merritt spent time in the bullpen, and in Indianapolis. But the problems of 1971 could not be attributed to pitching. The staff gave up 581 runs (an average of only 3.6 runs per game), which was third best in the league. Although Simpson and Merritt were never effective—they started a total of 32 games and finished a combined 5-18—the rest of the starters, led by Nolan, Gullett, McGlothlin and rookie Ross Grimsley (called up from Indianapolis in May) had a 3.12 ERA. Granger, Carroll and Joe Gibbon saved 37 games.

The problem lay with the offense. Bench and Perez consistently

1971 MONTHLY STANDINGS
NATIONAL LEAGUE EAST

April 30
	W	L	GB
New York	12	7	–
Montreal	9	6	1
Pittsburgh	12	10	1½
St. Louis	13	11	1
Chicago	8	13	5
Philadelphia	7	12	5

May 31
	W	L	GB
St. Louis	32	17	–
Pittsburgh	29	19	2½
New York	27	18	3
Chicago	21	27	10½
Montreal	18	24	10½
Philadelphia	17	30	14

June 30
	W	L	GB
Pittsburgh	49	29	–
New York	45	29	2
Chicago	39	36	8½
St. Louis	40	38	9
Philadelphia	31	45	17
Montreal	29	45	18

July 31
	W	L	GB
Pittsburgh	67	39	–
St. Louis	58	48	9
Chicago	55	49	11
New York	54	49	11½
Philadelphia	45	61	22
Montreal	43	64	24½

August 31
	W	L	GB
Pittsburgh	80	56	–
St. Louis	74	60	5
Chicago	71	62	7½
New York	66	66	12½
Philadelphia	57	75	21
Montreal	56	75	21½

Final Standings
	W	L	GB
Pittsburgh	97	65	–
St. Louis	90	72	7
Chicago	83	79	14
New York	83	79	14
Montreal	71	90	26½
Philadelphia	67	95	30

Baseball Men: Ray Shore

Baseball's first advance scout—and the man behind many of the great deals pulled off by Bob Howsam—had plenty of advance training.

Ray Shore's life was baseball. He grew up in Cincinnati playing Knothole ball and tagging along with his father to Crosley Field to follow the Reds.

"I saw one of the first night games in 1935," Shore remembered. "Even saw Babe Ruth play one time."

Shore signed his first pro contract when he graduated from high school in 1939. During World War II, Lt. Shore played on an Army team in Algiers.

"I struck out 19 guys once," recalled Shore, laughing. "I was called the 'Bob Feller of the African Algiers League.'"

Shore finally made the majors in 1946 with the St. Louis Browns, but his fastball wasn't as effective in the American League as it had been in the American armed forces.

Over three seasons, he won only one game with a career ERA of 8.23. "I gave up 16 runs in a game in Boston one year," Shore admitted. "That's hard on your ERA."

He hung on in the minor leagues until 1957 and then returned to Cincinnati to open a sporting goods store.

But after two years of struggling in the retail business, he wrote to the Reds new president, Bill DeWitt. DeWitt had signed Shore to his first contract with the Browns in 1946, and on the eve of Opening Day in 1961, he told Shore to report to Crosley Field to throw batting practice. That was the beginning of a 20-year career as a coach and scout with the Reds, where he pioneered the advance scout concept.

"In 1968, I wasn't one of the regular coaches, but Howsam respected my evaluation of players," Shore said. "So at the end of spring training, they had me scout the Cubs since we opened the season against them. I phoned in my reports, and (manager) Dave Bristol used them. But I really came into my own when Sparky got there."

Teams had used scouts for World Series preparation, but never to scout regular-season opponents. Shore developed the system and Anderson loved the reports.

So did Howsam who relied on Shore's advice to trade for such Big Red Machine stars as Joe Morgan, George Foster and Pedro Borbon.

"Sparky said I probably won five games a year directly with my information," recalled Ray Shore (right). Shore also played a key role in evaluating talent for trades and scouting playoff and World Series opponents.

failed to hit early in the season, especially with men in scoring position. The team average dropped to .241, down from .270. "If we're the 11th-worst hitting team in the league then I need my head examined," lamented Sparky.

The standings and the box scores were not hallucinations, however. In the first 62 games, the Reds had 25 complete games pitched against them. In one stretch, they went nine games without scoring more than three runs. By the end of May, the Reds were 20-29, buried in fifth place, sixteen games behind the Giants.

"It's just not any fun this year," admitted Rose.

Anderson also suffered. "I do not eat much anymore," he said. "I don't sleep. I've got pains in my back. I'm not so sure anymore. I've gotten snappy with the players. People who used to smile at me now look at me like I just killed their daughter."

One person who did show support, however, was his boss. In the middle of the season, Howsam took the unusual step of coming to visit Anderson in his clubhouse office. Anderson was surprised to see Howsam and was initially scared of what news he might be bringing.

"Sparky, you don't have many friends now, do you?" asked Howsam in his soft-spoken manner.

Anderson nodded.

"Well, I want you to know you've got a friend sitting across the table from you." Howsam said.

Anderson still had to reverse his team's dismal performance, but Howsam's vote of confidence eased the pressure. The timing of Howsam's appearance also revealed a style that Anderson saw repeated over the years. Howsam was much more likely to get on his manager when the club was winning than when it was losing. He did not want success to breed complacency. But when his club was down, Howsam, who valued loyalty, would stand by his manager.

Tolan began working out with the Reds in early May, and the club hoped to have him back by June. But on May 6, Tolan reinjured the Achilles tendon while jogging and required additional surgery. He was now out for the season, and Howsam scrambled to find another outfielder. The Reds picked up reserve outfielder Buddy Bradford on waivers from the Cleveland Indians and then traded Angel Bravo to the Padres for Al Ferrara.

Neither contributed much, although Ferrara had one of the better quips of the year. After a poor fielding performance had reporters questioning his ability, Ferrara retorted, "Who did you expect for Angel Bravo? Willie Mays?"

As it turned out, the Reds were on the verge of pulling off a deal that was almost as lopsided as Bravo for Mays. That was Duffy for Foster, as in Frank Duffy, a third-string shortstop for the Reds, for George Foster, who would develop into one of the premier sluggers in the National League.

With Dave Concepcion establishing himself as the everyday shortstop, prospect Duffy had little future with the club. Duffy had started the season with the team because of Concepcion's spring-training injury, but when Concepcion was activated, Duffy was sent back to Indianapolis. Duffy, a 1967 first-round draft choice who had already spent a season and a half at Triple A, refused to report and asked to be traded. Howsam began working the phones. The Pirates offered a minor league prospect, as did the Giants.

Howsam recalled his conversation with Rosie Ryan, who was the general manager of the Giants Triple A club in Phoenix.

"I called him and said we were looking for an outfielder, and what did he think. I didn't mention any names," said Howsam, invoking one of his trading rules. Never bring up a name first. Let the other guy tell you who's available. Among other players, Ryan listed Bernie Williams, a young outfielder with Phoenix.

Howsam dispatched his scouting director Rex Bowen to Charleston, West Virginia, to report on the Pirates' outfield prospect. Howsam himself wanted a look at Williams, but before he left, he arranged to have Ray Shore join him in Arizona.

The call to Shore came as no surprise. Since 1968, Shore had been an advance scout or "super scout," as the press often called him. Shore scouted the other National League teams during the season, staying just ahead of the Reds' schedule. An ex-player, he had been a coach with the Reds since 1961 and was the only coach from the DeWitt era whom Howsam retained into the 1970s. At the beginning of the '68 season Shore had no specific assignment, so manager Dave Bristol sent him out early in the season to scout the opposing clubs the Reds were about to play. No other club had ever used one of its scouts to gather this kind of information on a regular basis, so Shore defined the job the way it made sense to him.

"Using my background as a pitcher and catcher, I came up with my own advanced scouting forms," Shore remembered. "What would I want to know if I was pitching the game? What would the manager want to know about defensing players?"

Shore carried a 3x5 spiral notebook for each team with one page for each player. On the first line was *how to play* or how to position the defense (*pull hitter*, *spray hitter* and so on). The next piece of information was *bunt?* for bunting tendencies. This was followed by *hit and run?*, *will he run?*, *type of hitter* (dead-high fastball hitter, for example), *how to pitch*, and *arm strength* for catchers, middle infielders and outfielders.

Shore often added notes on players when he found a trend. Dodger first baseman Steve Garvey, for example, would rarely throw to second or third base when fielding a sacrifice bunt. Shore's note read, "In sac. situation, bunt to Garvey, not third."

He would make a copy of the notebooks for his manager, and then update it as new players came into the league or as players changed their hitting or pitching styles. Other clubs watched the Shore experiment with curiosity. Most felt it was a luxury.

"Some people would say why bother with advance scouts?" Shore remembered. "They figured they had coaches and managers that see these guys play. Which was true, but then they only saw the opposition play against *their* team. Maybe somebody else was doing a better job. I would say, 'Is there anybody you can't get out? Well, *somebody's* getting them out; they ain't hittin' .500 against everybody!'"

Shore's schedule and reports put the Reds a step ahead during the season. After Anderson arrived, Shore's stock rose even higher. Anderson used Shore's reports religiously.

"Sparky said I probably won five games a year directly, maybe ten or fifteen indirectly," Shore recalled.

Howsam began to treat Shore's opinions with utmost respect and to consult him on nearly all personnel decisions.

"Howsam used to call me during the season and he would say, 'Ray, we got a chance to deal with this club. What do you know about this guy?' I could tell him because I had just seen the club."

"You believed in what Ray told you," recalled Howsam. "Ray learned what it took to win in the major leagues, and that's what made him a great scout. He knew by observation what level of ability a player had to have."

A character trait Howsam admired in Shore, and Shore in Howsam, was frankness. Howsam wanted candid, definite opinions about players and Shore would provide it. Shore recalled that shortly after Howsam took the Cincinnati job, his new scouting director, Rex Bowen, had come back with a report on a Triple A player. Bowen said the player had some tools, but needed discipline, and if he came to the Reds, he "probably" could help the club. Howsam didn't like the "probably" answer. He pushed Bowen for a firm decision. Yes or no. Shore took the lesson to heart.

"That's why Bob and I got along well," said Shore. "I said what I thought. Wasn't no 'ifs', 'ands' or 'maybes'. If I was wrong, I was wrong. When you scout you're going to make some bad decisions. You only hope you make more good ones than you do bad ones."

In time, Shore became Howsam's most trusted adviser on personnel decisions.

"What Ray said carried more weight with Howsam than me or anybody," recalled Anderson. "The only input I had on trades was my opinion. But if Ray said 'Yes, I think we should,' then Bob would go with him I'd say 80 percent of the time. I thought Ray Shore had as much power as you could have being a guy who was an advance scout. That was good. Ray Shore was out there, looking at the big picture. That was a good way to do it."

So Howsam had called Shore to help him decide about young Bernie Williams. They arrived early at the ballpark in Phoenix, and found the best seats behind home plate to watch infield and batting practice. In the nearly empty grandstand, with the sound of bats slapping balls echoing across the park, the two men applied their 50 years of baseball wisdom to the evaluation of the outfielder.

Williams, 22, appeared to be a decent prospect and a good trade for Duffy. Howsam went to discuss the deal with Rosie Ryan in his office under the stands. When Howsam returned to his seat, he told Shore that the Giants had changed their mind. Williams wasn't available, but they could get George Foster. Shore couldn't believe it. This had to be a mistake. Although only a rookie, Foster was playing outfield for the Giants, and appeared to be their left fielder of the future. Shore had seen him a few days earlier in Atlanta.

"He was raw, but he showed some power," remembered Shore.

Foster had spent the previous year with Phoenix and had impressed the Giants with a .308 average, eight home runs and 66 RBIs. He had made the club in the spring of 1971, but through April and May, Foster had struggled against major league pitching. Still, Foster had shown enough promise to earn the roster spot. As Howsam and Shore talked, they realized they couldn't go wrong with Foster for Duffy.

"Foster had some pop in his bat," Shore said. "Duffy was a backup infielder who wasn't going to go anywhere with us."

Shore, who seemed to know everybody in baseball, knew the manager of the Tucson team that Phoenix was playing. He asked him for an evaluation. He told Shore, "Williams has some potential, but Foster is way ahead now." With the evidence mounting for Foster, Howsam called Rex Bowen from a pay phone at the stadium to check on the Pirates prospect in West Virginia. Bowen hadn't been impressed. Within an hour, after Howsam added pitcher Vern Geishert to the deal, George Foster was a Cincinnati Red.

Foster, a quiet and somewhat insecure young player, was not thrilled with the trade. He was playing left field, alongside his idol Willie Mays, and the "rejection" by the Giants hit him hard. Some of Foster's teammates didn't like the trade either. Bobby Bonds criticized the Giants for giving up on Foster too soon. Mays told Anderson he thought Foster was "going to be some kind of player." Just how good a player Foster would be was not evident in 1971 as he struggled at the plate, hitting .241 with a mere 13 home runs.

He was still a project, and his development would suffer some serious setbacks. But Foster more than fulfilled Mays' prediction.

That the Giants had given up on Foster confounded Shore until he learned that the scout who signed Williams was a good friend of Horace Stoneham, the president of the Giants. Williams eventually made the big leagues with the Giants, but was never more than a bench player in four undistinguished seasons. Years later, Charlie Fox, then the manager of the Giants would tease Shore.

"You stole my left fielder, you SOB."

Shore deduced that Fox had not been involved in the decision.

The Giants had made a hasty judgment based on peripheral issues that had little to do with player performance, exactly the kind of decision-making that Howsam never would have tolerated.

In July, the Reds showed signs of life by winning 13-of-17, but after losing five in a row in Los Angeles and San Diego, they found themselves mired in fifth place, 18 games behind San Francisco. The injustice of it all reduced Sparky to philosophical ramblings in the best tradition of Casey Stengel.

"Baseball is like life," mourned Sparky. "What was was and what is is. That's all there is to it."

Humbled by injured pitchers, slumping players and losing streaks, it should have come as no surprise that the sky, too, began falling. On September 6 in Los Angeles, the Reds trailed the Dodgers, 2-1, in the fifth inning. The Dodgers had runners on first and second, and shortstop Woody Woodward edged toward second base to set up a pickoff play. *Whooosh...Whump!!* A loud noise stopped the action.

A ten-pound sack of flour had landed about 15 feet from Woodward and exploded all over the grass. A small plane that had circled the stadium disappeared in the darkness. Woodward was shaken. "I don't drink much beer but I'm gonna have me a couple tonight," he admitted. No one was ever arrested.

Like the Reds of 1970, the Giants slumped in the second half of the season. The Dodgers nearly caught San Francisco, finishing only one game back. But the Reds had fallen so far behind, they could not make up any ground, and they finished fourth, tied with Houston. As late as August, Howsam publicly expressed hope for a miracle finish, but behind the scenes, his front office was engaged in a sober analysis that would lead to a restructuring of the team.

The Cincinnati Enquirer

George Foster found himself on the move in May of 1971 when the Giants traded him to Cincinnati. Foster became the Reds regular center fielder in '71, replacing the injured Bobby Tolan.

Bob Howsam loved his new Riverfront Stadium and its bright green artificial turf. It reduced maintenance costs, it prevented rainouts, and most importantly, Howsam genuinely believed it made for a faster, more exciting game for the fans. But Howsam could also see that Astroturf had created a huge set of problems for his club. The Reds were built more for the slow, lush grass and cozy fences of old Crosley Field than for the quick plastic turf of vast Riverfront.

These bigger multi-purpose stadiums (in Cincinnati, Pittsburgh, Philadelphia, St. Louis, Houston and San Francisco) were creating an environment for an offensive revolution in the National League. Baseball men could see that the bigger, slicker fields required faster, more agile players. A club that could blend speed with power would have a tremendous advantage in the plastic turf age.

No one saw this revolution coming sooner than Howsam, and no organization was quicker to adapt.

Speed and agility had always been important in baseball, especially to Rickey men, but the characteristics of the new stadiums now put these abilities at a premium. In 1970, the first year of Riverfront Stadium, home runs outnumbered stolen bases in the National League by a wide margin (1683 to 1045) just as they had every year in the N.L. since 1928. But in the next few seasons the gap would narrow. In 1976, for the first time in 48 seasons, stolen bases surpassed home runs. The Reds had made the transition four years earlier.

In 1970 and 1971, Howsam and Anderson watched, in game after game, as third base coach Alex Grammas held up the lumbering Cincinnati runners. Because the ball reached the outfielders so quickly on turf, slow runners could not score as often from first or second on base hits as they had on the thick grass of Crosley Field.

On defense, with Tolan gone from the lineup, the Reds had no real speed in the outfield. Balls that slower outfielders could cut off on grass, were scooting through to the wall. Even hard-hit groundballs on Astroturf, easily stopped for singles on grass, would scoot between the outfielders and go for triples.

With the all-Astroturf infield at Riverfront, runners enjoyed consistently good footing and had many opportunities to challenge for the extra base. In Rose, McRae, Carbo and Foster, the Reds had no arms that could consistently deter base runners.

"I started bearing down in my scouting on outfielders' defense because of Astroturf," remembered Shore. "At Crosley, you could get by with slower guys, but boy, the minute you move to turf, if you don't have speed, you can get killed."

In the infield, the Reds were strong up the middle with Concepcion and Helms. Concepcion was still developing, especially at the plate, but the Reds projected him as the prototype shortstop of the artificial surface era, tall and rangy with a powerful arm that enabled him to play deep on the quicker surface. Helms was never a stolen-base threat, but his quickness and instincts for playing second consistently ranked him among the top-fielding second basemen in the National League.

At the corners, however, the Reds were slow with May and Perez. Perez had come up as a second baseman, but his natural position in the major leagues would be first base, and the organization considered him a defensive liability at third.

Since his first year with the Reds in 1967, Howsam had focused the long-term efforts of the scouting department and the farm system on speed and defense in preparation for the move to

Riverfront, and in Concepcion that emphasis had already begun to pay off. There were some other youngsters (including prospects Ken Griffey, Dan Driessen, Joel Youngblood and Gene Locklear) with speed and quickness who were making an impact in the minors, but the club felt they were still a couple of years away. While Howsam always preferred to bring along his own players, the club had already considered trading for speed, and Tolan's absence in 1971 accelerated the decision.

Tolan had led the league with 57 steals in 1970, and the Reds had out-stolen their opponents, 115-45. But in 1971, Rose led the club with 13 steals, the club had only 59 stolen bases (ninth in the league) and had a slim 59-43 advantage over their opponents. While the Reds hoped to have Tolan back in the starting lineup in 1972, Howsam and others questioned whether the severity of his injury would prevent his return or diminish his speed.

As the front office evaluated the club, they saw a need for more overall team speed, improved defense at third base, and more speed and better arms in the outfield. Howsam also wanted another left-handed bat in the lineup. If Tolan could not return, the Reds had only Rose and Carbo from the left side, and Carbo had been disappointing in his second season. In addition, Howsam feared that Merritt and Simpson would not recover their effectiveness. Howsam hoped to add some more pitching.

Howsam relied on many people and several strategies to evaluate his club's needs, to rate opposing players and to gather information on other organizations. The process was fluid, with Howsam analyzing data from Chief Bender, Joe and Rex Bowen, Ray Shore, Anderson and others.

"He certainly didn't shoot from the hip," recalled publicity director Roger Ruhl. "He collected data, processed it. Sometimes I had the sense you could see the wheels turning, the computer computing."

Anderson recalled one strategy Howsam used to rate players at each position in the National League.

"We would lay out all the rosters of all the clubs, all the 14 first basemen, all the 14 second basemen, right on down," said Sparky. "Bob had a great theory that you could find out how strong you are

The Cincinnati Enquirer

Bobby Tolan's season-ending injury in 1971 crippled the Reds offense and revealed a lack of outfield speed, shortcomings that Bob Howsam addressed in the historic trade with Houston.

by numbers. You put a number 1 to 14 by your player. Catcher, there were 14 catchers. Bench got a number 1. That's one point. You keep going through all your players."

Bender, Shore, the Bowen brothers, Anderson and Howsam would methodically work through the positions, voicing their opinions about each player in the league. This was art, not science, and these opinionated baseball men thoroughly enjoyed the give-and-take. Sparky remembered he and Shore often disagreed on player rankings.

"We'd go into these meetings and I'd say, 'Ray, come on my side one time,'" laughed Anderson. "And Ray would say, 'If I think you're right I'd vote for you.' And I'd say, 'Well, you ain't thought I been right yet!' We would disagree, but we were the best friends and we never once would agree on players, deals, anything else. It would be funny."

Howsam recalled the give and take was essential. "To me that's just good business. That was the nice part of all these fellows, they would speak up and speak their minds. The only thing you want afterwards is an understanding that we wouldn't second-guess the decision."

The group would then run through the starters and relievers, ranking the pitchers. Finally, they would add up the rankings of the Reds and the other clubs. Anderson recalled it was a time-consuming exercising, but worth it.

"This is a lot of work. Ain't no flying in and flying out," Anderson said. "But when you're done—and this was Bob's theory and he was right—if your club had the lowest numbers, then you had the best team. If somebody else had a lower number, then you started looking at where you had to catch up. It's so easy. You stop kidding yourself when you put the numbers down."

Howsam relied heavily on Shore and Bender for American League rankings because they concentrated on the American League in the second half of the season. Shore had developed his own ranking system, beginning with a 5 for an average player, then 5+, 6, 6+, 7...all the way up to 10.

"I did that for every position, utility players and pitchers," Shore said. "Then I inserted in red ink where I thought our guys would rank. Then Howsam always had this list, and if somebody brought up a player for a deal, he could look at that list and say, 'Well, Ray ranks him here or there, Ray doesn't think he's as good as our guy, or whatever.'"

Concurrent with the ongoing evaluation of players during the 1971 season, Howsam was developing trade possibilities. Part of the process involved finding clubs that made a good trade match with the Reds. Ruhl recalled that this was done very pragmatically.

"It was not done to screw some team, but trying to anticipate what the other club's needs were and what would they logically expect," said Ruhl. "Then you play role reversal. Would we make that deal? That's how you would wind up with realistic trades."

Howsam relied heavily on Bender to hold exploratory talks with other clubs.

"Then we'd talk about it," recalled Howsam. "Who would we be willing to give up? I often found my people were willing to give up more players than I wanted to. I think that's normal, because when you know your own players, you misjudge their value, maybe over-emphasize their faults, and think the other players were worth more."

Organizational consensus was the key for Howsam. "I worked somewhat like Branch Rickey. I wanted my scouts to be able to tell me everything I needed and put it all together, and as a group we would talk about it. And we put everybody in priority."

The process was tempered, however, by the reality that certain clubs and certain general managers were easier to deal with than others. The Dodgers, in particular, were a tough club on trades. Sparky remembered that the Reds couldn't deal with the Dodgers.

"The first thing they always tell you, take a look at our (Triple A) Albuquerque club," said Sparky. "If I heard that once, I heard it 10 times."

Shore recalled that Dodger general manager Al Campanis never offered the Reds much hope.

"Al always held his players higher than what we had them," Shore said. "To hear Al talk, the Dodgers' minor league players could be playing for anybody else, they just weren't good enough to play for the Dodgers. He always wanted the moon."

While some clubs were going to be hard to deal with, Howsam felt other organizations were sloppy in the way they handled trades. When he first came to the major leagues with the Cardinals, he was surprised at how certain clubs made casual evaluations and snap judgments. Howsam often had the upper hand dealing with these organizations because his scouts knew more about the other clubs' personnel than their front offices did.

As Howsam and the others processed the information, the trades took shape in Howsam's office and in a nearby room. Behind Howsam's desk, names went up on a large sign board with plastic letters and name tags.

"We'd put names up there," Howsam remembered. "It had a curtain, and I would close it when somebody came in who I didn't want to see it. But I worked mostly in a back room where we had more room to lay out papers on a table."

Slowly the trade lists came together, with the top player the Reds wanted at the top of the page followed by other combinations. "We started small," Ruhl recalled, "but the list might wind up with 25 trades on it in priority order."

One name that dominated the top of the trade lists late in the 1971 season was Houston second baseman Joe Morgan. Morgan, 28, broke in with Houston in 1963 as a 20-year-old, but did not

The Cincinnati Enquirer

Tony Perez played a credible third base for the Reds from 1967 to 1971. But improving infield defense and returning Perez to first base were among Bob Howsam's goals as he plotted his moves in the 1971 offseason.

become a starter until 1965. Despite his size (5-feet 7-inches tall) and the conventional baseball bias against short players, Morgan had developed into an above-average second baseman who had been selected to two All-Star teams. Although he had never hit for a high average, he drew a lot of walks and had averaged 94 runs scored the preceding three seasons. He had excellent power for his size, played steady defense and the Reds coveted his speed. Morgan had averaged 44 stolen bases the past three years.

"We were all pushing Morgan," remembered Anderson. "I think Alex Grammas probably pushed the hardest. He felt that what he had to offer with his speed was what we needed. It would open up our whole offense for us."

As much as the Reds liked Morgan, their interest was tempered by the scuttlebutt that Morgan and his manager Harry Walker did not get along. Before the ever-thorough Howsam would proceed, he had to be convinced that the problems were not of Morgan's making.

"Bob was always very conscious of a 'Reds-type' player," recalled Anderson. "He wanted the scout's opinion on a guy's make-up: aggressive, clean-living, good attitude. Bob always had a thing about knowing the inside of a guy. I think sometimes he wanted us to be F.B.I. agents. The abilities, we could see. But Bob wanted to know inside a guy. What's he got? That was what Ray Shore was good at. He would sit around, kibitz with you, have a drink and before you know it, he's got your pockets picked."

For Howsam, knowledge was the ultimate weapon in trade talks.

"I always felt that I had the upper hand if I knew more than the other club did, about my player and their player. A lot of people say they don't care about what a fellow does off the field, but you'd better think about it. Is he a drinker? Is he running around with women? Is he fighting with his wife? We always hoped a guy was happily married."

The discreet Shore began to spend a little more time with the Houston club, working his contacts and keeping notes. Bender admired Shore's intelligence gathering.

"Ray talked to a lot of people on the Astros," Bender remembered. "He always seemed to have an 'in' to the manager's office on the other club. All he carried was a little notebook; other scouts would have a big clipboard, a lot of paper. Not Ray. He just had that notebook."

What Shore learned was that Morgan was not the source of the problems in Houston. Harry Walker was an abrasive manager who made a number of enemies in baseball, including several members of the Astros team after he arrived there in the middle of the 1968 season. Jimmy Wynn, Morgan and two first-base prospects, Bob Watson and John Mayberry, had run-ins with Walker. All were black, and the players had no doubts that among other ills, Walker was a bigot.

Morgan explained in his autobiography, *Joe Morgan: A Life in Baseball*, that he tried to remain aloof from Walker's machinations, but he finally had a confrontation with the manager.

After a questionable move that Morgan could not fathom, he yelled at Walker, "You're not trying to win!" His criticism of his manager, combined with his friendship with Wynn, was enough to label him a troublemaker.

Shore methodically put the story together, benefiting from several close contacts at Houston.

"They had guys I had known for quite a few years," Shore recalled. "Harry Kalas, who was the radio announcer with Houston, and I used to play golf and I got information from him, which you gotta do. Harry liked Joe. Harry was traveling with the club, and knew the gist of the thing."

Shore discovered enough to be convinced that Morgan would not be a risk. In fact, Shore became one of Morgan's biggest boosters, in part because he knew Morgan possessed one attribute that was vital to Howsam. Morgan was a winner. Many players have talent, but on a competitive club with the pressure to win, something extra was needed, something that didn't fit neatly on a scouting report. Howsam pushed his scouts on this elusive trait.

"I suspected Morgan was a great competitor," said Shore. "Walker didn't give Morgan the credit that Joe knew how to play the game. He over-burdened him with signs, and Joe felt he didn't need all those signs. I figured he had to be a great student of the game or else he wouldn't have been so indignant about how Walker treated him. I didn't know from personal knowledge that he was well-schooled, but I had an idea he wasn't a dummy."

The more Anderson learned, the more he, too, was convinced Morgan would not disrupt his club.

"We all felt that at Houston, for some reason, Joe wasn't right. We never had a problem at Cincinnati with the guy. We had Bench and Rose and Perez, three big dogs. They could take anybody and make 'em right. We always felt we could take the toughest guy you want to give us and our players could make him right. Now, that's a tremendous gift."

Before the deal was finalized in November, the discussions meandered, with both sides exploring different options, changing the mix of players. But Howsam always stayed true to Morgan.

"We didn't start out saying we had to get an infielder," recalled Howsam. "But when it's all put down, what did we need? Speed. We didn't want to give up too much power. Yet Morgan had some power. He had some leadership qualities we thought. He was a problem with Harry Walker, but we were confident he was a real competitor. He wanted to win."

Another factor in Morgan's favor was the Reds felt they had a good trade match with Houston. Houston needed a first baseman, and again, the Reds could thank Harry Walker. If Morgan was available in large part because of Walker's spitefulness, then Walker was also crucial in opening up first base. Walker had battled Bob Watson and John Mayberry over their hitting styles. Third baseman Denis Menke had filled in at first in 1971 while Watson and Mayberry stewed on the bench and toiled in the minors. While the Reds were looking at Morgan, the Astros had been scouting May and Perez.

In late September, Howsam initiated trade talks with a call to Houston general manger, Spec Richardson.

Frank Dale, then president of the Reds, remembered that Howsam was so thoroughly prepared that by the time he made the call to Richardson, Howsam knew more about the Astros than Richardson did.

"He could go to Richardson, and Richardson so respected Bob's judgment that he (Howsam) could sit down with him and say, 'I've studied and analyzed your team and here are my reports on what your team needs. What your team needs is this, and so on.' And he so convinced the Houston team about what they needed that he was then able to say, 'I just happen to have what you need.' It was thorough professionalism."

Howsam asked about Morgan's availability and told Richardson, "You need a first baseman; we've got a guy [May] hitting over 30 home runs. We'll trade you one for one."

The trade talks moved to San Francisco, Pittsburgh and Baltimore, site of the National League playoffs and the World

Cesar and Cactus Jack: The "Other Guys" in the Great Trade

The Cincinnati-Houston trade of November 1971 involved several quality players and appeared to benefit both sides. "You can't expect to trade a bucket of ashes for a bucket of coal," claimed Bob Howsam. He operated from this philosophy throughout his baseball career.

Yet, within a few years, the trade tilted heavily in Cincinnati's favor. Houston won no pennants with its acquisitions from the Reds, while the former Astros helped the Big Red Machine roar into high gear. Joe Morgan led the way with his back-to-back MVP seasons, but the steady and often brilliant play of Cesar Geronimo and "Cactus" Jack Billingham helped turn the deal into one of baseball's all-time best.

Billingham played Little League ball in his hometown of Winter Park, Florida, alongside another future pro, Davey Johnson. After high school in 1961, Billingham was drafted by the Dodgers. He reached the majors in 1968.

He was traded to Houston where he became a starter in 1970. When he was acquired by the Reds, Billingham, 29, had a mediocre lifetime record of 32-32 and a 3.55 ERA. But over the next five seasons, in the peak years of the Reds dynasty, Billingham became the leader of the Big Red Machine staff. Don Gullett and the bullpen captured the headlines, but Billingham led the Reds in victories (77) and durability (he averaged 222 innings per season).

Geronimo, 24, also came to the Reds with mediocre career stats. And no wonder. Unlike Billingham, who had grown up with the game, Geronimo had little formal instruction.

As a child, he played on empty lots in his native Dominican Republic, using a piece of cardboard for a glove. He entered the seminary at age 13 and played some basketball—but no baseball. When he left the seminary four years later, he took up slow-pitch softball, and soon discovered he had been blessed with a most powerful arm. "No one would catch my throws," Geronimo recalled.

His father arranged a tryout with a New York Yankee scout who signed him as a pitcher/outfielder. He struggled at the plate in the minor leagues, and was an erratic pitcher, but he impressed the scouts with his outfield play. He had only 127 major league at-bats when the Reds traded for him, but Howsam and his staff thought he had the arm and the speed (plus his nine-foot stride) to patrol the spacious Riverfront Stadium outfield.

Like Billingham, Geronimo blossomed in the Reds organization. He became the best defensive center fielder in the National League in the mid-1970s, winning four Gold Gloves. But the feat the former softball player was most proud of was finally hitting .300 (.307) in 1976.

The Cincinnati Enquirer

Cesar Geronimo credited batting coach Ted Kluszewski and Tony Perez with improving his hitting.

Series, respectively. Howsam and Richardson continued to explore the deal, but the Astros would not be rushed. They were shopping Morgan to other clubs as well. Morgan himself heard trade rumors that he would be dealt to Philadelphia for Deron Johnson (the ex-Red), pitcher Joe Hoerner and second baseman Denny Doyle.

Then he heard rumors the Reds wanted him, and in an unguarded moment, Morgan phoned Anderson to confirm the deal. Anderson, aware of baseball's rules against tampering, refused to verify the negotiations. He would only tell Morgan, "Things have a way of working themselves out."

At another juncture, the Astros nearly closed a deal with Los Angeles to trade Morgan for first baseman, Wes Parker. Anderson and Shore overheard the rumor during the Series and quickly contacted Howsam, who convinced Spec Richardson to hold off on any deals until the Reds had put together a final package. Richardson agreed to wait, but he had already given up on the Parker deal after Parker vetoed the trade.

In the month between the World Series and the winter meetings, the clubs discovered other common ground. With May gone, the Reds would move Perez to first, but that created a hole at third base. Houston's Menke, a veteran shortstop who could also play third base, was now available with May on first base. The Astros needed a second baseman to replace Morgan; the Reds were willing to deal Helms.

The conversations were exhausting and complicated, but Howsam had a routine he worked through with the GMs.

"I had a pre-printed sheet of questions so I wouldn't miss or overlook anything," recalled Howsam. "I would check off each one so I didn't miss a question. When I got through, there was a paragraph to write about what I felt, what he said. Then I'd talk to Chief and the group. I would go over this form and I would say, 'This is what I think we may be be able to do.'"

Now the Reds upped the ante. The Astros were going to have to give up more than Menke and Morgan to get May and Helms, who were perceived to have more value. The Reds turned to their other needs—pitching and outfield defense. Two Houston players graded high on the Reds scouting reports: pitcher Jack Billingham and outfielder Cesar Geronimo. Coach George Scherger had managed Billingham in the Dodgers minor league system and strongly

The Cincinnati Enquirer

First baseman Lee May hit 39 home runs and drove in 98 runs in 1971, tops on the Reds. But with Tony Perez able to play both first and third base, the Reds considered May more expendable, and he was included in the Houston deal.

recommended him. Geronimo had only 127 major league at-bats with one home run, but every report lauded his throwing arm and speed in center field. The Reds also knew one other important fact about Geronimo: he had a very long stride, a perfect running motion for Riverfront Stadium.

"He had a nine-foot stride," recalled Howsam. "Nine feet is about two feet more than the average guy has. He takes five steps, he's 10 feet closer. That became very important to us in evaluating the trade."

The more Howsam considered Geronimo's potential and the club's unsettled outfield situation, the more Geronimo became one of the essential elements of the deal. At one point Houston threatened to pull Geronimo's name from the deal, and Howsam replied there would be no trade. Anderson, who had barely heard Geronimo's name, was shocked.

"God, I kept getting worried and worried. I said, 'Who the heck is Geronimo?! My God, why are we worried about Geronimo?' Bob would not make it, though, without him."

The winter meetings convened in Phoenix in late November, and Howsam met with John Mullins, the Houston president, to finalize the deal. The Astros wanted one additional player in exchange for Billingham and Geronimo. Howsam agreed to popular pinch-hitter Jimmy Stewart—if the Astros would offer one last player from their farm system. After Howsam received a list of prospects, his scouts recommended Ed Armbrister.

Howsam alone attended these final discussions. While other clubs frequently included the general manager, the manager and others in meetings, Howsam preferred to work alone. He already had met with his people and knew their thinking.

"I already had my mind set, I knew what I wanted to get to, and I didn't want somebody in my organization to say something that might interfere," said Howsam.

The master of detail, Howsam had seen in other negotiations that a gesture, an off-hand remark could jeopardize a deal. Sparky also felt Howsam's strategy gave him an excuse to break off the talks for further reflection if the deal took an unexpected turn.

"He listened to their deal, and then he could say, 'I have to go talk to Sparky about this.' That would give Bob a chance to get out of the room," recalled Anderson.

On Monday morning, November 29, in his hotel suite, Howsam gathered all of his front-office people together who had made the trip to Phoenix. Everyone knew a deal was imminent, but they did not know that Howsam had just wrapped up the final details. The Astros needed time to contact their players and so the deal would not be announced until early afternoon. Howsam, who nearly lost a trade in St. Louis when the press discovered the news early, moved to ensure secrecy.

Howsam recalled asking his staff, "What have you got to do? Anything? Get it done right now, because I'm going to have a meeting. The door's going to be locked. I don't want anyone picking up a telephone, or going out of that door until I'm ready to announce the trade."

Press protocol at the winter meetings, however, required advance notice of any trade. Howsam wrote out a brief note that said a major deal would be announced at 3 p.m. No teams were mentioned. Someone summoned a bellman to take the note to the press room. In the clandestine spirit of the meeting, Dick Wagner grabbed the bellman and quickly ushered him into the bathroom and in hush-hush tones, gave him the note with $10 and instructions to post it.

1971 Scrapbook

The Opposition

Western Division

Against	Won	Lost
Atlanta	9	9
Houston	5	13
Los Angeles	7	11
San Diego	10	8
San Fran.	9	9

Eastern Division

Against	Won	Lost
Chicago	6	6
Montreal	7	5
New York	8	4
Philadelphia	5	7
Pittsburgh	5	7
St. Louis	8	4

The pitcher the Reds didn't want to face – **Al Downing** of the Dodgers was 4-1 against the Reds.

The pitcher they loved to see – **Tom Phoebus** of the Padres was 0-4 against the Reds.

The batter who loved the Reds – **Hank Aaron** of Atlanta hit .353 (18-for-51) with 8 HRs and 15 RBIs.

The batter who should have stayed home – **Ted Simmons** of the Cardinals hit .167 (5-for-30) with 0 HR and 1 RBI.

Club Leaders

Batting Average	**Pete Rose**	.304
Home runs	**Lee May**	39
RBIs	**Lee May**	98
Stolen bases	**Pete Rose**	13
Runs	**Pete Rose**	86
ERA	**Don Gullett**	2.64
Wins	**Don Gullett**	16
Saves	**Clay Carroll**	15
Games	**Wayne Granger**	70

Awards

Gold Glove	**Johnny Bench**
	Tommy Helms
Cincinnati Reds MVP •	**Lee May**
Outstanding Reds Pitcher •	**Don Gullett**
Reds Newcomer of the Year •	**Ross Grimsley**

• Awarded by Cincinnati Chapter of Baseball Writers Association

Trades

May 8	**Buddy Bradford** acquired from Cleveland for **Kurt Bevacqua**
May 13	**Al Ferrara** acquired from San Diego for **Angel Bravo**
May 29	**George Foster** acquired from San Francisco for **Frank Duffy** and **Vern Geishert**
Nov. 29	**Ed Armbrister, Jack Billingham, Cesar Geronimo, Denis Menke** and **Joe Morgan** acquired from Houston for **Tommy Helms, Lee May** and **Jimmy Stewart**
Dec 3	**Tom Hall** acquired from Minnesota for **Wayne Granger**
Dec 6	**Ted Uhlaender** acquired from Cleveland for **Milt Wilcox**

The Draft

Cincinnati drafted 48 players; four played in the major leagues:

Mike Miley •	New Orleans, LA	SS
Don Werner	Appleton, WI	C
Dave Revering	Fair Oaks, CA	1B
Dave Collins •	Rapid City, SD	1B-OF

• Drafted by the Reds, but signed with another club

Ruhl recalled the humor in the scene.

"I was wondering what the heck this bellman was thinking," Ruhl said. "Some guy grabs him, pulls him into the bathroom. There's a bunch of guys sitting around in this hotel room. He must have been wondering, 'What's happening to me?'"

The terse note posted in the press room intrigued reporters, some of whom thought it was a joke because it failed to specify teams. But there had been no major trades announced at the meetings, and when Ruhl stepped to the podium to announce the deal, he faced a full house.

After Ruhl read off the names—May, Helms and Stewart for Morgan, Menke, Billingham, Geronimo and Armbrister—the reaction was one of low whistles and murmurs. This was a huge deal. Many reporters were also surprised. Although the Reds were convinced they had made a good trade, the club feared that many writers and the fans would question whether the Reds received enough for two players the caliber of Mays and Helms. The first queries told the Reds their worries had been right.

Ruhl recalled one questioner wondering if Ruhl had misspoke. "I remember somebody saying, 'Don't you have the wrong Cesar?' when I read the list. They figured Cedeno, not Geronimo. There was a feeling that the Reds had given up too much."

Back in the suite, the publicity staff put Howsam in touch with the press in Cincinnati, hoping to put the Reds' spin on the trade.

"We got him on the phone with the TV stations back in Cincinnati," recalled Ruhl. "We started calling regional papers and sports editors so he could talk with them, and we went back and forth from room to room on the phones. We worked hard, but the initial reaction in Cincinnati was not very good. People tended to look at Helms, a very popular player, and say 'OK, we got Morgan for Helms, both second baseman. But then what did we get for May and Stewart? One pitcher and a couple of guys nobody had heard of.' But that wasn't the way to look at it; it was really May for Morgan."

But May for Morgan was not enough for Reds fans. *Enquirer* reporter Bob Hertzel, one of the most influential baseball writers in the region, sharply questioned Howsam's judgment.

"For Lee May you'd expect a Willie Mays, not just a guy named Joe," wrote Hertzel in an opinion he would later retract.

Reaction on the street was strongly against the deal. One fan said he was going to root for Houston. Another said, "May is a good ballplayer. What they traded for—all of them put together aren't as good as May." One fan imagined sabotage. "Somebody must have hypnotized Howsam."

It might have surprised some fans that Howsam agreed with them, to a point.

"Right after I made the decision, I told my people, 'We're going to make this trade, and for the future of our ballclub, I think this is going to the best for us. But to be honest, I've just given the pennant this year to Houston.'"

Howsam had considered the deal from Houston's viewpoint. "Just stop and think. Houston had a very fine ballclub. You add a 30-home run hitter and an All-Star second baseman and a 'super sub' (Stewart). They should have won it."

Anderson disagreed with his boss. After the deal was revealed, Sparky told Howsam, "You have just won the pennant for the Cincinnati Reds."

As it turned out, Anderson was correct. Even Howsam had short-changed his deal. The Reds had dealt for speed and the payoff would be quick.

George Foster dashed home with the pennant-winning run in the fifth game of the 1972 National League playoffs, giving the Reds a 4-3 comeback victory over the Pittsburgh Pirates. Foster scored on a wild pitch by Bob Moose to pinch-hitter Hal McRae (left).

The Cincinnati Enquirer

National League Champions • 95 wins-59 losses

Chapter 7

1972
Near Miss

Lost to Oakland in World Series, 4-3 • Johnny Bench, MVP

THE PLAYERS WHO WOULD COMPRISE the famous starting lineup of the Big Red Machine in the championship years of 1975 and 1976 were all in the Cincinnati camp in the spring of 1972: Rose, Morgan, Bench, Perez, Foster, Concepcion, Geronimo and the youngster, Ken Griffey. So were the leaders of the pitching staff: Gullett, Nolan, Carroll, Borbon and Billingham. But it was not obvious in early 1972 that all these players were destined for greatness in the Big Red Machine. Concepcion, Foster and Geronimo still had yet to capture starting roles, Griffey would return to the minor leagues, Billingham had not established himself as a dependable starter and Morgan had yet to prove that he belonged in the superstar category with Bench and Rose.

The 1972 Reds represented a team in transition, and a team surrounded by question marks. The 1970 version had hinted at greatness; 1971 had suggested mediocrity. Could these new-look Reds rekindle the dynasty talk on the banks of the Ohio?

Sparky Anderson blamed the 1971 collapse on pitching problems (Simpson and Merritt), injuries (Tolan) and slumps (Bench and Perez). But lack of execution and poor attitude topped his list of complaints.

"We didn't do the things a championship team has to do," said Anderson, promising a tougher camp in '72. He set weight limits for each player and $50 fines for each pound over the limit. Sparky declared an 11 p.m. curfew, banned TV from the clubhouse and announced the post-game food spreads would be curtailed.

"I'd come in before a game and a lot of players would be congregating in the food room. They'd be trying to find out from (equipment manager) Bernie Stowe what he was going to have to eat after the game. Here I was upset by losing and worrying about things like Simpson's arm and they'd be worrying about food."

Sparky himself took things more seriously in 1972. Ray Shore, whose nickname was "Snacks," would call Anderson with his scouting reports in 1970, and Sparky would say, "Wait a minute, Snacks, till I get a pencil and paper." The rookie manager wrote down every word.

In 1971, Shore would call to give the report, and Anderson, basking in the success of the '70 season, would say, "OK, Snacks, tell me."

Shore would say, "Sparky, you got a pencil?"

"Yeah, yeah, go ahead."

The Reds finished fourth.

In 1972, Shore would call in with the report.

"Wait a minute, Snacks," says Sparky. "I gotta get a pencil."

Unlike the spring of 1971, which was interrupted by bitter holdouts and ruinous injuries, the focus of 1972 was on the players and the competition for positions. Most eyes were on Bobby Tolan, and from the beginning of spring training he proved he had regained most of his speed. Rose moved from right field to left, leaving four players—Carbo, McRae, Foster and Geronimo—to compete for right field. Carbo, the 1970 Rookie-of-the-Year, had suffered from the notorious sophomore jinx in 1971. Shore thought Carbo was one of those players who found it easy to succeed as an unknown rookie, but hard to follow up when the expectations were higher. When Carbo had a mediocre spring in 1972, Anderson relegated him to pinch-hitting chores, and in early May, Carbo was traded to St. Louis for Julian Javier. Hal McRae excelled at the plate, but his questionable defense cost him a starting job. Geronimo eventually earned the start with a good spring; he and Foster split most of the right-field playing time in 1972.

Concepcion won the shortstop battle in spring training over Darrel Chaney, but Concepcion's carefree attitude did not always please his manager. Even Morgan admitted that during the 1972 season, he wondered why Anderson stuck with the young Venezuelan.

"I actually believed then that he should not have been playing every day," Morgan wrote in his autobiography. "He made too many mistakes, he didn't hit. He always seemed to be doing things that irritated Sparky or that got on the nerves of his teammates."

It would not be until 1973 that Concepcion claimed the shortstop position as his alone.

The annual uncertainty about the starting rotation surfaced when Merritt and Simpson continued to experience arm difficulties. Anderson decided to go with Nolan, Gullett and Billingham as his starters early in the season. Merritt spent most of the season at Indianapolis, starting only one game for the Reds. Howsam traded him to Texas after the season. Merritt never again regained his effectiveness and retired in 1975. Simpson began the year at Indianapolis, was recalled in May and started 22 games. Although he finished with an 8-5 record, he did not pitch in the playoffs or the World Series, and the Reds traded him in the offseason to Kansas City. Like Merritt, Simpson never fully recovered from his arm problems; he won only 10 games after leaving the Reds and retired in 1977.

The most critical move of spring training, however, happened off the field. The clubhouse chemistry had been jolted with the big trade. Helms, May and Stewart were popular players with leadership qualities and Anderson knew it.

"I told (Houston GM) Spec Richardson he'd never have to worry about them," said Anderson. "I can't tell you how many times I had May in for a little talk about something that was wrong and he'd say, 'OK, Skip, I'll take care of it.'"

Sparky recognized that with Rose, Bench and Perez he still had

William Schildman

During their six years together in Cincinnati, Joe Morgan and Pete Rose lockered next to one another in the Reds clubhouse. Their corner became a center of friendly "agitatin'," as Anderson recalled. The banter kept the team loose and egos in check.

great leadership. But Morgan, who came to the Reds with the reputation of being a trouble maker and what Anderson called a "yakker," presented something of a challenge. Sparky sensed the competitive fire in Morgan, and he had heard Shore's enthusiastic reports. How best to handle "Little Joe," or "Little Man" as Sparky came to call him?

"Joe's loaded with an essential asset of great players—pride," Sparky recalled. "In that respect, I learned early that he is very much like Pete Rose. I went to Bernie Stowe and suggested he put Morgan's locker in spring training next to Pete's. My feeling was that a little of what made Rose tick might rub off on Joe."

Rose immediately welcomed Morgan, just as he did with any new player. When Rose broke into baseball in 1963, most of the Reds veterans shunned him. Rose never forgot the courtesy and friendship Frank Robinson and Vada Pinson had shown. Early in spring training, he told Morgan to let him know if he could help him in any way with his accommodations in Tampa or in Cincinnati. Morgan appreciated the small, but genuine, gesture.

Now with their lockers side by side, Rose and Morgan discovered common ground, from their love of the game, to their burning need to excel, to their appreciation of the artful put-down. At Riverfront Stadium, the clubhouse featured a long row of stalls with three lockers at one end next to the players' lounge. Rose and Morgan had the two end lockers, with the one in the middle kept empty for mail and extra equipment. The area became a focal point of clubhouse camaraderie: Pete and Joe talked baseball, engaged in some serious one-upsmanship and directed sharp barbs at passersby. As Bench, Perez, Rose and Morgan grew to respect each other as players, they also challenged each other's skills and performance through a steady stream of invectives.

"To me they were what a baseball team should be," remembered Sparky. "They could eat each other's tail out, and it was fine."

"In spring training, I'd put Morgan, Perez, Bench and Rose at the same batting cage. I strolled around all the time, but I'd make sure I'd get back over there to hear 'em, 'cause I knew they'd be yapping at each other."

One night the Reds faced the Mets' Jerry Koosman, a tough left-hander who gave Morgan trouble.

"[Trainer] Larry Starr came in and said, 'Joe's got a temperature, high, about 104,'" said Sparky. "I said, 'Scratch him.' So pretty soon I heard the wildest yelling going on. I wondered what in the hell is goin' on? I went out in the clubhouse, and down by Joe's locker they had a sleeping bag with a pillow on it, a little glass of water, two aspirins and a note: 'Take these and you'll get over the Koosmanitis.' Well, it wasn't two minutes later, here comes Joe into my room. I mean, he's screamin', 'That no good Cuban so-and-so! I'm playing tonight. There's no way that Cuban's gonna tell me I've got Koosmanitis!'"

Anderson relented and started Morgan.

"He hit a home run off Koosman second time up," said Anderson. "Boy, you should have heard the things going on in the dugout then."

Morgan would ultimately become a two-time MVP on one of baseball's greatest teams, but in 1972, he still had to prove himself, and he accepted Anderson's challenge. With Bench and Perez grouped together at another spot in the clubhouse, it soon became obvious to Morgan that he had been included in the upper echelon.

"In most major-league dressing rooms, there is no design whatever in locker assignments," Morgan said. "Players will be thrown together by skin color, age, or the inclination of the clubhouse guy. In Sparky's game, the team that dressed together played together. And what these assignments told me and everyone else who ventured into the clubhouse was that this was a team built around four leaders.…"

Anderson remembered that Morgan told him he understood why he placed his locker next to Rose.

"You wanted me to see a guy who knew how to go about his business," said Morgan.

"Little Man," said Sparky, "we learn all the time."

The 1972 spring training schedule was interrupted in mid-March by a three-day trip to Venezuela where the Reds played the Pirates in a series of exhibition games. The Reds, who recruited heavily in Latin America, had gladly accepted the Pirates' invitation to join them in Caracas and Maracaibo for three games. But Venezuela proved to be a logistical nightmare for the usually thorough Reds.

The rigorous travel schedule, arranged by the Venezuelan promoters, was bad enough. But while the Pirates had been warned to upgrade their accommodations, the Reds were stuck with the promoters' arrangements. The Pirates flew on a non-stop Pan Am jet; the Reds flew in a no-frills Venezuelan airline that had to re-fuel in Jamaica. The Pirates booked large motor coaches for ground transport; the Reds piled into a rickety school bus.

The departure out of Miami was delayed for three hours, and then the pilot announced the plane was 1,700 pounds overweight. After some of the players refused to board the plane, all the baseball equipment was unloaded. Bernie Stowe slept with it overnight until it was flown south. At the ballparks, enthusiastic fans rushed the players for autographs during practice and even during the games. In batting practice before the first game, the Reds discovered another local custom. Kids raced onto the field grabbing the batting practice baseballs.

Publicity director Ruhl recalled coach George Scherger yelling at the uniformed officers on guard, "El policeman! El policeman! They are stealing our fucking baseballs!"

The police, perhaps not understanding Scherger's Spanish, failed to stop the pillaging. The Reds lost 60 balls the first night and didn't have enough left for batting practice the next two games.

"We were so anxious to get out of there," said Ruhl, "I remember even Howsam and [team doctor] George Ballou loading luggage onto the plane." Talking to reporters in Tampa, Howsam struggled to find something positive about the trip. Perhaps there had been some public relations value to the excursion, he offered.

The other disappointment from the spring of 1972 involved labor problems between the players and the owners over baseball's pension fund. The Major League Baseball Players Association had become much more aggressive in labor issues since Marvin Miller had become its director in 1966, and the Association had threatened a strike in 1969. In 1972, owners and the players failed to agree on increases to the pension fund. On April 1, the players voted to strike: it was the first work stoppage in the history of the game.

Howsam, who played a leadership role on the owners' Player Relations Committee, was well-schooled in the pre-Marvin Miller ways of doing business that invested all powers in the owners. That this grand game he had heard Branch Rickey so eloquently glorify—the game he had devoted his life to, the team that he had so carefully nurtured—could be jeopardized by *labor* problems was

Big Red Money Machine

The aggressive actions of the Players Association in the late 1960s and early 1970s to improve financial conditions for players led to the strike of 1972 and increased the attention given to salaries. Player statistics took on a new dimension.

In Cincinnati, the frugal Howsam-Wagner-Bender regime annually generated considerable off-season press with its hard-line stance against multi-year contracts, its disdain for the players union and agents, and a strict bottom-line philosophy. Rancorous holdouts were common throughout baseball, and the Reds were often league-leaders in that department.

Pete Rose spoke for many players when he recalled the Reds "were always kind of cheap." Rose, who was never shy about his salary demands or about becoming the first Reds player to use an advisor in negotiations, admired Marvin Miller's leadership of the Players Association.

"He was trying to even the playing field," recalled Rose. "Let's say you're a 23- or 24-year-old kid. You don't know anything about business. How would you like to go into an office when you got Chief Bender sittin' there. You got Dick Wagner sittin' there. You got Bob Howsam sittin' here. And you're sittin' there. Now what kind of advantage do they have on you? And they always wanted that advantage."

For Howsam, the issues were autonomy, fair pay for performance and fiscal responsibility. He did not begrudge raises, but he did not relish outsiders (i.e., Marvin Miller and agents) dictating the salary structure of *his* team. Howsam also feared that spiraling salaries would inevitably lead to higher ticket prices. That violated what he saw as his ultimate responsibility: fan satisfaction.

In 1972, the Reds payroll averaged $36,200, compared to the major league average of $34,000. These 1972 estimates (published by *The Cincinnati Enquirer*) revealed that salaries depended on a combination of seniority and sustained performance. Raises were not automatic. Rose led the list, but he had topped the $100,000 barrier in 1970 after two consecutive batting championships. Despite solid years in 1970 (.316) and 1971 (.304), his salary increased only marginally. (*The Enquirer* published estimated salary figures in the early 1970s, but discontinued the practice in 1973.)

Player	Estimated 1972 Salary
Pete Rose	$107,500
Johnny Bench	85,000
Tony Perez	75,000
Joe Morgan	70,000
Denis Menke	48,000
Clay Carroll	47,000
Gary Nolan	45,000
Jim Merritt	41,000
Bobby Tolan	40,000
Jack Billingham	35,000
Ted Uhlaender	35,000
Jim McGlothlin	30,000
Tommy Hall	27,000
Don Gullett	25,000
Pat Corrales	22,000
Wayne Simpson	20,000
Joe Gibbon	20,000
Bernie Carbo	19,000
Ross Grimsley	18,000
Hal McRae	18,000
Cesar Geronimo	17,000
Pedro Borbon	16,500
George Foster	16,000
Dave Concepcion	15,000
Darrel Chaney	14,000

simply inconceivable. Like most of the owners, Howsam thought that baseball's traditional structures had provided stability, prosperity and a benevolence towards the players for which they were now ungrateful.

Standing before his players on the morning of the strike, he asked them not to take such drastic action.

"This is a very sad day for baseball, for the fans, for all of us," Howsam told them. "Baseball has always been the great American game, something that people have identified with. Now this."

The strike of 1972 was over in 13 days, but those 13 days clearly signaled the end of the old era. Over the next few years, Miller and the Players Association would force baseball to confront a number of inequities in the owner-player equation, including the reserve clause that bound players to clubs for life. Howsam and the other owners would persist in the fight to preserve the system they had inherited and maintained. The evolution of the Big Red Machine continued against this backdrop of labor strife.

The collapse of the Reds in 1971 and the off-season moves of the Astros and the Dodgers created several favorites for the Western Division crown, including the defending champion Giants. The Reds were not even favored by the hometown *Enquirer*, which picked them second to Houston. Through the month of April and into early May, that prediction appeared generous. The Reds lost four of their first six and quickly fell five games out of first. The team ERA in April was a whopping 4.78. Nolan was the only starter who had won a game, and Billingham lost his first five decisions. On May 7, a struggling Don Gullett was diagnosed with non-infectious hepatitis and Sparky took him out of the starting rotation, calling up Ross Grimsley and Wayne Simpson from Indianapolis.

The poor start was magnified by the strong showing of the Astros and the memory of the slow start of 1971 that doomed the season. Howsam and Anderson both defended the Morgan trade against increasing speculation that the Reds had made a horrendous deal. On the bench one evening during another humiliating loss, Scherger warned Anderson, "The natives aren't just getting restless, they're getting serious."

When a dejected team filed into the clubhouse after losing its fourth straight game on May 10, Anderson, who was not given to clubhouse speeches, decided his players needed a jolt.

"What made me do it, I don't know," Sparky said. "But I got angry. I walked out in the middle of that room, and I said, 'Give me your attention. I'm going to tell everyone in this room something. We will win this thing this year. I don't want no more hangin' heads, I don't want no more being like a morgue in here. Get your ass up, and go get showered and get home, because this thing is going to be won by this ballclub.'"

Seldom do such histrionics have much of an impact, but the Reds immediately won four in a row from the Cardinals, getting victories from Grimsley and Simpson to start the streak, and launching another of their patented winning binges that characterized the Big Red Machine years. They went 22-6 and jumped into first place on June 9. From May 12 through August 28, a stretch of 100 games, the Reds went 68-32, nearly equaling their 70-30 start of 1970, and opened a lead of 8½ games.

The Reds' dominance in the second half of the season came despite several problem areas, including right field, third base and shortstop. With Menke at third, Geronimo in right and Concepcion at short, the Reds enjoyed solid defense. But the trio generated little offense from the 6-7-8 spots, respectively, in the batting order.

Sparky used Foster, McRae and Joe Hague some in right field, but none claimed a starter's role. Chaney platooned with Concepcion after the All-Star Game, and shared playing time in the postseason. Menke and Geronimo started in the playoffs and World Series.

The pitching staff fought injuries all season. Ten different pitchers started games and only Billingham threw more than 200 innings. Gullett's hepatitis limited him to just 16 starts and produced the highest ERA of his career, 3.93. Nolan was on his way to a Cy Young award through the first half of the year, with a 13-2 record and a 1.81 ERA. But then he developed muscle spasms and missed a month. He returned only to have something "pop" in his arm while making an off-balance throw on a ground ball.

Nolan complained of pain, but unable to find a specific injury, the club, especially Anderson, began to question if the problem was mental rather than physical. Nolan claimed he had pitched with pain many times, but that this injury was more serious. He grew bitter at Anderson and the club for questioning the injury. He did pitch enough innings (176) to qualify for season records, and had the league's best winning percentage (15-5; .750) and second-best ERA (1.99). Nolan finished fifth in the Cy Young balloting.

Fortunately for Anderson, the top half of the batting order produced. Rose, Tolan, Morgan, Bench and Perez all had excellent seasons. Bench led the way with 40 home runs and 125 RBIs, and captured his second MVP award. After a poor 1971, Bench regained the stature that made him one of the best players in the game. He graced not only the covers of sports publications, but he became one of the few baseball players ever to make the cover of *Time* magazine. (The last Cincinnati Red on the cover was manager Birdie Tebbetts in 1956 for a story on the slugging Redlegs.)

Bench had his own TV show in Cincinnati, which no doubt helped him retain his poise when he was surprised by the NBC program, "This Is Your Life," on September 16. After the game, he was summoned back to the dugout from the clubhouse for what he thought was a routine radio interview. Instead, host Ralph Edwards met Bench and conducted the show from the Riverfront Stadium infield. Bench's family members, who often attended games, knew of the surprise and appeared on the show. Bench's mother, who had been struck in the head by a high foul ball in the seventh inning and was taken to the first-aid room for treatment, rallied in time for the program.

Bench's many off-field activities had become an issue in 1971. Howsam and others questioned whether Bench's lackluster performance was due in part to these distractions. But 1972 ended such speculation. The 25-year-old from Oklahoma was surprisingly adept at handling the media, and continued to maintain a high profile. However, he sometimes battled with the fans, who criticized him for being aloof and unwilling to sign autographs. Bench never found mixing with fans to be as easy as Rose and some of the other players made it look. But Morgan remembered Bench chastising him for signing illegible autographs when he first came to the Reds.

"Somebody wants that to read it," said Bench, passing along advice that Anderson had once given him.

Bench's growing popularity was good for the franchise and for the game. The only problem developed with teammate Rose. John and Pete battled off the field about failed businesses. An antagonistic relationship developed. When Morgan came to the club in 1972, he was told by other players that he couldn't be friends with both Bench and Rose. One particular episode escalated the controversy. A weekly publication called *Pete Rose's*

The Cincinnati Enquirer

"Larger than life" was Joe Morgan's description of Johnny Bench. Bench earned the tribute with his great clutch performances in post-season games and the best defensive skills the game had ever seen.

Red Alert, which included features and analyses of the team, published an article critical of Darrel Chaney. Although Rose had no prior approval over articles, the front office and some players—including Bench—felt negative remarks about players in the magazine were out of line. Bench confronted Rose about it and there was a nasty exchange. Eventually, Howsam requested that Rose pull his support from the publication, and Rose complied.

The Bench-Rose feud continued to grow off the field, but the pair never let it affect the team's performance.

"Off the field they were like day and night," recalled Anderson. "But on the field, in uniform, they were truly professional and together."

Morgan, enjoying his first season playing with Bench, was amazed at Bench's intuitive sense of the game. Watching opposing pitchers from the dugout, Bench could often tell what pitch they would throw by reading subtle changes in their motions. Bench would predict a curve, fastball or off-speed pitch—and be right most of the time.

Morgan also appreciated Bench's arm, arguably the best of all time. Morgan, a man not given to hyperbole, thought the throw Bench made to him in the 1972 World Series against Oakland had to be caught to be believed. With Gary Nolan pitching, the A's stolen-base leader, Bert Campaneris, broke for second base.

"Nolan had a big, slow kick to the plate to begin with, and here he threw a big, slow curve on top of it," Morgan recalled. "I actually had my hands up, telling Bench not to throw. There was no way he was going to get Campaneris.

"Then he threw the ball and it was right on the corner of the bag. I just caught it there and the guy just slid in. *Bam!* If he had thrown the ball anyplace else, the guy would have been safe. It's the best throw I've ever seen, and the quickest release I'd ever seen of all the throws I ever saw him make."

Bench won the MVP award in 1972; Morgan finished fourth. Morgan led the league in on-base percentage, walks and runs, and finished second in stolen bases. His ex-manager, Harry Walker, continued to fire jibes at Morgan throughout the season, noting that the Astros clubhouse was more pleasant without Joe. But Morgan ignored the sniping and proved that Houston had underestimated him. Jack Billingham recalled that while Morgan was one of the better players on the Astros, "he was not a Hall of Famer" in Houston. Morgan thrived in the competitive atmosphere of the Big Red Machine, as did Billingham, Menke and Geronimo.

The Cincinnati Enquirer

After a dismal 1971, when he was routinely booed at Riverfront, Johnny Bench won his second MVP in 1972, and became one of the most popular—and marketable—players on the Big Red Machine.

"Being around the guys in Cincinnati made all of us in the trade better players," Billingham said.

Appropriately, the Reds clinched the pennant in Houston on September 22. The season that had begun with so many uncertainties now had just two: could the Reds beat the Pirates in the playoffs, and win the World Series?

The Reds had defeated Pittsburgh in the 1970 playoffs, but the Pirates had rebounded in 1971 to win the World Series (defeating the same Orioles who had handled the Reds in 1970). The Reds had great respect for the defending World Champions.

"Man for man I hope not to see a better team than Pittsburgh," said Sparky Anderson, before the playoffs. "Think of it. Roberto Clemente, Willie Stargell, Manny Sanguillen, Al Oliver, Dave Cash. Someday they'll be rated, man-for-man, with the great clubs like the New York Yankees."

It would be the Reds, not the Pirates, who would ultimately rate with the great dynasties. One reason was the playoff success Cincinnati enjoyed over Pittsburgh. The Reds defeated the Pirates in three National League Championship Series in the '70s.

The 1972 playoffs opened in Pittsburgh with Don Gullett facing Steve Blass, the 19-game winner and ace of the Pirates staff. Blass gave up a first-inning home run to Morgan, but the Pirates scored three in the bottom of the first off Gullett, then added two more in the fifth and won, 5-1.

Sparky started Billingham against Bob Moose (13-10, 2.91 ERA) in Game Two. The pressure was on the Reds, who needed to win to avoid having to sweep the Pirates at Riverfront. Anderson prepared a little pep talk telling his troops that the "shoe would be on the other foot" if they could win one in Pittsburgh. Clubhouse

The Revolutionary Reds

Baseball experienced a fundamental shift in offensive strategy in the 1970s, and the Big Red Machine led the revolution. In 1976, the National League, for the first time since 1927, recorded more stolen bases than home runs. Although the long ball remained a formidable weapon, teams began to emphasize the running game. The Reds led the charge in the N.L.: they flipped their offense in 1972 (140 steals, 124 homers), five years before the league as a whole reflected the change.

As the chart on the right indicates, the speed game, dominant at the beginning of the century, gave way to the home run in the 1920s. Through the 1940s and 1950s, speed was an afterthought, more a surprise element than an integral part of a club's offense.

With the move to Riverfront Stadium and Astroturf in 1970, Bob Howsam immediately recognized that the new stadiums appearing across the N.L. would reward clubs with overall team speed. He shaped his club accordingly: Tolan, Concepcion, Morgan, Geronimo, Griffey and Foster.

His "team speed" strategy immediately turned the Reds into a vastly superior offensive and defensive machine. The Reds were first or second in the league in runs scored every year from 1970 to 1976, except for 1971, when the injury to Bobby Tolan stripped the gears of the Big Red Machine. After Joe Morgan came to the Reds in 1972, the Reds led the league in stolen bases four of the next five seasons. In 1976, the Reds had eight players who stole 10 or more bases.

Howsam and Anderson not only devised a winning strategy for Riverfront and the Reds, they shaped a baseball revolution.

"Larry Shepard says I turned the National League into a monster because of running," recalled Anderson. "When I came into the league, nobody ran much. I believe, 'let her go!' Shep always said, 'You turned this into a disaster.'"

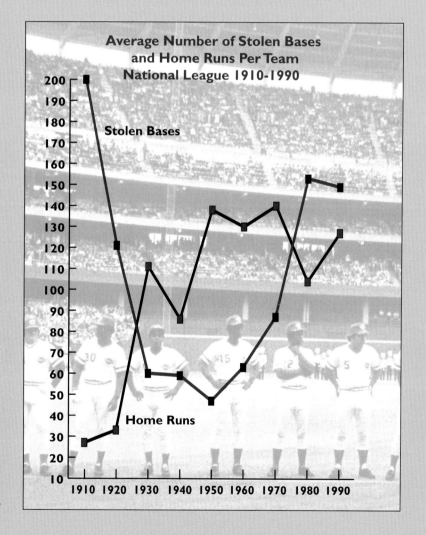

Average Number of Stolen Bases and Home Runs Per Team
National League 1910-1990

1972 Monthly Standings
National League West

April 30

	W	L	GB
Los Angeles	11	4	—
Houston	10	4	½
Atlanta	7	8	4
Cincinnati	5	8	5
San Francisco	6	10	5½
San Diego	5	11	6½

May 31

	W	L	GB
Los Angeles	26	16	—
Houston	24	17	1½
Cincinnati	23	18	2½
Atlanta	18	22	7
San Diego	16	26	10
San Francisco	15	31	13

June 30

	W	L	GB
Cincinnati	41	26	—
Houston	41	28	1
Los Angeles	36	31	5
Atlanta	31	36	10
San Francisco	27	46	17
San Diego	23	44	18

July 31

	W	L	GB
Cincinnati	57	37	—
Houston	54	44	5
Los Angeles	49	46	8½
Atlanta	46	50	12
San Francisco	44	54	15
San Diego	36	59	21½

August 31

	W	L	GB
Cincinnati	78	46	—
Houston	72	54	7
Los Angeles	66	57	11½
Atlanta	57	69	22
San Francisco	56	70	23
San Diego	46	78	32

Final Standings

	W	L	GB
Cincinnati	95	59	—
Houston	84	69	10½
Los Angeles	85	70	10½
Atlanta	70	84	25
San Francisco	69	86	26½
San Diego	58	95	36½

prankster Hal McRae responded by wearing his shoes on the wrong feet.

If McRae's antics were a hint the club was loose, the first inning proved it. In a performance that foreshadowed Game Five, Moose was totally ineffective, failing to retire a batter and giving up four runs before he was lifted in the top of the first. The Reds easily won, 5-3, and sent the series back to Riverfront tied at one.

Game Three was critical—the loser would face two consecutive must-win games. The sore-armed Nolan had recovered enough to start. He gave the Reds six strong innings and left with the lead, 2-1. But Borbon and Carroll gave up two runs, with the go-ahead run scoring in the eighth. With the score tied, the bases loaded and one out, Sanguillen hit a shot up the middle. Chaney dove for the ball and flipped to Morgan for the force, but Sanguillen beat the relay to first. Dave Giusti retired the final five outs for the save, and the Pirates were a game away from their second straight pennant.

The Reds' hopes for the pennant now fell to 22-year-old Ross Grimsley, who had won 14 games with a 3.05 ERA after his May call-up. After pitching well in his rookie season of 1971, Grimsley had been angered over his demotion to Indianapolis at the beginning of 1972. He complained to a reporter that Anderson didn't like him and that he wanted out of the Reds organization. Grimsley was something of a free spirit who often chafed at the rules of the club, but the Reds ignored the tirade. Grimsley made several excellent starts, and Anderson tabbed him for Game Four. With the pressure of the pennant on the line, Grimsley turned in his best pitching performance of the year, allowing the Pirates just two hits. The Reds won, 7-1.

For the first time since the division playoffs began in 1969, the National League pennant would be decided in the fifth and final game, a 3 p.m. start on a drizzly Wednesday afternoon at Riverfront. The weekday afternoon start and the weather kept the attendance under 42,000, but the crowd would see one of the most dramatic games in baseball history, a game that would substantially contribute to the legend of the Big Red Machine.

The Game One starters, Gullett and Blass, again squared off, and again Blass had the better of Gullett. The Pirates scored two runs in the second to take a 2-0 lead. With Sanguillen on first, Richie Hebner doubled. When the throw from Geronimo skidded through the infield on the wet turf, Sanguillen scored and Hebner moved to third. Cash followed with an RBI single and the crowd sensed a Pirate runaway. But Gullett throttled the rally and the Reds retaliated in the third. Chaney singled, Gullett sacrificed and Rose hit a bad-hop double over Stargell to drive in a run.

In the fourth, Gullett gave up singles to Sanguillen and Hebner, and Anderson summoned Pedro Borbon. The rubber-armed right-hander had appeared in 62 games in 1972, in short relief, long relief and even as a starter in two games. Borbon immediately gave up a looping single to left field by Cash that scored Sanguillen to make the score 3-1. Borbon retired Gene Alley on a fly to right and then Pirate manager Bill Virdon guessed wrong. He allowed pitcher Blass to hit away rather than sacrifice; Blass hit into a double play.

In the fifth, Geronimo, who was 1-for-17 in the series, hit Blass' first pitch, a slow curve, over the right field fence to pull the Reds within one, 3-2. In the sixth, Anderson brought in the second of his bullpen aces, Tom Hall. Howsam's Hall-for-Jim Merritt trade in December 1971 had been overshadowed by the Houston blockbuster. But in his first season in the National League, Hall had compiled a 10-1 record, a 2.61 ERA, and had 134 strikeouts in 124 innings. He had been the winning pitcher in Game Two in

1972 Monthly Standings
National League East

April 30

	W	L	GB
Montreal	9	4	—
New York	8	4	½
Philadelphia	9	5	½
Pittsburgh	5	8	4
St. Louis	5	8	4
Chicago	4	10	5½

May 31

	W	L	GB
New York	29	11	—
Pittsburgh	24	15	4½
Chicago	20	18	8
Montreal	18	22	11
Philadelphia	16	24	13
St. Louis	16	25	13½

June 30

	W	L	GB
Pittsburgh	40	25	—
New York	41	26	—
Chicago	37	29	3
St. Louis	34	33	7
Montreal	29	38	12
Philadelphia	24	42	16½

July 31

	W	L	GB
Pittsburgh	60	35	—
New York	52	41	7
Chicago	51	46	10
St. Louis	46	48	13½
Montreal	42	50	16½
Philadelphia	34	61	26

August 31

	W	L	GB
Pittsburgh	77	46	—
Chicago	67	58	11
New York	63	58	13
St. Louis	60	63	17
Montreal	57	65	19½
Philadelphia	44	79	33

Final Standings

	W	L	GB
Pittsburgh	95	59	—
Chicago	85	70	11
New York	83	73	13½
St. Louis	75	81	21½
Montreal	70	8	26½
Philadelphia	59	97	37½

relief of Billingham. Now, he retired the Pirates over the next three innings, allowing only one hit.

Blass was just as effective, but in this one-run game, every pitch carried the possibility of a rally-starting hit, a home run, a pennant-winning play. At one point announcer Al Michaels let out a sigh and said, "Oh boy. I don't have to over-dramatize anything. Just sit here and call 'ball one,' 'strike one.' Don't even have to use an adjective. I think you can feel what is going on."

In the eighth, with one out, pinch-hitter Joe Hague walked and Concepcion came in to run. The Reds had had great success stealing on Sanguillen, but Anderson called for the sacrifice, and Rose bunted Concepcion to second. Ramon Hernandez relieved Blass and ended the threat by getting Morgan to ground out and Tolan to strike out.

"I had butterflies," Tolan later admitted. "I'll never experience another game like this if I play ten more years. I was scared to death."

The Reds, down 3-2, were three outs from the end of the season.

Upstairs in the press box, publicity director Ruhl left his seat and headed for the elevator and the dressing rooms. The losing team had a five-minute grace period in the clubhouse before the press was admitted. Ruhl's responsibility was to enforce the delay. As Ruhl stepped onto the elevator, so did television announcer Tony Kubek, on his way to the Pirates dressing room to cover the post-game celebration. They parted ways at the clubhouse level. In the Reds clubhouse, Ruhl made a few last-minute arrangements, and then watched the ninth inning on TV with a couple of the players who had come out of the game.

Out on the field, Clay Carroll, the final star of Anderson's bullpen, pitched the top of the ninth. Carroll had set a major league record in 1972 with 37 saves and had been one of the top relievers in baseball the past three seasons. He quickly retired the side. With the roaring Riverfront crowd, Virdon brought in Dave Giusti, his top reliever, to face Bench, Perez and Menke in the bottom of the ninth.

Bench faced this moment with the additional burden of knowing that a spot had been recently discovered on his lungs. The Reds

© Cincinnati Reds

The Reds hired Al Michaels (left, with Sparky Anderson) from a Triple A Hawaii club in 1971 to be the club's radio announcer. Michaels' broadcast of Johnny Bench's dramatic home run in the 1972 playoffs is one of the most memorable calls in the club's history.

required physicals of all their players each September, and Bench's X-rays revealed a blur on his lung the size of a half dollar. Surgery was performed in the offseason, and a non-cancerous lesion was removed. But Bench did not know the eventual outcome as he waited in the on-deck circle for what he thought might be his last at-bat…ever.

Bench, however, had not dwelled on the melodramatic. He had told very few people of his condition, and he felt he had been successful in putting the upcoming surgery out of his mind. He had a great September (11 home runs and 33 RBIs) and he was five-for-17 in the playoffs.

As Giusti finished his warm-up throws, Bench's mother, who was sitting near the Reds dugout, left her seat and came down to the railing to wish her son luck.

"Hit a home run!" she told him, in a scene that could have been scripted by Hollywood.

As meaningful as that was to Bench, he already had a plan on how to approach Giusti. Before the game, Bench had made a slight adjustment in his swing.

"I felt bad in batting practice," he revealed. "I watched films before the game. I was crouching too much. I couldn't see the ball well."

He knew Giusti would likely pitch him outside, especially with his off-speed breaking pitch, a "palm ball," which broke down and away from right-handed hitters. Bench was determined not to try to pull the outside pitch, which often resulted in weak groundballs to the infield.

"I'm taking him to right field," Bench said to Morgan before he walked to the plate.

In the broadcast booth, Reds broadcaster Al Michaels set the outfield alignment for his listeners (deep and around toward left) and continued his call.

"Giusti winds and the one-one pitch to Bench is swung on and missed. Again a full rip on a sinker. One-and-two. Giusti, sinking fastball, slider, palm ball, good control. Tony Perez on deck.

"Giusti bends in, takes the sign. The right-hander winds and the one-two pitch to Bench. Johnny swings and drills it a mile, but foul. Boy, he had all of that one, but foul by plenty, hit it up in the red seats, the upper deck. One-and-two.

The wind and the pitch to Bench; change, hit in the air to deep right field, back goes Clemente, at the fence, she's gone! (Crowd roars for 34 seconds.)

Johnny Bench, who hits almost every home run to left field, hits one to right. The game is tied!"

Players leaped out of the dugout as the ball flew toward right field, and erupted in cheers, arms held aloft, as the ball cleared the fence. The Reds mobbed Bench after he crossed home plate. Sparky Anderson, however, was thinking extra innings. He dispatched Billingham to the bullpen to join Jim McGlothlin.

"My heart started going 90 miles an hour," Billingham remembered.

In the clubhouse, Ruhl and the players jumped with joy as though on pogo sticks. Suddenly there was a loud knock at the door. It was Tony Kubek.

Perez, the next batter, continued the rally with a single up the middle on Giusti's next pitch, and Anderson sent in George Foster to run for Perez.

With the National League pennant standing on first base and no one out, the strategy called for a sacrifice bunt. But Menke couldn't produce. With the count at three-and-two, Anderson started Foster and let Menke swing away. Menke fouled off two pitches, then singled to left. Foster stopped at second.

With Geronimo up, Anderson called for another bunt. Like Menke, Geronimo couldn't lay down the sacrifice, but the Reds' luck held. Geronimo hit a long fly to right field that moved Foster to third. Bob Moose, who had come in to relieve Giusti during the Geronimo at-bat, now faced Chaney. Anderson considered a suicide squeeze, but knew that Virdon would also be looking for it. Sparky didn't want to risk the run. Needing just a long fly ball to win, he let Chaney swing away. Chaney popped weakly to short left field. Gene Alley and Rennie Stennett bumped chasing the ball, but Alley held on. Two outs.

Anderson called on Hal McRae, his best pinch-hitter. Michaels continued his call.

"Foster at third, Menke at first, two down. Moose checking with Sanguillen, the stretch, the pitch on the way, McRae swings and misses, went after a slider on the outside corner. Oh-and-one.... The strike one pitch on the way is outside, ball one. One-and-one. On deck, Pete Rose. Moose turns his back on the plate, back of the rubber now, kicking at the rubber. Mops his brow, hunches over, takes the sign."

Sanguillen called for a slider, low and away, out of the strike zone, hoping McRae would chase a bad pitch. Moose nodded. He didn't want to throw the slider for a strike, either.

He didn't.

"The stretch and the one-one pitch to McRae. In the dirt! It's a wild pitch! Here comes Foster! The Reds win the pennant!" (Crowd roars for 22 seconds.)

"Bob Moose throws a wild pitch and the Reds have won the National League pennant. Four-three, Cincinnati. Foster scores. It's all over."

Third base coach Alex Grammas nearly beat Foster down the line, then jumped on him along with McRae and Rose. The rest of the players joined in. Fans raced on the field, trying to get into the dugout, and a couple actually made it all the way to the clubhouse. But the police, ably supported by Dick Wagner, cleared it out.

"We hadn't had any experience with this kind of thing with the crowd rushing the field," recalled Wagner. "I was in the dugout trying to help the police. We made a stand like Custer in there. I was standing guys up and pushing them back. My father called me after the game—he had seen some of this on TV—and said, 'Richard, you shouldn't be doing things like that.'"

But amidst all the joy and bedlam in the dugout, there was a moment of concern. Sparky was so overwhelmed he lost his breath and Ted Kluszewski had to escort the manager back to the clubhouse.

"I'm not feeling too good," admitted Sparky, but he was the only one.

"As far as I'm concerned," Bobby Tolan said, "the World Series is over. The two best teams have already played."

"Today's game represented the world championship," said Rose. "I know we've got to play the American League, but the two best teams in baseball played today."

The following day, the Oakland A's won the American League playoffs from Detroit and headed to Cincinnati for the first two games of the 1972 World Series.

Unlike the Orioles, who in 1970 were widely recognized as one of the great teams in baseball, the Reds' opponents in 1972, the Oakland A's, were an unknown quantity, recognized as much for their cantankerous owner and squabbling ways as for their accomplishments on the field. But like the Reds, the A's were on the verge of a dynasty. From 1971 to 1975, the A's would win five straight division titles, and they would triumph in three consecutive World Series, a feat matched only by the Joe McCarthy's Yankees of the late 1930s and Casey Stengel's Yanks of 1949-1953. Although most observers of the time would not have predicted it, the 1971-75 Oakland A's would ultimately rank among baseball's greatest dynasties.

But in 1972, the A's were still seen as more of a sideshow act than as deserving top billing in the World Series. The players often fought among themselves and with manager Dick Williams. The team wore gaudy green, white and gold uniforms that resembled softball jerseys. The players sported long hair and mustaches, and owner Charlie Finley was the most despised in the game.

Finley, who made his fortune in the insurance business, bought the Kansas City A's in 1960 and moved the team to Oakland in 1968. He was gruff and crude, accustomed to running his own business, and he showed little or no deference to the other owners or the hallowed traditions of baseball. He hated the gray and white tone of the standard uniforms, so he dressed his players in colorful jerseys and white shoes. He favored orange baseballs and he wanted to paint the bases different colors. He thought World Series games should be played at night. He lobbied for a permanent pinch-hitter in place of the pitcher because the fans wanted home runs and excitement, not low-scoring games.

NBC announcer Tony Kubek initially headed to the Pittsburgh dressing room for the 1972 playoff celebration. But he quickly changed venues after Johnny Bench's tying home run. A drenched and happy Pete Rose and Joe Morgan shared the interview stage with Kubek.

The Cincinnati Enquirer

HAWK

With a proboscis like Clay Carroll's, the nickname "Hawk" was inevitable. And with his Alabama drawl and country-boy persona, so were the stories and laughs.

Carroll was one of the genuine characters of the Big Red Machine. A fierce competitiveness on the mound gave way to an easy-going demeanor in the clubhouse that invited needling and practical jokes.

When weak-hitting Tommy Helms hit the first home run at Riverfront Stadium in 1970, Carroll taped an 'X' to the foul pole screen to mark the historic spot.

Helms immediately suspected Carroll when he saw the X. "I know who did that," Helms laughed. "Carroll left his signature."

Carroll was the first to acknowledge his lack of interest in formal education in his native Clanton, Alabama. When he was signed by the Milwaukee Braves in 1961, he was so anxious to play minor league ball, he forsook summer school and his high school diploma. Carroll made the major leagues in 1965 and Bob Howsam acquired him in a trade in 1968.

Carroll became a familiar figure on the Riverfront mound. He appeared in 486 games before being traded after the 1975 season. The durable Carroll averaged 58 appearances a year from 1970 to 1975, and along with Pedro Borbon, gave Sparky Anderson's bullpen great depth and flexibility.

When Anderson summoned the right-hander, he entered the game at a trot from the bullpen, accelerating as he approached the infield. Writer George Plimpton, in a 1975 *Sports Illustrated* article, noted that the Hawk's teammates often wondered if he would lose control.

"His teammates have speculated," wrote Plimpton, "that Carroll would get himself revved up to such a fearsome speed that he would run right past the mound, over the manager and the catcher standing there, and fetch up in a tumble in the dugout beyond."

Carroll conceded that relief pitchers were a little different. "You have to be cocky and flaky to be a reliever. You gotta think you're the best. Unbeatable."

But Carroll's teammates never let the Hawk soar too high. One of their favorite Carroll stories took place during the 1972 World Series.

While Carroll sat in a coffee shop in Oakland, a waitress approached, autograph book in hand.

"Are you a ballplayer?" she asked Carroll.

Clay sat up a little straighter.

"I'm Clay Carroll, ma'am."

"Oh, my mistake," apologized the waitress, quickly walking away.

The Hawk was grounded.

The Cincinnati Enquirer

"Hawk" (Clay Carroll) accepted the ball from Sparky Anderson in relief 347 times from 1970 to 1975, an average of 58 appearances a year. Carroll's 37 saves in 1972 set a major league save record.

Some of these innovations became staples of baseball, and some were dismissed, but it was never easy for baseball to ignore Finley. He even had the audacity to act as his own general manager. To the surprise of many, he signed some excellent talent, including Jim "Catfish" Hunter. Finley also signed a mule as the A's mascot and painted "Charlie O" on its hide.

In the late 1960s and early 1970s, as the long-hair revolution swept across America, many owners, including Bob Howsam, enforced traditional styles. Finley reveled in challenging baseball's conventions. He offered his players $300 if they would grow mustaches. By the fall of 1972, most of the A's sported facial hair, in part because wringing an extra $300 out of Finley was never easy. His parsimonious ways angered the team; most of the players were open in their disdain for Finley, and manager Williams. Williams seemed eager to confront players and encouraged dissension as a way of motivating his team.

In short, the A's and Charlie Finley were all the things the Reds and Bob Howsam were not. The Reds valued team discipline, a no-nonsense manager, a wholesome, family atmosphere and conservative, old-guard leadership in the front office. In sharp contrast to the A's, the Reds decreed short hair and clean-shaven faces. The 1972 World Series, wrote AP baseball writer Will Grimsley, would be a "battle of the mods and the squares."

The traditional appearance of the Big Red Machine—short hair, no facial hair, crisp uniforms, black shoes and socks with low-cut stirrups—was not invented by Howsam. It had dominated baseball for decades. But in a time of cultural upheaval that had many Americans abandoning tradition, Howsam was steadfast in his adherence to the old ways. Howsam had instituted regulations about players' appearances at St. Louis and he brought the same rules to Cincinnati. In Sparky Anderson, he found a kindred spirit. And in Rose, Bench, Morgan and others, he found players who not only agreed with the rules, but helped enforce them.

When veteran Bob Bailey, who often wore his uniform pantlegs low, came to the Reds in 1976, Bench delivered the club rules.

"Pull up your pants," Bench ordered. "Look right, the way the Reds are supposed to look."

Bailey, like most players, had never given much thought to the way his uniform looked.

"To him, the uniform was just something to play in," Bench said. "But to us, it's a discipline thing."

In part, the neat appearance of the players reflected Howsam's analogy of the baseball game as a stage show and the players as actors. The fans had a right to an impeccable production. Howsam enforced the look throughout the Reds system. Personnel director Bender recalled Howsam sending him notes about the appearance of minor league players after Howsam had visited the farm teams.

"Chief, get the manager to straighten this guy out, he's wearing his socks too low," Howsam would say. By the time a Cincinnati player reached the major leagues, he knew the rules.

Prior to the ceremonies before the first game of the 1976 World Series, the Reds were scheduled to line up on the foul line without their jackets. But on the cool evening, several players were wearing jackets in the dugout. When a TV producer muttered to Bench that the players were not supposed to wear them, Bench looked in the dugout and issued one stern word.

"Jackets!"

"I looked down the dugout and every jacket was coming off," said Blake Cullen, the producer. "Nobody said anything. Nobody asked any questions. And Bench just said that one word."

Anderson found the rules easy to enforce because he believed in team discipline, and players' dedication to team principles started with an allegiance to the uniform.

A popular song of the early 1970s was "It's Your Thing (Do What You Wanna Do)," by Sly and the Family Stone. It mirrored the changing attitudes of the era. But Sparky Anderson abhorred the message.

"I let my players do their thing *out on the field*. We let an athlete do what he can do best," he explained. "But on our club we need each other. We need all 25 guys; we are all part of something. We are not…in need of our own thing."

The club's rules extended to road trips as well; players wore ties to dinner, and dress codes were enforced on the plane.

"I've heard many stewardesses say we're the nicest group they have," said Rose. "That's good."

Morgan recalled that shortly after he joined the Reds, he wore a sports jacket over a T-shirt that depicted different signs of the zodiac with sexually suggestive figures. Sparky strongly recommended a more professional appearance. Morgan complied and became an enthusiastic supporter of the club's rules.

The rules applied to shoes, too. Although the team was famous for its well-shined black shoes, Howsam had experimented with red shoes in 1968. But two of the pitchers did not like the fit and switched back to the black shoes. Howsam wanted identical dress, so he dumped the red footwear. Later, as shoe companies began to put their logos on the sides of the shoes, Howsam ordered it blacked out. Clubhouse attendants carefully applied black polish to the companies' stripes and emblems. Howsam was not so opposed to the commercialism as he was to the color white.

"The movement of the white shoe detracts from the flight of the ball, and in watching the game, the ball should be the center of

Yes, the Abe Lincoln impostor at left is Peter Edward Rose. He joined fashionably coiffed pitchers Ross Grimsley (center) and Don Gullett at a winter banquet in 1972. The short-hair policy of the Reds sent the players scurrying to the barber shop in the days leading up to spring training.

attention," reasoned Howsam. He also felt white shoes exaggerated the length of the foot and made players look like circus clowns. He thought the Oakland A's looked like a "Sunday School softball team."

The rules also applied to equipment, including batting helmets. Each day before a game, the batboy shined the helmets with cleaning alcohol and placed them neatly along the top of the bat rack. Anderson recalled notes from Howsam about replacing smudged or chipped helmets. During an out-of-town game that was televised back to Cincinnati, Wagner noticed that Rose had written his number "14" on the back of his helmet. The number made it easier for Rose to locate his lid, but helmet hieroglyphics were forbidden. Such infractions could not wait until the team returned home. Wagner called the ballpark and relayed a message to Anderson. The number disappeared.

There were even rules for helmet-tossing. If a player hit a double, he did not stand at second and fling the helmet towards the first-base coach. He waited for the coach to jog out and then handed the helmet to him.

No one ever heard Howsam link his policies to the politics of the day. He never spoke of how his club's appearance was a stance against the moral decay that seemed to many to be overtaking America. But in the early 1970s, when appearance was a political statement, the Reds began to be seen as defenders of the silent majority. Of course that meshed quite well with the traditional values of Cincinnati and the Midwest where the club aimed its marketing strategies. Howsam claimed that if his team had been in Aspen, he would have permitted long hair; it was critical to the success of any team to mirror the mores of its market. But to all those who knew Howsam and his button-down staff, it was hard to picture them running anything but a tradition-bound club.

Had Howsam favored a more "mod" appearance, the history of the Cincinnati franchise would have supplied a precedent. The original professional baseball club, the Cincinnati Red Stockings of 1869, was celebrated in club publications. Half the members of the the Red Stockings wore mustaches, beards and extravagant sideburns. For years, the club's logo figure had sported a handlebar mustache and a 19th-century cap. But one year after arriving in Cincinnati, Howsam revised the logo; he put "Mr. Red" in a modern uniform and the mustache vanished.

Appearance, however, would not dictate the outcome of the World Series, and most pundits, no matter the length of their hair, picked the Reds. Las Vegas installed the Reds as favorites; the experience of the Reds and position-by-position comparisons favored the National League champs. But Ray Shore, who scouted the American League in August and September, reported that the A's were by far the superior team in the American League, and Sparky paid them a compliment when he referred to them as an National League-type club, with speed and a deep bullpen. Secretly, though, Anderson confided to a few associates that he thought the Reds could win in four games.

Part of his confidence stemmed from the injury to Oakland's premier power hitter, Reggie Jackson, who had severely pulled a hamstring in the playoff win over Detroit. The A's feared they might also lose shortstop Bert Campaneris for the Series as part of his suspension in the playoffs. Campaneris had missed the last three games of the American League playoffs for throwing a bat at a Detroit pitcher after he had been hit on the knee. But Commissioner Bowie Kuhn reinstated Campaneris, providing Pete

Rose with an opportunity for "agitatin" he couldn't refuse.

"Hey, Campy," Rose yelled during a practice session at Riverfront. "I just want you to know the bats don't carry too well in this ballpark!"

The Game One matchups featured Gary Nolan, who reported no problems with his arm, and Ken Holtzman. Holtzman had pitched for the Chicago Cubs in 1971, and in his last appearance at Riverfront Stadium had thrown a no-hitter. His opponent in that game was Nolan, who took the loss, 1-0. Holtzman was part of a strong Oakland rotation that featured "Catfish" Hunter, "Blue Moon" Odom and Vida Blue.

Holtzman earned the victory, but the hero was reserve catcher Gene Tenace who homered in his first two at-bats and drove in all the A's runs in the 3-2 victory. Tenace, who had gone only 1-for-17 in the A.L. playoffs, hit his first homer in the second inning with a man on. The Reds tied the game with single runs in the second and fourth. Tenace hit his second home run in the fifth and from then on, both bullpens pitched scoreless ball. The Reds threatened in the ninth, putting the tying run on third base with two out. Rose fooled the defense with a bunt, but it rolled foul. He grounded to second for the final out.

Williams used Rollie Fingers, the ace of his bullpen, in the sixth inning and brought in starter Vida Blue in the seventh. Blue earned the save. Williams didn't use his bullpen as much as Anderson, but like the Reds, the A's led their league in saves. Both managers were in the forefront of the development of the deep bullpen and the move away from the complete game, and the Series proved it. Sparky made 19 pitching changes and Williams, 15. No starter finished a game. It was only the second time in World Series history that had happened.

Hunter started Game Two against Ross Grimsley, and again the A's jumped off to a 2-0 lead. Hunter singled in a run in the second and Joe Rudi hit a long home run in the third. The Reds had only four hits against Hunter and entered the ninth still down by two. Perez led off the ninth with a single and Denis Menke drove a long fly to left field. Hunter thought Menke had hit a home run, but the ball hung up and Rudi, on the run toward the wall, looked over his left shoulder, and gauged the flight. He shortened his stride a couple of steps from the wall, then leaped with his left hand extended far above his head. The ball lodged in his glove just inches from the wall and nearly came through the back of the webbing. Perez, who was past second when the catch was made,

The Reds' traditional logo (right) featured a mustachioed old-time player in honor of the franchise's legacy of organizing baseball's first professional team (the 1869 Cincinnati Red Stockings). But the handlebar mustache was not representative of Howsam's image of the Reds, and a new logo appeared in 1968.

Logos, © Cincinnati Reds

Baseball honored Jackie Robinson during the 1972 World Series on the 25th anniversary of Robinson's history-making 1947 season. Robinson threw out the first pitch before Game Two at Riverfront Stadium. This was the final public appearance for the 53-year-old racial pioneer. He died of complications from diabetes nine days later.

The Cincinnati Enquirer

barely beat the throw back to first.

Geronimo lined a shot down the first-base line that first baseman Mike Hegan (a defensive replacement for starter Mike Epstein) dove for and knocked down. On his knees, Hegan picked up the ball and crawled towards the bag, touching first base with his hand. Perez advanced to second, but a promising rally had been crippled by two great defensive plays. Hal McRae pinch-hit and drove a single to left scoring Perez. Williams finally brought on Fingers who popped up Julian Javier for the final out.

Solid pitching and spectacular defense had shut down the Big Red Machine. As in 1970, the Reds were down two games to none. Part of the problem resided in the top of the batting order: Rose, Tolan and Morgan were a combined 2-for-23. Rose could not believe it.

"They're a good team and all that, but the Cincinnati Reds are a better team than Oakland and we know it."

Rose pointed to the controversies among the A's players as another good sign for the Reds. After Game Two, first baseman Epstein and Williams yelled at one another. Catcher Dave Duncan and Vida Blue criticized Finley in front of reporters. Yet it was the Reds who faced the must-win situation in Game Three.

Jack Billingham was up to the challenge. He pitched one of the best games of his career, a three-hit shutout over eight innings. The Reds needed every scoreless inning, for they could muster only one run off Blue Moon Odom. And that was a clunker. Perez led off the seventh with a single and was sacrificed to second by Menke. Geronimo then singled to right-center field. As Perez rounded third, he slipped on the wet turf and fell to his knees. He quickly scrambled to his feet and dashed towards the plate. The ball had slowed on the wet outfield grass and the A's assumed they had no play. Campaneris took the throw from the outfield with his back to home plate, and never realized he could have thrown out Perez.

Carroll relieved Billingham in the ninth and saved the shutout, It was a third straight one-run game, but this one belonged to the Reds. Bench could have been the goat had the Reds lost, but his strikeout in the eighth inning, courtesy of some A's chicanery, proved harmless. With one out and runners on second and third, Bench had run the count to three-and-two. Dick Williams suddenly headed for the mound, held up four fingers and gestured to first. It appeared he was giving pitcher Rollie Fingers instructions to intentionally walk Bench. In fact, he had told Fingers to fire a hard slider over the outside corner. Morgan, standing on third, sensed something was on and yelled to Bench, "Be alive!" But Bench was mesmerized by the perfect strike-three pitch, a slider he later said he didn't think he could have hit under any circumstances.

Now came the pivotal Game Four. Don Gullett started for the Reds and pitched seven strong innings, allowing just one run, another homer to Tenace. The Reds scored two runs in the eighth on a two-run double by Tolan off Blue, who had relieved Holtzman. The Reds led, 2-1, and Anderson turned the game over to his usually reliable bullpen.

Borbon retired the A's in the eighth, and after the Reds went down quietly in the ninth, it was Borbon's game to save. He got the first out in the ninth. Then came the critical play.

Williams called on pinch-hitter Gonzalo Marquez. Anderson recalled that Shore's scouting report said Marquez hit "everything in the air to left and everything up the middle on the ground."

The Reds had seen this in Game Three when Marquez singled up the middle on a ball that Billingham deflected. But Concepcion had played with Marquez in Venezuela and believed that Marquez hit groundballs in the hole. As Marquez stepped in, Concepcion took two steps toward third. Anderson nearly motioned him back to cover the middle, but didn't. Marquez bounced a high hopper up the middle over Borbon's head and into center field. If Concepcion had played Marquez straight away or shaded him towards second as Shore's report advised, he would have made the play.

Williams sent in speedster Allen Lewis to run for Marquez. Anderson visited the mound and told Borbon to check the runner, but not to throw over. But Borbon threw to first and fell behind in the count to Tenace. Anderson yanked Borbon and brought on Carroll. That strategy backfired when Carroll gave up a single to Tenace, putting the tying run on second. Williams called on his second pinch-hitter, left-handed Don Mincher. At that point, Anderson could have brought in lefty Tom Hall, but he stuck with Carroll. Mincher singled to right, tying the game.

With the winning run on third, Anderson brought his infield in to cut off the run at the plate. The third pinch-hitter of the inning, Angel Mangual, took advantage of the drawn-in infield and singled just between Morgan and Perez. Four straight singles brought the A's the victory and a 3-1 lead in the Series.

After the game, Anderson fumed. He was mad at Borbon for disregarding his instructions. He wondered if he should have brought in Hall. But Carroll had pitched well against left-handers all year, and Sparky didn't beat himself up over that. No, primarily he was angry at himself for not re-positioning Concepcion. When Ray Shore walked in the clubhouse, the frustrated Anderson picked up the scouting report on the desk and hurled it at the wall.

"I don't know what the hell these are good for if we don't use 'em," said Sparky, as much to himself as to Shore.

In a World Series made for second-guessing—six one-run

games, 19 Cincinnati pitching changes, and dozens of pinch-hitting and positioning decisions—Anderson would in later years question only this one move.

"I made one terrible mistake on where to play Marquez," Anderson admitted. "That was our game. It cost us the Series."

Anderson hoped to start Nolan in Game Five, but his arm had not recovered from the Game One appearance. Sparky turned to Jim McGlothlin. Hunter started for the A's. Rose stepped in to lead off; the A's fans booed lustily. Rose had angered Hunter and the A's loyalists when he said he was not overly impressed with Hunter in Game Two. At one point, after Hunter had gotten him out, Rose had yelled at him, "You're lucky to even be out here this long!" Hunter fired back, claiming that Rose "popped off" too much and that he would never get away with such insolence in the American League.

Rose, ever alert to needle an opponent, also had a running battle going with catcher Tenace. Rose thought Tenace went too far in complaining about pitches. He recreated a typical exchange for reporters.

"Ball one," said the umpire.

"That was a strike," complained Tenace.

"Come on, Gino," said Rose. "You don't really want that one, do you?"

"This is between me and the umpire. You stay out of it and just swing the bat."

Rose glanced at the umpire and said, with more than a hint of sarcasm, "Why don't you just give him a (ball and strike)

"Mr. October" in the 1972 World Series was not the A's Reggie Jackson, but his unheralded teammate, Gene Tenace. Tenace hit four home runs, drove in nine runs and won the MVP award.

The Cincinnati Enquirer

indicator?"

Tenace was offended. "No batter has ever said anything like that to me before."

Against this backdrop, Rose, with his team down three games to one, blasted Hunter's first pitch of Game Five for a home run.

But Tenace countered with a three-run homer in the bottom of the second. The A's led, 4-3, heading to the eighth, needing only six more outs to win the Series in front of the home-town crowd. But Morgan walked, stole second and scored on Tolan's single.

In the ninth, with Geronimo on first, Grimsley bunted, but popped the ball towards the mound. Fingers let it bounce with the hope of turning a double play, but his throw to first was wide. The A's got Grimsley, but had no chance for Geronimo. Rose singled sharply to center to give the Reds the lead. Game Five was proving particularly gratifying to Rose, who had dodged tomatoes, eggs and plenty of insults in left field during the three games in Oakland.

But the A's mounted one final threat. Tenace walked to lead off the ninth and Odom came in to pinch-run. With one out, Billingham replaced Grimsley and gave up a single to pinch-hitter Dave Duncan, putting the tying run on third. Campaneris then lifted a popup some 50 feet beyond first base. Morgan drifted over, waved off Perez and caught the ball just in foul ground. Morgan immediately looked to third and saw Odom streaking for home. Joe planted his foot to throw and slipped, but he immediately bounced up and zipped a strike to Bench, who blocked the plate and tagged the sliding Odom. The Reds had staved off elimination.

Five games. Five one-run games. The collective tension reached critical mass in Game Six and burst into a Riverfront Stadium laugher. With a two-run lead going into the bottom of the seventh, the Reds sent 10 men to the plate—a shocking hit parade compared to the 51 innings of nerve-wracking ball that had preceded it. The Reds scored five runs after two were out, four on singles by Tolan and Geronimo. The only episode marring the festive day was an anonymous phone call to police threatening the life of Tenace if he hit another home run. The threat, coming just weeks after the slaughter of Israeli athletes in the Munich Olympics, was taken seriously. The next day at a stadium ticket window, a beefed-up police force arrested a man with a gun who was making threatening remarks about the Oakland catcher.

The largest crowd in the history of Cincinnati baseball, 56,040, filled Riverfront for Game Seven on Sunday, October 22. The Big "Dead" Machine had been revived in Games Five and Six. Anderson was quietly optimistic.

"Just remember," he said softly to a reporter after Game Six. "This is a team that has won every game it's had to win."

The Reds had won the final two games of the playoffs, and two must-win games in the Series. Anderson still believed he had the better players and was backed by a better organization. But with a mere nine innings left in the season, subtle maneuvers, misplays and luck would count just as much as talent.

The first inning was a portent. With one out against starter Jack Billingham, Angel Mangual drilled a line drive to center. Tolan moved in, then suddenly pulled up and leaped. The ball skidded off the top of his glove. Mangual wound up on third; Tolan was charged with a three-base error.

"It looked like one of those line drives that sink," explained Tolan. "But all of a sudden it took off."

Tenace capitalized with a high bouncing groundball to third that hit a seam in the turf and took a bad hop over Menke's head. Video replays showed that Mangual would have scored even if Menke had been able to field the chopper. Mangual had run on contact.

Rose opened the first with a single, but Odom retired 10 in a row before walking Morgan in the fourth. Hoping to minimize the Reds' running game, Williams had moved Tenace to first base for Game Seven and put Dave Duncan behind the plate. (The Reds had stolen 11 bases off Tenace.) Odom threw to first base seven straight times to keep Morgan close. Finally Joe took off and Duncan threw him out on a close play.

Every pitch, every swing of the bat, every call became magnified under the pressure of the seventh game. But someone in the press box managed to find some time for humor. Early in the game, the phone rang in the commissioner's field-level box. Bowie Kuhn answered the phone.

"Hello, Chicken Delight?" asked the caller. "I want to order."

"I'm afraid you have the wrong number," Kuhn politely replied.

But the press box wag who had discovered Kuhn's number was not deterred. "The large size. The 24 pieces."

"You have the wrong number," Kuhn repeated, and hung up.

In the next inning, the phone rang again. "Hello, Chicken Delight? Do you deliver on Sundays? We're having a World Series party."

"You have the wrong number," Kuhn said.

"Isn't this 421-1430?"

"Yes, but this isn't Chicken Delight," said Kuhn, and he hung up again.

The joke finally wore off, and Kuhn, baseball's top boss, was able to enjoy the rest of the game uninterrupted by fast-food calls.

In the fifth, Perez doubled to start a rally. The Reds loaded the bases and scored one run on a sacrifice fly by McRae to tie the game. But Rose flied out to deep right-center to end the inning.

Oakland rallied again in the sixth. Borbon, in relief of Billingham, gave up a single to Campaneris. With two out, Tenace struck again with an RBI double. Bando crushed a long fly to center that sent Tolan running for the fence. The ball appeared catchable, but Tolan suddenly grabbed his leg and stumbled. The ball landed in the middle of the warning track. Tenace scored easily giving the A's a 3-1 lead. In the tightest moment of the Series, Tolan had not snapped, but his hamstring had. As he left the field, many in the stands and some in the Reds organization felt that Tolan's two miscues in Game Seven had all but doomed his future with the Reds.

In the eighth, the Reds threatened to tie the game and possibly win. Rose singled to center off Hunter. Williams brought in Holtzman to pitch to Morgan, and Joe rammed a low line drive past first base deep into the right-field corner.

"From the second I hit it, I was thinking triple," Morgan recalled.

But Rose, one of the club's best baserunners, got a poor jump.

"I had to hold back or it would have hit me," Rose said.

Mike Hegan, the Oakland first baseman, dove for the ball and sprawled in the basepath. Rose had to dance around him.

"I was just wondering whether I could reach third base, not about going home," Rose said.

Third base coach Alex Grammas could see the play in front of him as Rose headed towards third. Right fielder Matty Alou had trouble picking up the ball, and Grammas initially waved Rose around, but then threw up the stop sign. Morgan, intent on making third, was well past second when he saw Grammas stop Rose. He barely scrambled back to second before the throw. Rose kicked at third in disgust; a look of frustration etched Morgan's face.

1972 SCRAPBOOK

THE OPPOSITION

WESTERN DIVISION

Against	Won	Lost
Atlanta	9	9
Houston	11	6
Los Angeles	9	5
San Diego	8	10
San Fran.	10	5

EASTERN DIVISION

Against	Won	Lost
Chicago	4	8
Montreal	8	4
New York	8	4
Philadelphia	10	2
Pittsburgh	8	4
St. Louis	10	2

The pitchers the Reds didn't want to face — **Ferguson Jenkins** of the Cubs was 4-0 against the Reds; **Fred Norman** of the Padres was 4-1.

The pitcher they loved to see — **Al Downing** of the Dodgers was 0-4 against the Reds.

The batter who loved the Reds — **Hank Aaron** of Atlanta hit .463 (23-for-54) with 9 HRs and 14 RBIs.

The batter who should have stayed home — **Bill Buckner** of the Dodgers hit .172 (5-for-29) with 0 HR and 1 RBI.

CLUB LEADERS

Batting average	Pete Rose	.307
Home runs	Johnny Bench	40 •
RBIs	Johnny Bench	125 •
Stolen bases	Joe Morgan	58
Runs	Joe Morgan	122 •
ERA	Gary Nolan	1.99
Wins	Gary Nolan	15
Saves	Clay Carroll	37 •
Games	Clay Carroll	65

• League leader

AWARDS

Most Valuable Player	**Johnny Bench**
Fireman of the Year	**Clay Carroll**
Gold Glove	**Johnny Bench**
Cincinnati Reds MVP •	**Johnny Bench**
Outstanding Reds Pitcher •	**Clay Carroll**
Reds Newcomer of Year •	**Joe Morgan**

• Awarded by Cincinnati Chapter of Baseball Writers Association

TRADES

May 19 — **Joe Hague** acquired from St. Louis for **Bernie Carbo**

June 11 — **Bob Barton** acquired from San Diego for **Pat Corrales**

Nov. 30 — **Roger Nelson** and **Richie Scheinblum** acquired from Kansas City for **Hal McRae** and **Wayne Simpson**

Dec. 1 — **Hal King** and **Jim Driscoll** acquired from Texas for **Jim Merritt**

THE DRAFT

Cincinnati drafted 42 players; three played in the major leagues:

Tom Hume	Manatee, FL (JC)	P
Dan Dumoulin •	Kokomo, IN	P
Ron Hassey	Tucson, AZ	SS

• Drafted by the Reds, but signed with another club

"To this day," Morgan wrote in his autobiography, "I know the A's were not worrying about Pete Rose—he wasn't the tying run. I was. So Pete should have been able to score easily."

But with no one out, and runners on second and third, the Reds still appeared to be on the verge of a winning rally. Williams replaced Holtzman with his ace Fingers. Anderson pinch-hit Joe Hague for Javier, who had replaced Tolan in center. Hague popped up to short right, the runners holding. Up stepped Johnny Bench, who had predicted to Reggie Jackson prior to the game that he would get a big hit off Fingers in the late innings of the game.

"I looked over into their dugout and there was Reggie nodding his head and smiling at me," Bench said.

But Williams, fearing Bench would repeat his Game Five heroics against Pittsburgh, walked him. Putting the winning run on base defied traditional baseball strategy, but it worked. Perez lifted a sacrifice fly to right to score Rose; Morgan moved to third. But there would be no Bob Moose to throw a wild pitch. Fingers got Menke to fly to left to end the threat.

Tom Hall retired the A's in the top of the ninth and the Reds were down to their final three outs. Fingers got Geronimo and Concepcion, then nicked Chaney with an inside pitch. Once again the Reds had the tying run on base. Switch-hitter Rose was up and Williams hustled to the mound to discuss bringing in left-hander Vida Blue to turn Rose around. Williams felt Rose was less of a threat from the right side. But catcher Duncan jumped to Fingers' defense.

"If you take him out, I'll kill you," Duncan told Williams. "He's got great stuff."

Williams, who had been criticized throughout the Series—and the season—for over-managing, went with his catcher's judgment.

Rose hit a chest-high fastball good, but not good enough. Rudi caught it in left-center and threw his arms in the air. Rose kicked at the Astroturf in disgust. The A's were World Champs.

The unbelievable had happened: the upstart, underdog A's, without Reggie Jackson, had beat the heavily-favored Reds. The Reds pitching was superb, compiling a lower ERA (2.17 to 3.05) than the celebrated Oakland staff. The Reds outscored the A's 21 to 16, but as in 1970, one player almost single-handedly won the Series. The unheralded Tenace, with four home runs and nine RBIs, won the Series MVP.

Making his performance all the more galling for the Reds was the fact that Tenace hailed from Lucasville, Ohio, about 100 miles east of Cincinnati. But Cincinnati scouts had passed on him.

"Their scout in our area didn't think much of me," Tenace said. "Said I'd never make it."

The loss was painful for the Reds organization, made even more so by the sight of Charlie Finley and Dick Williams dancing on top of the A's dugout after the win. Howsam found the scene tasteless, but grudgingly admitted the A's had outplayed his club.

He found no reason, however, to make any radical moves. Howsam thought the Reds should have won the Series. But realistically, he had not expected the Reds to win even the pennant in 1972. He had believed it would take two years or more for the Houston trade to pay off, and he was pleasantly surprised at its quick results.

The loss to the A's would not deter Howsam from his master plan. He still had a club in transition (only 12 players on the '72 World Series roster were on the '70 squad) and Howsam felt the best years for the Big Red Machine were still ahead.

© Cincinnati Reds

Defiantly pumping his fist in the air, Pete Rose circled the bases after hitting the go-ahead home run in the fourth game of the 1973 playoffs. In the background stood shortstop Bud Harrelson, with whom Rose had scuffled the day before, setting off a near-riot at Shea Stadium. The Reds turned Rose's triumphant gesture into a poster for a 1974 promotion.

1973: Lost to Mets in N. L. Playoffs • Pete Rose, MVP

Chapter 8

1973-74
Dynasty Deferred

1974: 2nd to Dodgers in Western Division • 98 wins—64 losses

THE WINTER OF 1972-73, COMING off the Oakland loss, was an agonizing one for the Reds. Sparky Anderson complained that all he heard was the same question.

"'How did you lose to Oakland?' Not why, but how? I just tell them that we didn't play like we're capable of playing. There is no question that we were the best club."

Howsam agreed. "I wouldn't trade our team for theirs," he said. "I guess I feel that way in part because of the way Charlie Finley and Dick Williams acted. After the final game, they got up on the dugout and showed off. I wanted to beat Finley so bad. Finley wasn't a fool, though. He could get general managers to talk to him. He had a good ballclub. He put out the money for the players. But I still think we should have won."

At the winter meetings in December 1972, Howsam pulled off two quick deals to improve the pitching, the outfield and the bench. The Reds had decided to trade Hal McRae. There was no doubt McRae could hit, but his lack of speed and defensive skills—plus a carefree attitude that sometimes grated on Anderson—made him expendable. Ray Shore had scouted the American League in the second half of 1972, and came back with strong praise for right-hander Roger Nelson. Nelson was a hard thrower, the kind of pitcher Shore liked. "He was by far the best pitcher in the American League I saw in the second half of the season," Shore recalled.

Howsam initiated discussions with Kansas City. At the winter meetings in Honolulu, he met with the Royals' Cedric Tallis in the Reds' suite to package the trade. "We talked for an hour and a half, had a couple of ginger ales and made the deal," recalled Howsam.

The Reds sent McRae and Wayne Simpson to the Royals for Nelson and outfielder Richie Scheinblum. It would turn out to be one of the few poor trades Howsam made. In McRae, the Reds didn't give up a player for whom they had big plans, but Nelson and Scheinblum failed to produce. Anderson claimed Scheinblum never "got over being awed by the stars on our team," and he was traded mid-way through the 1973 season. Nelson came down with a sore arm in spring training and though he remained with the Reds for two years, he never came close to matching his performance that Shore saw in 1972.

"I guess I didn't do all my homework," admitted Shore. "Something must have happened to his arm." Nelson was traded after the 1974 season, having won just seven games in two years. He never won another game and retired in 1976.

The annual holdout derby began early in 1973, as Morgan, Bench and Rose all balked at the initial contract offers. Bench pointed to the big contracts being offered by other sports. "You've got to realize what they are making in sports like basketball and hockey," Bench argued. "We play more games and play before more people."

Of all the major sports, the National Basketball Association offered the highest average salary in the early 1970s ($60,000) in part due to the bidding war created by the rival American Basketball Association. Baseball and football had the lowest average salary at $28,000. But star baseball players could earn well into six figures, and in 1973, there were approximately 25 players earning over $100,000. Hank Aaron was the highest paid at $200,000, followed by Carl Yastrzemski at $167,000, Steve Carlton at $165,000 and Bob Gibson at $160,000.

A Big Red Machine Photo Album
1970-1976

The most honored starting eight in the history of baseball led the Cincinnati Reds to back-to-back World Championships in 1975-76. Catcher Johnny Bench (kneeling) infielders Pete Rose, Dave Concepcion, Joe Morgan and Tony Perez, (middle row), and outfielders George Foster, Cesar Geronimo and Ken Griffey (back row) won six MVP awards, 26 Gold Gloves, and 63 All-Star selections.

In 1970, the Reds commissioned an art print by sports cartoonist Willard Mullin depicting the Big Red Machine. Mullin created the original Brooklyn "Bum," a classic sports image. His Big Red Machine featured a "Joe Palooka" character smashing National League opponents, including (clockwise from top left) the Cubs, Braves, Padres, Dodgers ("Bums"), Pirates, Cardinals ("Cards"), Astros, Phillies, Giants, Mets and Expos.

Cincinnati Enquirer cartoonist Jerry Dowling drew dozens of Big Red Machine images during the 1970s. Many pictured the club as a monster vehicle, firing baseballs and squashing opponents. Dowling's critical eye also pictured the Big Red Machine in a trash dumpster or as an Edsel when the team floundered. This image captured the club after it swept the Pirates in the 1975 playoffs and roared into the World Series.

(© Jerry Dowling & *The Cincinnati Enquirer*, 1975)

Focus on Sports

Focus on Sports

Pete Rose crashed into Cleveland Indians catcher Ray Fosse in the bottom of the 12th inning of the 1970 All-Star Game in Cincinnati, scoring the winning run in one of baseball's epic collisions.

One of the most significant trades in baseball history brought Joe Morgan (left) to the Reds for the 1972 season. Bob Howsam gave up All-Stars Lee May and Tommy Helms and feared he had given the pennant to Houston. But Morgan, Jack Billingham, Denis Menke and Cesar Geronimo paid immediate dividends. Geronimo's (below, top) exceptional stride and arm strengthened the Cincinnati outfield. Billingham (below, bottom) became the workhorse of the pitching staff, averaging 15 victories from 1972 to 1976.

© Cincinnati Reds

"The wind and the pitch to Bench…change hit in the air to deep right field…back goes Clemente…at the fence, she's gone!"

— Reds announcer Al Michaels, October 11, 1972

(Tying home run, ninth inning of Game 5 of the N.L.C.S., Reds vs. Pirates)

© Cincinnati Reds

1972

"The stretch and the one-one pitch to McRae. In the dirt! It's a wild pitch! Here comes Foster!! The Reds win the pennant!!"

— Al Michaels, October 11, 1972
(Game 5 of the N.L.C.S., Reds vs. Pirates)

1972

© Cincinnati Reds

The Reds gathered for pre-game festivities before the second game of the 1972 World Series. In shirt sleeves, next to Sparky Anderson (far left) stood the starting lineup: Pete Rose, Joe Morgan, Bobby Tolan, Johnny Bench, Tony Perez, Denis Menke, Cesar Geronimo and Darrel Chaney.

1972

© Cincinnati Reds

Davey Concepcion started five games of the 1972 World Series and hit .308. Concepcion platooned with Darrel Chaney and Woody Woodward during his first seasons in Cincinnati, but earned the starting job for good in 1973.

© Cincinnati Reds

1972

Gary Nolan (shown during the 1972 World Series) was the best pitcher in the National League through the first half of the 1972 season. But arm problems, which eventually sidelined him for most of 1973 and 1974, limited him to just six appearances after the All-Star Game, and hampered his post-season performance. Nolan finished 15-5 and led the National League in winning percentage (.750).

1975

The 1975 World Series featured the odd couple of baseball parks: historic, quirky Fenway Park (below) for the first, second, sixth and seventh games, and bland new Riverfront Stadium (right, bottom) for the middle three games.

© Cincinnati Reds

Beginning in 1972, Reds management and their wives wore festive red jackets and dresses for all post-season games. Enjoying Game Three of the 1975 World Series were president Bob Howsam, chairman of the board Louis Nippert, Mrs. Louise Nippert, and Mrs. Janet Howsam. The only exception to the red jacket custom came in the 1976 Series when Howsam, fearful of hostile crowds at Yankee Stadium, ordered club officials to leave their red outfits in Cincinnati.

© Cincinnati Reds

1975

© Cincinnati Reds

Don Gullett started three games in the 1975 World Series compiling a 1-1 record. His strongest performance came in Game Five when he pitched 8 2/3 innings, allowing five hits and striking out seven.

Tony Perez began the 1975 World Series by going 0-for-15. But he hit two home runs in Game Five and resurrected the Reds hopes in Game Seven with a two-run homer in the sixth inning. Perez had five clutch hits in the Series, driving in seven runs.

Dick Raphael, *Sports Illustrated*

Pete Rose (14) grabbed a jubilant Will McEnaney as the 1975 World Series victory celebration erupted at Fenway Park. McEnaney had just retired Carl Yastrzemski for the final out on a fly to center field. Johnny Bench, batting practice pitcher Art Siefert (62), Clay Carroll (red jacket) and Tony Perez (far right) rushed to join the melee.

William Schildman

Joe Morgan hit his first World Series home run in the first inning of the first game of the 1976 classic at Riverfront Stadium off Doyle Alexander. Thurmon Munson was the catcher.

1976

Dennis Gruelle

Ken Griffey took batting practice before Game Three of the 1976 World Series. Most of the Reds, including Griffey, had never seen Yankee Stadium prior to the '76 series.

Even in hostile territory with his team ahead two games to none, Pete Rose found himself a popular target of Yankee Stadium autograph hunters before the start of Game Three. Rose hit just .188 in the Series, but his aggressive defense of Yankee leadoff hitter Mickey Rivers sent a "dare-you-to-beat-me" message that the Yankees could not answer.

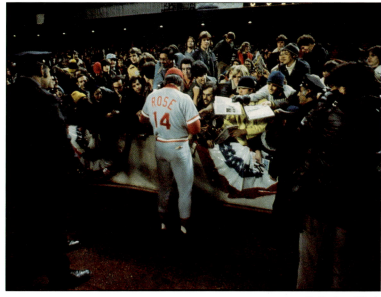

© Cincinnati Reds

© Cincinnati Reds

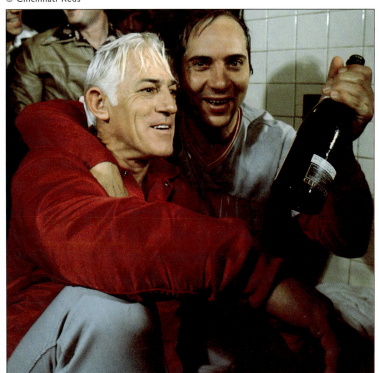

Johnny Bench and Sparky Anderson celebrated the sweep of the 1976 Series in the Reds clubhouse. It would be the final Series victory for Bench, but Anderson would enjoy one more taste of champagne with the Detroit Tigers in 1984.

© Cincinnati Reds

1976

Johnny Bench clinched the sweep of the '76 Series with this three-run ninth-inning home run in Game Four. The home run put the exclamation point on the Big Red Machine's seven straight post-season victories, and sealed the Series' Most Valuable Player award for Bench.

Bench again pleaded for a multi-year contract, but Howsam would not budge, giving Bench an opportunity to joust with his boss at the annual Ballplayers of Yesterday banquet.

"I see that Sparky got one (a multi-year contract) and Bob Howsam got a new three-year contract. Then, when I go in there Mr. Howsam acts like he's never heard of such a thing."

Even Howsam laughed at the joke but, as usual, Rose got in the last jab, asking Bench when he was signing his contract.

Bench said he didn't know. "Why?"

"I want to get in there before you while he still has some money to give out," Rose replied.

Bench and Morgan signed first, leaving Rose at home while the team reported for spring training. At one point, with Howsam and Rose $5,000 apart, a Cincinnati fan suggested in a letter to *The Enquirer* that 5,000 people each contribute a $1 to end the holdout. Rose and the Reds eventually split the difference at $117,500, and Pete remained the highest-paid player on team.

Two question marks in spring training involved shortstop and right field. The inconsistent Concepcion had platooned with Chaney at the end of 1972, but Davey's steady performance in the World Series and a good spring earned him the starting job. This would be the last spring until the mid-1980s there was any question about Concepcion being the starting shortstop. Geronimo and Foster competed for the right-field job, but Foster had a miserable spring and the Reds shipped him back to Indianapolis. Foster, plagued by a lack of confidence, was hurt over the demotion, and felt his days with the Reds were numbered.

"The next time you see me," he said to reporters, "I'll probably be wearing a different big-league uniform."

But the Reds were not prepared to give up on Foster. The organization recognized he was a project when they acquired him, and his all-around skills, speed, solid defense and an explosive bat kept the club interested. He had shown improvement in instructional settings. Shore recalled previous discussions of trading Foster to Montreal, but before a deal was made, Shore went to the Dominican Republic where Foster was playing winter ball.

"Hub Kittle was manager of the club in the Dominican, and as soon as I saw him, he said, 'I've changed your man.' Hub got him to stand up straighter, so he could follow the ball better, especially the outside pitch. I saw him smack a few balls. So I called Bob and said, 'Don't do anything. Foster has changed his style.'"

"By gosh, we've got something," Howsam told Shore, and put off the deal.

The Reds were hoping that a year in Indianapolis with minor league manager Vern Rapp would provide the final polish Foster required.

The pitching plans suffered a setback when Gary Nolan's arm failed to respond to treatment, limiting Anderson to a rotation of Billingham, Grimsley, Nelson and Gullett, his opening day pitcher. The Reds were favored in the Western Division, but the Dodgers, Astros and Giants figured to contend. Through the first six weeks, the four teams remained bunched. But then the Reds stopped winning and the Dodgers took off. The Dodgers went 21-8 in June; the Reds slumped to 12-16.

Tolan, Menke and Geronimo were all hitting miserably, and the pitching staff was hurting. Anderson and Howsam wasted little time making major moves. Sparky benched the slumping Tolan and Geronimo, and on June 9, the Reds called up Danny Driessen from Indianapolis to play third base. Driessen, originally a first baseman, had been moved to third at Indianapolis and was hitting .409. Menke and his .200 average went to the bench.

In the middle of June, with Nelson out indefinitely and Gullett still weak from the hepatitis illness of the year before, Howsam pulled off a quick trade, sending promising rookie Gene Locklear to San Diego for pitcher Fred Norman.

The Norman trade proved to be one of Howsam's best, but at the time, it had people shaking their heads. Locklear did not figure in the Reds' future, but Norman was only 1-7 when the Reds acquired him. Even Perez kidded the team about the trade at a luncheon. After reading about the trade in the morning paper, Perez joked he had called to his wife, Pituka, "Give me some more coffee. I want to read this when I'm awake."

Looking past the record, Howsam and Anderson saw a veteran pitcher who was struggling with the last-place Padres. Earlier in the season, Norman had beaten the Reds, 2-1, for his only victory, a win that impressed Anderson. Unlike most of the Reds pitchers, Norman did not rely on his fastball, which was less than overpowering. He threw a change-of-pace screwball that made his mediocre fastball look like a "blazer," according to Rose.

One reason the Padres were willing to deal Norman was the Reds' willingness to part with cash. The Padres had other offers for Norman, but none involved money, and the struggling franchise needed a quick cash infusion. With the approval of new majority owner Louis "Gus" Nippert, who had purchased controlling interest in the club prior to the 1973 season, Howsam was able to throw in enough cash to land Norman. Several weeks later, McDonald's magnate Ray Kroc bought the Padres and San Diego was flush. But the Reds already had Norman. Locklear played five seasons as a part-time player, while Norman became a consistent performer in the Cincinnati rotation.

Despite the roster moves, the Reds continued to slump. When the division-leading Dodgers arrived on Saturday, June 30, for a four-game series at Riverfront, the Reds were in fourth place, 10 games back. Seldom was a mid-season series seen as crucial, but this one qualified. The Reds' hopes for 1973 hinged on beating the Dodgers.

The Reds took a 5-1 lead into the eighth inning of the first game, only to give up six runs and fall behind, 7-5. Morgan then hit a two-run home run in the bottom of the ninth to tie the game, but a Lee Lacy single in the 13th won it for L.A. Devastated, the Reds were 11 games back.

The next day, more than 46,000 fans filled Riverfront for a doubleheader. Don Sutton started the first game for the Dodgers and took a 3-1 lead into the ninth inning. With the crowd pulling for a rally, Perez led off with a double. But Sutton retired the next two hitters. Desperate for a home run, Anderson sent Bench up to hit for Concepcion. The last time Bench had faced Sutton, he had hit a game-tying home run off the Dodger veteran. This time, Sutton pitched Bench like he was Babe Ruth reincarnate, and eventually walked him intentionally. This move defied conventional baseball strategy by bringing the winning run to the plate, but the Dodgers knew Anderson had little firepower left.

Sparky was forced to call on Hal King, the third-string catcher and a lifetime .217 hitter who had opened the season at Indianapolis. However, King could also remember past success against Sutton. He had hit a grand slam home run off him when King was with Atlanta in 1971. That homer came on a screwball. Sutton either forgot or thought it was a fluke, for he threw King another "screwgie." Swinging so hard that he tore a spike in his shoe, King lined a shot that easily cleared the wall, and the Reds had a miracle 4-3 comeback win.

The Dodger lead, which could have been 12 games, was now 10. In the second game of the doubleheader, the Reds again came from behind. Rose tied the game at 2-2 in the seventh with a single and, in the tenth inning, with two out, Perez singled home Morgan with the winning run.

The next night, on national television, Perez again had the game-winner, a two-run homer in the bottom of the ninth to beat L.A., 4-2. The Reds and Dodgers had played four games, each decided in the last inning, the winner in each game coming from behind. But most importantly to the Reds, they had pulled to within nine games and reversed the momentum of the pennant race.

King's blow triggered a 60-26 run to the end of the season, a .697 winning percentage. At first, the Dodgers dismissed the Reds' chances. By mid-July, they still had an 8½-game lead. Then Concepcion broke his ankle sliding into third base just before the All-Star Game. But the always-brazen Rose had the perfect pennant-race jab.

"The Dodgers may be in first place, but they're chasing us," said Pete, with a sneer.

The Dodgers played only five games over .500 in the final three months and, with the pennant on the line in September, the Dodgers finished 12-14 while the Reds roared home at 19-8. "They taught us a lesson," admitted L.A. third baseman Ron Cey. "We concerned ourselves about them too much."

Ironically, the spectacular finish by the Reds occurred in the midst of the roughest personnel problem the club faced in the Big Red Machine years. Bobby Tolan, who had fought a season-long slump, had been benched on a few occasions by Anderson. The proud and somewhat high-strung Tolan had not responded well. Usually one to join in the needling and verbal jousting of the clubhouse, Tolan withdrew, keeping more and more to himself.

One day around the batting cage, the players were calling their hits as they took batting practice. Rose smashed several line drives, which he called singles and doubles. The other players, including Tolan, threw in their opinion of each "hit." Then Pete blooped a fly to short center field.

The Cincinnati Enquirer

Hal King, the Reds third-string catcher, earned his place in the lore of the Big Red Machine with this ninth-inning home run that beat Don Sutton and the Dodgers, and launched the Reds' 1973 pennant drive.

1973 Monthly Standings
National League West

April 30
	W	L	GB
San Francisco	18	6	—
Cincinnati	13	8	3½
Houston	14	10	4
Los Angeles	11	11	6
Atlanta	7	13	9
San Diego	7	15	10

May 31
	W	L	GB
San Francisco	32	20	—
Los Angeles	30	19	½
Houston	29	22	2½
Cincinnati	27	21	3
Atlanta	17	30	12½
San Diego	17	33	14

June 30
	W	L	GB
Los Angeles	51	27	—
San Francisco	45	34	6½
Houston	43	36	8½
Cincinnati	39	37	11
Atlanta	33	45	18
San Diego	25	52	25½

July 31
	W	L	GB
Los Angeles	66	40	—
Cincinnati	63	44	3½
San Francisco	60	46	6
Houston	55	53	12
Atlanta	48	62	20
San Diego	35	70	30½

August 31
	W	L	GB
Los Angeles	83	52	—
Cincinnati	80	55	3
San Francisco	73	59	8½
Houston	69	68	15
Atlanta	65	70	18
San Diego	48	85	34

Final Standings
	W	L	GB
Cincinnati	99	63	—
Los Angeles	95	66	3½
San Francisco	88	74	11
Houston	82	80	17
Atlanta	76	85	22½
San Diego	60	102	39

"Triple!" shouted Rose.

The other players immediately hooted. "Triple? Are you kidding?"

"That's Tolan playing center," snapped Rose, a sharp reminder of Tolan's error in the seventh game of the 1972 Series.

Tolan couldn't take what he dished out. He barely smiled as his teammates howled at Pete's verbal rip.

Late in August, Tolan began to grow a beard, and after he defied Anderson's request to shave it off, Sparky threatened to take away his uniform.

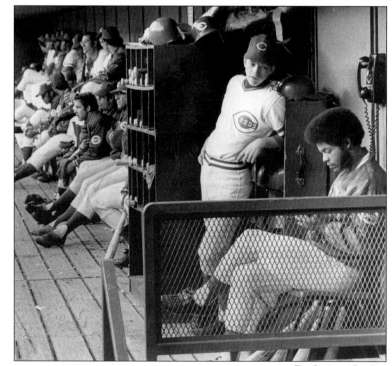

The Cincinnati Enquirer

Angry with club officials and estranged from his teammates, Bobby Tolan often sat alone in the final weeks of the 1973 season.

Tolan had also complained of a sore back, and the Reds scheduled a doctor's appointment for him on August 25. Tolan had missed an earlier appointment (miscommunication, said Tolan; insolence, claimed the Reds) and Chief Bender went to the clubhouse to remind Tolan of the appointment. Tolan and Bender began shouting, then pushing one another. Jack Billingham grabbed Bender, and other players held back Tolan before anyone was hurt.

The multiple acts of insubordination could not go unpunished by any regime, let alone one run as tightly as the Reds. Howsam fined Tolan, and Anderson banned him from the clubhouse. Tolan filed a grievance with the Players Association and was reinstated, and Anderson used him occasionally as a spot starter and a pinch-hitter in September. But Tolan, who had lost the support of his teammates, spent most of the month sitting alone on the bench.

"He's changed 100 percent," Rose said at the time. "He was hitting .200 and he had to face up to it. I guess bad years change a lot of people."

On the night the Reds clinched the pennant, Tolan left the clubhouse quickly, and a few days later he was again suspended. The Reds left him off the playoff roster, and in the offseason Howsam traded Tolan to San Diego.

T he Reds clinched the pennant on September 24, and then watched the Mets hold off the Cardinals and the Pirates to capture the Eastern Division. The Mets had finished with a mediocre 82-79 record, which would have put them 16 games behind the Reds in the West. Never had a team with such a poor record competed in post-season play. A position-by-position comparison clearly favored Cincinnati.

1973 MONTHLY STANDINGS
NATIONAL LEAGUE EAST

April 30

	W	L	GB
New York	12	8	—
Chicago	11	8	½
Pittsburgh	8	6	1
Philadelphia	9	9	2
Montreal	7	11	4
St. Louis	3	15	8

May 31

	W	L	GB
Chicago	29	19	—
Pittsburgh	21	20	4½
New York	21	22	5½
Montreal	19	22	6½
St. Louis	19	25	8
Philadelphia	19	27	9

June 30

	W	L	GB
Chicago	46	32	—
St. Louis	37	37	7
Montreal	34	37	8½
Pittsburgh	34	38	9
Philadelphia	35	40	9½
New York	32	39	10½

July 31

	W	L	GB
St. Louis	56	48	—
Chicago	55	51	2
Pittsburgh	51	51	4
Montreal	50	53	5½
Philadelphia	49	57	8
New York	44	57	10½

August 31

	W	L	GB
St. Louis	68	66	—
Pittsburgh	65	65	1
Chicago	64	69	3½
Montreal	63	70	4½
New York	62	71	5½
Philadelphia	62	72	6

Final Standings

	W	L	GB
New York	82	79	—
St. Louis	81	81	1½
Pittsburgh	80	82	2½
Montreal	79	83	3½
Chicago	77	84	5
Philadelphia	71	91	11½

Several Reds had excellent seasons, including Rose, Bench, Morgan and Perez. Rose, who would win the MVP award, hit .338, won his third batting title and set a club record with 230 hits. Bench hit 25 home runs and finished third in the league in RBIs with 104. Perez had one of his better seasons, hitting .314 with 27 home runs and 101 RBIs. Morgan hit .290, with 26 home runs, 67 stolen bases and 116 runs scored. All four finished in the top ten in the MVP voting.

The Reds also led the league in fielding and stolen bases, and their team ERA of 3.43 compared favorably to the 3.27 ERA of the pitching-rich Mets. Billingham (19 wins) and Gullett (18 wins) had outstanding seasons and matched up well with the Mets' Seaver and Koosman. Seaver had posted one of his most dominating seasons with 19 wins, a 2.08 ERA and a Cy Young award. But only one other Mets pitcher, George Stone, had a winning record.

The Reds had beaten the Mets eight of twelve games in the regular season, and on the eve of the playoffs, reporters were wondering how the Reds could avoid looking past the Mets to the World Series. But the prescient Anderson was uneasy as the playoffs began.

"I think people are being misled by the Mets," Sparky warned. "If that club had stayed healthy all year it would have won at least

A happy group of Reds greeted Johnny Bench after his winning home run off Tom Seaver in the ninth inning of the first game of the 1973 playoffs. Leading the welcoming delegation were Jack Billingham (with towel), Joe Morgan and Pete Rose (partially hidden behind umpire's arm).

The Cincinnati Enquirer

95 games. And the Mets we're facin' are healthy." Anderson believed his Reds were the better team, but in a short series, the Mets pitching could be the equalizer.

The playoffs opened on Saturday afternoon, October 6, at Riverfront Stadium. Seaver opposed Billingham, and in the shadows, both were tough to hit. Seaver put his team ahead, doubling in a run in the second. Going into the bottom of the eighth, the Mets clung to the 1-0 lead. Then Rose, who had gone 0-for-3, caught an inside fast ball and drove it over the wall to tie the game. Seaver came back to pitch the ninth and Johnny Bench once again provided the playoff heroics. Only 360 days after he had hit a game-tying home run against Pittsburgh in the 1972 playoffs, he hit a game-winning homer off Seaver.

Winning the first game at home against Seaver appeared to give the Reds a huge advantage. But Jon Matlack threw a two-hitter on Sunday to even the playoffs. Gullett started for the Reds and gave up only one run before Anderson pulled him for a pinch-hitter in the sixth. The 1-0 score held until the top of the ninth when the Mets battered Tom Hall and Pedro Borbon for four runs, giving New York a 5-0 victory. Suddenly, the advantage turned to the Mets. The Reds would have to win two of three in New York.

The brash Reds, who had been held to eight hits and two runs in the first two games, were annoyed at their failure to produce more offense in the playoffs. The comments of Mets shortstop Bud Harrelson only increased their irritation. The light-hitting Harrelson was quoted as saying the Reds were just "swinging from their heels."

"What the hell is he? A hitting instructor?" yelled an indignant Morgan.

Morgan and Rose, who yielded to no one in the trash-talking, intimidation phase of the game, plotted their reply. Whoever got to second base first in Game Three would let Harrelson know he had stepped over the line.

The final games of the playoff would be played in Shea Stadium, where the Mets' enthusiastic and often obnoxious fans created a hostile situation for visiting teams. The Mets' great comeback in 1973—they were in last place in early August, and won 18 of their final 24 games—had inspired the "You Gotta Believe" campaign that had the stadium draped in banners, and the fans in a frenzy.

Game Three matched Ross Grimsley against Jerry Koosman. Grimsley failed to make it past the second inning; the Mets scored seven runs in the first three innings, with Rusty Staub driving in four on two home runs.

The lethargic Reds trailed, 9-2, in the top of the fifth when Rose singled. Morgan hit a groundball to first baseman John Milner. Milner threw to Harrelson covering second for the force on Rose, and then Harrelson returned the throw to first to double up Morgan. Rose, trying to break up the double play and send Harrelson a message, slid aggressively into the shortstop. Harrelson jumped up and yelled an obscenity. Rose shoved Harrelson and the two ended up in a brawl at second base.

Players from both dugouts rushed the field. Mighty Ted Kluszewski, the Reds' 250-pound coach, played peacemaker, grabbing players from both teams and shoving them away from the pile. "Klu" also wrapped Rose in a bear hug to keep him out of the action. Just as things were calming down, the Reds' Pedro Borbon led a cavalry charge from the bullpen. Borbon was tardy because he couldn't open the bullpen gate.

"Pedro was so mad he couldn't get the gate open," said Clay Carroll. "He tugged at it twice. Then he just tore the thing off the hinges. Honest, he ripped it right off."

The crazed Borbon took on Mets pitcher Buzz Capra before teammates led him away from the melee. Walking off the field, someone mentioned to Borbon he had accidentally picked up a Mets hat. Borbon yanked it off his head and ripped it apart with his teeth.

Pete Rose (left) and Buddy Harrelson grappled in the Shea Stadium infield and launched a dugout-clearing brawl.

The fans in the outfield stands retaliated when Rose took the field in the bottom of the fifth. They threw beer cans, batteries and bottles; the bullpen players were doused. Finally, Anderson waved Rose into the dugout, and pulled all the players off the field.

"Pete Rose has contributed too much to baseball to be allowed to die in left field at Shea Stadium," Anderson told an umpire.

"They were all over me," Rose recalled. "Whiskey bottles, everything. The umps told Sparky to move me from left to center, but he wouldn't do it. Why should he and mess up two positions?"

National League president Chub Feeney conferred with the umpires and discussed the possibility of a forfeit. Yogi Berra, Willie Mays, Tom Seaver, Cleon Jones and Rusty Staub walked to the left field wall to plead with the fans. Staub carried a bat in case the New York fans turned on the goodwill mission. The peacekeepers were successful; the rest of the game proceeded without serious incident or a Reds rally. The Mets led, two games to one.

Fearing a resumption of crowd hostilities, baseball officials approached Rose and Harrelson to see if they would agree to a handshake at the start of Game Four. Although Harrelson and Rose agreed their dispute was not personal, Rose declined. He admitted to a hard slide, but to Rose it was all in the game. Why apologize?

"I honestly was trying to knock him into left field. But it was clean," insisted Rose. "It was just like 1970. All I did in the All-Star Game that year was try to win the game when I ran into Ray Fosse and I've been criticized for it for three years. I'm no little girl out there."

As it turned out, Rose had a far better response than a staged handshake. With the game tied, 1-1, in the 12th inning, Rose—who had been verbally pummeled and taunted throughout the game—launched a high fastball from Harry Parker over the right-field wall. The crowd, for the first time all day, was silenced. Rose ran the bases quickly, and as he neared third, raised a triumphant fist in the air. It would become one of the defining images of the Big Red Machine—Rose circling the bases with the go-ahead run, a dramatic payback to the New York fans in the heart of the hostile arena.

A storybook ending would have had Rose and the Reds winning the fifth game, but the Mets pitching and the continued abuse from the New York fans proved too much for Cincinnati. Seaver started against Billingham. The score was tied, 2-2, going to the bottom of the fifth when the Mets rallied for four runs, aided by a mental misplay by rookie third baseman Dan Driessen.

Wayne Garrett opened the inning with a double. Felix Millan, attempting to sacrifice Garrett to third, bunted towards the mound. Billingham picked up the bunt and threw to Driessen. The throw had the runner beat, but Driessen tagged the bag with his foot rather than tagging Garrett. Driessen mistakenly thought there was a runner on first and the force was in effect. Instead of one out and a runner on first, the Mets had two on and nobody out. A double scored one run, then a walk loaded the bases. Willie Mays hit a high chopper that Clay Carroll fielded, but the ball hung up in his glove, and his throw home was too late for the force. "You Gotta Believe" it was the Mets' year. New York built a 7-2 lead and Seaver kept the Reds handcuffed.

The crowd grew increasingly vocal as the game progressed. As the ninth inning began, the fans began leaving their seats, jamming the aisles, and crowding along the railing next to the field. The Reds rallied, putting two men on with one out, when a retaining wall that ran parallel to the first-base line collapsed. Several hundred fans spilled onto the field, and ushers and police rushed into the area. Behind the Reds dugout, the official Cincinnati delegation, easily identifiable in red blazers, was an obvious target for what had now become a mob. Debris rained on the group; some of the wives had their hair pulled. With the situation deteriorating, Howsam ordered his staff to evacuate the box. As the Reds brass left their seats, Mrs. George Ballou, the wife of the team physician, was pushed down and stepped on. The game had to be delayed so the entourage could walk onto the field and go through the dugout to the safety of the dressing rooms under the stadium.

Howsam later said he should have instructed Anderson to call the Reds off the field. Stadium security had lost control of the

© Cincinnati Reds
A disheveled and still-agitated Pedro Borbon was led off the Shea Stadium infield by teammates after the Rose-Harrelson donnybrook.

A tidal wave of Mets fans roared past helpless security officers and stormed the Shea Stadium field after the final out of the 1973 playoffs. Pete Rose, who was on first base, raced across the diamond (near the pitcher's mound) toward the Reds dugout. Danny Driessen (on the first-base line) also sprinted to safety. Several of their teammates stood on the top step of the dugout, bats in hand to rescue the players and protect themselves from the mob. Bob Howsam and the Reds delegation had been evacuated moments earlier from their seats behind the dugout.

crowd and the Reds on base appeared far more concerned with their safety than with scoring a run.

"I should have asked for a forfeit," Howsam said. "But I was so concerned about our people getting out. It definitely affected our players. They were trying to help us and they were worried."

With two out, Rose walked and stood on first base, just feet away from the howling mob, which continued to inch closer to the field. Bench urged Anderson to put in a pinch-runner for Pete. Sparky considered it, but he was still hoping for a miracle rally and didn't want to take Pete out of the game. But sensing a need for a rescue mission after the final out, Bench and several others grabbed bats and stood on the dugout steps.

Driessen grounded weakly back to the mound. Rose took a couple of steps toward second and then raced for the Reds dugout even before the final out was recorded. The two bulled their way through the fans on the field and made it safely to the dugout and dressing rooms. It is not unusual for fans to rush the field in celebration, but this crowd was bent on destruction. The mob tore up chunks of turf, leveled the pitcher's mound, demolished sections of the outfield fence and destroyed the field-level box seats.

In the aftermath of the loss, the Reds expressed both shock and anger. They had been upset by a team they felt they should have beaten, although they conceded the Mets pitching had been superior in the short series. But the hostility of the crowd had so muddled the outcome that the organization could not restrain its anger.

"This is more disappointing than last year's World Series," said Rose. "I wanted to beat all 55,000 of them. These fans don't deserve to have a champion."

"New York ought to be the next atomic bomb testing ground," groused Anderson.

Later, Anderson put the playoffs in perspective. "The Mets could no more play with us than the man in the moon. But anytime you can run those kind of pitchers out there, your chances of beating them three out of five are pretty tough. They just put a whipping on us."

A few weeks later, Rose won the MVP award in a close race with Willie Stargell. Although proud of the achievement, the hollowness of the playoff loss still echoed in his words.

"I've won three batting titles, two pennants, Gold Gloves and now this, the MVP award," said Pete. "But I haven't really won anything. I've never played on a championship team and that is my goal. I wanted to get in the World Series so bad that I almost started World War III."

When spring training opened in March 1974, some familiar faces were missing from the Cincinnati camp. Menke had been traded to Houston for pitching prospect Pat Darcy. Howsam had traded Tolan (and relief pitcher Dave Tomlin) to San Diego for pitcher Clay Kirby. Kirby had impressed the Reds with strong pitching performances against Cincinnati, winning 11 of 18 decisions, and he was expected to join the starting rotation.

The trades of Menke and Tolan were anticipated, but in a surprise move, the Reds sent 24-year-old left-hander Ross Grimsley to Baltimore for outfielder Merv Rettenmund. Since moving into the starting rotation in 1971, Grimsley had compiled a 37-25 record with the Reds and had impressed everybody with his two-hit complete-game performance in Game Four of the 1972 playoffs. On a club where starting pitching appeared to be in short supply, the exchange of a young arm for another outfielder seemed

1973 SCRAPBOOK

The Opposition

Western Division

Against	Won	Lost
Atlanta	13	5
Houston	11	7
Los Angeles	11	7
San Diego	13	5
San Fran.	10	8

Eastern Division

Against	Won	Lost
Chicago	4	8
Montreal	8	4
New York	8	4
Philadelphia	8	4
Pittsburgh	7	5
St. Louis	6	6

The pitcher the Reds didn't want to face – **Jerry Reuss** of Houston was 3-1 against the Reds, his only defeat a 1-0 loss to Don Gullett.

The pitcher they loved to see – **Claude Osteen** of Houston was 0-3 against the Reds.

The batter who loved the Reds – **Cesar Cedeno** of Houston hit .415 (27-for-65) with 4 HRs and 14 RBIs.

The batter who should have stayed home – **Al Oliver** of Pittsburgh hit .152 (7-for-46) with 1 HR and 3 RBIs.

Club Leaders

Batting Average	Pete Rose	.338 •
Home runs	Tony Perez	27
RBIs	Johnny Bench	104
Stolen bases	Joe Morgan	67
Runs	Joe Morgan	116
ERA	Jack Billingham	3.04
Wins	Jack Billingham	19
Saves	C. Carroll; P. Borbon	14
Games	Pedro Borbon	80

• League leader

Awards

Most Valuable Player	Pete Rose
Gold Glove	Johnny Bench, Joe Morgan
Cincinnati Reds MVP •	Pete Rose
Outstanding Reds Pitcher •	Jack Billingham
Reds Newcomer of the Year •	Dan Driessen

• Awarded by Cincinnati Chapter of Baseball Writers Association

Trades

March 27 **Andy Kosco** and **Phil Gagliano** acquired from Boston for **Mel Behney**

June 12 **Fred Norman** acquired from San Diego for **Gene Locklear, Mike Johnson** and cash

July 27 **Ed Crosby** and **Gene Dusan** acquired from St. Louis for **Ed Sprague** and **Roe Skidmore**

Oct. 2 **Steve Kealey** acquired from Chicago White Sox for **Jim McGlothlin**

Nov. 9 **Clay Kirby** acquired from San Diego for **Bobby Tolan** and **Dave Tomlin**

Dec. 4 **Merv Rettenmund, Junior Kennedy** and **Bill Wood** acquired from Baltimore for **Ross Grimsley**

Dec. 10 **Roger Freed** acquired from Cleveland for **Steve Blateric**

The Draft

Cincinnati drafted 43 players; two played in the major leagues:

Gary Lucas •	Riverside, CA (CC)	P
Jay Howell •	Boulder, CO	P

• Drafted by Reds, but signed with another club

questionable.

But for reasons of pitching style and hair style, Anderson had requested the trade. Sparky felt that Grimsley had a tendency to throw high in the strike zone, a habit that resulted in home run balls. But more telling was the often defiant attitude Grimsley displayed toward club rules. His roommate, Jack Billingham, recalled that Grimsley was a "free spirit with a nightclub reputation, which wasn't true."

Grimsley, who once professed a belief in witchcraft, received several reprimands from Anderson and suffered one particularly humiliating experience. Grimsley had naturally curly hair, and sometimes styled it into a Caucasian "Afro." Billingham recalled that Grimsley showed up in the clubhouse one day flaunting his bushy new Afro that stretched the club rules. Sparky had often threatened that Pedro Borbon would give the haircuts if players defied his orders. Upon seeing Grimsley, Anderson summoned Borbon. A few minutes later, Borbon had ruined the expensive cut; Grimsley was so mad at Anderson he had tears in his eyes.

When Anderson suggested the club move Grimsley after the '73 season, no one spoke in Grimsley's defense. There was a tendency to defer to Anderson's judgment when it involved players on the club.

"Bob probably listened to me more when it was a player on our staff," Anderson recalled. "But nobody jumped up in Grimsley's favor. He wouldn't have gone if, say, Ray (Shore) jumped up."

Shore agreed. "I liked Ross, but I didn't try to protect him. One thing I told Sparky was I will argue abilities with you, but I'm not going to argue personalities. You live with them. If you say this guy disrupts my clubhouse, he's uncoachable or whatever, I can't argue that point."

In exchange for Grimsley, Howsam acquired the right-handed Rettenmund who the Reds thought might contend for an outfield position. The trade proved to be one of Howsam's worst deals. Rettenmund became a pinch-hitter and a fifth outfielder, while Grimsley pitched well for the Orioles and later won 20 games for the Expos.

The Grimsley affair became one more very public reminder of the no-nonsense organization run by Howsam, Wagner and Anderson. Sometimes the club appeared to confuse demeaning rules with discipline. Orioles manager Earl Weaver thought Grimsley looked just fine and wondered if the Reds were turning away many fans because their ballplayers didn't "keep up with the styles."

Marvin Miller, head of the Players Association, thought Howsam was turning off a lot of young people. But suggesting that Bob Howsam did not know his market was like wondering if Miller had heard of the reserve clause. Howsam noted simply that since 1970, the short-haired Reds ranked third in attendance in all of baseball behind the Dodgers and the Mets.

Most of the Reds signed quickly in 1974, suggesting some degree of harmony between the players and the front office. Bench, who failed to match his 1972 statistics, disliked the haggling over salary, and took the risk of signing a blank contract. The Reds filled it in for an amount estimated between $125,000 and $150,000. Morgan received a raise to $132,500. Even Rose, who never shrank from a salary confrontation, signed quickly for $155,000—a $36,000 raise based on his MVP performance. Rose said he and Howsam had "become friendly" in 1973 due to frequent meetings. When Howsam accompanied the team on the road, he would invite Rose to his room for a breakfast conversation.

"We'd talk about little things on the team, things Sparky couldn't do, but that I could do as team captain. I think he looks at me as the team leader now. I guess that whiskey bottle did it," laughed Rose, referring to his battles at Shea Stadium.

But beneath the surface harmony, new circumstances in player-owner relations were beginning to affect negotiations. Based on the 1973 basic agreement between players and owners that Players Association president Marvin Miller had pushed through, the players in 1974 had the right to petition for arbitration if they could not reach agreement with the club. The player could submit a figure, the club could submit its figure, and after arguments for both sides were heard, an arbitrator would pick one figure or the other. No negotiated amounts were permitted at that point. For the first time in the 20th century, players had other options in salary negotiations besides the holdout, which in most cases was a weak and ineffective tactic.

While the players had fought hard for arbitration, the owners, led in part by Howsam and Reds president Frank Dale, had resisted any lessening of a club's power to set salaries. Just as Howsam had tried to balance his club on the field, he carefully balanced the players' salaries so that budgets could be met and players' expectations kept in line. If one of his star players—Rose, Bench, Morgan or Perez—won an arbitrated amount far above the others, Howsam's carefully crafted salary structure could collapse. Not only would the other stars demand similar increases, the second- and third-tier players would push to have their salaries remain relative to the superstars. The club would be faced with trading players or raising ticket prices, and Howsam's ability to control the fortunes of his club would be limited.

Tony Perez, who was represented by Jerry Kapstein, one of the most successful of the first generation of baseball agents, threatened to go to arbitration. But the Reds upped their offer to a reported $100,000—approximately a 20 percent increase in Perez's 1973 salary—and Tony signed. Perez, like many of the other players, deserved a raise, but it was also clear that Howsam did not want to risk arbitration.

The use of an agent in negotiations was also a new wrinkle that the Reds opposed, but could no longer prevent. Don Gullett, who loathed the salary haggling and didn't feel particularly adept at it, also hired Kapstein. In the first meeting with Chief Bender, Kapstein accompanied Gullett and began to make his case for a raise for the young pitcher. Howsam joined the meeting, but after a few minutes, walked out.

"Jerry starts talking about the great things Gullett was doing," remembered Bender. "Bob says after a while, 'We know all those things. I've heard enough. I'm leaving.' So he walked out. He was really perturbed."

Howsam could not bring himself to listen to an attorney with no baseball background cite a bunch of statistics and tell him how much his ballplayers were worth.

But eventually, Gullett signed for an increase and Bender sent Kapstein a letter acknowledging the deal. Bender also included some flattering remarks about Kapstein. When Wagner saw a copy of the letter, he blew up.

"I was stunned," Wagner recalled. "I told Howsam it would turn up in the first arbitration we had. And it did." Wagner was so upset he drove to the central post office in Cincinnati to retrieve the letter, but the post office could not help him recover it.

The next season, Howsam asked Wagner to handle more of the

The Reds on the Radio

The changes in the Reds lineup for 1974 included a new voice in the broadcast booth: Marty Brennaman.

Al Michaels, the Reds announcer since 1971, asked for a huge raise after the 1973 season and the Reds let him go.

"There was a sense that Al was a rising star," recalled marketing vice-president Roger Ruhl. "Here, he wasn't going to do TV, and he threw out a number so far beyond logic, it was just a matter of wishing him well."

Michaels left for San Francisco, and the Reds turned to Brennaman. Brennaman was broadcasting the Triple A Tidewater Tides and the Virginia Squires of the American Basketball Association. The Reds reviewed his audition tape and those of 15 others.

Dick Wagner listened to several of the announcers call play-by-play and eventually picked Brennaman.

"It wasn't very scientific," Wagner admitted. "But if a voice grated on me, I figured it would for the fans." Having passed the Wagner test, Brennaman came in for an interview.

"I was wined and dined by Wagner and Jim Winters (director of broadcasting)," Brennaman remembered. "But nothing happened until I had an audience with Mr. Howsam. No move was made until I met him and got his stamp of approval. And from that day forward, I never referred to him as anything but 'Mr. Howsam.' That's the ultimate compliment I could have paid him. I never called him 'Bob.'"

Following the popular and polished Michaels was no easy assignment. Brennaman hoped to put Michaels' memory behind him as he began the 1974 spring training broadcasts. But in his second game, the ghost of Michaels returned. At the Reds training camp, Al Lopez Field, Brennaman began his broadcast, "Good afternoon everybody, from Al *Michaels* Field in Tampa, this is Reds baseball!"

Brennaman quickly recovered and he and Joe Nuxhall became the longest-running broadcast team in Reds history, despite several run-ins with Wagner. Brennaman could be critical of players and Wagner didn't approve. But Brennaman recalled some excellent advice Wagner gave him.

"After a couple of years, I got close to Morgan and Rose socially and we had a hell of a time. Wagner found out and said you can't afford to socialize with these guys. I didn't want to hear it, but he was right. A broadcaster can't allow himself that luxury."

Broadcaster Marty Brennaman (center) flew back from the 1975 World Series with Karolyn and Pete Rose. Brennaman came to the Reds in 1974, replacing Al Michaels.

salary negotiations, especially those with Rose, Bench, Morgan and Perez. Bender had a tendency to involve Howsam in the negotiations as they proceeded, but Howsam was fed up with the whole process. He turned to Wagner, who had by far the tougher demeanor.

As the boss instructed, Wagner rarely brought Howsam into the negotiations.

"I would never pass the buck and say I had to take it to Bob," Wagner remembered. "I'd say let me think about it, give me a day. When I did the contracts, I determined the range and Bob would approve it."

Wagner had been involved in the business side of the operation, but he began to take a more active role in player relations, and eventually it would be Wagner and not Bender who would assume the general manager's position when Howsam stepped down in 1978.

With salary sessions out of the way, the news out of Tampa in 1974 was upbeat. Anderson called this version of the Reds "our best club," and much of his optimism revolved around several young players who had developed in the Cincinnati farm system. George Foster appeared to have turned around his career with a successful 1973 season in Indianapolis. Danny Driessen and Ken Griffey had moved quickly through the minors, and several other rookies appeared ready to break through.

For Howsam, the development of these young players was what he expected of his scouts and farm system. The 1973 Opening Day roster had included only three prominent players (Gullett, Grimsley and Concepcion) who had been signed and developed within the Reds organization since 1967 when Howsam had taken control of the club. But from 1973 to 1976, the Reds would add Driessen, Griffey, Will McEnaney, Rawly Eastwick, Doug Flynn, Santo Alcala, Manny Sarmiento and Pat Zachry.

All were signed in the late 1960s and early 1970s, and all would play critical roles in the winning of the two World Championships. This rich harvest of young players was even more remarkable because only Eastwick was a high draft choice. The others were either chosen low in the draft (meaning they were passed over several times by other clubs) or were signed as free agents (meaning they were not drafted at all). That they became members of the Reds was a tribute to the attention Howsam paid to scouting.

In the mid-1970s, other clubs began noticing that the Cincinnati scouts were driving bigger cars. Branch Rickey III, grandson of the legend and a scout for the Pirates in the '70s, recalled that a Reds scout drove up in a mid-size car, a step up from the smaller vehicle he had seen the man driving.

"Mr. Howsam wants us in heavier cars, doesn't want us to get hurt," said the scout.

Rickey couldn't believe it. Most organizations were telling their scouts to keep their mileage down, and here was Howsam putting his people in bigger cars. The change was slight, but it spoke volumes about Bob Howsam's respect for his scouts.

Within the first year of his arrival in Cincinnati, Howsam, who had been tutored in the ways of scouting by the original Mr. Rickey, brought two Rickey men, brothers Joe and Rex Bowen, to Cincinnati to run his scouting department. Howsam had known the Bowens since his days in Denver when the Bowens worked for Rickey's Pirates.

"Anybody highly regarded by Rickey was highly regarded by

Howsam," recalled Rex Bowen. "When Joe and I became disenchanted in Pittsburgh, I gave Howsam a call and said 'Are you interested in me?' We never even discussed pay or the exact position. I just flat out moved to Cincinnati."

Joe Bowen became scouting director for the Reds; Rex carried out special assignments as Howsam's personal scouting assistant.

The Reds employed 24 full-time scouts in 1967 when the Bowens arrived. Within three years, 15 of those holdovers from the DeWitt era were gone, and Joe Bowen increased the full-time staff to 36, bringing in 27 new people. In addition, the Reds employed more than 300 part-time "bird dog" or "recommending" scouts to identify prospects for the full-time staff to evaluate.

The challenge facing Bowen's staff was no different than the one he faced in Pittsburgh—or the one every baseball organization faces each year: how to cull from the hundreds of thousands of teenage boys playing baseball, the 50 or so players that have the best chance to make the major leagues.

Bowen's top 16 scouts, or area supervisors, were responsible for scouting and rating all of the best prospects in specific geographic areas. The size of these areas depended on population, and ranged from the Los Angeles-San Diego corridor (where the Reds assigned two of their area supervisors) to the Rocky Mountain region where one scout covered six states. Most of the players these scouts checked were first seen by one of the club's 300 recommending scouts.

Over the course of a prospect's junior and senior year in high school, he was seen several times by Cincinnati scouts. Under Howsam and Bowen, the Reds did not scout college players. At that time, the quality of most college programs did not meet the rigorous standards of the Reds. The Reds felt they would have to put a college graduate in their minor leagues for at least two years, and much of that time would be spent unlearning what they had been taught in college.

"We liked to draft young kids right out of high school," remembered Shore. "We could develop them in our system the way we wanted to develop them. The only bad part was that some kids at 18 are as good as they are ever going to be. But our kids knew how to play when they got to the big leagues."

Nearly all of the players drafted in the Howsam regime who made a major contribution to the Big Red Machine arrived in the majors by the age of 24 (Gullett, 19; Sarmiento, 20; Concepcion, Grimsley, Wayne Simpson and Driessen, 21; McEnaney, 22; Griffey, 23; Eastwick, Zachry and Flynn, 24).

Scouts filled out forms on each player, and ranked them according to major league potential. As the organization grew more serious about the player, he was investigated by one of the area scouts. Finally, each area scout submitted a list of top prospects from their region to Joe Bowen.

But the top prospect in one area might rate far down the list nationally. The job of "cross-checking" was accomplished in part by Howsam's theory of moving his scouts with the weather.

"In cold weather, we brought all of our scouts to the south and west, Florida, Texas, California," Howsam recalled. "This let our northern guys see the talent there. A lot of times scouts don't see all of the players. They think they've got the best player in the country, and then they see others and realize their kid isn't the best. Each scout sent Joe Bowen an evaluation of the best players he saw all year from anywhere, not just his area. Sometimes scouts would rate players high from other areas; a scout from Connecticut might say the best player he saw was in Georgia."

Each top prospect was also graded by the two Bowens and perhaps Chief Bender and Ray Shore. "The top boys will have been seen by at least six scouts," said Joe Bowen. Based on those final rankings, a committee of Howsam, the Bowens, Bender, Shore and assistant farm director Sal Artiaga set the final draft rankings.

The draft was organized in the reverse order of the previous year's standings of the major league teams, and many of the scout's top choices were already selected by the time the Reds drafted. From the initial pool of talent the Reds identified, only 60 or so would actually be drafted and signed by the club, and of that 60, only a handful would ever wear a major league uniform.

Those odds led Branch Rickey to propose his "quality out of quantity" prescription. Howsam and the Bowens agreed. The Reds evaluated more players than any other organization, and were one of only four teams to conduct regular tryout camps for boys whom the scouts may have overlooked. Tryout camps were a Rickey standard, in part because of another of his dictums: a scout may misjudge a young player, but he should never miss him altogether. The Reds always followed up on tips, no matter how obscure, and the tale of finding young Danny Driessen became one of the club's great success stories.

Driessen grew up on Hilton Head Island off the South Carolina coast. His high school had no baseball team, and he and his older brother, William, played in an amateur league for a coach in Hardeeville, about 30 miles north of Hilton Head. Each Sunday, coach Harold Young drove the 30 miles to pick up the Driessens and after the game he would drive them back home. Young thought both the Driessens, especially William, had big-league potential. But the amateur league was so out-of-the-way, it went unnoticed by area scouts.

Young took the initiative. He wrote a letter to all the major league clubs lauding his young players. "Bill hits the ball regularly well beyond 425 feet," wrote Young. He noted that 17-year-old Dan played both catcher and outfield, but he seemed to be better behind the plate. The Reds were the first club to contact the Driessens and arrange a tryout.

Eventually the pair was seen by Bill Jamieson, the Reds primary scout in the Carolinas. His report recommended against signing William Driessen, but he liked Dan. "A lot of speed and a good stroke," he wrote. The Reds signed him.

"For a yearbook and an airplane ticket to Tampa," recalled Driessen.

In the spring of 1970, 18-year-old Driessen was assigned to the class A club in Tampa, where coach Ron Plaza quickly switched Driessen to first base. After struggling his first season with only three extra-base hits and a .223 average, Driessen hit over .300 his next two seasons. In the middle of the 1973 season, as he was turning 22, Driessen made his big-league debut.

The Reds also discovered Will McEnaney through a tip from a high school coach. McEnaney, something of a free-spirit in high school, had starred for his Springfield, Ohio, school team as a junior, but his coach threw him off the team his senior year for drinking. McEnaney played in some independent leagues and a few scouts saw him, but the Reds had missed him. A coaching friend of McEnaney called the Reds and recommended they look at him. Cliff Alexander, the Reds' top Ohio scout who had signed Don Gullett, went to see McEnaney pitch. That night he pitched five innings and struck out 13 against a semipro team.

"You throw hard," Alexander said. "Why didn't you play in high school?"

McEnaney told him he been kicked off his team.

"Gosh, I remember when I was 17," sympathized Alexander. "Do you think you can handle it now on your own?"

"Yeah, I want to play ball," said McEnaney firmly.

Two weeks later in front of Alexander, McEnaney threw a no-hitter. The Reds drafted him in the eighth round.

The day of the draft was the day of McEnaney's high school graduation. "I was out all night with my buddies," he remembered. "The next morning I came home and the morning paper had already come, and my mom is saying you got drafted. Hell, I thought she meant the Army."

He signed for a $10,000 bonus and $500 a month. He worked his way up to the big-league club late in the 1974 season, and eventually gained immortality for recording the final outs of the 1975 and 1976 World Series.

Ken Griffey was also making his way to the major league level in 1974. He, too, was a testament to the tenacity of the Cincinnati scouting system—and the overall emphasis on drafting speed. Griffey was a high school sports star in Donora, Pennsylvania. He excelled in football and basketball, and also played baseball. As a youngster, he had played neighborhood pick-up games on the vacant lots around his housing project. He and his buddies used bricks for bases and cardboard for home plate. Griffey had few polished skills as a baseball player, and many scouts missed him. He didn't even make the local American Legion team (he was beaten out by the coach's son). And his high school played a very short season.

"The most games we got in during one season was six," Griffey recalled, "and we had to play a doubleheader to do that."

But Reds scout Elmer Gray saw Griffey in one of his few high school games and put the stopwatch on him. Griffey was not impressive as a hitter, but he was as fast an anybody Gray had timed. Griffey also showed some arm strength, and Gray recommended him as a low-round draft choice.

About 500 players were chosen in the 1969 draft before Ken Griffey's name was called by the Reds in the 29th round. The Reds offered him $500 a month ("All the money in the world," thought Griffey at the time), and sent him to their rookie league camp in Bradenton, Florida, where George Scherger was the manager.

"I hate to use the word, but when I had him he was 'crude,' especially at bat," remembered Scherger.

But Griffey made steady improvement and starred in spring training in 1973.

"Who in the world is that?" asked an admiring Tommy Helms after an exhibition game with Houston. Griffey had four hits, drove in two runs and ran to first base as fast as any player in the league. He made his major league debut at the end of the 1973 season and appeared ready to challenge for a starting position as the 1974 season opened.

Rex Bowen recalled that the Reds scouts also concentrated on players who showed signs of being able to hit with power to the opposite field, and had balance and body control in the field.

"One drill we had was to hit a slow chopper so they would have to charge the ball, field with two hands, and throw on the run," Bowen recalled. "But speed—it was absolutely the most important of all. If a guy was short on running, we'd look at him possibly as a catcher, first baseman or maybe third baseman. Otherwise, you've got to be able to run—for a championship team, that is."

The Reds' focus on speed cost them a few players. Ray Shore recalled that Mike Schmidt and Buddy Bell, both from the

Cincinnati-Dayton area, couldn't pass the club's speed tests.

"Basically we were a speed club," said Shore. "Right away our scouts would put the clock on them in the tryout camps, and if they couldn't run, boom, they were gone."

Schmidt played a lot of shortstop in high school, but the Reds weren't impressed.

"We didn't think he could run fast enough for a shortstop," explained Shore. "And we passed on Buddy Bell because we didn't think he ran fast enough."

The Reds also passed on prospects that appeared to fall in the "troublemaker" category. Howsam saw no point in bringing players of questionable character into the organization, and he wasted no time in weeding them out if they developed problems later on.

"Many years ago, I came to the conclusion that complainers and malcontents have a debilitating effect on your team," said Howsam. The search for "Reds-type players" of high character was never-ending.

"There are three kinds of ball players," Howsam told his scouts and his minor league managers. "Good players, major league players, and Cincinnati players. Cincinnati players must have something special. I want players who feel when they put on that uniform that says 'Cincinnati' across the front, they feel they are with the best."

One prospect who fell into the "troublemaker" category and was shunned by the Reds, was Cincinnati high-schooler Dave Parker. Parker, a dominating prep athlete, played little baseball his senior year due to a knee injury. But the Reds also passed on Parker because of rumors circulating among the tight-knit scouting fraternity that Parker used drugs. Nothing was ever proved, but the rumors were enough to scare off many teams.

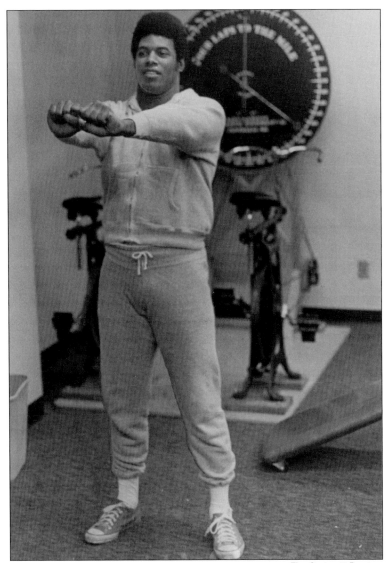

The Cincinnati Enquirer

Ken Griffey worked out in the Riverfront Stadium weight room in 1974. Griffey hit .343 in September of '74 to establish himself as the leading right-field candidate heading into the 1975 season.

The Pirates finally drafted Parker in the 14th round of the 1970 draft after some 200 players had already been selected. "Geez, you guys really picked a dandy," Joe Bowen remarked sarcastically to one of the Pittsburgh scouts.

But within a year, Parker was being compared to Roberto Clemente. Baseball men not familiar with the drug rumors couldn't understand how Parker had escaped the notice of the scouts. In pre-game practice before a spring training game between the Pirates and Cubs in 1971, Parker was hitting home runs to all fields, and showcasing his arm by throwing lasers to home plate from the outfield.

The Chicago manager, Leo Durocher, walked up to the umpires to exchange lineup cards before the start of the game. He looked at the umps and the Pirate manager. "Can you imagine that all the scouts in the whole country decided there were 200 sons of bitches better than *him*?"

Any organization could underrate some players and overrate others. The Reds were not infallible. Their drafts in 1972 and 1973 were rated as the worst in all of baseball by *Baseball America*. Of the 85 selections the club made in those two years, only five ever made the major leagues, and only one, Tom Hume, played extensively for the Reds. The failure of the '72 and '73 drafts played a role in the decline of the Reds dynasty in the late 1970s and early 1980s.

But the Howsam-led Reds succeeded more often than not because of the passion Howsam had for the development of young players, and the overall organizational commitment that stoked the enthusiasm of the scouts.

"The commitment to a top-level development program can only be held together with extraordinary leadership talent," Branch Rickey III explained. "Success is going to come when scouts believe information is being processed at the highest levels."

Howsam brought his scouts to Cincinnati each year in September for an organizational meeting. "We scheduled the meeting so they could see a club we were battling," Howsam recalled. "Usually it was the Dodgers. We wanted our scouts to see what we were competing against. So many scouts never see a major league game except on TV."

At these meetings and on other occasions, Howsam would go out of his way to talk to his scouts. If Bender couldn't find Howsam, he would know to look behind home plate.

"Bob would always sit with the scouts in the stands, always asking their opinions. 'How do you feel about this guy? What do you think of that kid?' Scouts respected him because he was one GM that would come down and talk to them."

George Zuraw, one of the most successful scouts in the Reds organization, recalled how Howsam could pull the best out of his people.

"I was on my way to Toronto from seeing a game in Baltimore," Zuraw said. "I stopped at a pay phone in Harrisburg, Pennsylvania, to call in my report. Trucks were whizzing by and here I was answering questions from Mr. Howsam about the Baltimore Orioles, questions that I hadn't even thought about. But Mr. Howsam was able to get the information out of me without me even knowing I had seen it. I saw it all, but I didn't chronicle it. I didn't think it would be important, but Mr. Howsam wanted to know. I told him about a guy hitting .400, but Mr. Howsam wanted to know about the guy hitting .220, too.

"I'll tell you how much respect I had for the man. When we talked on the telephone, I'd actually stand up for the entire conversation, even if I was in my home on the living room couch."

Once a player was signed by Bowen's scouting department, he became the responsibility of farm system director Bender and the minor league managers and coaches. In the mid-1970s, when the Reds had five farm clubs, some 115 prospects would be in the pipeline. Normal progress could move a player to the major leagues in about four years, but that could range from Don Gullett's one-year leap (from A ball in 1969 to the majors in 1970) to the six-year apprenticeship of Pat Zachry (from the rookie league in 1970 to the Reds in 1976). In a typical year, the Reds would graduate three or four players to the major league roster, and Howsam estimated that the average cost to develop a major leaguer from the farm system was about $500,000.

Bender's job was to orchestrate the development and movement of the players throughout the system.

"Our primary goal was to develop players for the major league club," said Bender. "But it's easier to develop a player on a winner than a loser."

When pitcher Pat Darcy came to the Reds farm system in 1974 from Houston in the trade for Denis Menke, he was immediately struck by the emphasis on winning in the Cincinnati organization.

"Houston's philosophy was to develop players and not worry about winning and losing," Darcy recalled. "But the Reds were really focused on winning. As it should be. I would lose in Houston (minor leagues), 2-1, and everybody would say, 'Good job.' In the Cincinnati organization, they said, 'We win games, 2-1, not lose them.' There was a lot more pressure."

The Reds wanted their minor league teams to be in a pennant race so the young players would have that experience before reaching the major leagues.

"A pennant race even in the minor leagues is still a pennant race," Darcy said. "You feel the tension and pressure. If you're not winning, there's no pressure, no importance to it."

The first stop for many of the young prospects was rookie camp held at the Reds minor league complex in Florida in June after high school graduation. It was here that the prospects were first introduced to the search for the "Reds-type" player. Will McEnaney had few fond memories of this tough introduction to professional baseball.

"I almost quit in Florida. Ron Plaza was an instructor, drill sergeant kind of guy, and he and Russ Nixon ran the camp. All we did was run. Florida in June! I wasn't used to it, the discipline, constantly being schooled on baseball situations. We would drill them, practice, practice, practice. We didn't play any games. All we did was practice and run. I had no idea it would be anything like that. I was miserable and homesick, but my Dad said stick it out."

McEnaney survived and spent the rest of the season in Sioux Falls, South Dakota, in A ball.

Each summer, Howsam arranged an unannounced visit to Sioux Falls and all his other minor league clubs, an opportunity to meet his "boys," as he always called the prospects, and to check on the status of the farm teams.

"I always went to the ballpark without the players ever knowing I was there," Howsam recalled. "A few times I even paid my own way into the park. I'd go through the gate, sit up there in the back and watch the club take batting practice, infield. After the game I wait until they'd settled down and I'd walk into the dressing room. Don't think I didn't see a few surprised faces."

Howsam usually took his boys out to a steak dinner. "I would sit

Davey Concepcion: Hall of Famer?

In 1973 and 1974, Davey Concepcion emerged as the starting shortstop for the Reds—and as the best shortstop in baseball. The Reds signed him as a skinny, 19-year-old pitcher out of Venezuela in 1968, but switched him to shortstop because of his athleticism and strong arm.

He made the major league roster in 1970, earned his first of nine All-Star selections in 1973 and won his first of five straight Gold Gloves in 1974.

Sparky Anderson marveled at how Concepcion developed. "He was 157 pounds, a little fawn whose legs were wobbly. But boy oh boy, he could play. Whew! What a player. I never thought he'd be the hitter he became, though. But Klu (hitting instructor Ted Kluszewski) believed it. Klu made him move up on the plate. One year he came back from winter ball and man, he was a great hitter."

Concepcion's eight-year run as the best shortstop in baseball (1974-1981) should earn him serious consideration for the Hall of Fame. From 1974 to 1980, he averaged 10 home runs, 28 doubles, 70 RBIs and 25 stolen bases. He led the league ten times in defensive categories, including fielding percentage, assists and double plays. Only Luis Aparicio, Mark Belanger and Ozzie Smith have won more Gold Gloves. One can argue that Concepcion is among the 20 greatest shortstops ever; as of 1996, there were 17 shortstops in the Hall of Fame.

Concepcion's career statistics closely resemble those of his boyhood idol, Aparicio, whose plaque hangs in Cooperstown.

Pete Rose waved Dave Concepcion home in a 1976 game. Concepcion was one of the best athletes on the Reds. Anderson claimed he could jump higher flat-footed than any player he had seen.

Concepcion, who perfected the now-common one-bounce throw to first base on Astroturf, was also a great clutch hitter and a key player on a dynasty team.

Pete Rose says Concepcion belongs in the Hall.

"I guarantee you Davey is as good as Pee Wee Reese and Phil Rizzuto. Davey was a better all-around player than Ozzie Smith. Not as good defensively, but offensively he was better."

The Cincinnati Enquirer

around and I would watch, frankly. It was an exercise. They didn't know that. I would watch to see if blacks sat together, if this group sat together. And if they weren't spread out, I knew then we had a problem."

Then, after watching a game and a team dinner, Howsam would meet with the manager. "At lunch we would talk over every player. I would ask to talk to certain players based on what he said or what I saw. Sometimes there was no problem at all, I just wanted to chat with a boy. I would walk around the field before the game, the outfield, the bullpen."

Howsam knew all these boys on paper, but had met few of them. One purpose of his visits was to make some personal contact. McEnaney recalled the first time he met Howsam was at the Three Rivers farm team in Canada. The players were in the clubhouse preparing for pre-game practice when Howsam walked through, stopping at each locker to greet each player by name. McEnaney was impressed by this feat—until he realized Howsam was glancing at the locker nameplates as he walked along.

"He would look at their name on the locker and say, 'Hi, so and so,'" the mischievous McEnaney recalled. "So I thought, I'll show him. So I put my shoulder up over the edge of the locker to hide my name sign."

Howsam came to McEnaney, shook his hand and glanced up at the nameplate, now hidden by McEnaney's arm. Howsam glanced down at McEnaney's glove.

"Hi there, how you doing, uh…Lefty."

One of the challenges all organizations confront is how long to hold on to marginal prospects. Some kids blossom late; some, as Ray Shore said, will never be any better than they are at age 18. Could a pitcher learn control? Could a fielder learn a new position? Could a batter learn to hit the breaking ball? Could a skinny young shortstop like Davey Concepcion ever fill out and learn to hit?

As he did in every other area of his operation, Howsam demanded as much information as possible before making a decision. Bender called the system one of organizational agreement.

"That was Rickey's theory," Bender remembered. "I was in Cardinal training camp when Rickey was there in the mid-'60s and we would go over players to release and if one guy stood up for a guy, Rickey would say, 'OK, we'll keep him.'

"Howsam felt the same way. If somebody didn't agree on a player, Bob always wanted to know why. And if they gave good reasons, then Bob would go along with them: 'Let's go with him for a while, keep him another year.'"

That philosophy saved Howsam his Gold Glove shortstop, Davey Concepcion. Concepcion fell in the category of a marginal prospect when he entered the Cincinnati farm system in 1968. After Concepcion's first year at Tampa in A ball, Bender recalled there were serious doubts about Concepcion making it. Anderson wondered why the Reds had bothered to draft him. When Pete Rose first saw the skinny young shortstop, he cracked, "At least you'll never pull a muscle. You'll have to pull a bone."

"David was so weak, you never thought he would hit anything," Bender recalled. "He could run, and had a great arm and was a good fielder. But you wondered with him being from a Latin country, if he would never develop physically (upper body). After his first year, there were some in the organization that didn't think he had a future in baseball. But Bob had seen him make some great plays and said we're not going to release him."

Griffey also came along slowly. "He could run," said Bender, "but he really didn't know how to play baseball. With that big swing, you questioned whether he would ever hit. He wanted to quit after the first year because he had a chance for a basketball scholarship. But we put him in the outfield (he came up as an infielder) and he improved."

One of the club's most dramatic success stories was Foster. Although he came to the Reds in a trade and not through the draft, Foster developed in the Reds farm system. After a woeful 1972, Foster opened the 1973 season at Indianapolis. Big-league pitchers had dominated him with breaking balls. The Reds didn't know Foster had been hit in the head twice while he was in the Giants organization and that he subconsciously feared the inside pitch. While at Indianapolis, Foster read an article about hypnosis curing ballplayers' fears. He asked the Reds if he could try it.

Howsam encouraged the experiment. Although the Reds GM was one to protect baseball's old-fashioned values, Howsam was eager to test new motivational strategies with his players. He had once sent his special assignment scout, Rex Bowen, on a research mission to gather information on psychological and motivational research. One thing Bowen discovered from a lighting expert was that the color green, which was on the underside of the bill of the Reds cap, could be distracting. The expert recommended a medium gray and Howsam ordered special caps with gray bills for the team.

Howsam also encouraged research into the effects of motivational recordings, music and which types of sunglasses worked best in baseball parks. He considered the idea of placing a library full of baseball books next to the Reds clubhouse where the players could relax, read and check out books. Howsam also examined hypnosis as an aid to relaxation and concentration.

"Certain players have mental blocks," he said. "How many times have you seen a pitcher with tremendous ability who can't get the ball over the plate? It might be mental and might be easily corrected."

So when Foster called asking for permission to visit a hypnotist, the Reds were not taken aback. The sessions paid off. Foster overcame his fear of the inside pitch, improved his batting stroke at Indianapolis and returned to the Reds in September of 1973. He hit four home runs in the final weeks of the season. Anderson predicted Foster would challenge for a starting position in 1974.

Three uncertainties faced the Reds as they prepared for the April 4 opening of the 1974 season. The first involved the starting rotation. Hopes for Gary Nolan's return to pitching faded; he had not responded to his 1973 surgery. Nolan would eventually go back under the knife in the spring of 1974 to remove a bone spur from his shoulder, causing him to miss his second straight season. Roger Nelson continued to battle arm problems, leaving the foursome of Billingham, Gullett, Kirby and Norman to lead the rotation.

The second area of concern was the outfield. The eventual Big Red Machine outfield of Foster, Geronimo and Griffey had yet to establish itself. Rose started in left, Foster and Griffey platooned in right, and Geronimo and newcomer Merv Rettenmund platooned in center.

The final question involved Henry Aaron. Aaron began the 1974 season with 713 home runs, one short of tying Babe Ruth's career home run record. With the Braves scheduled to open the season in Cincinnati, there were rumors that Aaron would not play so that he could tie the record in Atlanta. After weeks of speculation, Commissioner Bowie Kuhn ordered Aaron to play at

1974 Monthly Standings
National League West

April 30

	W	L	GB
Los Angeles	17	6	–
Houston	14	10	3½
Cincinnati	10	9	5
Atlanta	11	12	6
San Francisco	11	12	6
San Diego	10	14	7½

May 31

	W	L	GB
Los Angeles	36	14	–
Cincinnati	27	19	7
Atlanta	26	22	9
Houston	27	24	9½
San Francisco	27	25	10
San Diego	18	36	20

June 30

	W	L	GB
Los Angeles	52	24	–
Cincinnati	44	31	7½
Atlanta	42	35	10½
Houston	38	39	14½
San Francisco	34	45	19½
San Diego	35	47	20

July 31

	W	L	GB
Los Angeles	68	37	–
Cincinnati	63	43	5½
Houston	55	50	13
Atlanta	54	51	14
San Francisco	48	58	20½
San Diego	44	63	25

August 31

	W	L	GB
Los Angeles	83	49	–
Cincinnati	81	52	2½
Atlanta	73	60	10½
Houston	68	64	15
San Francisco	60	73	23½
San Diego	50	83	33½

Final Standings

	W	L	GB
Los Angeles	102	60	–
Cincinnati	98	64	4
Atlanta	88	74	14
Houston	81	81	21
San Francisco	72	90	30
San Diego	60	102	42

Riverfront Stadium. Ten minutes into the season, on a 3-1 pitch from Jack Billingham, Aaron rendezvoused with the Bambino beyond the left-field wall.

The Reds rallied to win the opener and took a one-half game lead in the standings. Shockingly, the club that Sparky had hyped as his "best ever" would not lead again the rest of the year.

As they had done in 1973, the Dodgers shot out of the starting blocks, and the Reds struggled. By mid-May, Cincinnati was eight games behind L.A., but the club retained its confidence. They remembered they had caught the Dodgers in 1973, and the players displayed a nonchalance that belied their predicament. Merv Rettenmund, in his first year with the Reds, watched the Dodgers pull away, and simultaneously observed the relaxed, laid-back atmosphere of the clubhouse.

"Tell me something," he whispered to Terry Crowley. "Are we eight games behind or eight games ahead?"

As the weather warmed, so did the Reds. They outplayed L.A. in July and August, and shrank the lead from 10½ games in early July to 2½ in September. For the second straight year, the pennant race came down to the season's final weeks. Baseball's premier teams would decide the race in two marquee series: three games in Cincinnati and three in Los Angeles. Every game was a sellout.

Anderson, who had been raised in Los Angeles and had come up through the Dodger organization, loved the rivalry. He respected the organization for its loyalty to manager Walter Alston and later Tommy Lasorda. "They are the most solid organization in the game of baseball," he would say in the 1990s. "Two managers in 43 years."

He took special pride in beating the Dodgers, but the losses came tough. "My mother and father wouldn't wait for me after a game in L.A. when we lost, because it bothered me so much."

But the rivalry energized him and he loved the drama. "I believe it's good for baseball to have two very strong teams. That's the monster out there. Everybody chases the monster."

The first L.A.-Cincinnati series in September was at Riverfront. The Dodgers won the first game to increase their lead to 3½ games; once again, the Reds seemed dead. In game two, the score was tied, 5-5, in the eighth inning when Joe Morgan stepped to the plate. Two innings earlier, he had sprained an ankle running the bases, but Sparky let him hobble to the plate. Morgan started to swing at Mike Marshall's first pitch…and fell in a heap. But he gathered himself and smashed a two-run homer to give the Reds a 7-5 victory. Whatever momentum the Reds gained faded quickly as the Dodgers won the next game. The Reds had not merely lost the series, they had lost a healthy Morgan, too. He could neither steal, nor field with any range the rest of the season. Sparky continued to start him, telling the press that half of Morgan was better than 100 percent of anybody else.

The Reds began a 10-game west coast trip a week later, opening against the Dodgers. The Reds took the first two games, narrowing the lead to 1½ games, but then lost the final game, and five of their next seven in San Diego and San Francisco. The pennant race was over. After the final game in San Francisco, Sparky shut the clubhouse.

"He don't want nobody in there," said the clubhouse man. "He's chewin' 'em out."

"I'm through being a nice guy!" screamed Anderson. He promised his players they would see a tougher taskmaster in 1975.

The 1974 Reds were not exactly failures. They won 98 games, the second most in all of baseball. But head-to-head with the

1974 MONTHLY STANDINGS
NATIONAL LEAGUE EAST

April 30
	W	L	GB
St. Louis	13	9	—
Montreal	9	7	1
Philadelphia	10	11	2½
Chicago	7	11	4
New York	8	13	4½
Pittsburgh	6	12	5

May 31
	W	L	GB
St. Louis	24	22	—
Philadelphia	25	23	—
Montreal	20	20	1
Chicago	18	25	4½
New York	20	28	5
Pittsburgh	17	27	6

June 30
	W	L	GB
St. Louis	40	34	—
Montreal	35	34	2½
Philadelphia	38	37	2½
Pittsburgh	32	40	7
Chicago	31	41	8
New York	30	44	10

July 31
	W	L	GB
Philadelphia	53	50	—
St. Louis	53	50	—
Pittsburgh	50	54	3½
Montreal	49	53	3½
New York	45	56	7
Chicago	42	59	10

August 31
	W	L	GB
Pittsburgh	70	62	—
Philadelphia	65	67	5
St. Louis	68	65	2½
Montreal	60	70	9
New York	59	71	10
Chicago	54	75	14½

Final Standings
	W	L	GB
Pittsburgh	88	74	—
St. Louis	86	75	1½
Philadelphia	80	82	8
Montreal	79	82	8½
New York	71	91	17
Chicago	66	96	22

THE REDS AND THE BLUES

The two clubs with the best records in baseball in the 1970s played in the National League West: the Cincinnati Reds and the Los Angeles Dodgers. They played 18 times a season. The rivalry was intense.

Off the field, Cincinnati and Los Angeles ran model organizations that were the envy of baseball; on the field, the two clubs waged furious division battles. The Reds and Dodgers finished first and second in the N.L. West for seven consecutive seasons, from 1972 to 1978.

In part, the rivalry was fueled by two relatively stable lineups. At a Reds-Dodgers game, the fans knew the players even without a scorecard. L.A.'s starting eight included several All-Stars:

	1973	1974	1975	1976	1977	1978
1B	Buckner	Garvey	Garvey	Garvey	Garvey	Garvey
2B	Lopes	Lopes	Lopes	Lopes	Lopes	Lopes
SS	Russell	Russell	Russell	Russell	Russell	Russell
3B	Cey	Cey	Cey	Cey	Cey	Cey
LF	Crawford	Crawford	Crawford	Smith	Smith	Smith
CF	W. Davis	Wynn	Wynn	Baker	Monday	Monday
RF	Mota	Buckner	Buckner	Buckner	Baker	Baker
C	Ferguson	Yeager	Yeager	Yeager	Yeager	Yeager

For Sparky Anderson, nothing was sweeter than beating the Dodgers. He had been signed by the Dodgers in 1953 and spent six years in their minor leagues, becoming indoctrinated in the organization's bedrock philosophies. He grew close to Walter Alston, and played alongside another Dodger hopeful, Tommy Lasorda. Lasorda replaced Alston as manager in 1977.

Lasorda's enthusiasm for "Dodger Blue" endeared him to the Los Angeles organization. At a luncheon in Cincinnati, Tommy rhapsodized about his club. "I want to work for the Dodgers even when I'm dead," he said. He urged the club to put a schedule on his tombstone. "That's so people can go to the graveyard and say, 'Let's go over to Lasorda's tombstone and see if the Dodgers are at home tonight.'"

Even Anderson had to admire his rival's style.

"In 1977, Tommy did one hell of a job feeding that club full of BS," recalled Anderson. "I always told Tommy, 'You ran me out of the league the last two years because of your BS!'"

Lasorda admitted his salesmanship was tested. "Pete Rose, Johnny Bench, Joe Morgan, Tony Perez…my God! People thought I was nuts. But I had to get my players to believe."

Third-base coach and future manager Tommy Lasorda watched Sparky Anderson call on Rawly Eastwick in 1976.

Dodgers, the Reds were 6-12, a six-game disadvantage they could not overcome. The Dodgers won the division by four games, with 102 victories.

The season typified the classic struggle these two clubs waged in the mid-1970s. Their one-two finish in 1974 was one of seven straight seasons (from 1972 through 1978) when the two clubs finished either first or second in the Western Division. Their rivalry did not have the post-season drama of the epic Yankees-Giants battles of the early 1920s or the Yankees-Dodgers matchups of the early 1950s, but no two teams in the same league or division ever sustained a one-two rivalry longer than Cincinnati and Los Angeles. The closest match was the Yankees and Indians from 1951 through 1956.

The Reds and Dodgers each would win three division titles between '72 and '78. The Dodgers won three pennants. The Reds won three pennants and two World Series. During this time, broadcaster Marty Brennaman proclaimed the Dodgers the second best team in baseball, and the statistics supported him. From 1972 through 1978, the Reds averaged 97 wins a season, the Dodgers, 94, and the Orioles, 90. Had the Dodgers beaten the A's in 1974 or the Yankees in 1977 or 1978, their 1970s club would be remembered with the great Dodger dynasties of the 1940s, 1950s and 1960s.

The decade-long duel between the Reds and Dodgers featured many taut series and a few brawls. At Dodger Stadium on August 7, 1974, with the Dodgers leading the Reds by 6½ games, the two teams tangled in the ninth inning after Bill Buckner slid hard in to Joe Morgan. The Reds won the game, 2-0, on a Jack Billingham shutout.

George Long, Sports Illustrated

Howsam and Anderson were not able to pinpoint the cause of the Reds' failure to win the division in 1974. There were few scapegoats. None of the players had a MVP-type season—but nobody had a bad one. Bench drove in 129 runs to lead the majors, Perez drove in 101 and Morgan was one of the most productive offensive players in the league (107 runs scored, 67 RBIs, 58 stolen bases). Rose slumped to .284 but led the majors with 110 runs scored. Concepcion hit .281 and stole 41 bases. Geronimo clinched the center field job with a .281 average. Geronimo, Morgan and Concepcion all won their first Gold Gloves. The pitching staff turned in a consistent performance. Billingham won 19, Gullett 17 and the staff ERA of 3.42 was nearly a run better than their opponents'.

If there was a weakness, it was third base. Danny Driessen hit .281 in his first full season, but committed 26 errors.

Howsam and his baseball men began meeting regularly in September and October to evaluate the club and discuss off-season moves. From the perspective that history affords, the 1970-74 period was but a prelude to the greatness the Big Red Machine would achieve with its back-to-back championships of 1975-76. From 1970 to 1974, the Reds won two pennants and three division titles. They averaged 95 wins and compiled a .590 winning percentage, a level of play that justifies dreams of dynasty.

But in the fall of 1974, with the World Series victories still in the future, there was a sense of dynasty unfulfilled. Not panic. Bob Howsam was not the type of man given to panic. But Johnny Bench knew as well as anybody what was at stake if the Reds could not win at least one World Series. Pride, self-fulfillment and the Big Red Machine's place in history were all on the line.

"You know you are going to hear the comments the rest of your life if you don't win it all: 'Yes, you were good, but…' or, 'How many World Series did you play in?' or, 'You didn't win it, did you?'" recalled Bench.

What would it take to put the Reds over the top? Were there other major moves that had to be made? Could the Reds win with Driessen at third base? Did the Reds need another starter?

Howsam and his staff pondered these questions and others. As the winter meetings approached, it appeared the Reds would turn to Atanasio Rigal Perez to solve their problems.

1974 Scrapbook

The Opposition

Western Division

Against	Won	Lost
Atlanta	11	7
Houston	14	4
Los Angeles	6	12
San Diego	12	6
San Fran.	11	7

Eastern Division

Against	Won	Lost
Chicago	7	5
Montreal	6	6
New York	9	3
Philadelphia	8	4
Pittsburgh	8	4
St. Louis	6	6

The pitcher the Reds didn't want to face — The Cardinals' **Bob Gibson** was 2-0 against the Reds, running his lifetime mark against Cincinnati to 22-16.

The pitcher they loved to see — The Reds were 3-0 against **Steve Rogers** of the Expos.

The batter who loved the Reds — **Steve Garvey** of Los Angeles hit .329 (24-for-73) with 4 HRs and 15 RBIs.

The batter who should have stayed home — **Willie McCovey** of the Padres hit .150 (6-for-40) with 0 HR and 1 RBI.

Club Leaders

Batting Average	Joe Morgan	.293
Home runs	Johnny Bench	33
RBIs	Johnny Bench	129 •
Stolen bases	Joe Morgan	58
Runs	Pete Rose	110 •
ERA	Don Gullett	3.04
Wins	Jack Billingham	19
Saves	Pedro Borbon	14
Games	Pedro Borbon	73

• League leader

Awards

Gold Glove	**Johnny Bench**
	Joe Morgan
	Davey Concepcion
	Cesar Geronimo
Cincinnati Reds MVP •	**Joe Morgan**
Outstanding Reds Pitcher •	**Don Gullett**
Reds Newcomer of the Year •	**Clay Kirby**

• Awarded by Cincinnati Chapter of Baseball Writers Association

Trades

Feb. 18   **Pat Darcy** acquired from Houston for **Denis Menke**

Oct. 25   **John Vukovich** acquired from Milwaukee for **Pat Osburn**

The Draft

Cincinnati drafted 47 players; eight played in the major leagues:

Mike Armstrong	University of Miami	P
Mike Grace	Pontiac, MI	3B
Mike LaCoss	Visalia, CA	P
Steve Henderson	Prairie View A&M Univ.	SS-3B
Ron Oester	Cincinnati, OH	SS
Lynn Jones	Thiel College	OF
Dan Norman	Barstow, CA (CC)	1B-OF
Andy McGaffigan •	West Palm Beach, FL	P

• Drafted by the Reds, but signed by another club

Will McEnaney jumped into Johnny Bench's arms after the final out of the 1975 World Series in Boston. Pete Rose led the rest of the Reds to the celebration.

AP/Wide World Photos

World Champions • Defeated Boston, 4 Games to 3

Chapter 9

1975
Champagne in Boston

Joe Morgan, MVP • Sparky Anderson, Manager of the Year

BEFORE TONY PEREZ LEFT Cincinnati after the 1974 season for his home in Puerto Rico, Bob Howsam called him to his office. In the organizational review meetings at the end of the season, Howsam and his staff had come to the conclusion that they would not open the 1975 campaign with Dan Driessen at third base. They liked Driessen's bat, and considered moving him to his natural position at first base. Putting him there, however, meant trading the veteran Perez.

At age 32, Perez was reaching a critical point in his career when offensive production tends to decline. True, Perez had remained a productive hitter into his thirties, but Driessen was nine years younger, and Howsam was mindful of the old Rickey maxim of not waiting too long to trade an older player.

The 1973 agreement between players and owners had included a provision that gave players with ten years service in the major leagues (and the last five with the same club) the right to veto a trade. Howsam asked Perez if he would waive the provision so that the Reds would be free to explore alternatives. "We wanted to be honest with him," said Howsam. "We told him we didn't know what the winter would bring."

Perez refused to sign a waiver, but said he would be agreeable to a trade if it was to a contending team. When Perez left for Puerto Rico, he thought he was leaving Cincinnati for good. The most likely deal the Reds would make would be Perez for a third baseman. Howsam publicly denied he wanted to trade Perez, but said he might—especially if he could find a third baseman with power to hit behind Johnny Bench.

"I would trade Tony if I believed the player or players we received in exchange would give us better balance (and) make us a better club. Our number one priority is to improve at third base," Howsam said.

As the clubs convened in New Orleans in early December for the annual winter meetings, several names were floated in the press: Graig Nettles of the Yankees, Sal Bando of the A's, youngster George Brett of the Royals and even ex-Red Tommy Helms, who had been moved to third base at Houston. But as the week-long meetings ground on, the deals slipped away, with only the Nettles deal still on the table.

Howsam wanted a young pitcher thrown in the deal, and the Yankees were not able to find a suitable replacement for Nettles. By the close of the meetings, Tony Perez was still a Red.

That prospect did not bother Sparky Anderson. "I think we can win without making a deal," said Sparky.

Bench, too, was happy his teammate would be back. "If Tony were traded, it would hurt me a lot. If you go back to 1968, there are only four of us left (Pete Rose and Clay Carroll being the other two). This is such a tough game for making friends. People like Tony become a part of you."

Howsam, too, seem relieved he had not pulled the trigger in what would have been a high-risk trade.

"This spring I may look at our ballclub and say I'm the luckiest son of a gun for not making a deal," admitted Howsam. "Our club won enough games last year to normally win a title, and with the young players we have, we should be as much a contender as last year and maybe better."

Howsam was right. His young players would improve, and he would bless the day he failed to trade Perez.

By not swinging the big deal, Howsam had thrown his manager a challenge. It would be up to Sparky to solve the third base situation. Howsam had acquired one new candidate, the slick-fielding, weak-hitting veteran, John Vukovich, from the Milwaukee Brewers. Vukovich joined a crowded prospect pool that included Darrel Chaney, and rookies Joel Youngblood, Ray Knight, Arturo DeFreites, Doug Flynn and Junior Kennedy. By Opening Day, Anderson decided to open with Vukovich, but admitted he expected to play several people there before the season was over.

Anderson also had to figure out how to use Driessen. He anticipated using Driessen at first base to give Perez an occasional rest. Sparky also talked of Driessen playing the outfield. But the Reds already had four legitimate candidates (Geronimo, Foster, Griffey and Rettenmund) for only two outfield positions. Sparky declared he would open the season by platooning Geronimo and Foster in center and Rettenmund and Griffey in right, with Driessen on the bench.

History remembers the 1975-76 Big Red Machine lineup with Foster, Geronimo and Griffey in left, center and right. But as of Opening Day, 1975, Anderson knew only that Pete Rose was in left.

The starting rotation appeared healthier than ever. Roger Nelson, who had battled arm problems for two straight years, had been traded; Gary Nolan, who had missed two seasons, was back in camp and throwing easily. A second operation on his shoulder to remove a bone spur that was piercing a muscle had been successful in eliminating the pain that had plagued Nolan since the middle of the 1972 season. Gullett, Billingham, Kirby and Norman rounded out the rotation, with Carroll, Borbon, Hall and McEnaney in the bullpen. Hall, who admitted to losing his confidence in 1974, was

The Cincinnati Enquirer

Johnny Bench's 1975 season started with a "bang," in a collision in April with Gary Matthews of the Giants. The injury to Bench's left shoulder required off-season surgery and affected his swing and offensive performance the next two years.

Money Talks

Reds players and management fought through the familiar contract battles in the spring of 1975. Don Gullett, Clay Carroll, Jack Billingham, Joe Morgan, Tony Perez, George Foster and Johnny Bench all entered into lengthy negotiations. Once again, Pete Rose argued the loudest.

Rose, 34, failed to hit .300 in 1974 for the first time in a decade. The club theorized Pete was beginning to decline. The Reds offered him an 18 percent pay cut from his 1974 salary of $155,000. In an early meeting, the club questioned his conditioning and his age.

Pete fired back. "I miss .300 for the first time in 10 years and suddenly I'm out of shape and a 'fatboy.' Well, I didn't miss a game in 1974."

The annual holdouts and Pete's "fatboy" comment inspired *Cincinnati Enquirer* baseball writer Bob Hertzel to lampoon Reds GM Bob Howsam. How would contract negotiations proceed between Howsam and his boss, chairman of the board Louis Nippert?

Hertzel's scene opens as Howsam reacts to his new contract calling for a pay cut.

"Now Mr. Nippert," Howsam begins. "I was shocked when I opened my mail and found a contract calling for an 18 percent pay cut. Over the years I believe I have been one of the most successful executives in baseball."

"True," answers Nippert. "But you know how it is in baseball. We pay off what you did last year."

"Exactly," says Howsam. "We drew more than two million fans. Our season ticket sale was at an all-time high…."

"But Bob," answers Nippert, "we finished second to the Dodgers."

"You can't fault me for that," said Howsam. "That was the players' fault."

"Oh really?" says Nippert. "I don't recall any of them approaching you and asking you to trade away Ross Grimsley…and it seems to me that a guy named McRae finished third in the American League batting race."

"Right. I thought I was helping the team. Besides, what about all those good trades I made over the years? I've had a couple of bummers. The law of averages caught up with me. That's all."

"Bob, to be honest with you, you are now 56 years old. I'm just not sure how many more productive years you have left. I think you may be about over the hill."

"But I feel good, Mr. Nippert. My weight is just the same as it was in 1972 when we won a pennant. I miss a division title for the first time in three years and suddenly I'm a fatboy…"

Nippert leans back in his chair. He is deep in thought…

"Okay, Bob," Nippert continues, "tell you what I'm going to do….I will sign you for the same figure you had last year."

"Gee thanks," says Howsam. "I really appreciate that. And I'll show you. We'll win this year."

"I expect it," answers Nippert. "By the way, who is going to play third base this year for us?"

"Quick, give me the contract," gushes Howsam.

Howsam seemed to hold all the cards in contract negotiations.

traded in May. Rawly Eastwick, who had looked sharp in spring training, was called up from Indianapolis.

The Reds could not afford another sluggish start. Six of their first 10 games were against the Dodgers. When the Reds swept L.A. in three one-run games in Cincinnati to start the season, heads nodded: the Big Red Machine was back. But when the "machine" headed west, the wheels fell off. The Reds lost two of three to San Diego and four in a row to the Dodgers. In two of the Dodger losses, the Reds had Rose on third late in the game with nobody out. Both times Morgan, Bench and Perez failed to deliver.

"A half-million dollars' worth of talent and they don't get me in," griped Pete.

The fast start was in ruins and so, too, was Sparky's confidence in Vukovich at third base. Although an offensive juggernaut like the Big Red Machine should have been able to overcome one weak bat in the lineup, Anderson could not tolerate Vukovich's hitting and his slow foot speed. In the second inning of the third game of the L.A. series, with the bases loaded and Vukovich due up, Anderson brought in Driessen to pinch-hit.

Vukovich, whose parents were in the stands watching the game, exploded. He smashed light bulbs all the way down the runway from the dugout to the clubhouse. Anderson said his reasoning was simple. "Who's my better hitter, Vukovich or Driessen?"

Despite Anderson's pre-season comments that his priority for third base was defense, the light-hitting third baseman was going to crack neither the lineup, nor the lightbulbs. Over the next two weeks, Anderson started Chaney and Flynn at third. By May 2, the Dodgers had a four-game lead. The Reds' record stood at a mediocre 12-12. The 1975 season was beginning to feel depressingly similar to 1973 and 1974, when the Dodgers pulled away to huge leads and the Reds struggled to catch up. Sparky felt he could no longer afford the status quo.

"I was starting to realize it could be lights out for me," Anderson recalled. "Like the party is going to be over here if we don't get going."

On Friday night, May 2, during infield practice, Rose was taking groundballs at first base, breaking in a new softball glove for his daughter, Fawn.

Anderson watched Rose from the dugout and considered his options. When Rose sprinted over to the dugout, Anderson stood up and went to the railing.

"Peter Edward, I wish you were playing over there," said Sparky.

"Over where?"

"Third base."

"You serious? Well, if you don't think it'll hurt the team, I'll try it. When?"

Anderson wanted to try Rose there right away; he also knew Saturday's game was on national TV. That was exactly the kind of challenge Rose loved.

"Tomorrow too soon? It's 'Game of the Week.'"

"Good, good," Pete said, rising to the bait. "How about having Sugar Bear (George Scherger) out here by 10 o'clock tomorrow morning hitting me groundballs from home plate, so I can see them coming off the bat?"

Presto. The Reds had a new third baseman.

There were several pivotal moments in the creation of the Big Red Machine: the day Howsam arrived, the day Anderson was hired, the day of the Morgan-May trade and the day Rose moved to third base. The position switch was as critical as any, but unlike the others, it was unplanned.

In spring training, Anderson had briefly considered switching Rose to third base from the outfield, but was aware that Rose had once sulked over moving to third. In 1966, manager Don Heffner announced Rose would play third base. He never consulted Pete. Rose, who later admitted his reaction was immature, griped about the move. His batting average fell under .200, and Heffner soon put him back at second.

Despite the magnitude of his decision, Anderson never consulted Howsam, Bender or Shore before he spoke to Rose. And if he had, the front office would have rejected the idea.

"Pete didn't have an arm," Bender explained. "The ball over the bag? He'd never throw anybody out."

But Bender was around before Saturday's game, so Anderson told him of the move.

"Well, Bob is in Arizona," Bender replied.

"Chief, I'm gonna tell you something," Sparky said. "It doesn't matter where Bob is. You know we haven't won yet, and we're starting off slow in '75. I look at it this way: it's me or nothing right now. I'm gonna play him at third base."

Anderson also told Marty Brennaman during his pre-game show that Rose would start at third. Brennaman refused to believe it until Sparky showed him the lineup card. Brennaman will never forget Rose's first chance.

"The first batter up, Ralph Garr, hits an absolute screamer to Pete's glove side. He breaks to his left, stumbles, fields the ball, recovers and gets up, and throws him out. He looked like a monkey playing with a football, but he threw him out. It was incredible."

The next morning, Bender's phone rang. It was Howsam.

"I looked at the box score this morning, Chief. I see Rose at third. That's a mistake, isn't it?"

"No, Bob. Sparky put him at third base."

"Oh, my God," said Howsam.

But Howsam never questioned Anderson about the move. He recognized it was the manager's prerogative to shape the lineup. And Howsam knew Rose would take the challenge seriously.

The Cincinnati Enquirer

"He looked like a monkey playing with a football," remembered announcer Marty Brennaman, but Pete Rose solved the Reds third base problem in 1975 with steady, if not elegant play.

"He worked his butt off," recalled Brennaman. "Pete was one of those few guys who loved the pregame as much as he loved the actual game. He'd take fly balls in the outfield. He'd go to first base and take groundballs. He just loved being involved. But once the decision was made to put him at third base, he was there every day well in advance of all of the rest of the guys. He'd take Alex Grammas with him or George Scherger, and take groundball after groundball after groundball. He was the only guy out on the field."

Scherger remembered that all throughout the 1975 season, Pete would come to him on off-days and plead for practice time.

"What are you doing tomorrow, Sugar Bear?"

"Goin' fishing."

"Nah, come with me to the park and hit me some groundballs."

"I'd hit him balls for an hour, sweat pouring off him," recalled Scherger. "Of all the guys I saw in baseball, nobody loved to play the game more than him."

For Rose, the challenge of playing a credible third base on a team of All-Star infielders—one that included three Gold Glovers in Morgan, Concepcion and Bench—was a matter of pride. He was never a smooth fielder, but he made the plays. "He knocked 'em down, picked 'em up, threw 'em out," Sparky said.

There was never any concern among the pitching staff that Rose would hurt the defense, Billingham recalled.

"I wasn't afraid to throw inside, never had a thought in my mind that, 'Oh hell, I got Pete at third.' I always knew he'd get in front of it. I remember more controversy when they had Driessen there. *That* did not make the pitchers confident."

For Rose, third base was like a new toy at Christmas. He had forgotten how much fun the infield was. He chatted with runners, traded insults with opposing third-base coaches and pumped up his pitchers with his constant chatter.

And of course, Rose had to defend himself from the "ripping" of his own teammates over his fielding prowess.

"That was right up his line 'cause that's what he liked," remembered Anderson. "Perez was all over him. Oh, Perez could get on him unmerciful."

"Come on, Pete, you need a bulletproof vest!" Perez yelled.

"You can't run, you can't throw, you can't catch!" Morgan cackled.

"I'll be an All-Star at third base!" Rose shot back. And he was.

Moving Rose to third served a dual purpose for Anderson. It allowed him to give more playing time to Foster and Driessen. Foster had never been a full-time regular since joining the Reds. He was philosophical about his time on the pine.

"I've seen more major league games than anyone else alive," he said. "Why, I even know some of the players personally."

On the night Pete opened at third, Anderson started an outfield of Driessen in left, Geronimo in center and Foster in right. Griffey was out because of a minor injury, but Anderson seemed serious about giving Driessen an opportunity. Driessen, however, stumbled in May and June, hitting only .232, while Foster had a productive two months, hitting 10 home runs and driving in 24 runs. By late May, Foster was the starting left fielder.

The other significant lineup shuffle in early May involved the batting order. Anderson had opened the season with Morgan batting second, a position he had usually occupied since coming to the Reds in 1972. But on April 18, Sparky dropped Morgan to third and began batting Concepcion second. On May 10, a week after Rose moved to third base, Anderson put Griffey into the second slot. The reconfiguring of the batting order was lost in the uproar of the Rose switch to third base. But batting Griffey second and Morgan third proved to be as critical to the success of the Big Red Machine as Rose's move to third base.

"Griffey is the key to our lineup," said Sparky in July. "If he hits .285, we can keep Joe third."

Griffey would hit .305 for the season, and Morgan stayed in the three hole. It allowed Morgan to blossom into the best offensive player in baseball. He won back-to-back MVP awards in 1975 and 1976. And, with Foster and Griffey becoming everyday starters, the Reds scored 840 runs, a club record. The next season they scored 857 runs for a two-year total of 1,697, the best in the N.L. since the 1953-54 Dodgers scored 1,733 in cozy Ebbets Field.

The Big Red Machine had been years in the making, but in one week in early May of 1975, Anderson made the two moves that solidified the lineup of Rose, Griffey, Morgan, Bench, Perez, Foster, Concepcion and Geronimo—and catapulted the team from the ranks of the very good to the very great.

The greatness that awaited this club, however, was not immediately evident. In the first two weeks after Anderson shifted Rose to third base, the Reds won only six of 13 games and continued to drop in the standings. When they lost three in a row on an East Coast trip, Sparky called a clubhouse meeting in Philadelphia.

He had always made spare use of such sessions. "I'd nail them once in a while just to keep the social atmosphere right," recalled Sparky. "Pete had a saying: 'Skip, we might need a meeting, why don't you just start yelling at me.' And I'd say, 'That's a good idea!'"

Among the suggestions Anderson made to his players in Philadelphia was to relax and quit swinging for the fences, and to stop the agitating, the "ripping" that sometimes bothered struggling players. Uninspired, the club lost three more and fell to 18-19. When Morgan suffered a spike wound in Montreal and Bench came down with the flu, it looked like the bottom might fall out.

Morgan had other ideas. The next day, May 17, with 14 fresh stitches in his shin, Joe burst through the clubhouse door.

"I'm playing!" he yelled, dead serious. "So screw you, Perez, and screw you, Rose, and screw you, Bench! And you, too!" he yelled at Anderson.

There was dead silence in the clubhouse for a moment…and then Anderson burst out laughing. The players joined in, and the tension in the clubhouse seemed to drift away.

"We needed to rip," Morgan later explained. "Maybe it makes us play harder or maybe it just makes us forget. We're not like the other teams. We can rip each other when we are going bad. We needed to get loose, to forget."

But the clubhouse fireworks weren't over. Bench, complaining of the flu, dragged himself into the trainer's room, and begged out of the starting lineup. But Bench did not have the flu. He and Brennaman had been out the night before touring Montreal's entertainment establishments. John was feeling the effects.

Brennaman, however, felt fine. "I woke up and I'm feeling like a million dollars," he recalled. "I'm not hung over, I feel wonderful. So I get to the ballpark and I couldn't wait to tell Sparky what I had done and who I had done it with. Before we start the pre-game show I say to Sparky, 'I went out with Bench last night and we had the damnedest time.'"

"Is that right?" responded Anderson.

Brennaman was green, but not from being hung over. He was in

Starting Lineups

Bob Howsam provided the players and the players provided the heroics, but in May of 1975, Sparky Anderson provided the tune-up the Big Red Machine desperately needed. Anderson made three critical alterations in the Cincinnati lineup:

- Switched Pete Rose from left field to third base;
- Gave George Foster an opportunity to start; and
- Put Ken Griffey in the number two slot in the batting order, moving Joe Morgan to third.

These moves created the familiar lineup of Rose, Griffey, Morgan, Bench, Perez, Foster, Concepcion and Geronimo, or a close variation of it. (The Big Red Machine lineup is defined as Rose, Griffey and Morgan followed by some combination of Bench, Perez and Foster in the 4-5-6 slots, and Concepcion and Geronimo in either the seventh or eighth spots.)

But, as familiar as these names would become, they did not immediately coalesce into the "Great Eight." The eight players first started together on May 9 (with Concepcion batting second and Griffey eighth), but Anderson continually juggled his lineup through May and June. When the Great Eight did appear in the same game, Foster batted seventh or eighth before moving up in the lineup for good in early July.

Appropriately, the historic Big Red Machine lineup was first used on July 4, when Anderson started Rose, Griffey, Morgan, Bench, Perez, Foster, Concepcion and Geronimo against Rich Folkers of the Padres. The Reds won, 7-6.

Injuries, the desire to give Danny Driessen more at-bats and the Reds' huge September lead limited Anderson's use of the starting eight to only 24 times in the regular season (with a 19-5 record). However, Sparky knew a winner when he saw it. He started the Great Eight in all 10 post-season games.

1975 Starting Lineup Summary

Player	Starts	Starts by Position								Starts by Batting Order							
		C	1B	2B	SS	3B	LF	CF	RF	1st	2nd	3rd	4th	5th	6th	7th	8th
Rose	162					137	25			162							
Morgan	141			141							19	119	3				
Bench	136	118	2				13		3			25	94	17			
Geronimo	133							133			3	3		7	50	41	29
Perez	131		131										54	61	16		
Concepcion	125				125						51	4		12	7	38	13
Foster	117						85	25	7			4	4	21	56	10	22
Griffey	116								116	86	4				6	18	2
Driessen	53		27				23		3	1		3	7	37	3	2	
Plummer	42	42													3	11	28
Chaney	41			8	27	6										16	25
Rettenmund	41						9	2	30	1				5	13	19	3
Others	58	2	2	13	10	19	7	2	3	1				2	8	7	40

only his second year as a major league broadcaster. He didn't realize he had just violated Bench's confidence. He didn't know that Bench was in the trainer's room sleeping off the "flu."

Which is where Anderson headed with a temperature of his own.

"I don't give a damn if your fever is 201!" Anderson yelled at Bench. "You're gonna catch, and if we play 30 innings you're gonna catch 'em all!"

Sparky then went on an equal-opportunity tirade, touring the clubhouse, yelling at everyone…and at no one.

He had his lightning rod now.

"We got too many guys that don't want part of the action!" he hollered. "If Cinderella's slippers fit, you put them on! If they don't, get the the hell out of our way, because we are gonna win and we will go right over the top of you guys that don't wanna play!"

That afternoon, the Reds ended their losing streak, beating the Expos, 5-3, in extra innings—on a Bench home run. The victory triggered a winning explosion. The Reds won 40 of their next 50 games (not 41 of 50 as has so often been reported) for a winning percentage of .800. They moved from 5½ games behind the Dodgers to 12½ games in front. By the All-Star break, the Western Division race was over.

As for Brennaman, he never again mentioned his after-hours activities to Anderson.

"That was the first time I understood you don't talk about what you did the evening before to people like Sparky," said Brennaman. "It got back to Bench that I was the one who told Sparky, and you could say Bench was not happy. It never happened again, I can tell you that."

The dominating stretch of baseball that moved the Reds into first place was marred by an injury to Don Gullett. On June 16, when the Reds were only 3½ games in front, Gullett was struck on his pitching hand by a line drive. It broke his thumb and sidelined him for two months. When the injury occurred, Gullett appeared to be on the way to a 20-win season and a possible Cy Young award. He was 9-3 with seven complete games. Anderson moved Fred Norman from the bullpen to the starting rotation and Norman went 9-1 over the last half of the season.

The Reds pitching staff concluded the season with an ERA of 3.37, well under the league average of 3.63. Gullett, Billingham and Nolan all won 15 games; Norman, Pat Darcy and Clay Kirby won 12, 11 and 10, respectively. The bullpen led the National League in saves, with 50. No pitcher had a losing record.

The pitching staff also led the league in fewest complete games, with 22. In one famous stretch of 45 games, the starters failed to complete a single game. The fans booed Anderson when he walked to the mound to change pitchers. On July 30, Pat Darcy broke the streak, and the fans gave him a standing ovation.

Darcy recalled the rare accomplishment. It had been a stifling mid-summer evening with high humidity.

"People were fainting in the stands," Reds beat writer Bob Hertzel said to Darcy.

"Over a complete game?" asked an incredulous Darcy.

Hertzel had to admit it was from the heat, not the feat, but the streak had become such an issue that Darcy's reaction was not far-fetched.

The 45-game stretch was a major league record, and it sharpened the image of the Reds as a club with weak pitching.

During the streak, Sparky heard a nickname he never resisted: "Captain Hook."

The players were quick to needle Anderson about it. After Anderson used Borbon, Carroll, McEnaney and Eastwick to preserve a win for Gullett, Concepcion summed up Sparky's effort.

"You've done it before, and you'll do it again. You've hooked them all!"

The perception that endures until this day is that the Big Red Machine lacked standout starting pitching. The only 20-game winner during the 1970-76 period was Jim Merritt in 1970. But when they were healthy, Gary Nolan and Don Gullett were among the most dominating pitchers in the league. In the three seasons Gullett made over 30 starts, he was 16-6, 18-8 and 17-11. Nolan's ERA between 1970 and 1976—except for 1973 and 1974, when he missed nearly all of both seasons—was 3.05, and he averaged 15 victories per year. Only Tom Seaver, Steve Carlton and Don Sutton averaged more wins in the National League during that stretch.

On a team that featured glamour names on offense, and a nickname and reputation that emphasized explosive hitting, the pitchers never received much credit. The only pitcher that earned the status of a Rose or Bench or Morgan in the 1970s was Seaver, who joined the Reds in 1977. He had developed his reputation long before coming to Cincinnati.

"We didn't really have a leader on the staff," remembered Darcy. "Gullett was pretty quiet. Billingham was really sarcastic. He was always close to being in the doghouse."

Billingham nearly cracked the 20-win barrier twice, winning 19 in 1973 and 1974. But it wasn't easy to win 20 with Anderson's quick hook. "I think Sparky pulled us too soon, but he could with

CAPTAIN HOOK

When Sparky Anderson took over the Reds in 1970, most teams recorded more complete games than saves. But Anderson took advantage of a deep and durable bullpen to offset inconsistent starting pitching. Sparky's bullpens were the "sweatshops of major league baseball," wrote George Plimpton. The chief toilers from 1970–1976 were Wayne Granger, Clay Carroll, Pedro Borbon, Tom Hall, Will McEnaney and Rawly Eastwick.

By 1977, saves had surpassed complete games in the National League. But Anderson and the Reds had made the transition seven years earlier.

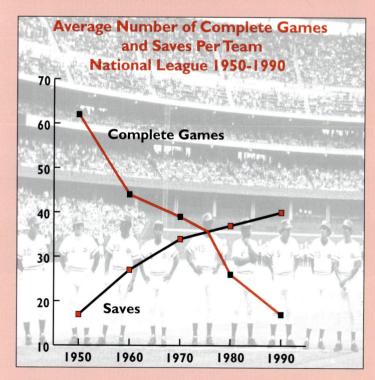

Average Number of Complete Games and Saves Per Team
National League 1950-1990

that great bullpen," Billingham recalled.

Darcy remembered pitching well against the Cubs in 1975, only to see Anderson heading out to the mound.

"When Sparky came to the mound, you weren't supposed to talk to him. He was coming out there to take you out," said Darcy. "But I thought I was throwing good and I said to him, 'No, Sparky, I feel good.' He grabs the ball and says, 'No, Pat, you'll feel better in the shower.'"

Anderson's quick hook cost his starters some wins and some respect around the league. But Sparky believed a strong bullpen was to the benefit of his starters. "I believe I know when to get a guy out of there. I like to think I can save games for my pitchers by getting them out of there before the damage is done."

Said Sparky to his starters: "Boys, if you want that game, I suggest you go out and get them 1-2-3. Play this song in your mind [Sparky assumes a waltz tempo here.]: 1-2-3…1-2-3…1-2-3. You got no problems from me. But if you start going 1-2-3…4-5, we'll see you later, and we'll get somebody that wants to get 'em out."

Some of the Reds starters chafed under the Arthur Murray approach, however. Saying that pitching could be as easy as 1-2-3 didn't necessarily make it so. Billingham recalled the night Gullett dominated slugger Willie Stargell with blazing speed inside.

"Sparky says, 'That's how you do it,'" remembered Billingham. "Well, I'm right-handed with an 87 mile-per-hour fastball. Give me a 96 mile-per-hour arm and I could do that, too."

Despite the Reds' powerful offense and the talented bullpen, it was no easy task being a Cincinnati starting pitcher.

"You were always expected to win," said Billingham. "Sparky seemed to take it personally when you lost. He wouldn't talk to you. If you won, you were best buddies. He'd slap you on the back. But he would ignore you if you lost. Some guys couldn't handle it. You could be satisfied with a losing performance if you pitched well for some clubs, but in Cincinnati that wasn't good enough."

Pitching coach Larry Shepard was also a tough taskmaster. "I'd pitch a one-run game," Billingham recalled, "and 'Shep' would congratulate me. But the next day he'd say, 'Jack, here's where you made your mistake, here's why you gave up that run.' Always thinking, always teaching. Larry was a perfectionist."

Shep would needle his pitchers, saying it was tough to win with

The Cincinnati Enquirer

Sparky Anderson's "Captain Hook" reputation was nurtured in part by the rubber arm of Pedro Borbon. From 1972 through 1976, Borbon (right) averaged 70 appearances a year.

the Reds, because the offense didn't *always* score six runs. "There was always that sort of edge that the hitters carried the club," recalled Billingham.

Shepard also knew that some of his guys needed more rope. The free-spirited Borbon was a constant challenge.

In a staff meeting prior to the 1976 season, Shepard drilled the pitchers and catchers on the signs. Borbon listened with some curiosity, then turned to Bench when Shepard finished.

"Yahnny," said Borbon. "We use the same signs as last year."

"OK, Pedro" replied Bench.

"What signs are you using?" asked a puzzled Shepard.

"I just put down fingers, and he throws whatever the hell he wants," said Bench, laughing.

Shepard gave his pitching crew some funny moments, even if they were unintentional. Shepard had undergone hip replacement surgery and had lost considerable mobility. When starters were throwing before a game in the bullpen, Shepard would stand near the plate watching them warm up and he would offer encouragement. Once, Billingham unintentionally buzzed Shepard with an inside fastball.

"Shep fell down getting out of the way, and somebody had to help him get back up," Darcy recalled. "He's screaming, 'Goddammit, Billingham!' Here you are trying to get your mind on the game and your pitching coach is on the ground."

Shepard wasn't one to take things lying down—it just always seemed to work out that way.

"Sparky had a little meeting with the pitchers and was yelling at us pretty good," Darcy remembered. "He turns to Shep and says, 'You got anything to say?' Shep tilts back in his chair and before he can say anything, the chair tips over and somebody had to help him up. We were all trying not to laugh."

Despite the pratfalls, Shepard had Anderson's ear about the staff. "I've always said, if we had the Dodgers' pitching in the years of the '70s, these guys could have won 130 games," said Anderson. "But we didn't have that, so what we had to do, Shep would call it, was 'defense from our bullpen.' We'd start a guy, and our offense would dictate when to make a change. Our offense would give us enough leeway to do that. We had that bullpen, four or five deep at times, down there."

Anderson's machinations seemed excessive in the early 1970s, but baseball would adopt them within a decade. In eight of his nine seasons in Cincinnati, from 1970 to 1978, Sparky's clubs had more saves than complete games, a shift in pitching statistics that the league as a whole would not reflect until 1977.

Anderson built his bullpens around Clay Carroll and Pedro Borbon. Both had durable arms and Anderson used both as set-up men and closers. He complemented Carroll and Borbon with several excellent relievers including Don Gullett (in his rookie year), Wayne Granger, Tom Hall, Joe Gibbon and Manny Sarmiento (or, as Sparky called him, "Sarmentino"). In 1975 and 1976, Anderson had his best bullpens with the addition of Will McEnaney and Rawly Eastwick.

Sparky would also send his fifth or sixth starter to the bullpen and use him frequently. Nearly all of his starters saw significant bullpen action, including Billingham, Gullett, Norman, McGlothlin and Merritt.

"Top to bottom, our staff would beat any other," Darcy said. "L.A. might have had three better starters, but our 10-man staff matched up against anybody. Most staffs had two or three guys that they hardly ever used. Not Sparky. He used everybody."

Using everybody was a delicate juggling act for Anderson and Shepard. Many of the starters, feeling unrecognized and unappreciated, grew to despise their manager. Shepard protected his boss—and Anderson acknowledged Shepard's crucial role.

"In the nine years I was with him, he literally kept the pitching staff away from me that hated me," admitted Anderson. "I could hear them yelling in the coaches room and Shep saying, 'You ain't gonna change that SOB, so there ain't no use in trying.'"

The reputation of the Reds pitching staff was reflected in the annual All-Star selections. From 1970 through 1976, the Reds captured 34 All-Star spots, but only five pitchers made the team: Jim Merritt, Wayne Simpson, Clay Carroll, Jack Billingham and Gary Nolan. In the championship years of '75 and '76, no pitchers were selected. When the 1975 team was announced, Bench, Concepcion, Morgan, Perez and Rose were on the squad. But one omission stung the Reds. Dodger manager Walter Alston selected L.A. reliever Mike Marshall instead of Cincinnati's Will McEnaney, who had eight saves, a 1.38 ERA and a 3-1 record. "He should have made the team," said Billingham.

McEnaney, in his second season at age 23, had become a valuable asset in Anderson's bullpen. Along with rookie Rawly Eastwick, the two were becoming a younger version of the Carroll-Borbon tandem that had anchored the bullpen since 1971.

McEnaney's development and graduation to the big leagues was typical of many of the Reds players in the early 1970s. It involved training, discipline, an ability to adapt to changing circumstances—and a strong dose of veteran minor league manager, Vern Rapp.

Rapp had first come to Bob Howsam's attention as a player

Vern Rapp (left), manager of the Reds Triple A farm club at Indianapolis, had many opportunities to review new talent with Bob Howsam. Rapp managed Indianapolis throughout the early 1970s and guided the development of Ken Griffey, Dan Driessen, Will McEnaney, Rawly Eastwick, Pat Zachry and several other stars of the Big Red Machine.

when Howsam signed him to catch in Denver. Howsam then hired him as a manager for the Cardinals farm system in 1965. He brought Rapp into the Cincinnati organization to manage the Triple A club at Indianapolis in 1969, where Rapp remained for the next seven seasons.

Rapp first encountered McEnaney in 1973. McEnaney had been groomed as a starter during his first four seasons in the minors, and had moved steadily up the farm system to Triple A in '73. He made the American Association All-Star team that year. In 1974, after evaluating McEnaney in spring training, the organization shifted him to the bullpen.

The Reds' brass liked McEnaney's fastball and changeup, but believed his curve was too slow. A two-pitch pitcher, especially one with a good fastball, could have success in the bullpen. But McEnaney felt he was being demoted.

"I thought they had lost confidence in me," he recalled. "All the way through the minors, the relievers were the less-talented guys. I thought they were going to phase me out."

But McEnaney was the only left-handed prospect at Triple A, and Rapp knew the Reds wanted him.

"Vern was brutally honest, so I believed him when he said the Reds liked the way I pitched," said McEnaney. Rapp was recognized throughout the Reds organization as a great developer of young talent. McEnaney thought Rapp was the best manager he had in the Reds system, and had come to appreciate Rapp's concern for his players even though the two had some run-ins.

In 1973, the carefree McEnaney was escorting a date through the lobby of a hotel just as curfew time arrived. Rapp caught him and threatened to fine him for having a girl in his room. McEnaney yelled that Rapp couldn't prove it and the two screamed back and forth. The next day Rapp called in McEnaney.

"Will, you gotta settle down. Why don't you get married?"

McEnaney, ever the practical jokester, also tested Rapp's patience and his sense of humor. "We were in Des Moines playing one night getting the crap beat out of us," McEnaney recalled. "I had a dog leash for an invisible dog. It had a wire loop on the end of the leash so you could hold it out in front of you like you were walking a dog. So I'm out under the stands behind the dugout farting around with it."

Pretty soon Rapp, who was not happy with his team losing, noticed the commotion.

"McEnaney!" yelled Rapp. "Get that fuckin' dog in here!"

Rapp believed in McEnaney despite the shenanigans and taught him a new pitch.

"Vern taught me a slider. I never had to rely on one before because my curve was good enough in the minors," said McEnaney. "But one day Vern pulls me over and brought out his old catcher's mitt, the round one that looks like a pie. He says, 'I want you to learn the slider.' We stood 40 feet apart and he showed me the spin. The next day I was on the mound and Vern says, 'You got it.' It came to me pretty easy. In about 10 days, I started throwing it in games, getting strikeouts, using it a lot against right-handers."

McEnaney developed into the number one relief pitcher on the Indianapolis club in early 1974. The Reds called him up in July.

"Rapp put the polish on me," said McEnaney. "He had a bigger smile than I did when he told me I was going to the big leagues."

When McEnaney arrived in the Reds clubhouse, he was prepared for almost anything. Stories of the hazing of rookies were common in major league baseball. McEnaney was also in awe of the superstars. But he was immediately welcomed by none other than Mr. Rose.

"I started to unload my equipment," remembered McEnaney. "My shoes were really horrible, all scuffed up, the cleats were all worn down."

In the early 1970s, players were responsible for buying their own shoes, and rookies often did not have many pairs. Rose watched as McEnaney started to pull on the old shoes.

"Hey, you can't wear those," scolded Rose. "Can you fit into a 9½?"

With that, Rose pulled open a nearby locker. Inside were 30 pairs of shoes, given to Rose by a shoe company.

"Pick out a couple of pair," offered Pete.

"Oooh," purred McEnaney.

"Good luck," said Rose. "Have fun up here."

"That," McEnaney recalled, "was my first day in the clubhouse."

McEnaney's snub from the 1975 All-Star team did not long remain an issue for the rampaging Reds. Even McEnaney dismissed it. "They can have the All-Star game. We'll take the 'fall classic.'" That sentiment reverberated throughout the organization. The Reds had seen their share of All-Star games, pennant races and playoffs. The Big Red Machine roared toward its final obstacle: winning the World Series.

Despite a few troublesome injuries—most notably a sore left shoulder that bothered Bench nearly all season—the Reds continued to lengthen their lead. The team excelled in come-from-behind finishes and late-inning wins. The Reds captured 28 victories in their last at-bat in 1975.

Their lead was 17½ games on September 1. Despite the starters resting much of September, the club went 18-9 to win by 20 games, the biggest margin in the major leagues since 1906. The Reds' 108 victories were the third highest in National League history.

"If it's October, it must be the Pirates," had become a theme for the Reds in the '70s. For the third time in five seasons, the Reds faced Pittsburgh in the playoffs. It figured to be a battle of power (Pirates) versus speed (Reds). Scout Ray Shore encouraged Anderson to turn the troops loose on Pittsburgh catcher Manny Sanguillen. To bolster the blitzkrieg, Anderson moved Morgan into the two hole and dropped Griffey to seventh.

"I can put more pressure on Pittsburgh batting second," Morgan said.

Griffey wasn't happy with the move, but Foster offered him some incontrovertible advice.

"No matter where you are in the batting order," reasoned Foster, "you eventually have to come up."

Game One, at Riverfront, opened in the Pirates' favor when they scored two early runs off Don Gullett. But in the third inning, with the Reds trailing, 2-1, Joe Morgan walked and stole second and third. Pirate starter Jerry Reuss then walked Bench, and gave up RBI hits to Perez and Griffey to put the Reds ahead for good. Under the hard gaze of "Captain Hook," Gullett pitched a complete game. But afterward, Gullett was more thrilled with his fifth-inning home run, his first in the major leagues.

The Reds' speed was the focus of attention in the clubhouse. Although Morgan went hitless, his romp around the bases in the third inning ignited the club. "Joe Morgan did more for us today than anyone else," Anderson claimed. "When he stole third base you could sense it. It was like everyone saying, 'Now, let's go!'"

Morgan had held his regular "coaching" clinic before the

playoffs began, using the videotape machine in the Reds clubhouse to break down the moves of the Pittsburgh pitchers. Foster, Concepcion and Griffey gathered around. "I'm not so sure how much it helps them technically, but it gives them confidence," said Morgan. And in Game Two, the confidence paid off.

The Reds stole seven bases on their way to a 6-1 victory. The Pirates pitchers could not keep the Reds close, and Sanguillen could not throw them out. Morgan, Griffey, Foster and Concepcion each stole bases, and Perez picked up three RBIs with a home run and a single. Once again, the starting pitching stopped the Pirates. Fred Norman gave up four hits and five walks in six innings, but continually pitched out of trouble.

The playoffs headed to Pittsburgh where John Candelaria, in his rookie season with the Pirates, got the start. He was the third Pittsburgh left-hander to start against the Reds, and he pitched brilliantly through seven innings. He struck out seven of the first nine batters, but one of the batted balls was a Concepcion home run that put the Reds ahead, 1-0. The Pirates then went ahead in the sixth on a two-run homer by Al Oliver.

Candelaria had 14 strikeouts and appeared on the way to a win when he faced Rose with one on and two out in the eighth. Rose ripped a fastball over the left-field wall to put the Reds in front.

McEnaney set down the Pirates in the bottom of the eighth, but Eastwick walked in the tying run in the bottom of the ninth. It only postponed the inevitable for the Pirates. In the tenth, pinch-hitter Ed Armbrister hit a sacrifice fly to drive in Griffey with the go-ahead run, and Morgan drove in an insurance run. Borbon came on to retire the Pirates in the bottom of the inning, getting a young rookie named Willie Randolph for the last out. In the broadcast booth, Marty Brennaman called the final pitch.

The Cincinnati Enquirer

Ken Griffey greeted Don Gullett after his home run in Game One of the 1975 playoffs. Gullett pitched a complete game on route to a Cincinnati sweep of the Pirates.

"Randolph, right-handed batting rookie infielder. Borbon looking for the sign. He kicks and deals. The pitch is hit to Morgan. He's up, he throws to Tony. And the 1975 pennant belongs to the Reds!"

On the day the Reds won the pennant, the Boston Red Sox completed a three-game sweep of the defending World Champion A's, and set up a World Series between two of baseball's oldest franchises.

The two clubs were linked in history through the "Father of Professional Baseball," Harry Wright, who captained both clubs in the early days of the professional game. In 1869, Wright helped create the original Cincinnati Red Stockings, baseball's first professional club, and gave them their bright red leggings that begat the team's nickname. In 1871, Harry moved to Boston along with his brother George, the Red Stockings' star shortstop. Harry organized the Boston club, and also outfitted that nine in red hose. One hundred and four years later, Wright's two clubs, the Reds and Red Sox, would face off in what would come to be regarded as the greatest World Series of all time.

The Red Sox were a surprise entry in the 1975 series. Boston had last been in post-season play in 1967, when the "Impossible Dream" team lost the World Series to a St. Louis Cardinals team that Howsam helped build. Only Carl Yastrzemski and Rico Petrocelli remained as starters from that Boston club. In the early 1970s, the Red Sox began to rebuild with a collection of young talent: Carlton Fisk, Dwight Evans, Rick Burleson, Cecil Cooper

In one of the Reds' few unsuccessful ventures on the basepaths in the 1975 playoffs, Cesar Geronimo was thrown out at the plate. Manny Sanguillen applied the tag while Joe Morgan offered his call of the play. The Reds stole 11 bases in the playoffs, without being thrown out once.

The Cincinnati Enquirer

Sparky Anderson's "Captain Hook" image was well established by the eve of the 1975 World Series.

1975 Monthly Standings
National League West

April 30

	W	L	GB
Los Angeles	15	8	–
San Diego	11	10	3
Cincinnati	12	11	3
Atlanta	12	12	3½
San Francisco	10	11	4
Houston	8	16	7½

May 31

	W	L	GB
Los Angeles	30	20	–
Cincinnati	28	21	1½
San Francisco	23	22	4½
San Diego	24	24	5
Atlanta	22	27	7½
Houston	20	31	10½

June 30

	W	L	GB
Cincinnati	49	28	–
Los Angeles	43	36	7
San Francisco	37	39	11½
San Diego	36	41	13
Atlanta	32	43	16
Houston	28	52	22½

July 31

	W	L	GB
Cincinnati	69	37	–
Los Angeles	55	52	13½
San Francisco	52	53	16½
San Diego	50	56	19
Atlanta	46	56	22½
Houston	38	70	32

August 31

	W	L	GB
Cincinnati	90	45	–
Los Angeles	72	64	18½
San Francisco	67	68	23
San Diego	61	75	29½
Atlanta	59	77	31½
Houston	52	85	39

Final Standings

	W	L	GB
Cincinnati	108	54	–
Los Angeles	88	74	20
San Francisco	80	81	27½
San Diego	71	91	37
Atlanta	67	94	40½
Houston	64	97	43½

and, in 1975, rookies Jim Rice and Fred Lynn. Although several of these players were not as familiar to the baseball public as the heart of the Big Red Machine, Fisk, Rice, Lynn, Cooper and Evans would each play more than 1,800 games and become frequent All-Star Game participants. Fisk, Rice and Evans would amass career statistics worthy of Hall of Fame consideration. Rice, who broke his arm in September, did not play in the Series.

In 1975, Boston led the American League in runs scored and batting average, but did not dominate the pitching statistics. They had no 20-game winners. The staff was led by the veteran Luis Tiant. Their team ERA of 3.99 was above the American League average of 3.79, while the Reds ERA of 3.37 was better than the National League mark of 3.63. Nor could the Red Sox match the Reds in speed and defense. The Red Sox stole 66 bases; the Reds 168. Howsam had shaped his team to exploit the artificial turf of Riverfront (and the other artificial turf parks in the National League); Boston was built for the thick grass of snug Fenway Park and the grass fields of the American League, where only one franchise, Kansas City, played on carpet.

This was a classic American League team from the 1950s mold against a sleeker 1970s National League model.

The Series opened in Boston, where fabled Fenway Park and Luis Tiant took the spotlight. The most conspicuous feature of Fenway, the imposing left-field wall, loomed. The "Green Monster" was 315 feet from home plate. It seemed like a sure home run target, except that it stood 37 feet high. Both right-handed and left-handed hitters had ruined their swings trying to capitalize on the inviting wall, and many an outfielder had looked foolish trying to judge the bounce of balls off the tin barrier. The speculation was that the Reds' right-handed power and outfielders Foster and Geronimo would be humbled by the "Monster."

Broadcaster Brennaman recalled the club's first look at the ballpark from behind the first-base dugout.

"The first thing they saw was the left-field wall. Bench's eyes lit up like a Christmas tree, then Perez's and Foster's. And that, of course, was absolutely the worst thing that could have happened. Rettenmund (who had American League experience) was saying, 'Hey, don't get carried away with that thing now.'"

If the Green Monster added one idiosyncratic feature to the Series, Tiant offered several more. The Cuban-born Tiant, whose heavy dark mustache made him appear at least 10 years older than his stated age of 34, had a disconcerting pitching motion that featured head twists and a quivering glove. His eccentric delivery, his competitive fire and his success at Fenway had made him the favorite of the Boston fans, who chanted "Loo-ie, Loo-ie" when he pitched. And on this first night of the Series, "El Tiante" had two extra fans in the stands: his parents had received permission from Cuban authorities to attend the games. Their son gave up several hard-hit balls, but only five hits and no runs, and the Red Sox surprised the pundits with a 6-0 opening victory.

Rose wasn't that impressed. "His (Tiant's) best ball was the 'at-'em' ball," said Pete, referring to the hard-hit outs the Reds made. But Morgan gave the wily pitcher credit. "Tiant put nine zeroes up on the scoreboard. That's what he was supposed to do. That impresses me. It doesn't matter whether he had good stuff or not."

In 1970 and 1972, the Reds had lost the first two games of each Series, deficits they could not overcome. In Game Two of the '75 edition, Anderson turned to Jack Billingham to pull the Reds even. Ray Shore had scouted Boston the final weeks of the season and

1975 MONTHLY STANDINGS
NATIONAL LEAGUE EAST

April 30

	W	L	GB
Chicago	12	5	—
New York	9	7	2½
Pittsburgh	9	7	2½
Philadelphia	8	10	4½
St. Louis	7	10	5
Montreal	5	11	6½

May 31

	W	L	GB
Pittsburgh	24	18	—
Chicago	25	20	½
New York	21	19	2
Philadelphia	22	23	3½
St. Louis	19	24	5½
Montreal	15	24	7½

June 30

	W	L	GB
Pittsburgh	45	29	—
Philadelphia	42	34	4
New York	37	34	6½
St. Louis	36	37	8½
Chicago	36	40	10
Montreal	31	39	12

July 31

	W	L	GB
Pittsburgh	63	41	—
Philadelphia	59	46	4½
New York	54	48	8
St. Louis	52	52	11
Chicago	49	57	15
Montreal	42	58	19

August 31

	W	L	GB
Pittsburgh	75	58	—
Philadelphia	72	63	4
St. Louis	72	63	4
New York	71	64	5
Chicago	62	74	14½
Montreal	58	75	17

Final Standings

	W	L	GB
Pittsburgh	92	69	—
Philadelphia	86	76	6½
St. Louis	82	80	10½
New York	82	80	10½
Chicago	75	87	17½
Montreal	75	87	17½

his detailed notes indicated that Boston was a fastball-hitting team. Anderson initially doubted the report, but as he watched the Red Sox pick up 10 hits off the fastballing Gullett, he decided to test Shore's report with Billingham.

The festive atmosphere of the Series contrasted sharply with the dank reality of another cool, wet New England day. Red Sox starter Bill Lee, however, was anything but a wet blanket. He had won 17 games in 1975 and led the Red Sox in memorable quotes. The writers loved him, and the fans thought his nickname of "Spaceman" was well-deserved.

Prior to the start of Game Two, a reporter commented on Lee's status as the starting pitcher.

"Well, you're it," said the reporter.

"No," said Lee, hitting the reporter lightly. "You're it! You're it! No tag-backs!"

On this night, the Reds found Lee's pitching as bewildering as his sense of humor. He retired the first 10 batters, before giving up the Reds' first run of the Series in 13 innings when Bench singled home Morgan in the fourth. That tied the score at one. The Red Sox regained the lead in the sixth, 2-1, on a Petrocelli single.

Lee maintained the one-run lead going into the ninth. The Red Sox were only three outs away from a two-game lead. But Bench woke up the Reds with a double to right field. Red Sox manager Darrell Johnson called for ace reliever Dick Drago, who induced Perez to ground to short as Bench took third. Foster popped out weakly to shallow left.

Concepcion, who had made the final out in Game One, redeemed himself with a soft single up the middle to tie the game. Although Fisk had thrown out two would-be base stealers, Anderson flashed the steal sign and Concepcion made it. Ken Griffey then lined a double to left-center and the Reds had their first lead of the Series, 3-2. Eastwick earned the save with a 1-2-3 ninth.

By the end of the game, Anderson had become a believer in the accuracy of Shore's report. He had watched Billingham baffle the Red Sox with breaking stuff. Said Sparky cryptically to a reporter: "Billingham taught us some things we thought were right, but now we're assured of."

Rose thought the Reds had made too many mistakes in the first two games, and he was pleased with the split in Boston. But he admitted the Boston fans must have been wondering, *"That* team won 108 games?"

Afterward, Lee was asked his impressions of the Series thus far. "Tied," he said.

The teams left drizzly Boston for Cincinnati and Game Three. Whereas the memories of the 1972 and 1970 Series were of late afternoon shadows and soft fall sunlight in Cincinnati, the 1975 Series was to be played under the bright white lights of Riverfront Stadium. Rick Wise, who had thrown a no-hitter at Riverfront when he pitched for the Phillies in 1971, started for the Red Sox; Gary Nolan opened for the Reds. Had Game Six of this Series not upstaged all the others, it is likely that the third game would have been the most remembered.

Fisk started the scoring with a home run in the second, but Bench put the Reds in front in the fourth with a two-run homer, the Reds' first hit of the game. In the fifth, Concepcion and Geronimo unloaded back-to-back home runs, and Morgan's sacrifice fly drove in Rose to make it 5-1.

But in the seventh, with the score 5-2, ex-Red Bernie Carbo hit a pinch-hit home run off Clay Carroll, and in the ninth, Evans hit a two-run homer off Eastwick to tie the score at five.

Geronimo led off the bottom of the 10th with a single. Anderson called on Ed Armbrister to pinch-hit. All season long, the little-used Bahamian had drawn big laughs from his teammates by bragging that he would play a big role in the Reds' success in 1975. "I'm the key man," he would say.

Now, the "key man" knew his job: lay down a sacrifice to move Geronimo to second base. Armbrister bunted the pitch into the dirt in front of the plate and the ball bounced high into the air. On the spot where Bernie Carbo, umpire Ken Burkhart and Orioles catcher Elrod Hendricks had collided five years before in the Cincinnati-Baltimore World Series, Armbrister, Fisk and umpire Larry Barnett were drawn into another memorable maelstrom.

Armbrister hesitated a split second before running. In that instant, the quick Fisk threw off his mask and lunged forward to catch the ball. As Armbrister took his first step, he saw Fisk reaching for the ball. Armbrister pulled back and ducked to avoid Fisk, but the two brushed. Fisk caught the ball, took a full step forward to clear himself of Armbrister, and airmailed a throw into center field. Instead of a double play, the Reds had runners on second and third with no one out.

The Red Sox pleaded for an interference call. They were livid over Barnett's decision that Armbrister did not hinder Fisk. But it appeared the collision was accidental, and Barnett indicated that influenced his call. The rules were vague. Rule 7.08 (b) stated a runner was out when "he intentionally interferes with a thrown ball; or hinders a fielder attempting to make a play on a batted ball." Did "intentional" refer to only the thrown-ball segment of the rule, or also to fielding, which followed the semicolon in the rule? Rule 7.09 read that a runner committed interference when "he fails to avoid a fielder who is attempting to field a batted ball." Later the umpires

Heinz Kluetmeier, *Sports Illustrated*

Heinz Kluetmeier, *Sports Illustrated*

As Ed Armbrister's bunt bounced high in front of the plate in the 10th inning of Game Three, Boston catcher Carlton Fisk reached for the ball. He and Armbrister brushed (left). Fisk stepped free of Armbrister (right), but threw high to second base. The Red Sox claimed interference.

revealed they interpreted the rules in light of supplemental instructions provided by baseball for the World Series that said no interference should be called in case of a runner and catcher colliding.

If Fisk had made an accurate throw—it appeared he had righted himself and had the time to do so—it is likely Geronimo and Armbrister both would have been out. There would have been no protest by the Red Sox. (Of course, then the Reds would have argued that Fisk had hindered Armbrister.) From the moment Armbrister bunted the ball until Fisk caught it took less than one and a half seconds. Even with video replay, announcers and sportswriters did not agree on the call.

After the argument died down, the Red Sox walked Rose to load the bases and set up a double play. Pinch-hitter Merv Rettenmund struck out, and the Red Sox looked as though they might escape. But MVP Morgan lifted a long fly ball to center field over the head of Fred Lynn, and the Reds won, 6-5.

Anderson refused to be drawn into the bunt controversy after the game. But what if the call had gone the other way?

"I would probably have gone insane," admitted Sparky.

In the Boston clubhouse, Fisk fumed. "It's a damn shame to lose a ballgame like that."

Bill Lee said he would have chewed Barnett's ear off if he had been close enough during the argument.

"I would have Van-Goghed him," he said.

Up two games to one with two games remaining at Riverfront, the Reds hoped they could win the Series in Cincinnati. But Tiant ruined the Reds' plans with his second complete-game victory. The Reds scored two runs off the Cuban in the first inning, but "El Tiante" survived all 163 pitches he threw, and the Red Sox won, 5-4.

Cincinnati had the tying run on base in the fifth, sixth and eighth innings, but couldn't score. In the sixth, with two out and Geronimo on first, Anderson chose light-hitting Darrel Chaney to pinch-hit instead of Driessen. Chaney struck out.

After the game, Anderson took shots from his own family about the move. "Dad," said Sparky's 14-year-old son, Albert, "I'm really sorry to hear Danny Driessen died."

Anderson claimed he had to save Driessen in case he needed him later in the game. The Reds rallied one final time in the ninth, but Anderson had two left-handers, Griffey and Morgan, due up and Driessen remained on the bench. With one out and Geronimo on second, Lynn made a superb, backhanded running catch to rob Griffey of the game-tying hit. With Morgan up, Geronimo unexpectedly took off for third. Momentarily distracted, Joe popped up for the final out, and the Series was tied at two games apiece.

Lost in all the drama and controversy of the first four games was Perez's batting slump. He had gone 0-for-14, and Anderson kidded him that he might go in the record books if he didn't hurry up and get a hit. But Tony was not worried. "I not pressing," said Perez. "I just in a slump. I too old to be pressing."

In the second inning of Game Five, which pitted Boston's Reggie Cleveland against Gullett, Perez made his 15th consecutive out. But in the fourth, Perez broke the slump with a home run to tie the score, 1-1. Then in the sixth, with two on, Perez hit his second home run to give the Reds a 5-1 lead. Gullett pitched one of the best post-season games ever in the Big Red Machine era. He took a two-hitter into the ninth, but gave up three hits and one more run before Anderson brought in Eastwick to record the final out.

Heinz Kluetmeier, *Sports Illustrated*

Johnny Bench congratulated a determined Tony Perez after his three-run home run in Game Five gave the Reds a 5-1 lead. Bench and Joe Morgan (behind Perez) were on base.

The Reds were a confident team after the win. "We're in the driver's seat now," declared Morgan. "The pressure is on them because they have to win both games. We've got champagne riding with us."

The announced starters for Game Six were Billingham and Lee, but storms descended on Boston and Saturday's game was postponed to Sunday. Then, it was postponed to Monday. Then, it was postponed to Tuesday. After Sunday's game was called, Anderson decided to hold a team practice at an indoor facility at Tufts University. The Reds, in uniform, climbed aboard a school bus at their hotel, and headed to Tufts. "This is the first time I've ever been to college," cracked Carroll.

But getting Carroll to college was not easy. The driver took the wrong exit and the Reds were lost. Twice the driver had to stop for directions. The scene turned surreal at a gas station.

"We've all got our uniforms on," recalled Pat Darcy. "Sparky got off the bus and it was like "Candid Camera." It was real busy and everything just stopped. It was like, that can't be Sparky Anderson. But there's Sparky saying to the attendant, 'How do you get to Tufts University?'"

By this time, everybody was looking for Allen Funt, but Sparky finally navigated the bus to Tufts—with a relaxed group of Reds "agitatin'" their manager all the way.

The New England monsoons finally abated on Tuesday, and a full October moon shone above the historic ballpark that evening as the teams lined up for the opening introductions to Game Six. Up in the NBC television booth, Joe Garagiola, Tony Kubek and Dick Stockton completed their pre-game comments for the estimated 62 million viewers. The 1975 Series was the fifth to include night games, and the thrilling come-from-behind performances in the

In the first inning of the fifth game of the 1975 Series, Carlton Fisk tagged out Pete Rose for the third out. Rose attempted to score on a fly ball to left field by Johnny Bench. Tony Perez later hit two home runs to lead the Reds to a 6-2 win and a three games-to-two lead in the Series.

earlier games, the Armbrister-Fisk controversy, and the do-or-die aspect of this game for the Red Sox generated a huge television audience. The weather helped, too.

"All that rain in Boston turned it into Super Bowl week," recalled Rose. "It was just us, the Red Sox and all that mass media. There were interviews all the time. It had already been a helluva of a World Series to that point, and the rain just increased the anticipation for Game Six."

Both managers switched starting pitchers after the rain delays. Johnson started Tiant, figuring he needed his most successful hurler on the mound in a game Boston had to win.

Anderson called Billingham into his office.

"Jack, you're going to be mad at me, and Jolene (Billingham's wife) is, too, but I'm puttin' you in the bullpen."

Billingham was furious. He could not understand the move. "(Dwight) Evans said I had the best stuff on the club," recalled Billingham.

Anderson started Gary Nolan. "Nolan has not pitched in relief this year," explained Sparky. "If I don't start Nolan, he is useless to me." Anderson used Billingham in relief in both Game Six and Game Seven. Although Cactus Jack did not earn a decision in the Series, his ERA of 1.00 (in 9 innings) was tops on the Reds.

The second-guessing of Anderson's choice to start Nolan in Game Six began in the first inning. Yastrzemski and Fisk singled and Fred Lynn hit a long home run into the right-field bleachers for a 3-0 lead. The crowd, which had barely settled into their seats, erupted in a long cheer, and continued the clamoring as Tiant dipped and danced through the first four innings.

This was the third time in 10 days that the Reds were facing El Tiante. Most of the lineup had batted against him a dozen times. In the fifth, Tiant began to struggle, walking Armbrister and giving up a single to Rose. Griffey then launched a fly ball over Lynn's head in deep center. Lynn had run down a similar Griffey drive in Game Four, but in smaller Fenway, he ran out of room. Turning at the last moment, he leaped against the wall, missing the catch and landing hard on his back.

Two runs scored and Griffey made third, but all eyes were on Lynn who remained slumped against the wall in a grotesque position. The exuberant crowd suddenly quieted, and even after Lynn shakily got to his feet and remained in the game, the crowd seemed stunned. Moments later, the Reds tied the game when Bench flicked a low outside pitch off the Green Monster to drive in Griffey.

In the previous four games, the team that scored first had lost the game, and the Reds were now poised for another come-from-behind victory. In the seventh, with none out, Griffey and Morgan singled and Tiant again had to scramble. He nearly survived the inning, getting Bench and Perez to fly out, but Foster boomed a double high off the center-field wall to give the Reds a 5-3 lead. Leading off the eighth, Geronimo homered to right to make it 6-3. The magnificent Tiant was through, and the crowd gave him a standing ovation. As he lumbered off the field, a familiar sense of post-season despair settled over Fenway: the 57-year-old curse would continue.

Pedro Borbon, the fifth Reds pitcher, opened the eighth inning. Anderson had relieved Nolan in the third with Fred Norman, and then used Billingham, Carroll and Borbon. Anderson had saved his aces Eastwick and McEnaney for the late-inning kill.

"All good managers are good defensive managers for the last six outs of the game," explained Anderson in his book, *Sparky!* "Everything hinges on them. You might blow out a team once in a while. A few times you're going to get blown out, too. Basically, though, most games are decided in the eighth and ninth innings."

Borbon had pitched a scoreless sixth and seventh, but gave up a single to Lynn and a walk to Rico Petrocelli to lead off the eighth. The Fenway crowd was buzzing again. Anderson, in his familiar Captain Hook stroll to the mound, gingerly stepped over the foul line with his familiar stutter step, and tapped his right arm, signaling for Eastwick. The thin right-hander had already won two games and saved another. He appeared set to pick up the World Series MVP award if he could record the final six outs.

With the crowd roaring, Eastwick quickly retired two right-handed hitters, Dwight Evans and Rick Burleson. Johnson called upon left-handed Bernie Carbo to pinch-hit for pitcher Roger Moret. Anderson considered bringing in his lefty, McEnaney, but was certain Johnson would have countered with the right-handed hitting Juan Beniquez. With the Green Monster looming, Anderson did not like that matchup.

"If he (Beniquez) had lost the ball into the screen, I would have been sick," Anderson later explained.

Eastwick jumped ahead of Carbo, one ball and two strikes, causing Anderson to reconsider. He could bring in McEnaney with two strikes on the hitter, making it nearly impossible for Johnson to bring in a pinch-hitter. "I was all set to make the move. I took one step up the dugout steps. Then for a reason I simply do not know, I changed my mind."

The episode was eerily similar to the non-decision Anderson made in the 1972 Series when he failed to re-position Concepcion in the ninth inning of Game Four, a game the Reds lost.

The count moved to two-and-two. In the stands behind home plate, Ray Shore and Chief Bender discussed the impending victory celebration. Shore thought Carbo looked overmatched against Eastwick. He told Bender he didn't want to get caught in all the commotion on the field, so he was heading to the clubhouse as soon as the inning was over. He began to gather his papers.

Crack! Carbo launched the next pitch deep into the center-field stands, a three-run homer that tied the game.

Carbo raced around the bases, first with his arms above his head, then stretching them out at his side as though he were floating, riding the wave of the crowd's cheers. Behind home plate, Shore sunk back into his seat. Out in the bullpen in right-center field, the Cincinnati pitchers watched in disbelief as Carbo's drive landed in the seats above them. They knew as soon as Carbo hit it that it was gone. But they couldn't believe Carbo had hit it off Eastwick.

"It was really smoked," remembered Darcy. "One second, we're up, 6-3, with our ace reliever. Now I'm thinking, God, I could be in this game."

Carbo's home run was one of the most dramatic in World Series history, but on this wild night at Fenway, it would prove to be second best.

In the bottom of the ninth, the Red Sox launched what appeared to be a game-winning rally. Doyle walked and Yastrzemski singled to right. Doyle raced to third and Yastrzemski dashed to second on Griffey's throw to third. Anderson summoned McEnaney, who walked Fisk intentionally to load the bases, and bring up Lynn. Hoping for a double-play ball, Bench called for a slider down and away, but instead McEnaney unloaded a fastball.

Bench was crossed up; his immediate thought was the ball would get by him for a wild pitch. But in the next fraction of a

Denny Doyle's desperate dash to score the winning run in the bottom of the ninth inning of Game Six fell victim to a strong throw from George Foster and a sweep tag by Johnny Bench.

Heinz Kluetmeier, *Sports Illustrated*

second, Lynn swung and lifted a high fly to short left field. Foster moved toward the foul line and caught the ball in foul territory just two feet from the wall along the edge of the stands. Doyle, on third, looked over his shoulder at the play behind him.

"Go, go, go!" he thought he heard third-base coach Don Zimmer yell.

In fact, Zimmer had yelled, "No, no, no!"

Foster's location required that his throw home follow a precise arc, just over Doyle's left shoulder. Too far right, it would hit Doyle; a couple of feet to the left, Bench would not have time to snare the throw and make the tag. Foster's one-bounce throw was perfect. Bench grabbed the ball, swung his big mitt around and tagged the diving Doyle for a double play.

Bench accompanied McEnaney back to the mound.

"Will, what the hell?" said Bench. "You crossed me up!"

"Yeah, I guess I did," McEnaney admitted. "But heck, John. These things work out, don't they?"

In the 11th inning, it was the Reds' turn to think they had the game and the Series won. With one out and Griffey on first, Morgan smashed a long line drive to right field that appeared to be a home run. As Morgan headed to first base, he noticed that Dwight Evans continued to chase after the ball.

"Whoa, where does he think he's going?" thought Morgan. "He can't get to that!"

But Evans never gave up. While on the full run a few feet in front of the fence, he leapt awkwardly with his glove extended and snared the ball. It appeared from the replays that Morgan's drive would have landed in the first row of the right-field seats. Evans bounced off the fence, turned and threw back to first base to double up Griffey. Fenway shook in the deafening roar. The game had become a feast of baseball riches.

In the 12th, the Reds again rallied, putting the go-ahead run on second, but Concepcion and Geronimo failed to deliver. Pat Darcy

AP/Wide World Photos

A step in front of the right-field wall, Dwight Evans jumped for Joe Morgan's drive in the 11th inning. Evans' miraculous catch was one of four historic, heart-stopping plays in the final innings of Game Six.

returned to the mound for the bottom of the 12th. Since coming into the game in the 10th inning, Darcy had retired all six men he had faced. Now he faced Fisk to lead off the 12th.

"No one had hit the ball hard," recalled Darcy. "I'm thinking, 'Don't walk anybody, don't walk anybody.' The first pitch to Fisk was high, and I tried to throw the next one for a strike, but harder, tried to muscle it, but I didn't throw it as hard as I had been throwing."

Fisk swung at the thigh-high fastball, sending it soaring to left field. The ball started fair, but kept hooking toward foul ground. Fisk dropped his bat and waved his arms toward fair territory, willing the ball to stay in play. It did, landing flush against the foul pole for a home run and a 6-5 Boston win, triggering a Fenway celebration that was as emotional as any the old yard had ever seen.

If ever a team had reason to be demoralized, it was the Reds after Game Six. They seemed to have the game won twice, before Carbo's homer and Evans' catch had robbed them of the Series victory. Yet, as Darcy recalled, the players never hung their heads. "Billingham told me, 'You pitched really well; don't let it bother you.' Morgan said same thing. Most people were saying what a great game it was."

"With the Big Red Machine, you never got down," Billingham recalled. "How many times did we lose two in a row?"

Rose had set the tone. In the 11th inning, in his last at-bat, he had turned to Fisk and said, "Can you believe this game?" And that was *before* Evans' catch and Fisk's homer.

Pat Darcy pitched two scoreless innings for the Reds before facing Carlton Fisk to lead off the 12th inning in Game Six. Fisk's home run swing ended the most memorable game in World Series history.

AP/Wide World Photos

All during the 10th and 11th innings, Rose kept Darcy pumped up with infield chatter. "After every out, Rose tossed the ball back to me after it had gone around the infield," Darcy remembered. "He'd say, 'What a game. This is a great game. I'd pay to see this game.'"

On the way to the team bus after the game, Rose told Anderson, "That's the greatest baseball game I ever played in." He promised Sparky that the Reds would win Game Seven.

Anderson, though, could not shake the feeling that he had lost the game, and perhaps the Series, by failing to relieve Eastwick with McEnaney during Carbo's at-bat.

"The only thing that kept running through my mind was that I cost us two World Series," said Anderson, thinking back to the 1972 loss to Oakland.

Ray Shore joined Sparky in his hotel room, and kept Anderson company until the Reds skipper fell asleep at four in the morning.

Through the first five innings of Game Seven, it appeared Boston would derail the championship hopes of the Big Red Machine. Gullett started, and in the third inning gave up three runs on two singles and four walks. But his clutch strikeouts of Fred Lynn and Rick Burleson with the bases loaded kept the score close.

Meanwhile, Red Sox starter Bill Lee baffled the Reds. With Cincinnati trailing, 3-0, in the sixth, Tony Perez walked to the bat rack. He looked around the corner and there was his manager, pacing nervously, scratching his head of white hair.

"What's wrong with you, Sparky?" asked Perez in the high-pitched squeal he used when he was ribbing a teammate. Perez's normal voice was a deep, thick bass.

"Damn, Doggie!" said Sparky. "We're down three to nothing!"

"Don't worry 'bout it," said Perez. "Get somebody on base. I'm going to 'heet' one. I'm going to heet a bomb."

From the on-deck circle, Perez watched Bench bat with one out and Rose on first base. Bench grounded to short for what appeared to be an inning-ending double play. But Rose slid hard into second base and Denny Doyle hurried his relay throw to first to avoid Pete.

AP/Wide World Photos

In a video moment frozen in time, Carlton Fisk danced along the first-base line, urging his long fly ball to stay fair.

Dennis Gruelle

With two out in the sixth inning of the seventh game and the Reds trailing Boston, 3-0, Tony Perez crushed a Bill Lee blooper curve far over the left-center field wall for a two-run home run. Johnny Bench scored from second base. The arrow points to the ball in flight.

The throw sailed past Yastrzemski; Bench was safe at first. Nowhere would Rose's hustle appear in the box score, but he had kept the bat in Tony's hands. The Reds were still alive.

In the back of his mind, Perez believed he might see Lee's blooper pitch again. In Game Two, he had swung at the blooper and missed it badly. In the second inning of Game Seven, Lee had thrown him another floater and Perez timed it.

"Throw me that again," Perez prayed.

Lee began by throwing Perez sinkers away. Then, Perez watched intently as the "Spaceman" came to a slight "stop" in his windup.

"I knew right then it was coming," said Perez. "I stayed back and said, 'Here it comes.' As soon as I hit it, I said to myself, 'We're back in the game.' I felt right then we were going to win."

The ball shot off his bat, high and deep, and disappeared in the New England night, far beyond the left-center field wall. The Boston outfielders did not even turn to follow the flight.

The two-run blast brought the Reds to within one run, at 3-2. Out in the bullpen, Perez's blast revitalized McEnaney. "Before he hit it, I thought 'I'm not going to get a ring, not going to get a World Series share.' And when he hit it I thought, 'My God, what's our ring going to look like? How much money are we going to get?'"

In the seventh, the Reds drew even. Griffey walked, stole second and scored on a two-out single by Rose. Bench fouled out with the bases loaded to end the rally. Neither team mounted a threat in the eighth. For the first time since 1924, the seventh game of a World Series went to the ninth inning tied.

In a move that Boston fans would long question, manager Darrell Johnson had pinch-hit for Jim Willoughby with two out and nobody on in the bottom of the eighth. Until that point, Willoughby had pitched six shutout innings against the Reds. He was Boston's most effective reliever. Johnson now called on Jim Burton, a rookie left-hander who had pitched only one-third of an inning in the Series, to pitch the ninth. Burton immediately walked Griffey.

Anderson usually shunned the sacrifice, but he now gave the bunt sign to Geronimo. "Chief" successfully moved Griffey to second. Driessen, in only his second at-bat of the Series, advanced

Tony Triolo, *Sports Illustrated*

Joe Morgan's flare single to center field with two out in the ninth inning drove in the winning run in Game Seven of the 1975 Series. The Reds scored all four of their runs in Game Seven with two out.

Griffey to third on a grounder to Doyle. Pitching carefully to Rose (who had been on base in 11 of his previous 19 at-bats), Burton walked him. Up stepped Morgan.

Morgan had faced Burton in Game Three. Burton had a "late-breaking" slider that was tough for Morgan to follow. With the count at 2-2, Burton threw it again. It was a good pitch, on the edge of the strike zone, low and away. Morgan managed a defensive swing, and flared a soft liner, almost a bloop, over second base and far in front of hard-charging center fielder Lynn. Griffey trotted home. For the first time in the game, the Reds led, 4-3.

AP/Wide World Photos

Tony Perez (left) hugged Clay Carroll, batting practice pitcher Art Siefert grabbed Johnny Bench, and Joe Morgan raced to join the mob as the Reds celebrated the 1975 Series win.

In four of the seven games, Morgan had come to bat with the winning or tying run on base in what could have been the Reds' final at-bat. In Game Three, he singled in the game-winner in the bottom of the tenth; in Game Four, he popped out in the bottom of the ninth; in Game Six, Evans robbed him of a game-winning home run in the top of the eleventh; and now in Game Seven, he had driven in the winning run of the World Series. It was a champion's performance in baseball's ultimate pressure-cooker.

Standing on base, Morgan glanced into the Reds dugout. Usually after a flare hit, the bench would ride the hitter, telling him he had just embarrassed the Big Red Machine. But now, the players in the dugout were jubilant, not jeering. "I couldn't have gotten a bigger reaction from them if I had sent one over the scoreboard on top of the bleachers in dead center field," recalled Morgan.

Anderson turned to McEnaney to preserve the lead. Since Boston's run-scoring third inning, the Reds pitching had been outstanding, allowing only two hits. It was vintage Big Red Machine: the hitters had grabbed the spotlight, but the pitching had kept Cincinnati in the game. Relievers Billingham and Carroll had allowed only one hit in their four innings, and now McEnaney had three outs to go.

Pinch-hitter Juan Beniquez led off the Boston ninth. Bench signaled for a fastball. "We went against the scouting reports unintentionally," recalled McEnaney. "Beniquez was a first-ball fastball hitter. We just forgot. We got lucky."

Beniquez flied to right. The second hitter, pinch-hitter Bob Montgomery, grounded out to Concepcion, bringing up Yastrzemski.

McEnaney couldn't raise enough saliva to spit. "I was scared to death," admitted McEnaney. "John gave me a sign for a slider on the first pitch. I missed it low. He called for another slider. Low, ball two. You couldn't give Yaz a good fastball to hit. You had to pitch around his strike zone. We tried to throw him breaking balls, hoping he would swing. I always had confidence in my slider, but I missed on both of them. The next pitch was a fastball up and he took it for a strike. I figured he would take it.

"The next pitch was another fastball, and it's middle in. He took a batting-practice swing, kind of a lazy swing. As soon as as he hit I knew it was an out. I saw Geronimo camping under it. I looked back at John. I just jumped in his arms."

Every person in a Reds uniform joined the pile in the middle of the infield, except Anderson. He felt too emotionally spent to join the crush of players. Most baseball people had agreed with his annual assessments of the past few years that the Reds were the "best club in baseball." But the boasts had put additional pressure on Anderson. Nineteen seventy-five had also been difficult for him with the discovery of cancer in a close friend, and an emotional reconciliation with his son after a year-long feud over the youngster's hair. In a tearful speech after the game, Sparky dedicated the win to the terminally-ill Milt Blish, the car dealer who had befriended Anderson in the mid-1960s when baseball had cut him adrift.

Next to the Cincinnati dugout, waving a Reds pennant, Bob Howsam cheered the final out with the rest of his delegation. But there would be no dancing on the dugouts, the way Charlie Finley had gloated at Riverfront Stadium after Oakland's win in 1972. Howsam's fine sense of decorum would never have allowed that.

Bob Howsam (left) maintained a calm exterior during the seventh game of the Series, but he enthusiastically joined chairman of the board Louis Nippert in a champagne shootout after the Reds won. The championship was Howsam's first since his St. Louis Cardinals won in 1964.

Howsam was never good at being a "fan," merely enjoying the spectacle of the game. He was working all the while.

"I always tell people I sit next to that I'm not going to be a good person to sit by because I'm not going to talk much," said Howsam.

The Cincinnati Enquirer

A crowd of 30,000 gathered on Fountain Square plaza in the heart of downtown Cincinnati to cheer the 1975 World Champions. It was the Reds' first championship since 1940.

"I'm too interested in what's happening on the field. Even in the seventh game of the World Series, I wanted to see how my players could do. Lee MacPhail (President of the American League) said to me during the winter meetings, 'I watched you during the seventh game, and I wondered what the hell you were thinking about. All you did was sit there and you never showed any reaction.'"

But as cool as Howsam was *during* the game, his genuine excitement burst forth in the celebration in the clubhouse. He and owner "Gus" Nippert thoroughly soaked one another as they drowned five seasons of frustration in the spray of champagne.

In the post-game euphoria, there were tributes to the "organization," recognition that it was Bob Howsam who had built the foundation for the success of the Reds. The victory was a tribute to the old-fashioned way of building a baseball team, through scouting, development and astute deal-making; through discipline, teamwork and industriousness; through always paying homage to the needs of the fans; through adherence to the bedrock values and principles that Howsam had been taught and practiced. And, if one practiced them well enough and worked harder at them than anyone else, one was bound to succeed.

In the following days and weeks, the club enjoyed a victory parade through downtown Cincinnati, the toasts of the winter banquet circuit, $19,000 World Series checks and a celebratory cruise in the Caribbean. Howsam and Anderson finally had their championship, and for the first time since the creation of the Big Red Machine, the Reds had undeniably earned the title they had claimed all along: *"the best team in baseball."*

1975 SCRAPBOOK

THE OPPOSITION

WESTERN DIVISION

Against	Won	Lost
Atlanta	15	3
Houston	13	5
Los Angeles	8	10
San Diego	11	7
San Fran.	13	5

EASTERN DIVISION

Against	Won	Lost
Chicago	11	1
Montreal	8	4
New York	8	4
Philadelphia	7	5
Pittsburgh	6	6
St. Louis	8	4

The pitcher the Reds didn't want to face — **Randy Jones** of the Padres was 3-1 against the Reds.

The pitcher they loved to see — **Phil Niekro** of the Braves was 0-6 against the Reds.

The batter who loved the Reds — **Bill Madlock** of Chicago hit .538 (28-for-52) with 8 HRs and 9 RBIs.

The batter who should have stayed home — **Rick Monday** of the Cubs hit .176 (9-for-51) with 0 HR and 2 RBIs.

CLUB LEADERS

Batting Average	Joe Morgan	.327
Home runs	Johnny Bench	28
RBIs	Johnny Bench	110
Stolen bases	Joe Morgan	67
Runs	Pete Rose	112 •
ERA	Don Gullett	2.42
Wins	Billingham, Gullett, Nolan	15
Saves	Rawly Eastwick	22 •
Games	Will McEnaney	70

• League Leader

AWARDS

MVP	Joe Morgan
Sporting News Player of the Year	Joe Morgan
Manager of the Year	Sparky Anderson
Gold Glove	Johnny Bench, Joe Morgan, Dave Concepcion, Cesar Geronimo
Cincinnati Reds MVP •	Joe Morgan
Outstanding Reds Pitcher •	Don Gullett
Reds Newcomer of the Year •	Rawly Eastwick

• Awarded by Cincinnati Chapter of Baseball Writers Association

TRADES

May 20	**Mac Scarce** acquired from New York Mets for **Tom Hall**
Dec. 12	**Mike Lum** acquired from Atlanta for **Darrel Chaney**
Dec. 12	**Jeff Sovern** and **Rich Hinton** acquired from Chicago White Sox for **Clay Carroll**
Dec. 12	**Bob Bailey** acquired from Montreal for **Clay Kirby**

THE DRAFT

Cincinnati drafted 35 players; five played in the major leagues:

Frank Pastore	Upland, CA	P
Paul Moskau	Asuza Pacific Univ.	P
Scott Brown	DeQuincy, LA	P
Don Welchel •	Dallas, TX	P
Bill Paschal •	Univ. of North Carolina	P

• Drafted by the Reds, but signed with another club

Johnny Bench approached home plate and a happy Tony Perez, Danny Driessen and Cesar Geronimo (right to left) in the ninth inning of Game Four of the 1976 World Series. Bench's home run, his second of the game, clinched the Reds 7-2 victory and a World Series sweep.

World Champions • Swept New York Yankees, 4-0

Chapter 10

1976
Sweep to Greatness

Joe Morgan, MVP • Set Reds attendance mark of 2.6 million

THE 1975 SEASON AND WORLD Series answered whatever questions remained about the domination and character of the Big Red Machine. The Reds won 108 games, the most in the National League since 1909, and their winning margin of 20 games tied the major league record. Joe Morgan captured the MVP award, the team's fourth in six years. Four Reds—Morgan, Bench, Concepcion and Geronimo—won Gold Glove awards.

In the Series, the Reds had come from behind to win each of their four victories. The drama of the seven games, highlighted by the many memorable plays that quickly became enshrined in baseball video lore, helped establish the Reds as one of the game's great teams.

The Series also helped revitalize the sport. In the mid-1960s, baseball had led all other sports in popularity. But by 1968, suffering from television's new love affair with football and the hype of the Super Bowl, baseball lost its lead. The decline continued through the early 1970s, and by 1975 only 16 percent of all fans named baseball as their favorite sport.

Sport demographics in the early 1970s revealed that baseball was favored by those over 50 and those making less than $5,000. Football, by contrast, captured the under-35 fan and those making more than $10,000.

"Baseball has had trouble attracting the younger, more affluent fans who are more likely to attend games in person and who form the kind of audience that is attractive to television sponsors," wrote pollster Lou Harris.

But the 1975 Series spurred a baseball revival. Attendance reached an all-time high in 1976 at 31 million fans, and began an upward trend that would continue for the rest of the decade. Television and newspapers began to praise the game for its pastoral qualities in comparison to the violence of football. In 1977, Harris reported that for the first time since 1968 more sports fans in the country followed baseball than football.

Of all the franchises in baseball, none had helped promote this revival more than the Reds. And, thanks to the marketing vision of Bob Howsam and Dick Wagner, none was better positioned to capitalize on it.

When Howsam took over the Reds in 1967, the club was a perennial also-ran that averaged 800,000 a year in attendance. By the mid-1970s, the Reds fielded a championship club of All-Stars with the most charismatic players in the game. The Reds regularly drew more than 2 million fans annually, and were recognized as one of the best-run clubs in all of baseball.

The 1973 attendance mark of 2,017,601 was the first of eight straight seasons over 2 million. In 1976, Cincinnati would lead the major leagues in attendance with 2,629,708, a club record that still stands. At the time, that was the fourth-highest season attendance figure in major league history. What made the attendance figures even more remarkable was that Cincinnati was the second smallest metropolitan market in all of baseball.

The success Howsam had in Cincinnati at the gate repeated the success he enjoyed in Denver and St. Louis. He set minor league attendance records in Denver and established the attendance base that ultimately brought major league sports to the Rocky Mountains. In St. Louis, where his association with long-time aide and marketing strategist Dick Wagner began, Howsam's Cardinals set the all-time club attendance mark of 1.7 million in 1966 and he laid the groundwork for the club's first 2 million season in 1967. Howsam is one of the few general managers to set attendance records with two different franchises, and to push both over the 2 million mark.

A part of the surge in attendance under Howsam in Cincinnati could be attributed to new Riverfront Stadium. But Pittsburgh, Philadelphia and Kansas City had recently opened new parks and none had come close to cracking 2 million. The organization benefitted greatly from a contending club with Hall of Fame talent, but other clubs in bigger cities had similar success in the standings without the attendance spike. In the final analysis, Howsam and Wagner were simply very good at one of baseball's fundamental challenges: they knew how to put fannies in the seats.

This particular skill was tested almost immediately when the Howsam regime opened for business in Cincinnati. Filling new Riverfront Stadium pushed Howsam and Wagner into uncharted territory. For the franchise to be successful in the new facility, it would have to double the typical attendance at a Crosley Field game (10,000), and during the peak summer months average 30,000, the equivalent of a Crosley sellout. Could Cincinnati sustain that level of support for its baseball team?

As he had in St. Louis, Wagner ran the business side of the operation, which included ticket sales, marketing and promotion. Under Howsam's direction, Wagner focused the marketing effort on three main goals: increasing season ticket sales, building upon the regional appeal the club already enjoyed and aiming promotions at families and young adults.

The Reds' season ticket base was about 900 when Wagner arrived in 1967. He developed season ticket and group sales

The Cincinnati Enquirer

The Reds attracted 10 capacity crowds of over 50,000 fans in 1976 and drew 2.6 million, the fourth highest total in baseball history.

brochures to take advantage of the move to Riverfront. By the early 1970s, the club annually sold over 15,000 season tickets. Wagner fought hard to retain his season ticket holders. The club mailed them classy souvenirs in the offseason; after the World Championships of 1975 and 1976, the Reds sent commemorative bats stamped with the players' signatures.

Long before Howsam arrived, the Reds had benefitted from a strong regional presence that included Indiana, Kentucky and West Virginia. To be successful at Riverfront, the Reds had to boost their regional appeal. They took advantage of two developments: the new interstate highway system and radio.

Roger Ruhl, the publicity director and later the vice president of marketing, recalled that the new stadium, the success of the Big Red Machine and the interstate highway system all came together to jump-start the marketing effort.

"Now, instead of being two and one-half hours from Columbus, it was an hour and a half," said Ruhl. "You had the ability to put 50,000 people in the ballpark on a Saturday or Sunday, or any day of the week if the Dodgers were in town. At Crosley on weekends, you didn't have the capacity to kick that up to 50,000, but that's what the interstate and the new stadium meant to the Reds."

If Cincinnati was a small metropolitan market, the region more than made up for it. Wagner liked to cite the statistic: there were more people within 150 miles of Cincinnati than in any other major league market. The Reds' domain included Indianapolis, Dayton, Columbus, Lexington, Louisville and even parts of West Virginia and Tennessee. The Reds put more emphasis than ever on the region, especially the annual media caravan which blitzed all the major metropolitan areas before the start of spring training.

The speakers bureau, inaugurated by Howsam in 1968 and headed by popular ex-Red Gordy Coleman, worked overtime. Coleman received 15 to 20 requests a day; in the winter, he spent nearly every day on the road making appearances. During the season, Coleman targeted his schedule at the Reds' opponents.

"If the Cubs are the next team coming to town, I go out into northwestern Indiana," Coleman said. "That's where the actual Cub fans are. I get on radio shows, call-in shows. I promote the series and the game of baseball, just like an advance man. If it's the Cards coming, I'll go into Cardinal territory."

In 1974, surveys revealed that 51 percent of a typical Riverfront audience hailed from Ohio, 30 percent from Indiana and 12

Courtesy of Roger Ruhl

In 1976, Kentucky Fried Chicken became the Reds' largest season ticket holder when the company purchased $18,000 worth of tickets for a promotion. Company founder Colonel Sanders was thanked by marketing vice president, Roger Ruhl.

percent from Kentucky.

Much of the regional success of the Reds could be traced to the Reds Radio Network which for years had broadcast into Ohio, Indiana, Kentucky and West Virginia. In 1971, the Reds went into the radio business themselves, taking back the broadcast rights from sponsors. The club aggressively expanded the network. From 70 stations in 1970, the Reds jumped to 115 by 1977, extending their coverage into Virginia, Tennessee and Florida.

Retaining the broadcast rights proved to be more profitable than selling the rights, and it also allowed Howsam and Wagner more editorial control over the broadcasts. The announcers were now employed and paid by the Reds, not the radio stations.

"It let us get our side of the story out," admitted Wagner in a time when ownership was engaged in bitter disputes with Marvin Miller and the Players Association. Howsam and Wagner refused to allow their announcers to mention the Players Association unless the club deemed it was a legitimate news story.

"I don't think the average fan is interested in the Players Association as such," declared Wagner.

Al Michaels, the Reds announcer from 1971 to 1973, and Marty Brennaman, who replaced Michaels, knew their broadcasts were monitored by Wagner. Michaels remembered that Wagner would not let him mention Marvin Miller's name during the Bobby Tolan incidents of 1973. Tolan had asked Miller and the Players Association to intervene on his behalf when Tolan was suspended.

"How could you report the Tolan case," wondered Michaels, "without using the name Marvin Miller?"

Wagner tried to avoid other unpleasant news for the Reds by discouraging his announcers from mentioning bad weather. Wagner thought it extraneous to dwell on rain because games at Riverfront

The Cincinnati Enquirer

The tough-minded Dick Wagner shrank from no challenge; when bees swarmed the Riverfront Stadium infield on April 18, 1976, Howsam's top lieutenant led the fight to repel the invaders.

were rarely rained out.

Brennaman believed that the Reds "imposed much greater restrictions than other announcers had to deal with." He recalled one of Wagner's admonitions: "Say it and forget it." If you had to mention bad news, say it once, then move on. But Brennaman could not heed that dictum.

"Say a guy makes an error in the second inning that leads to three or four unearned runs, and the Reds are behind. In the seventh or eighth inning, I might bring it up again. Wagner would let me know about it."

"Dick," Brennaman would plead, "by your own admission people are constantly turning on the radio and we've always got brand new people to our broadcast. I've got to say in the seventh or eighth inning what happened in the second because it impacts what happens."

Wagner would be unmoved. "Say it and forget it."

"But I wasn't of a mind to say it and forget it, and therein was the reason we fought so much," recalled Brennaman. "I had to measure everything I said."

Whatever tension existed between the announcers and the club did not interfere with the success of the Reds on radio. Michaels and Brennaman were both relative unknowns when they came to Cincinnati, but they forged a strong rapport with Reds fans. They developed into strong play-by-play men and became popular ambassadors for the club.

The growth of the radio audience was also due to the research background Howsam and Wagner shared. Howsam did not make snap judgments about players; his thorough intelligence-gathering was legend. On the business side, Wagner set up a sophisticated research system to aid marketing decisions.

Old-line baseball people may have been skeptical about the worth of such an effort, but Wagner had the benefit of his experience with the Ice Capades in the 1960s. He was eager to borrow ideas from a well-run business.

"I really got into the marketing with the ice shows," Wagner recalled. "They had early IBM equipment. We tracked ticket sales and did fan surveys."

Wagner and Howsam brought the Reds into the computer age.

Wagner believes the Reds were the first major league club to have a computer, an early Digital behemoth. In an era when software was not available off the shelf, the Reds hired two professors from Miami University to write programs. Wagner's staff devised questionnaires that were distributed at Crosley Field and later at Riverfront Stadium.

"We did about a dozen games a year, different days of the week," Wagner explained. "We asked fans their residence, how often they attended games, their TV and radio listening habits, and so on." The club conducted phone interviews and surveyed license plates in the parking lot.

For years, baseball had seen itself as a blue-collar game, a refuge for bleacher bums soaking up sun and beer and enjoying a day off work at the ballpark. But Cincinnati fans fit a different profile, Wagner's research revealed.

"We discovered we had 50 percent women and children in the ballpark in the summer months, and a well-educated audience," Wagner said. "At the new stadium we were upscale."

As for the venerable bleacher bum, he was not appreciated. The surveys showed that the two biggest complaints people had were profanity and fans without shirts.

"We looked into making fans keep their shirts on, but decided against it," Wagner recalled.

One of the biggest payoffs from the data was in selling radio and TV time. The crowd surveys provided far more information about the demographics of Reds radio listeners and TV watchers than did typical media research. Advertisers and media outlets had to take notice. "We were able to say, 'Here's our audience, here's where they live, here's what kind of income they have,'" recalled Wagner. On more than one occasion, the Reds could tell the TV and radio stations more about their listeners than the stations knew.

The data buttressed Howsam's conviction about baseball's greatest strength: it was a "family sport." His mentor, Branch Rickey, had looked upon baseball similarly: it was "wholesome entertainment."

"Our consumer was Ozzie and Harriet and David and Ricky," recalled Ruhl, referring to the archetypal American family of 1950s TV fame. "Before it was became fashionable to have a passion for the customer, Howsam had that. The fan wanted a good product and it needed to be priced fairly. It just wasn't solely baseball; it was the entertainment experience at the ballpark."

Ruhl pointed to Howsam's policy of immediately removing litter from the playing field during a game as a small but telling example of Howsam's approach. Between half innings, if anyone had thrown any litter on the field near the outfield wall, the Reds sent a member of ground crew racing out to pick it up.

"Somebody would wonder: 'Why do that? They're just going to throw more cups.'" recalled Ruhl. "But Howsam said, 'Not if you pick up the first one. They'll see how hard the kids work to run out there.'"

Because Howsam felt family attendance was the heart of a healthy franchise, he believed in keeping ticket prices affordable. Wagner countered that survey data showed the "typical fan" at Riverfront could pay a higher price. Howsam resisted. He held the line on ticket prices from 1968 to 1972; when he raised them for the 1973 season, it was a modest 50 cents across the board.

On the other hand, Howsam and Wagner avoided discounting tickets. Many other teams offered discounts, but the club's philosophy was "don't cheapen your product," recalled Ruhl. "Condition the fan to put down the full price, and then get added value on a particular game with Jacket Day, Bat Day or Cap Day."

Not surprisingly, Reds promotions were heavily marketed to families. The merchandise went to youngsters under 14 accompanied by an adult. The promotion dates were carefully targeted. Jacket Day came early in the season when jackets could be worn.

In early 1976, Jacket Day fell on Sunday, April 11 (vs. Houston), the same day Joe Morgan was to receive his MVP award. An early-season weekend game against the Astros would have typically drawn 20,000. Instead, 53,390 jammed the yard—it would be the biggest crowd all season. The Reds grossed an extra $90,000 (at an average ticket price of $3). The net profit was $60,000, because 25,000 jackets cost the club $30,000. In reality, the total profit was a lot more: all those extra kids ate a lot of popcorn, hot dogs and soft drinks.

The most successful promotion, however, and one that many other clubs copied, was the Straight A program. Junior high and high school students were rewarded for scholastic achievement. Howsam began the program in Denver, then transplanted it to St. Louis and Cincinnati. *The Cincinnati Enquirer* and *The Dayton Daily News* sponsored the program, printing the names of the winners. Each student received two free tickets to three games. The promotion paid off because most families bought additional tickets.

In 1967, the first year of the program in Cincinnati, 6,000 students qualified. By 1974, the program had expanded to 29,000 students in 18 counties in Ohio, Indiana and Kentucky. That year alone, the club handed out nearly 175,000 tickets. Wagner believed the Straight A program, along with the radio network, were the two cornerstones of the marketing effort.

"In 1976, we drew 2.6 million paid fans in the park and we also had 625,000 kids as guests of the Reds," Howsam recalled. "You have to get kids into the ballpark. Get them and you often get their moms and dads, too." In addition to the Straight A kids, the club also brought in students from economically disadvantaged areas and students with disabilities.

Cincinnati's marketing strategy also owed a debt to football. "Baseball had fallen into second place behind pro football," recalled Ruhl. "Part of the challenge was how to keep kids interested in the game."

Youth baseball programs captured kids early, but their interest in football and other sports peaked from ages 15 to 30. The Reds fought back. "That's where a lot of our promotions were directed," recalled Ruhl. "Teen Nites, College Nites and Straight A. When you surveyed our crowds against other clubs, you saw a much younger audience at Riverfront. Bob worked at that."

The Reds could also thank football for another marketing ploy: the Reds gift shop, the first of its kind in baseball. Wagner had read an article about a Washington Redskins gift shop, clipped it and sent it along to Ruhl for the "future projects" file. When the Reds opened a new downtown ticket office in 1974, they found a location with enough room for a gift shop. The club added a second shop in the Kings Island amusement park.

"We tried to go with upscale things," Wagner recalled. "We sold nicer things than you could typically get at the ballpark. We got into the art print business. Now we had a place to sell those, as well as our posters from Poster Days at the ballpark." Officials from other teams made visits to investigate the concept.

The people of Cincinnati had always had a great affection for the Reds. Now, Riverfront Stadium and a fan-friendly front office made the love affair more fun and more accessible. A few blocks north of the stadium stood the corporate headquarters of Procter & Gamble, a company that could appreciate a superb marketing effort. Wagner often repeated an observation he heard from a P&G executive: "Every home I went into when I interviewed for the job in Cincinnati had some Reds memorabilia in it."

The Cincinnati Enquirer

Bob Howsam (right) congratulated participants in the Straight A program at Crosley Field in the first years of the program in Cincinnati. Howsam's program, aimed at bringing in youngsters and their parents to the ballpark, was copied by many other clubs.

Two weeks before the opening of the 1976 season, the Reds announced that they had pre-sold over 1 million tickets; mail order and group sales had doubled over previous seasons. The World Championship and the overwhelming success at the gate gave Howsam great satisfaction. But it was tempered by baseball's labor problems, which to Howsam, not only threatened his carefully constructed Big Red Machine, but the integrity of the game itself.

The owner's hallowed reserve clause, the linchpin in baseball's rules that "reserved" or bound players to clubs for life, had been under attack by the Players Association since 1970 when Curt Flood challenged it in court. Flood lost his case, but Marvin Miller continued to test its legality. In 1975, pitchers Dave McNally, of the Expos, and Andy Messersmith, of the Dodgers, played out the season without signing contracts. Under the original interpretation of the reserve clause, the clubs could simply renew the contracts; players would remain the property of the clubs. But baseball's arbitration panel, established to hear owner-player disputes, re-interpreted the language in the reserve clause to give Messersmith and McNally their freedom. They were declared "free agents," able to sign with any club. The revolutionary decision was upheld in Federal District Court in early 1976, and baseball was forced to establish a new working arrangement between players and owners to take effect in 1977.

Howsam had spoken forcefully of the need to save the reserve clause. He had come to believe, after 30 years in baseball, that the game could not survive without it. From his earliest days in Denver, Howsam had developed and refined the skills of stadium management, fiscal responsibility, promotion and the ability to judge young talent. He developed a great respect for the game, a profound appreciation for the enjoyment it brought to people. But he also was brought up in a system in which ownership held absolute control of players through the reserve clause. Howsam mastered the system well, trading players from one club to another, and buying and selling contracts. There was no reason to question the system or wonder how things might be different if the reserve clause did not exist. Only after the laws of baseball began to be challenged in the 1970s did old-line baseball men have to confront the issue of player mobility. Howsam could not bring himself to support a system so foreign.

Howsam feared the loss of the reserve clause would reverberate throughout baseball, leading to rapidly escalating salaries, increased player mobility, the loss of the farm system and the loss of competitive balance. Free agency, he maintained, would drive fans away and lead to the collapse of the game itself.

"If costs escalate and salaries in particular go up so that we have to charge prices that the fans are not willing to pay, we are going to be getting away from the family sport which has made the game the great game it is," Howsam declared.

Like many other owners, Howsam feared that a few rich franchises would attract the best players, ruining the competitive balance in the leagues and perhaps driving a few of the weaker clubs out of business. In Howsam's view of the future, players jumping from club to club would also undermine fan loyalty.

Without a reserve clause, Howsam was also afraid clubs would abandon the farm system. If players had unlimited freedom to jump their teams, Howsam believed the clubs could not justify the high costs of developing young players.

"Baseball is different from basketball and football because they are able to get most of their talent from the colleges," said Howsam. "It would be impractical for us to maintain a large scouting staff and sign and develop young ballplayers, only to have some other team take them away from us. Clubs spend nearly $500,000 to develop a player. They won't do that if they can't keep that player, if that player is simply going to walk away."

Some of Howsam's fears would eventually materialize. Others, such as the abandonment of the farm system, would not. But he faced more immediate concerns in 1976: the makeup of his championship club. Howsam had to sign his players to contracts, and under the new rules general managers could no longer dictate all the terms. To Bob Howsam, who cherished the opportunity to manipulate and refine a ballclub through calculated trades and shrewd scouting, the loss of control was onerous.

The embodiment of evil in this changing order were agents, and Howsam and Wagner despised dealing with them. Marty Brennaman experienced the depth of that rancor when Wagner gave him an ultimatum.

"I will never deal with an agent when it comes to negotiating your contract," Wagner told his broadcaster. "Because I will not talk to him."

"It killed him to have to deal with agents," Brennaman recalled. "In my case, he didn't have to. And I never used an agent until he (Wagner) was fired."

Ray Shore remembered a telling scene in Boston during the 1975 World Series. "(Agent) Jerry Kapstein and his brother came in the clubhouse. Bob had (publicity director) Jim Ferguson tell them to leave. They didn't take it too kindly. Bob didn't think they had any place in the clubhouse. He let it be known."

But with salary levels far more market-driven than in the past, and multi-year contracts an increasingly viable option, players throughout baseball were turning to agents to help them negotiate complex and potentially lucrative deals. Reds players had additional incentive: the Cincinnati club always held a tough line in salary talks. Rose, Bench and Perez used Cincinnati attorney Reuven Katz. Morgan, Foster and Griffey relied on Tom Reich. But most of the Reds turned to Kapstein.

A native of Providence, Rhode Island, and a graduate of Harvard, Kapstein began representing athletes in the early 1970s. By 1976, the 32-year-old Kapstein was widely recognized as the leading sports agent in the nation. Perez was among his first Cincinnati clients; Kapstein helped him negotiate a large raise in 1974. Perez later dropped Kapstein, but in 1975-76, Kapstein was the pitchers' best friend: he represented Carroll, Gullett, McEnaney, Eastwick and Darcy. But Kapstein's presence had a Grim Reaper quality to it: by the middle of the 1977 season, all of these players had been banished from Cincinnati. The only Kapstein Red to survive was Davey Concepcion.

Gullett hired Kapstein in 1974. Like most clubs, the Reds opened salary negotiations by sending players a contract in the mail.

"If you liked the figure, you signed," recalled Gullett. "If not, you went in and talked. It wasn't my bag, going and tooting my own horn in salary talks. I didn't like telling them how much I needed. And the way Wagner looked at you, he always looked disappointed or mad."

Gullett was able to face down National League hitters, but not the dour Mr. Wagner. So, Gullett acted on a tip from Pete Rose to hire the gunslinger named Kapstein.

"Jerry negotiated my '75 contract and I was very satisfied with it," Gullett remembered. "The club told me they wished I hadn't sought his services, but I was happy."

In the winter of 1976, the Reds and Kapstein could not agree on new terms for Gullett. Gullett wanted a multi-year contract. The front office reminded Kapstein the team had raced off to its big lead in 1975 while Gullett had a broken thumb. The impression was that the Reds didn't need Gullett—they certainly didn't need him enough to warrant a multi-year deal.

Gullett was infuriated. He never signed a new contract in 1976. He played out his option and became the first Red to qualify for free agency.

Of the last seven Cincinnati players to sign contracts in 1976, five were represented by Kapstein.

"That should tell you something," said Wagner.

Bench, Morgan and Rose signed their 1976 contracts for approximately $200,000 apiece. The club's opening offer to Perez was about $117,000, and Perez initially refused to sign. Eventually, he wrangled a raise that put him closer to the vicinity of the club's three big non-Latino stars.

But Perez's holdout and the logjam with Kapstein's players were not the biggest news stories of the spring. The opening of spring training was delayed 17 days in March when the owners closed the camps until a new bargaining agreement was signed with the Players Association. The most controversial issues dealt with the length of service players had to accrue before they would be eligible for free agency. The players demanded six years; owners lobbied for an eight- or nine-year period.

By closing the camps and threatening to postpone the opening of the season, the owners hoped to pressure the players into an agreement favorable to management. Many of the Reds were already in Florida and anxious to play, including Bench and Rose. They organized informal workouts and appeared to favor a quick settlement.

"We busted tail to bring baseball back to the popularity it now has," said a frustrated Rose. "We can't let it slip back with something like this. We must remember that it is give and take. It can't be all take for the players."

As he waited for a softball game to conclude on a public diamond where the Reds had gathered to practice, Rose couldn't believe his predicament.

"Look at me!" he said. "I'm in the position I've wanted to be in for 13 years. I'm coming to spring training as a World Champion. And what do I do? Sit here in a sweat suit watching a beer league game going on! I can't even wear the Cincinnati Reds uniform!"

It was exactly this impatience that Howsam and other owners hoped would drive a wedge in the Players Association. But 17 days into the lockout, Commissioner Kuhn ordered the camps opened. Kuhn feared the public relations fiasco of a long impasse and he acted in accord with what he considered to be the "best interest of baseball." But many of the owners, including Howsam and his staff, felt betrayed. They believed Kuhn had destroyed any chance they had of negotiating a favorable agreement. In mid-season, a new bargaining agreement was finally signed, awarding free agency to players with six or more seasons of major league service.

"Great!" said Rose when he heard the news the camps were open. "I'll be ready to play a game in a week!"

Rose's comment reflected the mood of the Cincinnati players as they started workouts in Tampa. Any animosity the players felt toward the club over contract negotiations or the lockout melted away in the hot Florida sun. The Reds were an eager bunch. No National League team had repeated as World Champs since the 1921-22 New York Giants, and nothing short of tying the record would be acceptable.

The ribbing started almost immediately. During a strenuous calisthenics workout, Bench yelled, "Let's take a strike vote!"

Morgan and Perez exchanged barbs over the big Cuban's salary squabbles.

"'Doggie,'" cried Morgan. "You trying to undermine the game of baseball?"

"I no undermine nothing," retorted Perez. "I just try to get my money."

"You gonna play out your option? An old man like you. How old are you? Forty?"

"I not any older than you," Perez reminded Morgan. "How come you and Bench, you never have trouble getting what you want. You just go in and say, 'Bob, I want my $200,000,' and he give it to you. You no leave any money for me."

Sparky liked what he heard. "The boys are well tuned," he said.

The Reds entered the 1976 campaign with the most talented and established club Anderson had managed. Coming off a championship season, Howsam made few significant moves. The only major change was the trade of Clay Carroll to the White Sox. Carroll, a Red since 1968, had been the club's most consistent relief pitcher and one of its more likeable characters. But the development of McEnaney and Eastwick, along with Carroll's age (34) and salary ($95,000), made "The Hawk" expendable.

Howsam traded or released pitcher Clay Kirby and utility players Darrel Chaney, Terry Crowley and Merv Rettenmund. He acquired bench players Bob Bailey and Mike Lum, and rookie pitchers Santo Alcala and Pat Zachry made the team.

Anderson considered Alcala and Zachry to be the only question marks on his squad. "The way I manipulate a pitching staff, I can't just get along with eight pitchers," Captain Hook said.

As always, Anderson had his pitching questions, but for the first time since taking the helm in 1970, he had no doubts about his starting lineup. Rose, Griffey, Morgan, Perez, Bench, Foster, Concepcion and Geronimo were the established starters. With a rotation of Billingham, Nolan, Norman and Gullett, Anderson predicted a world championship, three 20-game winners and

The Cincinnati Enquirer

Rookie Pat Zachry (with pitching coach Larry Shepard) made the big league club in 1976 after spending six seasons in the Reds minor league system. Zachry was a 19th round draft choice in 1970.

another MVP award for the Reds.

The 1976 season did not go exactly to Anderson's script. No pitcher won more than 15 games. But Morgan won another MVP, the Reds won 102 games and firmly established themselves as one of the great dynasties of all time with their seven-game sweep of the playoffs and World Series.

Considering the dominance of the 1975 Big Red Machine, it is surprising there were any questions about the 1976 edition. But early in the season, the Reds stumbled. That was typical. Except for the 1970 campaign when the Reds jumped to a 34-14 start, April and May were the club's worst months. Anderson's theory? Cold weather.

"I always used to say, 'If we can just go 20-20 in our first 40, I promise you we'll win,'" Sparky remembered. "Concepcion could not play in it. He couldn't hit nothing in cold weather. Just get us into May, then we'll take over."

From 1972 through 1975, the Reds had begun each season unimpressively, trailing the division leaders at the end of May. They improved their record in June and played their best baseball in July and August.

In 1976, the Reds started the season at 28-17, but still trailed the Dodgers. Several players started slowly, including Concepcion. On May 9, at Chicago's Wrigley Field, he tried to shake his early season slump. He happened by a large clothes dryer in the clubhouse. Claiming he was trying to "warm up," Davey wriggled into the dryer to the delight of his amused teammates.

Pat Zachry couldn't pass up the opportunity to shut the door. But when he did, the dryer unexpectedly clicked on and took a startled Concepcion through a couple of quick rotations. Zachry jerked the door open and out tumbled Davey, with several singed hairs. But he had properly "warmed up." Freed from the "unfriendly confines," he went three-for-five in the game.

Meanwhile, Captain Hook struggled with the pitching staff. The Reds were scoring runs, but not six per game, as pitching coach Shepard had put it. Gullett, who had begun the season in the bullpen, missed several starts with lingering injuries. Billingham and Norman were ineffective. The starting rotation needed help. In early May, Anderson demoted Darcy and Norman to the bullpen and inserted rookies Zachry and Alcala into the rotation. As had happened with Simpson and Gullett in 1970, with Grimsley in

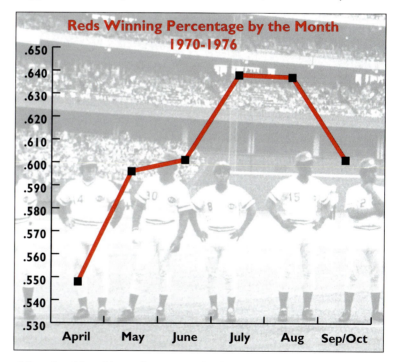

After sluggish cold-weather starts, the Big Red Machine revved into top gear in the summer and coasted in September.

1972, and with Darcy, Eastwick and McEnaney in 1975, the youngsters made a significant contribution. They combined for a 25-11 record. Zachry's ERA of 2.74 led the starters and he had a 5-1 record against the Dodgers. He was co-winner of the N.L. Rookie of the Year award with San Diego's Butch Metzger.

Alcala was not as consistent as Zachry, but the 6-foot-7 native of the Dominican Republic won seven of his 11 games in May and June when the Reds most needed the pitching lift. Alcala's broad smile and confident attitude meshed well with the friendly "agitatin" of the clubhouse.

"My fastball, she was 'fan-tass-teek!'" Alcala would shout after a big performance.

"The turning point in the season," recalled Anderson, "was when the two kids went into the rotation and did so well."

Morgan agreed. "Without Zachry, it would have been awfully tough. He beat L.A. five times. He beat them early in the year when we needed to show them we were best."

Zachry first beat the Dodgers and Don Sutton in Los Angeles in mid-May, pulling the Reds into first place. The Dodgers regained the lead, and ten days later came to Cincinnati ahead by two games. Zachry reprised his performance, winning the first game of the series. The Reds went on to win three of four and move one game ahead of the Dodgers.

The Dodgers returned to Cincinnati in mid-June, down three and one-half games. The Reds swept the two games, with Zachry and Norman earning complete-game wins. The sweep pushed the Reds lead to five and one-half games. The Dodgers never again threatened.

Zachry and Alcala were not the only unexpected stars of the first half of the 1976 season. In his first full year as a starter, George Foster was putting up MVP numbers. He was selected N.L. Player of the Month in May and July. By the All-Star break, he had 17 home runs and 72 RBIs, tops on the club. Had he kept up the

The Cincinnati Enquirer

Utility infielder Doug Flynn (23) and Pete Rose collaborated on a rundown play in a game against Atlanta. Flynn was part of a very active and productive Cincinnati bench in 1976.

Would you believe 128-34?

The memory of the lineups of the 1976 season is one of Sparky Anderson starting Rose, Griffey, Morgan, Perez, Foster, Bench, Concepcion and Geronimo, and then turning his attention to the bullpen.

In fact, Sparky started the regulars in only 46 regular season games.

When the season began, Anderson went with the "Great Eight" for six of the first seven games and the Reds were off to a 5-2 start. But then Anderson returned to his 1975 pattern, working in the reserves and resting either Geronimo or Griffey against left-handers. On such occasions, Sparky started Foster in center or right, giving Bob Bailey 25 starts in left field. Against righties, Anderson put Danny Driessen and Mike Lum in the lineup. Doug Flynn wound up with the most starts of any of the reserves due to minor injuries to Morgan and Concepcion.

When Anderson started all eight regulars in 1976, the Reds were 36-10, a .783 percentage. In the remaining games, the Reds were 66-50 (.569). The history-making lineup, which Anderson used in all 17 post-season games in 1975 and 1976, started only 70 regular-season games together over the two seasons.

Perhaps it was only humane that Sparky did not use the heart of the Big Red Machine more often. In the 87 games they started in 1975-76 (including regular- and post-season games) the Great Eight won 69 and lost 18, a winning percentage of .793. Projected over a 162-game season, Rose & Co. would have won 128 games.

1976 Starting Lineup Summary

Player	Starts	Starts by Position								Starts by Batting Order							
		C	1B	2B	SS	3B	LF	CF	RF	1st	2nd	3rd	4th	5th	6th	7th	8th
Rose	156					156				156							
Concepcion	142				142					1	24	7			12	49	49
Foster	137						84	31	22			11	64	39	21	2	
Perez	131		131									1	49	37	43	1	
Morgan	131			131						1	130						
Geronimo	128							128		1		1	6	23	54	43	
Griffey	128								128	125	1				2		
Bench	123	120				3						4	31	56	32		
Flynn	52			31	20	1				1						11	40
Driessen	51		31			20				7	8	15	19	1	1		
Plummer	40	40													15	25	
Bailey	30					5	25							19	11		
Lum	27						24		3	2		2	4	11	8		
Others	20	2				6	3	9		4	2		1		8	5	

1976 Monthly Standings
National League West

April 30
	W	L	GB
Cincinnati	10	7	—
Los Angeles	10	9	1
Houston	11	10	1
San Diego	9	10	2
Atlanta	8	9	2
San Francisco	7	10	3

May 31
	W	L	GB
Cincinnati	28	17	—
Los Angeles	28	19	1
San Diego	24	21	4
Houston	21	27	8½
San Francisco	18	30	11½
Atlanta	16	30	12

June 30
	W	L	GB
Cincinnati	46	29	—
Los Angeles	42	34	4½
San Diego	39	36	7
Atlanta	34	41	12
Houston	34	41	12
San Francisco	31	47	16½

July 31
	W	L	GB
Cincinnati	66	38	—
Los Angeles	55	46	9½
Houston	54	52	13
San Diego	49	56	17½
Atlanta	46	56	19
San Francisco	46	58	20

August 31
	W	L	GB
Cincinnati	84	49	—
Los Angeles	74	56	8½
Houston	67	68	18
San Diego	63	70	21
Atlanta	59	73	24½
San Francisco	56	76	27½

Final Standings
	W	L	GB
Cincinnati	102	60	—
Los Angeles	92	70	10
Houston	80	82	20
San Francisco	74	88	28
San Diego	73	89	29
Atlanta	70	92	32

pace, he would have edged out Morgan for the MVP award. But Foster admitted he started swinging for the fences in the second half of the season and his production fell off. He still finished first in the league in RBIs, won *The Sporting News* Player of the Year award and finished second to Morgan in the MVP vote.

Fred Norman rebounded from his bullpen stint to be the Reds' most effective starter through June and July, winning seven games. By the All-Star break, Norman led the league in ERA; Sparky called him the "best pitcher in the National League."

Despite his age, 35-year-old Rose had one of his best seasons, leading the league in hits (215), doubles (42) and runs scored (130). It marked the eighth time he had over 200 hits, just one short of Ty Cobb's record.

Bench, though, was not himself. He still suffered the effects of the injury to his left shoulder early in 1975. He slumped so badly early in 1976, he asked Anderson to drop him in the lineup. He batted fifth or sixth until September when Anderson moved him back to fourth. But Morgan, Foster and Perez took up the slack; the Reds scored a club-record 857 runs, the best in baseball, and the most in the majors since the 1962 San Francisco Giants.

Minor injuries and slumps also forced Anderson to juggle his anticipated starting lineup. The starting eight of Rose, Griffey, Morgan, Bench, Perez, Foster, Geronimo and Concepcion started only 20 times before the All-Star break, and only 46 times all season. The longest the starting eight played together was five consecutive games, which they did twice. Only Rose and Concepcion started more than 140 games. Flynn, Driessen, Plummer, Bailey and Lum all had 20 or more starts.

"Doug Flynn may be the only utility infielder in the history of baseball to have enough at-bats to qualify for the batting title," joked Sparky after Flynn had started nine of ten games.

Bob Bailey, who earned most of his starts in left field, took Sparky aside at one point and kidded him.

"Skip, you've got to get the regulars back in there," urged Bailey. "The extra men need a rest!"

When the regular eight started, they were nearly invincible. The Reds were 36-10 in the 46 games started by Rose & Co., a .783 winning percentage. Anderson turned to the Great Eight when he needed it. In the first six games against the Dodgers, when the pennant race was still in doubt, Anderson started the Great Eight four times. The regulars won all four. In late August, the Phillies invaded Riverfront for what was billed as a preview of the playoffs. Anderson started the regulars all four games and the Reds took three of four.

Rose couldn't but help admire his club. "I wonder if people realize what a great team we have?" he mused after the Reds had swept four from the Dodgers in early August.

The Reds knew they were a great club. Their confidence—which to other clubs often bordered on arrogance—created an atmosphere that kept the Big Red Machine focused on winning. Bench referred to the winning attitude as "inner conceit."

"I don't think there was ever a time we thought we were going to lose," Bench later recalled. "We just didn't lose."

Baseball is the most individual of the team games, and no player embodied this like Pete Rose. He was unabashed in his pursuit of his personal goals each season (200 hits, .300 average, 100 runs scored), but he was also the consummate winner.

"I believe in winning one hundred and ten percent, and I think the rest of the Reds do, too," Rose said. "Anyone who doesn't, wouldn't last long on our team. You try not running out a ball, and

1976 MONTHLY STANDINGS
NATIONAL LEAGUE EAST

April 30

	W	L	GB
New York	13	7	—
Philadelphia	8	6	2
Pittsburgh	8	8	4
Chicago	9	10	3½
St. Louis	8	10	4
Montreal	6	11	5½

May 31

	W	L	GB
Philadelphia	30	11	—
Pittsburgh	25	19	6½
New York	24	24	9½
Chicago	20	24	11½
St. Louis	20	25	12
Montreal	16	23	13

June 30

	W	L	GB
Philadelphia	50	20	—
Pittsburgh	41	29	9
New York	39	37	14
St. Louis	31	41	20
Chicago	30	43	21½
Montreal	24	43	24½

July 31

	W	L	GB
Philadelphia	67	32	—
Pittsburgh	56	44	11½
New York	52	52	17½
St. Louis	42	56	24½
Chicago	43	59	25½
Montreal	34	61	31

August 31

	W	L	GB
Philadelphia	83	47	—
Pittsburgh	72	57	10½
New York	66	64	17
Chicago	60	72	24
St. Louis	56	70	25
Montreal	43	81	37

Final Standings

	W	L	GB
Philadelphia	101	61	—
Pittsburgh	92	70	9
New York	86	76	15
Chicago	75	87	26
St. Louis	72	90	29
Montreal	55	107	46

let Joe Morgan get on your tail. He'll shout at anybody, no matter how big a star the guy is. He'll do it in a way that'll make you feel this big, and you won't forget it. We've got pride, you know?"

Morgan thought the secret of the club's success was its "baseball smarts."

"I know I'll get an argument on this," Morgan conceded in an interview years later, "but I'd take that 1976 team and play the '27 Yankees or the '61 Yankees or anybody, and we'd win four of seven. Not so much because of ability, but because of this: We weren't Phi Beta Kappas off the field, but on it we were. Everybody on that team knew how to play, how to win, and what their roles were. It was a very smart team, and I'd take them in any short series."

Anderson recalled the atmosphere surrounding the club.

"They were arrogant, but arrogant in their play on the field, not as people. They didn't agree with what everybody did on the team, but they loved one another. That was the difference between this group (1975-76) and the group we started with in 1970. And these guys had a love for the game. They were a team full of professionals."

Although the outcome had been clear for weeks, the Reds officially clinched the pennant at home on September 21. This was the fifth division title in seven years. The Reds' clubhouse was a bit subdued.

Bottles of champagne stood unopened when Bob Howsam walked in. "Some of these guys are acting too dignified," he observed. "They should take advantage of this."

With that, the usually dignified Howsam opened a couple of bottles and began spraying champagne around the room. Howsam, it turned out, knew the difference between Cold Duck and Dom Perignon—and not just in ballplayers. Morgan saw that Howsam picked the less expensive bottles for the ritual dousing. Morgan, too, had reason to know. His distributorship sold the champagne to the club.

If Howsam drenched anyone in the clubhouse, it should have been his second baseman. Morgan wrapped up his second consecutive MVP award. He led the league in two critical offensive categories, on-base percentage and slugging average, a feat that placed him in the company of such National League Hall of Famers as Willie Mays, Willie McCovey, Stan Musial, Duke Snider and Rogers Hornsby. With career highs in home runs (27) and RBIs (111), and 60 stolen bases in 69 attempts, nobody personified excellence like "Little Joe." And he accomplished all this despite starting in only 131 games.

Morgan's speed continued to delight fans, amaze his teammates and bedevil his opponents. In a game against the Phillies, Morgan and Bench pulled off a double steal. Morgan, who was on second, got a tremendous jump on the pitcher, and when the throw went to second, Morgan never hesitated rounding third. Second baseman Dave Cash applied a late tag on the sliding Bench and realized a moment too late Morgan was heading home. Cash recovered, but his throw was high. Morgan had stolen two bases on one pitch. There was no provision in the scoring rules to account for such grand larceny. Morgan was credited with one stolen base and awarded home on a fielder's choice.

"He plays a game with which I am not familiar," golfing legend Bobby Jones once said about Jack Nicklaus. It was a sentiment baseball men shared about Morgan. Joe always credited his Big Red Machine teammates (especially Rose, Bench and Perez) for bringing out the best in him as a player. But the relationship was reciprocal. Without Morgan, the Reds had not won. With him, they became a dynasty. During the 1972-1976 period, Morgan *averaged* 22 homers, 85 RBIs, 113 runs scored, 119 walks and 62 stolen bases. In 1976, he became the first second baseman since Rogers Hornsby (in 1929) to lead the N.L. in slugging percentage.

"Just the way he stood at the plate, flipping his arm like a penguin riled opposing pitchers," Perez said. "He was cocky as hell, and they always wanted to knock him on his behind, but they knew he was so tough he could never be intimidated."

The only drama left in the final days of the 1976 season concerned Perez's streak of 90 RBI seasons and the race for the batting title. Perez entered the final game with 88 RBIs. He picked up one early in the game, and then in his final at-bat of the season, stroked a two-run single to put him over 90 RBIs for the tenth straight year.

The batting race looked as though it might be an all-Cincinnati affair going into the final week of the season. Three Reds were in contention. Bill Madlock led the league with a .337 average, Griffey followed at .332, Rose .329 and Morgan .327. Over the final week, Griffey surged ahead and Rose and Morgan fell back. After 161 games, Griffey appeared to have the title won. He led Madlock .338 to .333. Sparky considered resting him on the final day. Madlock had regularly rested against tougher pitchers; Morgan, in particular, saw no shame in giving Griffey the final day off.

Anderson did take Griffey out of the starting lineup, but Madlock had a career day, going four-for-four. Aware of Madlock's hits, Anderson inserted Griffey into the game, but he was hitless in two at-bats, and Madlock had the title, .339 to .336.

But in nearly all other categories, the Reds dominated. As a team, they led the majors in victories and runs scored. Five of the eight regulars—Griffey, Rose, Morgan, Geronimo and Foster—hit over .300. The Reds led the majors in hits, doubles, triples, home runs, stolen bases, slugging percentage and on-base percentage.

The Cincinnati Enquirer

Joe Morgan's combination of speed and power clinched his second MVP award in 1976. Morgan had career-highs with 27 home runs and 111 RBIs, and was second in the league with 60 stolen bases.

1976 Scrapbook

The Opposition

Western Division

Against	Won	Lost
Atlanta	12	6
Houston	12	6
Los Angeles	13	5
San Diego	13	5
San Fran.	9	9

Eastern Division

Against	Won	Lost
Chicago	9	3
Montreal	9	3
New York	6	6
Philadelphia	5	7
Pittsburgh	8	4
St. Louis	6	6

The pitcher the Reds didn't want to face – **Jim Barr** of the Giants was 4-0 against the Reds.

The pitcher they loved to see – **Don Sutton** of the Dodgers was 0-4 against the Reds.

The batter who loved the Reds – **Mike Schmidt** of Philadelphia hit .348 (16-for-46) with 5 HRs and 11 RBIs.

The batter who should have stayed home – **Manny Sanguillen** of the Pirates hit .186 (8-for-43) with 0 HR and 2 RBIs.

Club Leaders

Batting Average	Ken Griffey	.336
Home runs	George Foster	29
RBIs	George Foster	121 •
Stolen bases	Joe Morgan	60
Runs	Pete Rose	130 •
ERA	Pat Zachry	2.74
Wins	Gary Nolan	15
Saves	Rawly Eastwick	26 •
Games	Rawly Eastwick	71

• League Leader

Awards

MVP	Joe Morgan
Sporting News Player of the Year	George Foster
Co-Rookie of the Year	Pat Zachry
Fireman of the Year	Rawly Eastwick
Gold Glove	Johnny Bench, Joe Morgan, Dave Concepcion, Cesar Geronimo
Cincinnati Reds MVP •	Joe Morgan

• Awarded by Cincinnati Chapter of Baseball Writers Association

Trades

Dec. 16 **Woody Fryman** and **Dale Murray** acquired from Montreal for **Tony Perez**

The Draft

Cincinnati drafted 52 players; nine played in the major leagues:

Duane Walker	San Jacinto JC (TX)	P-OF
Paul Householder	North Haven, CT.	OF
Bill Dawley	Lisbon, CT	P
Eddie Milner	Central State Univ. (OH)	OF
Jay Howell	Univ. of Colorado	P
Tim Laudner •	Minneapolis, MN	C
Scotti Madison •	Pensacola, FL	SS
Pat Sheridan •	Wayne, MI	OF
Bruce Bereyni	Northeast Missouri State Univ.	P

• Drafted by the Reds, but signed with another club

They led the major leagues in fielding average, and had the fewest errors of any club. Bench, Rose and Foster led catchers, third baseman and outfielders in fielding percentage. Seven of the Great Eight made the N.L. All-Star team, and the one who didn't—Geronimo—wound up hitting .307 and won his third straight Gold Glove.

The Reds had no 20-game winners, but Anderson found the depth he coveted. Seven pitchers won 10 games or more—another first in National League history. The bullpen led the league in saves and Eastwick picked up the "Fireman of the Year" honor.

No team since the Dodgers of the 1950s—not even the great Yankee teams of the 1950s or the Orioles of 1969-71—had dominated in so many categories.

Nearly all of baseball's dynasties had won two or more World Championships in a five-year period (the 1950s Dodgers being one notable exception), so history's verdict on the Big Red Machine awaited the games of October.

First up for the Reds were the Philadelphia Phillies, who had won 101 games, and showcased some excellent talent in Mike Schmidt, Greg Luzinski, Garry Maddox, starter Steve Carlton and reliever Tug McGraw. Nineteen seventy-six was the first of three consecutive years the Phillies would win the N.L. East. The Reds were favored, but the perilous five-game format and the infamy of the '73 loss to the Mets were never far from Anderson's thoughts.

"The playoffs is a nightmare," said Sparky on the eve of the opener in Philadelphia.

As always, Anderson summoned Ray Shore to huddle with the players and remain available during the playoffs.

"I focused on the American League in the second half of the season," Shore recalled. "I would put a book together on them, the teams that were out in front. But I didn't scout the A.L. playoffs. Sparky wanted me to be with our club. He said, 'Snacks, I want you here when we are playing in the playoffs so we can make adjustments. Nobody ever hears about the team that gets beat in the playoffs.' Sparky wanted to make sure we got to the Series."

Shore's presence paid immediate dividends. In preparing the pitching matchups against the Phillies, Anderson favored opening with Zachry and following with Gullett. Although Gullett seemed to return to form in September, Anderson still considered Zachry his most consistent starter.

But Shore recommended that Anderson switch the order. Shore did not like the idea of starting the Reds' number one starter against Carlton, the Phillies' best pitcher.

"If we pitch Zachry and he gets beat, then we got a question mark in our second game," Shore reasoned.

Additionally, Shore knew that Tim McCarver always caught Carlton; both were left-handed batters. That matchup would work against right-hander Zachry and in favor of left-hander Gullett.

Shore also felt Gullett's contract status might help the Reds. Gullett figured to become a free agent after the season was over.

"Gullett's out there pitching for his life," Shore said to Anderson. "He's liable to rack up a good one."

Anderson and Shepard agreed, and Gullett opened for the Reds. As Shore predicted, he "racked up a good one." He out-pitched Carlton, allowing only two hits in eight innings. He left with a 6-1 lead, having driven in three of the runs himself. The Phillies made several fielding mistakes and mental errors, and appeared to be bothered by the playoff pressure.

"We were World Champs with all that experience," recalled

Shore. "It wasn't going to bother our guys. But the Phillies were playing like they were just happy to be there."

The Reds stole four bases in the first game, inflicting what Roger Angell of *The New Yorker* referred to as "a debilitating nervousness on the Philadelphia defense." The veteran baseball writer appreciated the way the Reds bedazzled their opponents.

"Their speed and power and opportunism and experience breed the conviction in the opposing team that it must play an almost superhuman level of baseball to have any kind of a chance. This is the same brain fever that used to afflict opponents of the old, all-conquering Yankees," wrote Angell.

In Game Two, Phillies starter Jim Lonborg no-hit the Reds through five innings, while the Phillies grabbed a 2-0 lead off Zachry. But in the sixth, the Reds' speed again proved decisive—only this time it was not the stolen base.

Concepcion started the rally with a walk. With one out, Rose singled him home. Griffey singled and Rose headed for third. He beat the throw with a head-first slide, and Griffey took second. No team in baseball was better at taking the extra base than the Reds, and no one took better advantage of first-to-third opportunities than Peter Edward.

The Phillies walked Morgan to set up a force play, but Perez ripped a shot off first baseman Dick Allen's glove that scored two runs, and gave the Reds the lead for good. Borbon relieved Zachry and pitched four scoreless innings. The Reds had won both games in Philadelphia and the playoffs now headed to Riverfront Stadium.

Sparky credited Rose's dash to third on Griffey's single with sparking the winning rally. "It changes everything, second and third instead of first and second," said a smiling Anderson. Rose elaborated.

The Cincinnati Enquirer

George Foster ignited the pennant-winning rally against Philadelphia in the ninth inning of Game Three of the 1976 N.L. playoffs with a 480-foot home run. Johnny Bench followed with his game-tying blast.

"Look at it this way. I single. If I steal, Griffey or whoever is hitting next, has to take a pitch they might hit. Suppose I make it. Now they hit a groundball in the hole that the first baseman fields. One out, man at third. But if I'm still on first and they hit that groundball, it goes through for a hit. I go to third, he goes to second on the throw. Second and third, none out."

Sparky had a somewhat simpler explanation for the victory.

"We don't play too bad when we're playing pretty good."

Game Three of the 1976 playoffs was a classic come-from-behind victory for the Reds that has been somewhat overshadowed by all the other great moments of the 1970s. It did not have the drama of a deciding game, but it was as thrilling a game as any played in the Big Red Machine era.

Jim Kaat and Gary Nolan held the offenses in check through six innings. The Phillies led, 1-0. Then, Manny Sarmiento gave up two runs in the seventh, and Anderson began to ponder the next day's matchup against Carlton. The Reds had beaten Carlton once, but Anderson did not like their chances of beating him twice in a short series. Then, salvation: the Big Red Machine rallied for four runs in the seventh. Perez smacked an RBI single, Foster drove in a run with a sacrifice fly and Geronimo tripled in two more for a 4-3 lead.

Anderson's glee was short-lived. Back roared the Phillies with two runs in the eighth off Rawly Eastwick. They added one more in the top of the ninth to go up, 6-4. With three outs remaining, the Reds needed two runs to tie. Foster and Bench quickly provided the firepower. Facing reliever Ron Reed, Foster led off the inning with a home run.

That brought up Bench. As he had in the fifth game of the 1972 playoffs and in the first game of the 1973 playoffs, Bench had an opportunity in the ninth inning to tie or win a game with a home run. Marty Brennaman continued his play-by-play from the Riverfront press box.

He's behind at one-and-two. That was the count and the pitch that Foster took Reed downtown on. Bench is back in and Reed serves it up. Swung on…fly ball…deep left-center field…Maddox on the warning track…looking up! IT'S GONE! Johnny Bench with a home run to left-center and the Reds have tied it up on back-to-back ninth inning home runs! They're on their feet at Riverfront and it is tied at six runs apiece!

Sparky's playoff nightmare abated. "I knew right then we had it won," he said.

Concepcion singled and Geronimo walked. Armbrister, Anderson's "designated bunter," laid down a perfect sacrifice, moving the pennant-winning run to third base with only one out.

Tom Underwood, the third Phillies pitcher in the inning, walked Rose intentionally to pitch to Griffey. From the booth, Brennaman called the final play of the 1976 National League season.

One ball and no strikes on Griffey. Underwood with the slow comedown to the belt. He throws. Griffey swings…slow chopper…right side. Here comes Concepcion! Tolan boots the ball! And the 1976 pennant belongs to the Reds! (Crowd roar, five seconds.) It was a high chop along the first-base line. Bobby Tolan could not come up with it cleanly. Concepcion scores and it is pandemonium down on the field…as the Reds have scored three in the ninth inning and have swept the Philadelphia Phillies to move into the 1976 World Series.

ho did the Reds want to play in the fall classic? "The New York 'Jankees'," said a champagne-drenched Tony Perez in

The Reds were an overwhelming favorite in the Cincinnati media, as well as among national baseball experts, to win the 1976 Series.

his thick Cuban accent.

He got his wish. The Yankees, in post-season play for the first time since Howsam's Cardinals defeated them in the 1964 World Series, beat the Kansas City Royals on a ninth-inning home run by Chris Chambliss in the fifth game of the A.L. playoffs.

"A good team, but not in the class of the Reds," said Alex Grammas, Sparky's former third base coach, who managed the Milwaukee Brewers in 1976.

Ray Shore agreed. He had scouted the Yankees in August and September and was unimpressed. He predicted a Reds romp.

"If we lose more than one game in the World Series, I'll be disappointed," Shore declared to a reporter. He also promised the Reds would run on the Yankee outfielders ("They have no arms in the outfield at all") and on catcher Thurman Munson ("We'll run all over him").

He realized his comments could have backfired. But frankness won out. "I wasn't trying to take anything away from Yankees," Shore later explained. "But they weren't in the same class as us."

Yankee general manager Gabe Paul, who was the GM of the Reds in the 1950s under Powel Crosley, had pulled off a series of trades in 1976 that joined Mickey Rivers, Willie Randolph and pitchers Ed Figueroa, Doyle Alexander and Dock Ellis with Yankee stars Catfish Hunter, Munson, Graig Nettles and Chambliss. The temperamental but successful Billy Martin managed the club.

Martin was never accused of lacking chutzpah. On the eve of the Series, the writers asked him to compare his team to the Reds.

"We've got better pitching," he boasted. "And I'll take Thurman Munson over Johnny Bench (at catcher), Roy White over George Foster (left field), Chris Chambliss over Tony Perez (first base) and Willie Randolph over Joe Morgan (second base)."

Clearly, Martin and Shore were not on the same page.

Martin had just picked Munson over the best catcher to ever play the game, Randolph over the defending N.L. MVP, White over the left fielder who would finish second to Morgan in the 1976 MVP balloting, and Chambliss over the game's most consistent RBI man.

How could Martin possibly pick Randolph over Morgan?

"My guy has more range and is a better fielder," said Martin, with a straight face.

Morgan could not be bothered.

"We don't care what the Yankees do," he said. "If we play our game, we can beat anyone, anytime."

Anderson decided not to stir things up further. At least on the surface. When reporters asked him for a prediction, Sparky said, "I believe we'll win in seven."

His eyes twinkled. Sparky was talking about the seven games it would take to sweep the playoffs *and* the World Series.

Shore saw several weaknesses the Reds could exploit.

"I didn't think their pitching was that good. Hunter was the only guy that scared you a little, but even with Hunter I thought we had a good enough hitting club. I really based it on trying to keep Rivers off base and trying to keep Munson in the ballpark. I thought I had it pretty well figured out."

Rivers, the leadoff man who had hit .312 and stolen 43 bases during the regular season, had been the catalyst for the Yankees all year.

On October 16, the World Series opened in Cincinnati. It was a cool Saturday afternoon. Gullett started for the Reds, Doyle Alexander for the Yankees. Martin would have preferred to start Hunter, but he had pitched three days earlier in the playoffs.

As Rivers settled into the batter's box to open the game, Rose began to creep in from his third-base position. By the time he stopped and the ball was on the way to the plate, Rose was almost 25 feet down the line—only 65 feet from Rivers.

"I told Pete to play in," Shore said, "but when I looked up I didn't expect him to be shaking *hands* with him."

Shore's strategy was to take the bunt away from Rivers, and dare him to slap the ball past Rose. It was Rose's idea to turn it into a strategy of intimidation.

"He does not have the bat control to hit it by me," Rose declared.

Rivers struck out.

Morgan put the Reds in front in the bottom of the first with a home run and the Reds held a 2-1 lead after five innings. If there was a pivotal inning to this game, it was the sixth. The Yankees put four of their first five hitters on base, but failed to score. Shortstop Fred Stanley walked, but Rivers failed to execute the sacrifice when Gullett picked up his bunt and threw Stanley out at second.

Rivers was then caught stealing. Concepcion gave the Yankees another life when he misplayed White's pop fly for a two-base error. Munson shot a hard single to right but a strong throw from Griffey held White held at third. Lou Piniella, the designated hitter, popped to Morgan, and the Yankee threat fizzled.

In the bottom of the sixth, the Reds did the little things right—and scored. Griffey, on first base through a fielder's choice, stole second. With two out, Perez singled him home. The Reds added two more in the eighth on a Bench triple and a wild pitch.

After allowing only one run and five hits through seven innings, Gullett appeared on his way to a rare complete game. But in the eighth inning, he felt something pop in his ankle. He had dislocated a tendon and was through for the game and the season. As it turned out, it was his last appearance as a Cincinnati Red.

Perhaps the most memorable action in the Reds' 5-1 victory took place off the field. The Reds had given the Yankees permission prior to the start of the Series to use walkie-talkies to monitor their defensive alignments. Scouts, sitting in the press box, could relay information to the bench electronically.

But Howsam learned that the Yankee scouts had taken seats in the ABC booth, where they could not only see the game, but the TV pictures as well. Suspecting the scouts might be stealing signs from the TV monitors, Howsam informed the commissioner. Despite the whining of the Yankees, Kuhn ordered the scouts out of the booth.

After the game, the Reds hosted a party for the World Series delegations. But Yankee owner George Steinbrenner forbid his

After Game One of the 1976 World Series, (left to right) Johnny Bench, David Concepcion, Tony Perez, Joe Morgan, Pete Rose and Pedro Borbon saluted the victory. No boisterous high-fives, just handshakes. The matter-of-fact Reds knew they would win.

The Cincinnati Enquirer

employees from attending. "Stay in your rooms," he ordered. "Parties are for winners. We're losers." Barely 48 hours after Yankee employees had reveled in the ecstasy of the Chambliss home run and the playoff victory, the Reds had brought them and their walkie-talkies back to earth.

Game Two's crowd on Sunday night shivered in a 40-degree chill, but commissioner Bowie Kuhn wore only a suitcoat to Riverfront Stadium. Kuhn hoped to emphasize he hadn't sold out to TV by going for prime time evening ratings while allowing the National Football League to hog the warm afternoon weather.

It was the first weekend World Series game played at night. Howsam, who was often at odds with the commissioner, found the situation intolerable.

"Football has to be laughing their heads off at us," he said. "They played this afternoon. When do we play? At night! I think we're the number one sport. I don't like football and TV telling us what to do. But the most important thing is this weather is a hardship to the fan who pays the money to come to the game."

When a reporter asked Howsam about Kuhn's suggestion of possibly moving the World Series to a neutral, warm-weather site in the future, Howsam spit out a vulgarity. It was totally out of character.

"He'd damn well better not try that," said Howsam.

When someone wondered if the commissioner might not know the situation better than Howsam did, the Reds' president bristled.

"*I* fill ball parks," he snapped.

Howsam and Kuhn uncomfortably shared the same box for the game. Howsam's overcoat was pulled up around his neck.

In the second inning, the Reds jumped ahead with three runs off Hunter. The last was the most telling. With Geronimo at third base, Griffey lofted a shallow fly to center fielder Rivers.

"Run on Rivers every chance you get," Shore had told the coaches.

"Tag and go!" now yelled third-base coach George Scherger.

The Cincinnati Enquirer

Fred Norman, who in three-plus seasons with the Reds had compiled a 49-29 record (.628 winning percentage), started Game Two of the World Series.

Geronimo slid under Munson's tag. In the dugout, Anderson clapped his hands.

Hunter retired 14 of the next 16 hitters, while the Yankees rallied with one run in the fourth and two in the seventh to tie the game.

In the bottom of the ninth, with the temperature dipping into the low 30s, Concepcion and Rose flied out. Griffey stepped into the batter's box. Hunter moved ahead with two quick strikes.

"Keep it in play! Keep it in play!" reminded Anderson from the dugout.

Ever since Griffey had joined the Reds, Anderson had been singing this tune with his young speedster. He wanted Griffey to put the bat on the ball and leg out a lot of hits. The players were so accustomed to hearing Sparky yell, "Keep it in play!" to Griffey, they began calling Griffey, "Kip."

The mindful Griffey nubbed a soft grounder to shortstop. Fred Stanley charged hard and made a hurried, off-balance throw. The TV replays showed that a perfect throw would have nailed Griffey, but Stanley's toss sailed past Chambliss into the Reds dugout, and Griffey went to second. Griffey's speed kept the inning alive for Morgan and Perez.

With first base open, Martin weighed his unenviable options: pitch to MVP Morgan, or walk Joe and face the RBI king, Perez.

Out at second, Griffey didn't care who batted. "Man, I hope someone drives me home," said a shivering Griffey. "I'm freezing."

Martin ordered the intentional walk. As Morgan took ball four, he yelled two words to Munson.

"Big mistake!"

Nine years had passed since Perez and Hunter were in a confrontation this dramatic. In the 1967 All-Star Game, in the top

A chilled Ken Griffey streaked across home plate with the winning run in the bottom of the ninth inning in Game Two. Tony Perez's single scored Griffey on the cold Cincinnati evening. Thurman Munson waited on the ball.

of the 15th inning, Perez had homered off Catfish to give the National League a 2-1 victory. But Morgan wasn't thinking of that when he said, "Big mistake!" to Munson. What Morgan was thinking was this:

"With a man on second base and two outs, there is no better hitter in all of baseball than Tony Perez."

Before Perez headed for the plate, he turned to the on-deck hitter, Danny Driessen, and said, "All you got to do is tell Griffey to slide when he comes around third. You won't be hitting no more tonight. I'm going to win *theees* one."

Perez settled into the batter's box, his fingers flexing and unflexing on the bat in his familiar style. Right away, he saw the pitch he was looking for—a fastball. It was out over the plate more than Hunter wanted. Perez ripped it on a hard line to left. Griffey scurried around third. Driessen urged him home. Griffey scored standing up, as a disgusted Munson waited for the tardy throw.

Jack Billingham picked up the victory, pitching 2 2/3 shutout innings in relief of Freddie Norman. Overlooked at the time, Billingham's scoreless relief stint set a World Series record. In seven World Series games, dating back to 1972, Billingham had allowed just one earned run in 25 1/3 innings to give him an ERA of 0.36, the lowest in Series history.

But the evening belonged to Perez. "I remember that night," he said years later. "It was a big hit. It was very, very cold that night."

Colder, really, than anybody knew. It would be Perez's last at-bat in Riverfront Stadium as a member of the Big Red Machine.

The World Series entourage now moved to New York, where the ghosts of past dynasties prowled the vast reaches of Yankee Stadium. Most of the Reds had never played there, yet many had grown up following the great Yankee teams of the 1950s. Anderson recalled his idol, Joe DiMaggio. Zachry, who started Game Three, remembered playing games in his Texas backyard with an imaginary teammate: Mickey Mantle. Several of the players walked out to center field to view the monuments of Babe Ruth, Lou Gehrig, Miller Huggins and DiMaggio.

Howsam had seen his first major league game in New York some 35 years before. He had learned many of his general manager skills from the Yankees' George Weiss. But he did not allow nostalgia to cloud his concerns about security at the big park.

The last time the Reds had faced a New York team in post-season play (the Mets in 1973), Howsam had watched his traveling companions and his players nearly mobbed. He had also seen on television the week before the riotous actions of the Yankee crowd as they celebrated Chambliss' pennant-winning home run. Lacking confidence in New York security, Howsam brought along a Cincinnati police captain to coordinate the protection of his club. Howsam also ordered his party to leave their red Cincinnati blazers at home and declined use of the field-level box seats. Their colorful attire and visible location had made them an easy target at Shea Stadium three years earlier.

"We set up away from the field in dark clothes," recalled Howsam years later, still indignant over the circumstances. "I always felt so angry inside that we couldn't express our excitement, our pride in red. But we were afraid somebody would get hurt."

The Yankees started former Pittsburgh pitcher Dock Ellis in Game Three. Ellis was 6-7 against Cincinnati lifetime; the Reds greeted him like a long-lost, batting-practice pitcher, powdering him with four runs in 3 1/3 innings.

Meanwhile Ellis' supporting cast was treating "The House That

Ruth Built" like the little house of horrors. In the second inning, the Reds parlayed two infield hits, two stolen bases, two close calls at first, one blooper, a long double by Foster and three Yankee miscues into three runs. Munson dropped a pitch as he tried to throw out Driessen stealing. Randolph and Stanley failed to execute a double play, and Stanley dropped a pick-off throw from Munson.

Driessen started every game because Kuhn permitted the use of the designated hitter for the first time in a World Series. Anderson, who opposed the DH, toyed with the idea of not using one, but capitulated. Driessen hit .357 in the Series and was the hitting star of Game Three. After his rally-starting single in the second, he homered in the fourth and doubled in the sixth. Driessen, Foster and Bench combined for seven hits and three RBIs.

The Reds had kept Rivers from scoring in the first two games, but he stirred the crowd in the first inning when Zachry made a bad throw on Rivers' bunt attempt. With the fans roaring in anticipation, Rivers took his lead. Zachry promptly picked him off. In the fifth, with the Yankees trailing, 4-1, Rivers led off with a single, and advanced to second when White walked. Munson then lined to a leaping Perez, who threw quickly to Concepcion to double off Rivers.

Many first basemen would have tried to nail White—he was only a couple of yards in front of Perez when Tony speared the ball. But Perez knew instantly the proper play to make, and never hesitated. The Reds played baseball the way it was meant to be played. Yankee lapses were immediately exposed and zapped.

"You're taught when you're losing to take a holding lead, go nowhere on a line drive," said Anderson of Rivers' meandering. "He took off, bless his heart."

Zachry pitched into the seventh inning, having allowed only two runs before Sparky called on a surprised McEnaney. McEnaney had suffered through a miserable season, accumulating an ERA just under 5.00.

After McEnaney had blown a game to the Dodgers on September 24, Anderson called the left-hander into his office.

"Will, why don't you forget about this season?" said a disgusted Anderson. "Just prepare yourself for the playoffs."

McEnaney figured it was just Sparky's way of saying he was through for the year.

"I was pissed," remembered McEnaney. "I didn't expect to pitch at all in the Series. Sparky didn't have any confidence in me. I didn't have any confidence. I was scared."

But in the seventh, with the score 4-2, the Yankees put the tying runs on base against Zachry. Up stepped the left-handed hitting Chris Chambliss. Sparky, playing a hunch, called on McEnaney.

"Will was a herky-jerky left-hander, hard to pick up," Sparky later explained. "His stuff wasn't overwhelming, but he had that quick little breaking ball. I thought he might give Chambliss some problems."

Anderson's hunch paid off. McEnaney recalled he threw Chambliss "a bad pitch, up and in." Chambliss grounded to Perez and the threat died. In the ninth, McEnaney gave up two singles. But with two outs and Chambliss again coming to bat, Anderson stuck with his "herky-jerky" lefty. McEnaney retired Chambliss on a fly to left, and the Reds had their third straight victory.

Rose told reporters after the game that he was bored with the way the Series was going.

"It just isn't as exciting as last year," he complained, referring to the Boston-Cincinnati masterpiece.

"We have not played as well as we are capable of playing,"

Sparky said.

Comments like these did not sit well with the Yankees, down three games to none.

"I think we're being belittled and I don't like it," said an exasperated Munson.

"We've been out-blooped so far," whined Martin, who refused to acknowledge the Reds' dominant performance.

The National League's first designated hitter in a World Series, Danny Driessen, homered in Game Three against Dock Ellis. Driessen started in all four games and hit .357.

Morgan, not surprisingly, had a different perspective.

"The New York Yankees? Hell, they ain't even the best team in New York. With Jon Matlack, Jerry Koosman and Tom Seaver pitching for the Mets, the Yankees might not score three runs in an entire series. There are about seven teams in the National League better than the Yankees. People say we're cocky. I call it confidence, total team confidence. We have adopted a professional demeanor befitting a championship team. And if the Yankees don't like it, well, let 'em try to win at least one game from the Reds."

In 1975, the Reds and Red Sox had respected each other's abilities, and such disparaging remarks were rare. As defending champions and favorites to repeat in '76, the Reds were brash and confident. They had earned it. They had nothing but contempt for the Yankees who failed to acknowledge the obvious.

Rain postponed Wednesday's Game Four to Thursday, giving everybody an extra day in New York. The Yankee wives did not organize any outing for the Reds spouses, perhaps as a result of a muddled shopping excursion in Cincinnati. The Reds wives had organized a shopping trip for the Yankee wives that was to include downtown shopping and a lunch at the Playboy Club. But when the trip was postponed from Friday to Sunday, only Karolyn Rose attended. She escorted the Yankee wives to a neighborhood shopping center and to lunch at her husband's restaurant. Several of the Yankee wives expressed surprise and disappointment at the itinerary. Left on their own in New York, the Reds players and wives still managed to find plenty of shopping and sight-seeing to fill the day.

Sparky took advantage of the off-day to challenge the New York press to a game of "How Good are the Reds?" Anderson said he wanted a four-game sweep so the press would have to ask, "Are they as good as the old Dodgers?"

To Anderson, the Dodgers of the 1950s—the Dodgers of Jackie Robinson, Duke Snider, Roy Campanella, Gil Hodges and Pee Wee Reese—were the most impressive club he had seen. Until now.

Sparky launched into his comparison: Bench over Campanella; Perez and Hodges even at first base; Morgan over Robinson and Concepcion over Reese. He gave Billy Cox the edge at third base defensively, but Rose was the overwhelming choice offensively.

Anderson picked Foster over the Brooklyn candidates in left, gave Snider a big edge offensively in center and liked Griffey over Carl Furillo in right because of Griffey's speed. He rated the Dodgers' pitching as superior.

He noted that the Dodgers had two players (Campanella and Robinson) in the Hall of Fame and predicted that the Reds would eventually have four: Bench, Gullett, Morgan and Rose.

(After the Reds' sweep of the Series, the national press, led by *Sports Illustrated*, would begin comparing the Reds not only to the Dodgers of the 1950s, but even to the fabled 1927 Yankees.)

The weather threatened to push the fourth game into Friday, which would have set up another TV rhubarb. President Gerald Ford and Jimmy Carter had a presidential campaign debate

The rain delay after Game Three sent the Reds out to enjoy the "Big Apple." (From left to right) Tony Perez, Manny Sarmiento, Joel Youngblood and Davey Concepcion headed for a New York restaurant. Club rules required jackets and ties for most public appearances. Few players complained. Broadcaster Marty Brennaman recalled that the Reds enjoyed making a fashion statement.

scheduled for prime time Friday evening. But the skies cleared Thursday afternoon, and Gary Nolan and Ed Figueroa squared off.

In the first inning, the Yankees took their first lead of the Series. They scored on a Munson single and a Chambliss double. Meanwhile, the Reds did not look immortal. Rose was trapped off second base in the first inning and Munson threw out Foster trying to steal second in the third inning.

In the fourth, the Reds took the lead when Foster singled home Morgan, and Bench lined a two-run homer off the left-field foul pole. Bench was having a spectacular World Series. He had fought nagging injuries all season, but aided by several days rest in September, he was healthier than he had been all year. And he had discovered a new "timing" tactic. Stepping into the box, he pointed his bat toward the pitcher, then pulled it back as the windup began. His home run was his seventh hit.

In the fifth, the Yankees pulled within one run when Munson drove in Rivers. Munson and Bench were staging a head-to-head duel in the middle of the Series. Bench was considered the best catcher in baseball and Munson was arguably the best in the American League. Each respected the other, but had tired of the questions from the media. Both felt they had something to prove.

On the bases, the Reds tested Munson. He fared slightly better than National League catchers. The Reds had a success rate of 73 percent against Munson (7 steals in 11 attempts); they stole at a 79 percent clip against the N.L. The Yankees, who had stolen 163 bases during the regular season, hardly challenged Bench's arm; they were 1-of-2. Offensively, Shore's scouting report emphasized keeping Munson "in the park" by pitching him away. It worked. Munson got his hits—he hit .429 and tied a Series record with six hits in a row—but all his hits were singles and he drove in only

THE *REAL* MR. OCTOBER

Reggie Jackson earned the nickname, "Mr. October," after his home-run performances in the 1977 and 1978 World Series.

But impressive as Jackson's long-ball binge was, it did not compare with the clutch hitting of Johnny Bench in post-season play. Bench's late-inning heroics in the pressure-cooker moments of baseball's October games earns him the accolade of the best post-season clutch hitter in baseball history.

His game-clinching home run in Game Four of the 1976 World Series was his *fifth* dramatic post-season hit in the Reds' final at-bat. Three of the hits came in a deciding game. Here are the big five:

- **1972 Playoffs vs. Pirates**: In the bottom of the ninth inning of the deciding fifth game, Bench homered off Dave Giusti to tie the score, 3-3. The Reds won the game, 4-3, and the pennant.
- **1973 Playoffs vs. Mets**: In the bottom of the ninth inning of the first game, Bench homered off Tom Seaver to win the game, 2-1.
- **1975 World Series vs. Red Sox**: In the top of the ninth inning of Game Two, with the Reds trailing, 2-1, Bench started the winning rally with a double off Bill Lee and scored the tying run. The Reds won, 3-2.
- **1976 Playoffs vs. Phillies**: In the bottom of the ninth inning, with the Reds trailing, 6-5, Bench homered off Ron Reed to tie the score, 6-6. The Reds won the game, 7-6, and the pennant.
- **1976 World Series vs. Yankees**: In the top of the ninth inning, with the Reds ahead, 3-2, Bench hit a three-run homer off Dick Tidrow to clinch the Series victory.

two runs.

With the Reds leading, 3-2, neither team seriously threatened in the sixth, seventh or eighth. Anderson had summoned McEnaney in the seventh to face Chambliss after a two-out Munson single. McEnaney repeated his Game Three success against the big first baseman, retiring him on a grounder to Morgan. Anderson stuck with his suddenly rehabilitated reliever in the eighth and ninth.

In the Reds' half of the ninth, Figueroa walked Perez and Driessen. Martin called on one of his top relievers, Dick Tidrow, to face Bench. Tidrow had gotten Bench to bounce into a double play in Game Two, but now Bench pointed his bat ominously at the right-hander. Marty Brennaman picked up the call:

"Danny Driessen holding his ground at first base. Here's a pitch to Bench. Swung on…and hit to deep left field. That might be his second of the game! It's gone! A home run! Johnny Bench with his second home run of the night!"

The Reds' dugout exploded. "We are going to be World Champions again, boys!" shouted Sparky over the uproar.

The Reds added one more run on back-to-back doubles by Geronimo and Concepcion for a 7-2 lead. For the second straight year, McEnaney walked to the mound to record the final outs of the World Series. He struck out pinch-hitter Otto Velez, then faced Rivers. Rivers finally lined one hard at Rose, but Pete snatched the ball out of the air and shouted, "Take that, Mickey!"

"It was great," recalled McEnaney. "We threw the ball around the horn and, you know that flip of Pete's, he flipped it to me and said, 'Here, get one more.'"

Brennaman told the tale.

"Two outs. Here's the 2-0 pitch to Roy White. Swung on! High fly ball to left-center field! That should do it! Foster has it and the 1976 World Championship belongs to the Reds!"

The Reds became the first National League team in 54 years to win back-to-back World Series, and the 13th team to sweep.

There was no question about the Series MVP. Bench hit .533 with six RBIs and two home runs. His slugging percentage of 1.133 was the fourth best in World Series history. For the fourth time in his career, he had struck a dramatic home run in the heat of post-season play.

Afterwards, Anderson claimed Bench was blessed by divine intervention.

"God touched Johnny Bench's mother and said, 'I'm gonna give you the best baseball player who ever lived,'" said Anderson, who for once could be excused for the hyperbole.

As a team, the Reds hit .313, and that was with Rose and Griffey batting a combined .121. The other seven regulars hit over .300. At the time, it was the second-highest team batting average in the history of the World Series. The Reds' slugging percentage of .522 was the third highest in Series history. And all of it came off of a pitching staff that had led the American League in ERA.

The 1976 Series stamped Concepcion as the great shortstop he was. In the fourth inning of the first game, he had quelled a Yankee uprising by stopping a wild throw behind second base by sticking out his leg. He ended the inning with a sparkling catch and throw of an apparent hit by Randolph—all of this saving two runs. In the first inning of the last game, with a runner on second, he ranged well behind the bag to nail a bullet by Carlos May, snuffing out another rally. Davey hit .357 for the Series.

Unexpectedly, the Reds' pitching proved almost as dominating as the hitting. Each starter lasted into the seventh inning and the bullpen pitched $8\frac{1}{3}$ innings of shutout ball.

Pedro Borbon (left), Santo Alcala and Joel Youngblood haul Will McEnaney off to the showers as the Reds celebrated their second straight Series victory.

The Cincinnati Enquirer

Years later, reflecting on the consecutive World Championships, Anderson recalled that the 1975 club was "tight."

"That might have been the worst Series we played as far as playing like we could," said Sparky. "But the Yankee Series, I thought we played just the way we should. I didn't think we overly played. I thought we played exactly how we were supposed to. Just dominate and do it."

Baseball fans, even some Reds fans, were disappointed that the '76 "Fall Classic" was anything but. The epic clash of 1975 had whetted their appetites. But baseball's poet laureate, Roger Angell, put the sweep in perspective:

"The 1976 World Series, in spite of its brevity and skimped drama, was a significant one. It profoundly enhanced and deepened the reputation of the Cincinnati Reds, who must now be considered seriously with the two or three paramount clubs of the last half-century."

Only one question remained: How long could the Big Red Machine roll on?

Sparky Anderson could not bear to watch his Big Red Machine dynasty slowly crumble in 1977 and 1978. Hampered by the absence of Tony Perez, injuries and ineffective pitching, the Reds finished second to the Dodgers both years. In 1978, Bob Howsam resigned as president, Pete Rose left the Reds for Philadelphia and new president Dick Wagner fired Sparky Anderson. The Big Red Machine era was over.

The Cincinnati Enquirer

1977: 2nd place • Perez traded • George Foster, MVP

Chapter 11

1977-78
End of the Run

1978: 2nd place • Howsam, Anderson, Rose depart

AMIDST THE TUMULT OF THE YANKEE Stadium clubhouse, as the champagne-laden coronation of the Big Red Machine gleefully proceeded, a surprisingly subdued Bob Howsam accepted congratulations on his club's success. Howsam had reached the pinnacle of his profession. His club had won back-to-back World Championships and his organization was widely regarded as the best in baseball. Yet he could not shake the foreboding that his beloved game was doomed, that forces loosed by the coming of free agency had changed the game for the worse.

When confronted by an interviewer and asked the inevitable question about his reaction to the Reds victory, Howsam could not mask his emotions. "We may never see what we had before," he said in a husky voice.

These few words were Howsam's eulogy for the game he had mastered. He feared that championship teams would now be bought, not hand-crafted through scouting, development and trading. He understood that the Big Red Machine was the last great club of the old order.

His sentiments would also serve, unwittingly, as the eulogy for his own dynasty. Despite free agency, Howsam thought his Big Red Machine still had championship years left. Here was a team of not-too-old veterans and several impressive young players approaching the prime of their careers. His farm system was rated among the best in major league prospects. Even with the anticipated loss of Don Gullet to free agency, the Reds were early favorites to win their third consecutive World Series in 1977.

But dynasties die. Players grow old. They suffer injuries. Young players don't measure up. Trades backfire. Clubhouse chemistry wanes. Management misreads its personnel. For seven seasons, Howsam and Anderson had carefully steered the Big Red Machine around most of these potholes. But over the next two years, the Reds hit every one.

Baseball's free-agency era began just weeks after the 1976 World Series. The owners gathered in New York in early November to participate in a draft of the first 30 players eligible for free agency under baseball's new labor agreement (signed in July 1976). Among the eligible players were Reggie Jackson, Don Baylor, Bobby Grich and the Reds' Don Gullett. Gullett had never signed his 1976 contract and with six years of major league service, he qualified for free agency.

The defection of Gullett was the first step in the dismantling of the Big Red Machine. But Howsam did not mourn the loss. Gullett had missed significant portions of the '75 and '76 seasons with a broken thumb and shoulder problems and had won only 26 games. For a team that had won 210 games over those two years, Gullett did not seem irreplaceable. Of even more significance to the front office was the nature of Gullett's shoulder problems in 1976. Gullett had claimed he had fallen off a ladder repairing a barn in the offseason, but the Reds had reason to think otherwise.

Several Cincinnati players, including Gullett, had been invited to participate in ABC television's *The Superteams* program in Hawaii during February of 1976. During the obstacle course competition, Gullett missed a jump, and landed heavily on his shoulder outside the area cushioned by a protective mat.

"When Gullett came in late to spring training and couldn't throw," recalled Dick Wagner, "we couldn't figure out what was wrong. Then, later in the year, Morgan and Rose told us they had seen him hurt his shoulder at *Superteams*."

Unsure of Gullett's future and unwilling to sign him to the long-term contract that he and his agent Jerry Kapstein demanded, the Reds let Gullett go.

At the draft, Howsam watched as the Yankees and several other clubs bid for Gullett and the remaining free agents. But Howsam would not allow the Reds to participate. He had been steadfast in his view that baseball could not survive free agency, and he would not relinquish his principles. When the Reds' turn came in the draft order, Howsam read a statement.

"In fairness to the players who have won the World Championship for us two years in a row, and considering the way our organization is structured, we do not think it would be right for the Cincinnati club to get into bidding contests that must come out of this draft."

Howsam was immediately criticized as a reactionary who could not accept the new order. Years later, in discussing Howsam's stewardship of the Reds, Johnny Bench said that Howsam's intransigence to free agency likely cost the club some more World Championships.

"He wanted to prove that he could still put together a club that could win," Bench said. "And Howsam was the only one who had the ability to do it. But if had taken the other road, we probably would have continued at a greater level for many more years."

Broadcaster Brennaman felt, too, that Howsam had miscalculated. "Howsam was one of the great doomsayers. 'Free agency is going to be the ruin of baseball.' Well, it turned out to be great for baseball. But Howsam and Wagner thought it was going to ruin the game."

Sparky Anderson agreed with Bench that Howsam's decision hurt the Reds, but he refused to blame his boss.

"I believe the problem was not that we had Bob Howsam. It was that baseball didn't have enough Bob Howsams. If everybody had stood up and said, like Bob did, 'You're not going to re-shape the game this way,' things might have been different. But for that to happen, everybody has to have the courage of their convictions like Bob did. Unfortunately for baseball, there was only one Bob Howsam."

Most of the owners had originally stood with Howsam against free agency, but once the courts agreed with Marvin Miller and the Players Association about the fundamental inequities of the reserve system, there was no turning back. Now, only the Reds were left to tilt against the windmills. The other owners who cried they could not afford free agency were suddenly transformed into frenzied shoppers. They frantically outbid one another for that one star who would bring a title. It all angered and saddened Howsam. He stubbornly clung to his hopes that free agency would not last and that he could field a winner without honoring the new conventions.

Refusing to sign Gullett was not a dynasty-breaking decision. Gullett enjoyed only one more successful season before arm problems ended his career. But on December 16, the Reds announced a deal of much greater significance: they traded Tony Perez and Will McEnaney to Montreal for pitchers Woody Fryman and Dale Murray.

Of all the decisions and events of the 1977-78 period, the trade of Perez is most often cited as the deal that toppled the dynasty. That analysis overlooks an anemic pitching staff and key injuries that contributed just as much to the club's failure on the field. But clearly, the trade of Perez sapped the spirit of the team. The impetus for the deal was to give Dan Driessen the first-base job. He had a good year in 1977, putting up Perez-like numbers with 91 RBIs and a .300 batting average. But Perez's absence was felt more off the field than on it.

"I don't think Howsam understood Tony's value," Rose recalled. "I know he did as a player, but not as a leader. Take any of those kids that spoke Spanish. They all looked up to Tony like he was their dad. Tony was a pretty good stabilizer between me and Bench and Morgan, too. He kept us from getting big-headed. In a quiet way, Tony's the biggest agitator you ever seen."

"Tony had the personality and the ability to hold down and cool off clubhouse situations that could have grown ugly," remembered trainer Larry Starr. "When guys got hot under the collar, Tony would come in with that Cuban accent and make fun of it. Pretty soon everybody would be laughing."

Brennaman agreed that Perez provided a unique force in the clubhouse. "He was a guy who was a buffer between everything. He was the guy who could maintain a friendship with Bench and with Rose and carry on his own special brand of foolishness with both of them. He could say things to guys that a lot of people couldn't say because of the type of person that he was and the respect people had for him. With all the leadership abilities the 'Big Four' had, Tony embraced more of those attributes than any of them did."

For an organization that prided itself on thorough research—prior to the Morgan trade, the Reds knew more about the Houston clubhouse than the Astros did—the failure to understand Perez's importance to the team was inexcusable. On a team full of big egos and awash in braggadocio, Perez policed the excesses.

Yet when the management team gathered together at the end of the 1976 season, the consensus was that Perez, despite *averaging* 103 RBIs over the past 10 seasons, was expendable. There were many reasons to move Perez, reasons as old as the game itself and reasons as new as free agency.

For Howsam, the challenge was age-old: "You have to turn the club over enough so you don't get caught with a lot of older

The Cincinnati Enquirer

Tony Perez hugged Johnny Bench, his teammate of 10 years, at the press conference announcing Perez's trade to Montreal.

ballplayers." The cold logic of baseball's truncated actuarial tables drove the decision. Players decline in their mid-30s. Thirty-four-year-old Perez was the one veteran the Reds had an immediate replacement for: 25-year-old Driessen.

"Driessen could give us more speed and he could help us in a way that we weren't going to grow old," Howsam recalled.

An alternative was to platoon the left-handed Driessen and Perez, or to allow the two to compete for the job. But Perez vetoed the idea.

"I had 10 straight years of driving in 90 or more runs," Perez explained. "I'd been in the starting lineup for nine years, and then my playing time started being reduced in '76. I didn't want to go through another year of that. Sometimes I get upset. I don't like to miss when I'm not tired. The only answer Sparky gave me is, 'Danny needs a chance to play.' So I told the Reds finally, 'I love my teammates, but please, I must play every day—somewhere.'"

The usually hardheaded Howsam was sympathetic to Perez's plight.

"I respected him and his family too much to just put Tony on the bench. I was trying to do a good thing, but it was a mistake."

In hindsight, Anderson felt the platoon might have worked.

"We should have kept Tony. Let it happen how it's gonna happen. Let Tony be upset if he's upset. We could live with that. Tony was one of those guys, he might be upset, but he's not going to hurt the ballclub. But that's so easy to say now. Danny was ready to play."

Platooning Perez might have worked for one season, but it was not a long-term option for the club. Perez had the leverage of free agency. He could have played out 1977 without signing a new contract and then tested the market. Free agency, recalled Wagner, was another factor pushing the trade.

"All these new rules come into play and make you pay attention to your younger people," Wagner said. "You have to make room for the younger guy because of the restrictions we're getting at the higher level where fellows can go for a trade or just ask to be free agents. The whole thing puts more pressure on the older player as we see it and makes us want the younger player. This was basically the reason behind the Tony Perez trade."

With no thought of trading Driessen, the club could find no compelling reasons to keep Perez—except for the intangibles. At the time no one made those arguments. Anderson admits his failure to stand up for Perez was one of the biggest mistakes he made as a manager.

"I never knew until Tony Perez left after the '76 season that he was probably the number one leader. Tony Perez was a great leader who didn't do it with a big mouth. He had a way. But I never knew that. That's how stupid I was."

The only decision remaining for the Reds was which club could give them what they needed in exchange for Perez. The loss of Gullett intensified the search for a left-handed pitcher, and uncertainties about relief pitchers McEnaney and Eastwick argued for more bullpen help. When the Expos offered lefty Woody Fryman (an All-Star in 1976) and the hard-throwing reliever Dale Murray, the Reds jumped.

Howsam completed the deal at the winter meetings in Los Angeles. Anderson met Ray Shore and Chief Bender in the team hotel, where they told him the details of the deal. Only when Anderson heard the news did the reality of Tony's absence hit him.

"I had not given much forethought to what it would be like not

RBI Kings

The trade of Tony Perez broke up not only the historic starting eight of the Big Red Machine, it also broke up one of the great power pairings in baseball history.

From 1967 through 1976, teammates Perez and Johnny Bench drove in 1,957 runs.

They rank seventh on the all-time list behind Babe Ruth/Lou Gehrig (2,884), Hank Aaron/Eddie Mathews (2,627), Gil Hodges/Duke Snider (2,483), Mickey Mantle/Yogi Berra (2,403), Willie Mays/Willie McCovey (2,306), and Met Ott/Bill Terry (2,095).

From 1968 to 1976, when they anchored the middle of the Big Red Machine lineup, Bench and Perez averaged 205 RBIs a year.

to have him," Anderson said. "But when they told me the deal had been made, all of a sudden I realized we have just lost a *very* good hitter, and a *very* good guy."

The Reds informed Perez of the trade by phone. One of the first calls Tony made was to McEnaney.

"Will, nobody knows this yet, but they traded me to the Expos."

McEnaney, who had not yet been informed of the deal, and who was not one of Perez's close friends, could not quite figure out why Perez was calling him.

"Oh, Tony, I'm so sorry," McEnaney said, wondering all the time what was up.

"Don't worry about me," said Perez in his deep Cuban bass. "You comin' to."

Perez's attorney, Reuven Katz, recalled the press conference to announce the trade.

"Tony's press conference was in my office," said Katz. "I knew that Bench and Perez were very close. I couldn't tell Bench before the press conference what it was about, but I called him and said, 'Be at my office at 12 o'clock. It's very important.'

"A few minutes later a friend of Bench's calls and says, 'Why do you want him in your office? He's worried.' I said, 'Tell him not to worry, just come to the office.' So John walked in and saw Tony. They didn't say a word. They just went up and hugged each other. He knew Tony was gone. They embraced for some time. It was so real and it was the story. Something had been taken out of Bench's life, and Perez's."

At the press conference, Perez spoke with dignity about the trade. He took no shots at the Reds.

But years later, he was still confused about why Howsam ripped apart a starting lineup that had yet to be beaten on the field.

"To this day, I ask myself this question," said Perez. "Why would anybody want to break up that starting eight?"

The trade of Perez upset many of his teammates, but their more immediate concerns were their own situations. Enlightened by the free-agent contract figures, the players became much more conscious of their own bargaining power. The average major league salary would climb from $52,300 in 1976 to $74,000 in 1977, and Morgan, Rose, Concepcion, Foster, Griffey, Nolan, Eastwick and others began aggressive negotiations for lucrative, long-term deals. Whatever harmony had existed between players and management after the glorious sweep of the Yankees, quickly disappeared in a fierce war of words that played out all over the newspapers.

"I think a lot of the Reds will play out options—including me, if I don't get my million," Concepcion declared.

"If push comes to shove, I'm thinking about playing out my option," Foster threatened.

"I can't tell you what management is thinking," Morgan groused after his negotiations stalled. "And, right now, I don't give a damn."

Even the club's "PR" events backfired. In Dayton, on the annual media caravan designed to tout the upcoming season, Eastwick called his employers "stupid" for trading McEnaney. Eastwick then went on to complain that he had been underpaid in 1976 and lobbied for a four- or five-year deal.

Some of the harshest words came from Nolan.

"If the Reds don't want to pay me what I'm asking, then they should trade me," he challenged. Nolan had blasted Anderson after the World Series about his handling of the pitching staff.

"It's always the same. 'Joe Morgan this.' 'Pete Rose that.' 'Tony Perez this.' 'John Bench that,'" he complained. "We don't have a Cy Young or a Walter Johnson, or a Tom Seaver or even a Catfish Hunter. Yet we go out there and get the job done. Then we hear our manager say things like, 'The only thing I'm concerned about is our pitching.'"

Nolan signed a one-year contract, but made it clear he would leave after the season.

The Reds had signed all their players to one-year contracts for 1976, except a two-year deal for Bench in the club's first multi-year package. Although Howsam had not compromised on his stand against free agency, the new era forced a reappraisal of his policy against multi-year contracts. Wagner, in particular, feared that a player's productivity would fall if he played under a guaranteed contract. But the club realized the only way to secure the heart of the team was to negotiate long-term deals. By March 1977, Morgan, Foster and Griffey had received three-year deals, and Concepcion, represented by Kapstein, had been rewarded with a five-year package. The length of Concepcion's deal was something of a surprise, but the Reds had agreed to the contract when Concepcion pushed Kapstein aside and made the deal himself.

Wagner had once before tried to pull an end run around Kapstein in negotiations with McEnaney. Wagner shot McEnaney an offer that Wagner claimed was "three times" McEnaney's previous salary. McEnaney gulped and said, "I'll take it."

Kapstein dragged McEnaney out of the room before he could sign and informed the reliever that the offer was insulting. "Let me handle it," Kapstein said. McEnaney obliged, and wound up with a better contract.

Wagner now challenged Concepcion to make his own deal. Concepcion took the bait.

"I make up my mind," Concepcion responded. "He (Kapstein)

The 1977 Reds: The Highest Paid Eight

The marathon salary talks between the players and Cincinnati management in the 1976-77 offseason were often acrimonious. Howsam and Wagner lost the public relations battle because the press and the fans were critical of the Reds tight-fisted policies.

Yet the signings produced the highest paid starting lineup in the history of baseball. An unofficial payroll survey by United Press International revealed that the starting eight of the Reds was the highest paid at $1,630,000.

The Phillies ranked first in overall team payroll at $3,497,000. The Yankees were next at $3,474,000 and the Reds were third at $2,759,000.

Player	Estimated Salary
Joe Morgan	$400,000
Pete Rose	$365,000
Johnny Bench	$235,000
Dave Concepcion	$200,000
George Foster	$185,000
Cesar Geronimo	$100,000
Ken Griffey	$85,000
Dan Driessen	$60,000

Despite the executive-level salaries, the players still faced rules and fines. Anderson's curfew was 1:00 a.m.

Violation	Fine
Missing curfew	$100 first violation; $200 second
Failure to take fielding practice	$50
Failure to take batting practice	$25
Alcohol on plane	$200

work for me, I no work for him. I call him and I tell him I think I got what I want."

The contract may have been sweetened by more negotiating, but Concepcion's five-year, $1 million deal was among the most generous ever offered by the club.

Concepcion's signing during spring training ended the holdouts except for Rose's. Once again, Pete and management were miles apart on contract terms. Rose was a chart-defying anomaly: 35 years old, he still showed no signs of decline. In 1976, he had led the major leagues in runs scored and doubles, and tied George Brett of the Royals for the lead in hits. He played in 162 games, made the All-Star team and finished fourth in the MVP vote. Rose's hit total stood at 2,762; he seemed to be a lock for 3,000 hits and the Hall of Fame.

Rose made $188,000 in 1976. With the free-agent salaries driving the market price of star players sky-high, Rose asked for a raise to $400,000 annually over one, two or three years. Because of the possibility of Rose playing out his option year and declaring himself a free agent, Rose's familiar holdout took on unfamiliar urgency. If there was one player Cincinnati fans thought was worth an outrageous salary, it was their own Peter Edward. The club soon found itself fighting a public relations nightmare. A poll in *The Enquirer* revealed that 55 percent of the fans thought the Reds should agree to Rose's demands. On Howsam's weekly radio show, the Reds GM was besieged by irate callers.

Katz felt the public outcry probably saved Pete.

"I don't think the Reds really wanted him in 1977," Katz recalled, remembering the tone of the negotiations. "But the fans pushed them into it."

The club finally took the unheard of tactic of buying a full-page ad in *The Enquirer* and *The Dayton Daily News* to explain its position. Not only did Reds management blast Rose in the ad, they accused the media of becoming biased.

Enquirer reporter Bob Hertzel recalled that the Reds put themselves in the awkward position of having to rely on paid advertising.

"They could have gotten their position out for free if they had just talked to me," Hertzel said. "But they were always tight-lipped, so it was hard to report their side. That's the way Howsam was."

None of Rose's previous holdouts had ever persisted past mid-March, but the 1977 logjam was not broken until the evening before Opening Day. Rose, Katz and Wagner met in a final session. The talks turned nasty before Rose finally agreed to an estimated $365,000 a year for two years. But the intensity of Wagner's approach left a sense of repugnance that Katz could not shake.

The Reds belittled Katz, Rose remembered. "The club always called him an 'agent.' Reuv was a lawyer. He wasn't an agent. They used that to embarrass him and they did it purposefully. There were times when I don't think Reuven was a hundred percent sure about wanting to go in there (for negotiating sessions)."

The 1977 contract would be Rose's last with the Big Red Machine.

With the off-season soap opera finally over, the regular season began. But it provided no better story lines. By April 25, the defending champions were 5-10, seven games behind L.A.

"And we haven't even played *that* good," admitted a despondent Anderson.

Tommy Lasorda, the Dodgers' new manager, had led his team to a blazing start, keyed by Dusty Baker and Reggie Smith. How hot were the Dodgers? In late April, the Reds won five in a row—and still lost a half game to L.A. in the standings. After the Reds lost two straight to the Dodgers at Riverfront Stadium, shortstop Bill Russell observed, "They look dead. They just weren't as up as they usually are against us."

"We're playing like we don't realize the season has started," Rose moaned.

Gaffes mounted and tempers flared. After watching George Foster run through the "stop" sign of third-base coach George

The Cincinnati Enquirer

Dick Wagner (left) and Pete Rose joked about a microphone at the press conference announcing Rose's signing in 1977. Despite the apparent cordiality, the contract negotiations left permanent scars.

1977 Monthly Standings
National League West

April 30

	W	L	GB
Los Angeles	17	3	—
Cincinnati	9	10	7½
Houston	9	11	8
San Francisco	8	11	8½
Atlanta	8	12	9
San Diego	8	15	10½

May 31

	W	L	GB
Los Angeles	33	15	—
Cincinnati	22	23	9½
San Diego	24	28	11
San Francisco	20	27	12½
Houston	20	27	12½
Atlanta	17	32	16½

June 30

	W	L	GB
Los Angeles	50	26	—
Cincinnati	40	33	8½
San Francisco	34	43	16½
Houston	33	43	17
San Diego	32	46	19
Atlanta	28	42	21½

July 31

	W	L	GB
Los Angeles	66	38	—
Cincinnati	51	51	14
Houston	48	57	18½
San Francisco	47	58	19½
San Diego	45	62	22½
Atlanta	37	65	28

August 31

	W	L	GB
Los Angeles	80	53	—
Cincinnati	72	62	8½
Houston	64	69	15
San Francisco	62	72	18½
San Diego	59	76	22
Atlanta	48	84	31½

Final Standings

	W	L	GB
Los Angeles	98	64	—
Cincinnati	88	74	10
Houston	81	81	17
San Francisco	75	87	23
San Diego	69	93	29
Atlanta	61	101	37

Scherger, collide with the startled coach, fall down, get up and be thrown out at home with his team behind by six runs, Sparky exploded.

"We've got Hall of Fame players over here! Hall of Fame!"

A few days later, Anderson earned his first ejection of the season. As Anderson headed onto the field to confront umpire Paul Pryor, Pryor warned him, "You're getting in trouble, Sparky."

"Trouble?!" cried an incredulous Anderson. "Trouble? What do you know about trouble? My team is 15-19! That's trouble."

But Anderson did not blame the players alone. He admitted he had let up in spring training.

"I'm not saying the team has gotten fat," Sparky said. "But our biggest problem is that when you win two years in a row, it's just hard to gear up and start another long haul."

Years later, Anderson revised his critique. He had been too soft.

"I believe I allowed them to sit back early. The Dodgers got off to such a fast start, but I still felt we would peck away and come and get them. I let it go too far. Had I pushed them harder, say from May 1st on, they would have got going a little quicker."

There was something else missing besides Sparky's prodding: Perez. Anderson knew the players missed "Doggie," even if they didn't openly acknowledge it.

"Doggie was a part of the time in baseball where you had more of a family spirit," Sparky recalled. "Tony was part of the family. Now he's gone. You've broken up the family. Guys like Davey and Rose and Bench and Morgan, I think they felt that if the club would do that to Tony, they would do that to them. It created a very bad animosity among the players."

From the very first day of spring training, Brennaman had noticed Perez's absence.

"I can remember walking into the clubhouse in Tampa and you knew intuitively that something was wrong," Brennaman said. "And it wasn't a case of saying Tony's not here. It was Tony's not here and it's a much bigger absence than we had anticipated. With Tony there, they never got too high or too low. I'm not so sure that was true in '77."

"If Tony were here, things would be different," declared one regular early in the season. "Right now, we're afraid to get all over each other. But if he were here, he'd get it started."

Clubhouse chemistry created huge problems for the Reds in 1977, but the starting eight, including Driessen, continued to score runs. Rose, Morgan and Concepcion declined offensively, but Bench and Foster improved dramatically over their 1976 production. The Reds would score 802 runs in 1977, second in the league, led by Foster's 52 home runs and 149 RBIs, both all-time club records.

Foster, who had been nicknamed "Yahtzee" by Rose ("My Uncle George's nickname was Yahtzee and I just figured everybody named George is Yahtzee," explained Pete), had become a favorite of Reds fans. Here was the heir apparent to the Reds' aging power structure, a steel-forearmed, bible-toting disciple of Teddy Roosevelt's philosophy: "Speak softly and carry a big black-stained hickory stick." He had gone from project to superstar. His 52 home runs tied his old Giants' teammate, Willie Mays, for the third highest total in N.L. history.

But there was no George Foster on the pitching staff. Overlooked in the hubbub of the Perez trade, the pitching underwent significant changes in the offseason and in the early part of 1977. The rotation opened without three of the regulars from

1977 MONTHLY STANDINGS
NATIONAL LEAGUE EAST

April 30

	W	L	GB
St. Louis	12	7	–
Pittsburgh	10	7	1
Montreal	8	8	2½
New York	8	9	3
Chicago	7	9	3½
Philadelphia	7	9	3½

May 31

	W	L	GB
Chicago	28	16	–
St. Louis	28	18	1
Pittsburgh	26	17	1½
Philadelphia	25	19	3
Montreal	18	26	10
New York	16	29	12½

June 30

	W	L	GB
Chicago	47	24	–
Philadelphia	40	32	7½
St. Louis	41	33	7½
Pittsburgh	39	34	9
New York	31	42	17
Montreal	30	42	17½

July 31

	W	L	GB
Chicago	60	41	–
Philadelphia	59	43	1½
Pittsburgh	59	44	2
St. Louis	56	48	5½
Montreal	48	54	12½
New York	43	58	17

August 31

	W	L	GB
Philadelphia	81	50	–
Pittsburgh	77	56	5
Chicago	71	60	10
St. Louis	71	62	11
Montreal	60	72	21½
New York	51	80	30

Final Standings

	W	L	GB
Philadelphia	101	61	–
Pittsburgh	96	66	5
St. Louis	83	79	18
Chicago	81	81	20
Montreal	75	87	26
New York	64	98	37

The Kapstein Factor

Did player agent Jerry Kapstein break up the Big Red Machine? Although no one in Bob Howsam's front office will admit that any personal vendetta was directed toward Kapstein, the record shows that by mid-1977, all the Cincinnati players Kapstein had represented (except Davey Concepcion) had been traded or released. The victims included Clay Carroll, Pat Darcy, Will McEnaney, Rawly Eastwick, Gary Nolan and Don Gullett.

In the long term, these moves reflected sound baseball judgment. Few of these players had memorable careers after leaving the Reds; none matched their best year in Cincinnati. But if some of Kapstein's cast-offs had been retained—given the horrendous pitching problems the club had in 1977 and 1978—they may well have been the difference between a first- and second-place finish.

Jerry Kapstein (right) and Davey Concepcion met the press after Concepcion signed his five-year pact in 1977.

the 1976 campaign: Gullett, who was in a Yankee uniform, Nolan and Alcala. Nolan suffered a foot injury and did not pitch until May 10. Anderson admitted he rushed Nolan back into the rotation because of the team's poor start, and Nolan again developed arm problems. Alcala's lackluster spring and exasperating work ethic earned him a trade to Montreal in May after two ineffective starts. (He retired after the 1977 season.) McEnaney had been traded, and Manny Sarmiento was left behind in Tampa with a lingering illness that kept him sidelined until mid-July.

It was only May of 1977 and already half of the Reds' 1976 staff was either sidelined or sent packing. In the dynasty years of the Big Red Machine, new acquisitions (Norman, Billingham, Kirby) or youngsters (Gullett, Simpson, Grimsley, McEnaney, Eastwick, Zachry) had stepped in and pitched well, often beyond expectations. But early in 1977, the newcomers and rookies failed miserably. Through June 14, Murray, Fryman, rookie Tom Hume and Mike Caldwell (acquired in a trade with St. Louis) had a combined ERA of 5.52. Zachry provided little stability. He won only three of his first 10 decisions.

Howsam watched his pitching staff disintegrate and his team fall farther behind the Dodgers. Not a single off-season move had worked. No pitcher had been able to provide the intimidation, the "stopper" factor of a Don Gullett. The bullpen blew game after game. And the future looked dim. Nolan and Eastwick, both represented by Kapstein, were not likely to be Reds in 1978. Eastwick, bitter over the McEnaney trade and the club's failure to offer him a multi-year deal, had already said that 1977 was his last year with the Reds.

The situation was desperate. "We made a decision about two weeks before the June 15th trading deadline," Anderson recalled.

"We didn't feel we could catch the Dodgers with what we had."

Howsam worked the phones as the deadline approached. His most frequent calls were to the New York Mets.

"It kept coming out in the press and in the reports we got that Tom Seaver was not getting along with (owner) Donald Grant," Howsam recalled. "So I started working that angle. Could we get Seaver? They were hot and cold. I kept after them."

Unlike the trade that brought Joe Morgan to Cincinnati in 1972, the Seaver deal involved a player of unsullied reputation.

"Morgan was more of an unknown," Howsam said. "Seaver wasn't like that. The questions had to do more with what they wanted. My style was to talk enough to find out what positions they were trying to strengthen. You would be foolish to make a deal by starting out saying, 'I'll give you so-and-so.' Everybody is trying to build a club and all do it different. 'What are you looking for?' Now, you can put together a package."

The Mets began with Zachry and expanded their list. Eastwick was included, but he balked at going to New York, and delayed the deal. With Seaver involved, the New York media aggressively pursued the news. On the evening of the June 15, the Riverfront Stadium press box rocked with rumors. Meanwhile, the war room, Howsam's office, was a jangle of nerves and ringing telephones.

"Eastwick was in the deal, but Kapstein intervened and we had to substitute players," Wagner recalled. "That was a real fire fight to get that done. The National League called us four times during the game to tell us to take our players off the field that were in the trade. I kept saying, 'What trade?' I'd been in Howsam's office and I knew the trades weren't a done deal. The league office said, 'The media is reporting the trade has been made!' But it hadn't. 'Goddammit, the deal hasn't been made!' I was yelling back."

The Cincinnati Enquirer

Tom Seaver's Riverfront Stadium debut came on June 26, 1977. His introduction to the Reds included the traditional hosiery. As Seaver gingerly examined his new low-cut socks, Johnny Bench commanded, "You will wear them and you will like them. You WILL like them!"

Just hours before the trading deadline expired, Howsam and the Mets agreed to a package of Zachry, Doug Flynn and top minor league outfielders Dan Norman and Steve Henderson for Seaver. Although Howsam had turned his back on free agents, he had acquired in "Tom Terrific" a player of more stature than anybody available in the free-agent derby. And Howsam had given up very little to do it. Zachry never matched his rookie year and wound up 41-49 with the Mets. The highly touted prospects, Norman and Henderson, had undistinguished major league careers. Had Seaver led the Reds to another World Series, as everyone thought he would, the trade would have ranked among Howsam's legendary deals.

But Howsam wasn't done on this June 15. He also wanted to move Nolan and Eastwick before their trade value expired at the end of the season. Because of Nolan's arm problems, he had limited value and was dealt to the Angels for minor league infielder Craig Henderson (who never made the majors). Eastwick was traded to St. Louis for reliever Doug Capilla. And Howsam sent the disappointing Mike Caldwell to Milwaukee for two more prospects (who also never made the majors).

To replace the pitchers lost in the deal, the Reds turned to their Indianapolis club and brought up 23-year-old Paul Moskau and 40-year-old player-coach Joe Hoerner. Reds fans cringed. A 40-year-old pitcher? Had their championship club really sunk this low? Although the Reds had landed Seaver, the loss of Zachry, Eastwick, Gullett, Nolan, Alcala and McEnaney had turned the staff gray overnight. The starters included Fryman, 37, Norman, 35, Billingham, 34, and Seaver, 32. Relievers included Hoerner, 40, Joe Henderson, 31, and Borbon, 31. The only pitchers in their 20s were the unproven: Murray, 27, Capilla, 25, and Moskau, 23.

On the day of the trades, the Reds had pulled within sight of the Dodgers. Observed Morgan, "The season can't be over in June when you're 6½ back."

Seaver pitched well, winning 14 of his 17 Cincinnati decisions,

© Jerry Dowling & *The Cincinnati Enquirer*, 1971

The club's poor 1977 showing transformed the Big Red Machine from a steamrolling juggernaut to a classroom dunce.

but the remainder of the revamped staff failed to contribute. Any hopes of a third consecutive World Championship collapsed in July. On the tenth of July, the Reds trailed the Dodgers by eight games. But when the Reds lost 16 of their next 20 games, they fell 14 back, and it was over.

In the midst of the collapse, Fryman headed south—literally and figuratively. His shoulders had buckled from the burden of heavy expectations from the Perez trade. Angry at Anderson for banishing him to the bullpen, Fryman bolted the club for his farm in Kentucky. Despite a personal visit from Wagner, Fryman could not be cajoled into returning. With Murray ineffective in the bullpen and Fryman tending his tobacco crop, the Perez trade had yielded absolutely nothing. Meanwhile, Doggie was racking up another 90+ RBI season north of the border.

The Reds called up several rookies over the last half of the season, including Mario Soto and Ray Knight, but the Dodgers were long gone. With the pitching rotation in shambles—10 pitchers started at least 10 games and only Fred Norman pitched over 200 innings—Cincinnati couldn't draw any closer to L.A. than 8½ games.

Sparky was so embarrassed he suggested a novel promotion for the 1978 season if the Reds' play didn't improve.

"If things aren't different, then I hope they have 'Spear Day' here at the ballpark. Give out spears with poison on the ends."

He also suggested "Explosion Day."

"If this team isn't straightened out next year, I ought to take this room and blow it up…with me in it!"

"What has happened?" Sparky asked. "I'll tell you. The pitching has allowed 4.70 runs a game! But every one of us has to share some of the blame."

Referring to the 1971 fiasco, Anderson said, "That was not a failure. We just didn't have the team. But this, this is total failure."

The professional attitude that had so characterized the 1975-76 team was so lacking on the 1977 club that Anderson could not stand it. In early September, after an embarrassing 13-4 loss in Houston, the Reds rode to the airport. Anderson and some of the coaches heard laughter from the rear of the bus.

Morgan walked back to inform his teammates that it wasn't all smiles up front. But absent the crackling thunder of a Tony Perez, the players continued their snickering.

With reporters on the bus, Anderson would not risk an outburst. But his face was red and his demeanor was barely controlled as he shouted at the players that there would be a clubhouse meeting when they returned to Cincinnati.

Morgan believed that all the roster moves had taken their toll on the Reds. By season's end, the Reds had lost eight players—roughly one-third of their roster—from the 1976 club. Many of the new players were not schooled in the Reds farm system.

"We held up well for certain periods," Morgan recalled. "But our attitude was inconsistent. A team with character, as we're supposed to have, should never get like that. In losing, you cut away a little confidence. It takes special people with a special attitude to be a winner."

This new group of Reds, untutored by Perez, never did learn their lessons.

In mid-September, Howsam convened the annual organizational meetings. Once again, he brought together Anderson, Ray Shore, Chief Bender and Rex and Joe Bowen to evaluate the club. Following the failure of 1971, these same men had restructured the

Reds. But now, despite the debacle of 1977, the brass rated the Reds starting eight as the best in baseball. No major overhaul was recommended.

That conclusion proved to be a huge miscalculation. The "Great Eight" had peaked offensively in 1976. The turndown in offense in 1977 was not a temporary dip, but the beginning of a permanent decline for the group as a whole and for most of the individual players. The veterans could have been expected to decline, and they did. Morgan, 34, suffered an unexpectedly sharp drop in offensive production, brought on by a stomach muscle pull in 1978. Bench, 29, and Rose, 37, could not duplicate their peak years of the early to mid-1970s, but continued to have productive seasons. The biggest problem, however, was not the veterans; it was the failure of the young players to continue their development. Only Foster and Concepcion were able to sustain and improve on their 1976 performances.

Griffey, who was 27 in 1977, never bettered his 1976 season. Geronimo, 29, began a fast downhill slide in 1977 that he never reversed. Driessen, 26, had a productive 1977 in his first full season as a starter, but never improved.

The starters might have been challenged by a hot crop of rookies, but the poor drafts of 1972 and 1973 failed to produce any significant talent. Not one new player from the Reds farm system made a significant contribution in his debut year of 1977 or 1978.

The Reds were in need of another blockbuster deal. A bold gamble—one that would have turned baseball wisdom on its head—would have been to retain the veterans and trade some of the *wunderkinds*. In December 1971, Howsam plucked a future MVP from the talent pool in Morgan, and gave up some impressive talent. Could the Reds have pulled off a similar deal six years later, trading perhaps Driessen, Griffey or Geronimo for a superstar-in-waiting, such as Andre Dawson, Eddie Murray or Rickey Henderson? The normally prescient Howsam organization never considered such a strategy because it never saw the collapse coming.

The pitching woes did receive some attention. Howsam heard favorable reports from the farm system that led him to believe the Reds could expect significant contributions from several young pitchers, including Tom Hume, Paul Moskau, Mario Soto and Mike LaCoss. But Howsam knew he needed some veteran arms, so in his first significant off-season move, he sent Fryman to the Cubs for 29-year-old right-hander Bill Bonham.

For the second consecutive year, Howsam refused to use the free-agent draft to improve his team. Howsam abstained in all 43 rounds. At the winter meetings in Honolulu, the other owners roasted Howsam about his draft tactics. At a dinner, the emcee tossed the Reds boss a red-and-white football in recognition of all Howsam's "passes" at the draft. But Howsam had his reply ready. On December 9, the Reds announced they had acquired Vida Blue, the 28-year-old Oakland A's pitching star, for minor league outfielder Dave Revering and $1.75 million in cash.

The enormous cash deal was unlike the Reds, but club ownership had agreed when Howsam proposed it.

"We needed a left-hander," Howsam recalled. "We had some extra cash. I had almost given up on the deal when I got a call from Oakland. (Owner Charlie) Finley was willing to make the deal for Blue for $1.75 million plus a player."

Howsam would not stoop to enter the free-agent market, but in this transaction, he had accomplished the same result: he had purchased a star player whose presence might return the team to pennant contention. With Blue and Seaver dominating the rotation, Howsam had largely solved his starting-pitching problems for 1977. Here was a twosome that more than made up for the loss of Gullett and Nolan, the club's dominant one-two punch during its dynasty run. With two former Cy Young winners on the mound, the Big Red Machine appeared to be refueled.

At the winter meetings, Howsam had quietly informed Commissioner Bowie Kuhn of the deal. Kuhn made no comment, but when the deal was publicly announced, he quickly issued a sobering statement saying he wanted to investigate the transaction.

This was the second time Kuhn had held up a deal for Blue. In 1976, Finley sold Blue, Joe Rudi and Rollie Fingers to the Yankees, but Kuhn voided the deal as violating the best interests of baseball. Now he threatened to do the same thing.

"I told him we were within the rules," Howsam recalled. "We had quite a go-around. He felt no more than $400,000 in cash should be exchanged. And he claimed that Revering wasn't good enough for Blue. But there was no rule that we were breaking."

No *official* rule was broken. But the deal did violate a recommendation that Kuhn had announced in 1977 that cash transactions between clubs should not exceed $400,000. Howsam thought there was one other critical factor involved.

"I think Bowie had a strong dislike for Finley."

On January 30, Kuhn blocked the transaction, claiming he was protecting the competitive balance among the teams.

Howsam was livid.

"I don't think that baseball intended the commissioner to decide which teams would be allowed to win pennants and how often," he said, skewering Kuhn.

The ruling left Howsam in a quandary. Unwilling to enter the free-agent bidding, he was now being told he could not rebuild his club through long-accepted means. The Reds threatened to appeal the decision in court, but backed off. Finley eventually sold Blue to the Giants for seven prospects and $390,000.

Unable to purchase Blue from Oakland, Howsam returned to the trading bazaar. The A's were shopping reliever Doug Bair. Ray Shore had recommended the hard-throwing right-hander, so Howsam acquired him for Revering and cash on February 25. It was Howsam's final trade. On March 1, the 60-year-old Howsam stepped down as president and turned the club over to Dick Wagner. Howsam announced he would remain with the club in an advisory capacity as vice chairman.

The Cincinnati Enquirer

The decline of the Big Red Machine in 1977 and 1978 left Sparky Anderson with much to explain to the new club president, Dick Wagner. Wagner fired Anderson in December, 1978.

Howsam's departure did not surprise club insiders. In 1967, Howsam had told Bender that he wanted to retire at age 60. Howsam also suffered from a lingering back injury.

"If you are going to do your job, you have to put in many hours and they were hard days," Howsam recalled. "I just couldn't sit at a desk. I'd go to a game in the evening and then go home and lie down flat as I could. I was in misery all the time."

But those with whom he worked believed the volatility of the new free-agency era had drained Howsam's enthusiasm. Howsam admitted as much. The "fun" had gone out of the game for him.

"The trading, that's the fun, the competition," he said. "It is like being a player competing with the other guy, building your team. But now it is so restrictive. You have a player you want to trade. It's hard enough to find someone else who has a need for that player. And has what you're looking for. But that isn't the end of it. Now you have to worry if the man is signed or if he will play out his option."

The problem with the new rules was that there were no rules—at least, few that Howsam recognized.

"You put all the effort in, the scouts, the instructors and coaches in the minor leagues and bring these boys along, and you work hard when they get to the major leagues," he said. "And when they are in their prime, they walk away from you. That isn't right."

Years later, Roger Ruhl explained Howsam's dilemma. "Bob liked to see pieces come together, the puzzle completed. Control your destiny. Work hard. Out-think the other person. Howsam preached (team) balance, and free agency made that so much more difficult. Just as you put the pieces together, free agency threw another wrinkle into that."

Shore concurred. "Here was a guy who went out and did his homework, and built what should have been a great club for another four or five years. Then all of a sudden it's all going to be taken away. I don't think Bob felt he could operate under the new conditions. He wanted to build something and once he built it he wanted to keep it."

Any hope of resurrecting a dynasty in Cincinnati faded with Howsam's retirement from the day-to-day management of the organization. In Wagner, Howsam had a no-nonsense, experienced baseball man who was supremely loyal. But if the Perez trade had undermined the spirit of the team, the Wagner move eventually had a similar effect on the front office. Driessen was no Perez and Wagner was no Howsam.

Wagner possessed neither Howsam's ability to judge young talent, nor his excellence at reading his scouts. Wagner did not seek out opinions as thoroughly as his predecessor. The organizational consensus, the inclusiveness that characterized Howsam's approach to major decision-making, evaporated. Wagner ordered employees to keep the doors shut that opened onto the long hallway that cut through the middle of the office.

Where Howsam exhibited a steady, congenial public image, and a pleasant, if firm, demeanor with his staff, Wagner was the dark force, explosive and unpredictable.

"Dick was an enigma," Brennaman recalled. "You could be in a social situation and he could be the greatest guy. But he had an awesome temper. He could fly off the handle like that. One minute we could be talking and the next second he could be raving."

Under Howsam, Wagner rarely had to worry about whom he pleased—as long as he pleased his boss. Now, as the head of the organization, Wagner's image mattered, but he didn't seem to notice.

"I don't think Wagner gave a damn about what people thought about him," Brennaman said. "When he made a decision, he didn't even think if it was going to be unpopular. He didn't care. He had his convictions like nobody I've ever known."

What Wagner *didn't* have was a hard-headed number-two man to carry out the tough assignments.

"Bob Howsam had a Dick Wagner," Brennaman explained. "Dick Wagner didn't have a Dick Wagner. Had he had a Dick Wagner, history might have treated him better."

Howsam left the organization on the eve of spring training with the 1978 roster set. Wagner made one minor move, sending 35-year-old Jack Billingham to Detroit for two prospects. Billingham, who had won 87 games for the Reds since 1972, finished the 1977 season pitching out of the bullpen, and did not figure to be in the starting rotation.

The Reds had four MVPs in the starting lineup (Bench, Rose, Morgan and Foster), a luxury never previously enjoyed by any N.L. club. Anderson's primary concern was fine-tuning the pitching staff. The rotation would be anchored by veterans Seaver, Bonham and Norman, and would be filled out by Hume, Moskau and Capilla, three youngsters who would have to improve upon their 1977 performances. Bair and Murray headed up the bullpen, and Anderson hoped for depth in Borbon, Dave Tomlin (acquired from San Diego) and Sarmiento.

Anderson also toughened his training camp. Howsam believed the club had been "complacent" in 1977. More than one reporter had commented on the "country club" atmosphere in spring training. Anderson agreed. He had been embarrassed by the Reds' lackadaisical performance.

"We're going to be doing things differently this year, right from the start," Sparky promised.

The Reds began 1978 with one of their best starts under Anderson, rolling to a 30-19 record by the end of May. But the

The 1978 Reds lined up on Opening Day at Riverfront Stadium. To help promote the club's fall goodwill trip to Japan, the game was televised in 23 Japanese cities.

Giants and Dodgers kept pace, and through July no team enjoyed more than a four-game lead.

But as exciting as the three-way pennant race was, the spring and summer of 1978 belonged to Pete Rose. On May 5, at Riverfront Stadium, Pete smacked a line drive to left field to become the 13th player in history to reach the 3,000 hit mark. Five weeks later, the 37-year-old Rose went two-for-four against the Cubs. A common occurrence for Pete, but it was the beginning of a hitting streak that would reach 44 games, and put him second in the record books to Joe DiMaggio's 56-game streak.

When the streak reached 30 games, Rose set his sights on the N.L. record of 37 held by Tommy Holmes. The media barrage began.

"Fine with me," said Pete. "I like talking about my basehits."

Pete's enthusiasm for the game and his passion for the craft of hitting were displayed daily. After he broke Holmes' record, he revealed one of his secrets.

"If you sandpaper or alcohol-rub your bat every day, you can see exactly where you hit every pitch," said Pete. "On the first out in game 38, I hit the ball well, but when I looked for the spot, it was right on the label. So I knew I had to choke up another inch to hit that pitch. Next time up, same pitch, line drive, and I had the record."

On July 31 in Atlanta, Rose tied Willie Keeler's 1897 record of 44 straight with a sixth-inning single. But Braves pitchers Larry McWilliams and Gene Garber—and third baseman Bob Horner—stopped the streak the following night. Rose hit two hard line drives, but Horner speared one and McWilliams made a sensational catch of the other. In the ninth, with two out and the Reds down, 16-4, Garber struck out Rose on a changeup. Pete was

The Cincinnati Enquirer

Former teammate Tony Perez greeted Pete Rose at first base after Rose singled for hit number 3,000 on May 5, 1978.

Forty-Four in a Row

The streak began with a run-of-the-mill Pete Rose leadoff single in Chicago and built slowly through June and July. Once the streak reached 30 games, the sporting world turned its spotlight on Rose. Pete thrived in the media heat.

Rose held court on the techniques of hitting and Joe DiMaggio. He discovered Tommy Holmes (who held the modern National League record at 37 games) and Willie Keeler (who held the all-time National League mark with 44 games, set in 1897). The streak even inspired the weak-hitting Sparky Anderson to reminisce about his "epic" batting streak in 1959, his only year in the major leagues.

"Eleven games," bragged a joking Anderson. "Longest streak of the year by a Phillie."

And how did the streak end for "Ever-Lovin'?" (Ever-Lovin' was the nickname Sparky occasionally used for himself.) Robbed of a line-drive smash?

"They *pinch-hit* for me in the fifth inning," said Sparky laughing. "Yep. Eleven-game streak and I got pinch-hit for!"

Rose did not have to worry about Anderson lifting him. Rose was helping his team win (the Reds went 26-18 during the streak and kept pace with the Giants) and he was filling the seats. For games 32 and 33 in Philadelphia, the Reds drew 11,000 over the average crowd. In Montreal, games 34-36 drew an additional 8,000 per game, and in New York, the crowds increased by an average of 14,000 per game. Back home for games 40-43 (including a doubleheader), the Reds drew an average of 48,000, 14,000 over their season average.

Powerful ammunition for a player in the final year of his contract.

Pete Rose's 44-Game Hit Streak

Game	Date	Opponent	H/AB	Notes
1	6-14	Chicago	2-4	1B in 1st and 5th
2	6-16	St. Louis	2-4	2B in 5th; 1B in 7th
3	6-17	St. Louis	2-4	1B in 1st and 9th
4	6-18	St. Louis	1-4	bunt 1B in 5th
5	6-20	@ San Fran.	2-5	2B in 1st; 1B in 9th
6	6-21	@ San Fran.	1-4	1B in 1st
7	6-22	@ San Fran.	1-4	1B in 8th (last at-bat)
8	6-23	@ LA	1-4	1B in 1st
9	6-24	@ LA	4-5	2B in 1st; 1B in 3rd, 5th and 9th
10	6-25	@ LA	2-3	1B in 1st and 5th
11	6-26	@ Houston	1-5	1B in 3rd
12	6-27	@ Houston	1-4	1B in 7th (last at-bat)
13	6-28	@ Houston	1-4	1B in 6th
14	6-29	@ Houston	1-3	2B in 1st
15	6-30	LA	1-5	1B in 9th (last at-bat)
16	6-30	LA	3-5	1B in 3rd, 8th and 9th
17	7-1	LA	1-5	2B in 3rd
18	7-2	LA	1-4	2B in 1st
19	7-3	Houston	3-5	2B in 1st; 1B in 6th and 8th
20	7-4	Houston	1-4	1B in 1st
21	7-5	Houston	1-4	bunt 1B in 7th (last at-bat)
22	7-7	San Fran.	3-5	1B in 3rd, 5th and 9th
23	7-7	San Fran.	1-4	1B in 3rd
24	7-8	San Fran.	1-4	1B in 6th
25	7-9	San Fran.	3-4	1B in 3rd, 6th (bunt) and 9th
	ALL-STAR BREAK			
26	7-13	New York	2-5	2B in 7th; bunt 1B in 9th
27	7-14	New York	2-5	1B in 3rd and 5th
28	7-15	New York	1-2	1B in 1st
29	7-16	New York	1-5	2B in 7th (last at-bat)
30	7-17	Montreal	1-4	1B in 5th
31	7-18	Montreal	2-4	2B in 1st; 1B in 3rd
32	7-19	@ Philadelphia	1-4	bunt 1B in 8th (last at-bat)
33	7-20	@ Philadelphia	1-5	1B in 5th
34	7-21	@ Montreal	1-3	1B in 1st
35	7-22	@ Montreal	1-3	1B in 6th
36	7-23	@ Montreal	2-6	1B in 6th; 2B in 10th
37	7-24	@ New York	2-5	1B in 7th and 9th
38	7-25	@ New York	3-4	1B in 3rd and 7th; 2B in 9th
39	7-26	@ New York	1-3	2B in 5th
40	7-28	Philadelphia	1-2	2B in 3rd
41	7-28	Philadelphia	1-4	bunt 1B in 6th
42	7-29	Philadelphia	3-4	1B in 1st, 2nd and 4th
43	7-30	Philadelphia	2-5	1B in 5th and 6th
44	7-31	@ Atlanta	1-4	1B in 6th

1978 Monthly Standings
National League West

April 30

	W	L	GB
Los Angeles	13	7	—
Cincinnati	13	8	½
San Francisco	10	10	3
Houston	10	12	4
San Diego	7	12	5½
Atlanta	6	14	7

May 31

	W	L	GB
San Francisco	30	16	—
Cincinnati	30	19	1½
Los Angeles	27	20	3½
San Diego	21	26	9½
Houston	20	25	9½
Atlanta	18	27	11½

June 30

	W	L	GB
San Francisco	47	29	—
Los Angeles	44	33	3
Cincinnati	44	33	3½
San Diego	37	39	10
Houston	33	39	12
Atlanta	31	43	15

July 31

	W	L	GB
San Francisco	63	43	—
Cincinnati	62	43	½
Los Angeles	61	44	1½
San Diego	54	52	9
Houston	48	56	14
Atlanta	48	56	14

August 31

	W	L	GB
Los Angeles	79	54	—
San Francisco	77	56	2
Cincinnati	72	61	7
San Diego	70	65	10
Houston	62	70	16½
Atlanta	59	73	19½

Final Standings

	W	L	GB
Los Angeles	95	67	—
Cincinnati	92	69	2½
San Francisco	89	73	6
San Diego	84	78	11
Houston	74	88	21
Atlanta	69	93	26

incensed and accused Garber of treating the at-bat like it was the "seventh game of the World Series."

Rose didn't expect Garber to groove a pitch. Pete was upset Garber didn't treat the at-bat as he should have under the game circumstances. Facing a 12-run deficit in the top of the ninth inning, hitters expect pitchers to challenge them, to throw strikes, not changeups. Rose couldn't take a walk, so he swung at borderline pitches; he couldn't risk the umpire's call. Garber had violated baseball's unwritten code of conduct, and that irked baseball's ultimate competitor.

On the day Rose's streak ended, the Reds were only one-half game behind the Giants. On August 6, after beating the Padres, Cincinnati moved into first place for the first time since April 25. The team appeared poised to mount a late-season surge that would reclaim the legacy of the Big Red Machine. But Anderson and the Reds had been living dangerously with a thin bench, a wobbly pitching staff, unending injuries and a porous defense.

Further, the club had never filled the void left by Perez's absence. Reporters noted that unlike in years past, the players rarely socialized together outside the ballpark. Morgan admitted the needling and "ripping" of the dynasty days were gone.

Bench, who suffered with a season-long back injury, found the lack of team intensity puzzling.

"We haven't played good fundamental baseball this year. We're playing like a team that's let down because it's lost a couple of games—or because a couple of guys are hurt. We're in the wrong frame of mind."

Fred Norman felt the team had never regained the spirit of the dynasty years.

"The team just wasn't as close as it was before. Used to be that after games a lot of us would go out together and maybe have a beer or two—not all the time, but enough, and that kind of thing helps. Now, instead, this guy goes here, and this guy goes there and we aren't together.... And now this guy's talking about this guy, and this guy's talking about this guy and it's just not the same."

The loss of Perez and failure of 1977 had shaken the team's confidence and destroyed its cohesion. The Reds had to reestablish the dynasty mentality, but as Morgan admitted, "no one was quite sure how that would happen."

With the pennant on the line, and the chance to reclaim the dynasty mantle, the Reds collapsed, going 6-16 while the Dodgers burst past, grabbing a seven-game lead by the end of August. Although the Reds regained their poise in September, they could not catch the Dodgers. The Reds finished with 92 victories, 2½ games behind L.A.

Given the injuries and the pitching problems, 92 wins was remarkable. Sparky admitted, "I don't know how we were flirting for so long a half-game out, one game out, two games out. We always patchworked our pitching…but this year has been a total patchwork of the whole club."

Once again, the pitching was abysmal. The staff allowed 688 runs, only ninth best in the National League. In the peak dynasty years, the Reds staff never ranked lower than fifth. Seaver was under .500 as late as the first of September, and finished 16-14. He pitched a no-hitter in June (the first of his career), and would have had to pitch several more to win consistently. The Reds scored only two runs in 15 of his 36 starts.

Bonham had elbow problems and missed a dozen starts. Norman pitched well the first half of the season, but in the critical weeks of the pennant race, he was 3-4 with a 5.07 ERA.

1978 MONTHLY STANDINGS
NATIONAL LEAGUE EAST

April 30

	W	L	GB
Philadelphia	10	7	—
Montreal	11	8	—
Chicago	11	9	1½
Pittsburgh	9	9	1½
New York	10	12	2½
St. Louis	9	11	2½

May 31

	W	L	GB
Chicago	24	20	—
Montreal	25	22	½
Philadelphia	22	21	1½
New York	23	27	4
Pittsburgh	21	25	4
St. Louis	18	31	8½

June 30

	W	L	GB
Philadelphia	40	31	—
Chicago	38	35	3
Montreal	37	38	5
Pittsburgh	35	38	6
New York	33	45	11½
St. Louis	30	47	13

July 31

	W	L	GB
Philadelphia	55	45	—
Chicago	51	51	5
Pittsburgh	48	52	7
Montreal	50	57	8½
New York	45	62	13½
St. Louis	40	64	17

August 31

	W	L	GB
Philadelphia	71	59	—
Pittsburgh	66	64	½
Chicago	66	65	5½
Montreal	61	73	12
St. Louis	56	75	14½
New York	53	79	19

Final Standings

	W	L	GB
Philadelphia	90	72	—
Pittsburgh	88	73	1½
Chicago	79	83	11
Montreal	76	86	14
St. Louis	69	93	21
New York	66	96	24

Prospects Hume, Moskau and Mike LaCoss, unlike the Gulletts, Simpsons and Grimsleys of the past, failed to contribute. They finished 18-23 with a combined ERA over 4.00. In the bullpen, Bair was the only standout (28 saves; 1.98 ERA). No one else was consistent. Sarmiento had the *second-best* bullpen ERA at 4.39.

The Reds might have overcome the pitching problems if the offense could have performed at its 1976 levels. But the offense continued to struggle. The Reds scored 710 runs, second best in the league, but only 65 runs over the league average (as compared to their whopping 212 runs over the league average in 1976). Seven of the eight starters declined in offensive output from 1977; Concepcion was the only exception.

Injuries fed the decline. Morgan pulled a stomach muscle in June, and never recovered. Anderson said half a Joe Morgan was better than anybody else he had, but Morgan went two months without attempting a stolen base. He hit only three home runs from June through August. Morgan played in 132 games, his lowest total since 1968.

Bench, even though only 29 years old, was beginning to show the strain of having caught more than 100 games for 11 consecutive seasons. He hurt his back early in the season and missed nearly all of June. He appeared in 120 games, the fewest since he had become a starter.

Geronimo sprained his shoulder in May. Unable to swing a bat with any consistency, he appeared in only 122 games, his fewest since joining the Reds. Driessen, who was twice drilled in his right arm by pitched balls, continued to play but changed his swing as a result of the injuries. He hit only .197 after the All-Star break.

In the dynasty years, Anderson had capable reserves, but the bench was bare in 1978. Bench's replacements, Don Werner and

The Cincinnati Enquirer

As the Reds endured a critical six-game losing streak at the end of August, Bob Howsam flew to Cincinnati to talk to the team. "I built this club and take great pride in it," he said. Hitting instructor Ted Kluszewski (left) sat in on the session.

Vic Correll, managed only one home run and 17 RBIs between them in 228 at-bats. Mike Lum, Junior Kennedy and Ken Henderson (acquired from the Mets in May for Dale Murray) could not match the production of Doug Flynn, Driessen, Bob Bailey and Bill Plummer, the top reserves in 1976.

Despite the season-long struggles, Anderson somehow managed to keep the Reds close. The Reds scored only 22 more runs than they allowed, which historically has produced a record of about six games over .500. Yet Anderson guided the Reds to a 92-69 mark, 23 games over .500. Much of the success—and a tribute to Anderson's managing skills—was the Reds record in one-run games. They finished 33-19, their best mark in the 1970s.

As Dick Wagner watched his club stumble through the second half of the 1978 season, he came to two personnel decisions that forever ended the reign of the Big Red Machine. Despite the batting heroics of Rose and the adept managing of Anderson, Wagner determined neither would return to the Reds in 1979. The domination of the Reds had ended on the field in 1976, but with seven-eighths of the legendary starting lineup in the fold and Anderson at the helm, the image of greatness persisted as did the hope that the Reds could still add a link to the dynasty chain. But Wagner's decision to jettison Rose and Anderson unequivocally brought the era to a close.

Rose's contract expired at the end of the 1978 season. He had hit .302, scored over 100 runs and collected 198 hits. He had hit in 44-straight games, but common sense suggested that even the great Pete Rose was headed for a decline.

"You know I love Pete and I want you to know everything about him," Sparky confided to Rose's attorney, Reuven Katz. "His bat

WHAT WENT WRONG?

The failure of the Reds to win a third World Championship and extend the reign of the Big Red Machine dynasty in 1977-78 has been attributed to the trade of Tony Perez. As critical as Perez's presence was to clubhouse chemistry, the decline in the fundamental areas of hitting, pitching and defense, and injuries to key personnel, also accounted for much of the team's failure on the field.

Team Statistics	1976	1977	1978
Runs scored & rank	857 (1)	802 (1)	710 (2)
League Average	645	713	645
Runs allowed & rank	633 (5)	725 (8)	688 (9)
Expected wins •	105	89	84
Actual wins	102	88	92
Record in 1-run games	31-24	24-23	33-19
Errors & rank	103 (1)	95 (1)	134 (4)

• Expected wins is derived from a formula using runs scored and runs allowed. Teams that score and allow the same number of runs, for example, have historically played .500 baseball. The formula will usually predict a club's actual record to within four games. A large positive discrepancy, such as in the Reds' 1978 record, can be attributed to managerial skill, and can mask underlying problems.

Runs Produced (Runs scored + RBIs)			
	1976	1977	1978
Rose	193	159	155
Griffey	185	174	153
Morgan	224	191	143
Bench	136	176	125
Foster	207	273	217
Perez/Driessen	168	166	138
Concepcion	143	123	142
Geronimo	108	106	55
Starter Totals	1364	1368	1128
Reserve Totals	295	184	251
Starter At-Bats	4315	4470	4092

speed is really slowing down."

"It could be that Sparky was saying he didn't have much more to go," Katz remembered. "And so maybe they thought he was reaching the end."

Rose would be 38 at the start of the 1979 season, and Wagner rebuffed Katz's efforts to talk about a $400,000 long-term contract.

Dennis Gruelle

Pete Rose's much-publicized divorce, his fast lifestyle and his rumored association with gamblers helped convince Reds president Dick Wagner to take a hard line on re-signing Rose for 1979.

By all accounts, Pete wanted to stay in Cincinnati. He was willing to accept less than what the inflated free-agent market could surely bring him.

Wagner, however, offered a much lower figure, a figure that represented a cut from Rose's 1978 salary. It was an offer the Reds chairman, Louis Nippert, supported.

"I reviewed 1978 with Mr. Nippert," recalled Wagner, "and I said this is what we will offer Rose. He said, *'That's enough*, Dick Wagner.' He had never spoken in that tone of voice to me."

The promotions-conscious Wagner certainly recognized Rose's value to the Reds. But Wagner's decision to hold the line was also colored by the rumors of Rose's gambling activities. Rose was aware of the reports.

"A guy from the commissioner's office came to town because someone told someone I owed bookies money," Rose recalled. "The two guys they said I owed money to were friends of mine. He came in and I picked him up at the airport and I took him to these guys. He looked them right in the eye and asked them did I bet with them. They said, 'No,' which was true. 'Did I owe them money?' They said, 'No,' which was true. That was the end of it, but I think Wagner was worried about that."

Unsure of Pete's past off the field and uncertain of his future on it, the Reds made little serious effort to negotiate with their aging superstar. Rose, feeling unwanted and unwilling to turn his back on offers that could bring him twice as much as the Reds offer, entered the free-agent draft in November.

If there was any question about his future, a photo shoot for a *Sports Illustrated* story confirmed his feelings. Pete posed for photos with the caps of the eight teams he hoped would draft him.

"Ahhh, endorsements," sighed Rose, as he put on the blue

Dodgers cap.

"They *need* me," he beamed, as he tried on a Phillies cap.

"OK, Pete, how about a frown?" the photographer asked.

"You want a frown? I'll give you a frown. Give me the Reds cap."

After a carnival-like tour of baseball cities in pursuit of the best offer from a club he felt he could put over the top, Rose eventually signed with the Phillies for $810,000 annually for four years.

"It is very sad," said former teammate Tony Perez. "Pete Rose, he always was something special. He was the man who put the 'go' in the Machine. I hate to see this team broken up. It was such a great team when it was all together."

The Rose issue had dragged on all fall, marring even the Reds' celebratory trip to Japan in October and November. Wagner had taken his lumps. But on November 27, just a week after Rose had broken off all talks with the Reds, Wagner staggered fans with another bombshell. He fired Sparky Anderson.

If the hiring of the unknown Anderson in 1970 had surprised Cincinnati fans, the firing of the by-now very popular Anderson was unfathomable. The Reds had finished first or second in eight of Anderson's nine seasons. But the signs of discontent had begun to build in 1977.

In spring training, coming off the back-to-back championships, Anderson had softened his training regime. He allowed Rose, Bench, Morgan and some of the other stars to skip the long road trips. Sportswriter Pat Harmon wrote, "What do you say to a high-priced star who has had a super season in 1976 and tells the manager he knows how to prepare himself? In some cases, the manager gives in and Sparky did."

Anderson's training camp in no way resembled the "Stalag 17" camps of the early 1970s.

"The only thing we lead the league in is suntans," sniped Rose at one point in 1977, implying that the club was too laid back.

Anderson did not have the "grip" on the players that he once had, Billingham recalled.

Pete Rose and his attorney Reuven Katz were baffled by the Reds' negotiating stance in 1978.

The Cincinnati Enquirer

The Cincinnati Enquirer

Sparky Anderson returned to Riverfront Stadium to clear out his office after he had been fired by Dick Wagner.

"He got to be too friendly. He couldn't get on them any more.…When you have nine superstars, they almost handle you, instead of you handling them."

"Sparky gave a lot the first few years to cultivate these guys," explained Ray Shore. "Then, later on, it probably wound up costing him his job. When he started to lose, he started to take some of it (privileges) away. Like (players') kids in the clubhouse. Things got out of hand. You'd go in the clubhouse, there were 9,000 people in there. Seaver didn't have any boys to bring in, so he brought in friends, neighbors, and then Pete would have his kids and so on. Then Sparky cut it back to only when we win were the kids allowed. Pete never understood that; he sort of resented it."

Wagner admitted considering a change as early as the summer of 1978. He consulted Howsam about the idea. Because of Howsam's continuing involvement with the organization, Anderson and others assumed he was behind the firing.

"I think Sparky thinks that, but it was not my decision at all," Howsam said. "Dick called me and said he was thinking about making some changes. I said to him, 'The general manager and the manager have to get along. If not, you'll have to do something. But that's your decision to make.' That was my comment and I don't believe that would have fired anybody."

Wagner agreed with Howsam's interpretation of events.

"I talked to Howsam, but he didn't fire him. I don't pass the buck. It was no real mystery. We were in a change in times with our team, in the relationships with players. I was unable to get Sparky to adjust to some things. I would do the same thing again."

It was vintage Wagner, unconcerned with the popularity of the decision, and not given to second-guessing himself. Would Howsam have made the move? It is unlikely that Anderson's magnificent on-field success with the Reds in 1978 would have escaped Howsam's thorough evaluations. Sparky squeezed every victory possible out of his injury-riddled, pitching-impoverished team. But Howsam would not stand in Wagner's way. Howsam was a man who appreciated the customs of organizational settings. Wagner was now in charge. It was his call.

Wagner flew to Los Angeles to meet Anderson in an airport hotel and said simply, "I'm not bringing you back." He offered no reasons and Anderson did not ask. While Anderson was stunned by the move, he recognized Wagner's prerogative to install his own man. To this day, Anderson and Wagner have remained friends.

The departures of Anderson and Rose, on top of the failure of the Reds to maintain the superior performances of 1975-76, jolted the legions of Big Red Machine loyalists. Even though the Reds won a division title in 1979 and finished with baseball's best record in the strike-shortened 1981 season, those clubs were never recognized as part of the Big Red Machine dynasty. They were "little red machines" with no claim to the reign that had preceded them.

But how could any team not suffer in comparison? How could any organization hope to replace a once-in-a-century lineup? In Bench, Rose, Morgan, Perez and Concepcion, the Reds fielded five Hall of Fame-caliber players. *Total Baseball*, the official encyclopedia of Major League Baseball, lists Bench, Rose and Morgan as among the 100 best players of all time. Concepcion and Perez rank among the top 20 or 25 players to ever play at their positions. And, in George Foster, the Reds had the best power hitter in baseball in the mid-1970s. A testament to their greatness is that together they dominate the club's all-time career and single-season records. Few franchises have so many club records held by players who were part of the same starting lineup.

That level of talent is what made the Big Red Machine great—and what made it impossible to prolong.

"You couldn't replace them," Howsam admitted. "Just be happy you had the ballclub like the Big Red Machine."

The Big Red Machine faded faster than it should have because of the Perez trade and the gutting of the pitching staff in 1977. But the disappointment of 1977 and 1978 can neither mask the greatness the team achieved, nor diminish the excellence of the organization Howsam assembled.

In a reflective moment years later, Howsam said of that club, "You could be so proud."

In the context of the statement, he spoke for himself and his organization. This was a team of which you could be exceptionally proud.

But in another sense, he spoke for the fans and history as well. Here was a team that gave baseball everything it could ask. In its dynasty run, the Reds played with a level of enthusiasm, professionalism and skill that had seldom been seen before and has not been rivaled since. The Big Red Machine showcased some of the most compelling personalities in the history of the sport and won two of the the game's most memorable World Series, a nerve-wracking seven-act thriller and a stately four-act coronation. For two glorious seasons the Reds gave a gift of excellence to the fans that is not always granted to every generation.

Here. These seasons are for you. They are for the ages. This is how you play the game.

You could be so proud.

Big Red Machine Scrapbook
1970 – 1978

All-Star Selections

1970
Bench
Merritt
Perez
Rose
Simpson

1971
Bench
Carroll
May
Rose

1972
Bench
Carroll
Morgan
Nolan

1973
Bench
Concepcion
Morgan
Rose

1974
Bench
Morgan

Perez
Rose

1975
Bench
Concepcion
Morgan
Perez
Rose

1976
Bench
Concepcion
Foster
Griffey
Morgan
Perez
Rose

1977
Bench
Concepcion
Foster
Griffey
Morgan
Rose
Seaver

1978
Bench
Concepcion
Foster
Morgan
Rose
Seaver

MVP Award (votes & place finished)

1970
BENCH   326   (1)
Perez   149   (3)
Rose   54   (7)
Tolan   17   (15)
Merritt   21   (21)
Granger   1   (28)

1971
May   28   (12)
Rose   1   (22)

1972
BENCH   263   (1)
Morgan   197   (4)
Rose   19   (11)
Carroll   16   (12)
Tolan   6   (17)

1973
ROSE   274   (1)
Morgan   102   (4)
Perez   59   (7)
Bench   41   (10)
Billingham   6   (21)

1974
Bench   141   (4)
Morgan   72   (8)

Concepcion   5   (15)
Billingham   4   (16)

1975
MORGAN   321½   (1)
Bench   117   (4)
Rose   114   (5)
Perez   18   (15)

1976
MORGAN   311   (1)
Foster   321   (2)
Griffey   49   (7)
Eastwick   26   (11)
Geronimo   3   (22)

1977
FOSTER   291   (1)
Rose   15   (15)
Bench   3   (20)
Seaver   1   (22)

1978
Foster   104   (6)
Rose   35   (11)

Gold Glove Winners

1970
Bench
Helms
Rose

1971
Bench
Helms

1972
Bench

1973
Bench
Morgan

1974
Bench
Morgan
Concepcion
Geronimo

1975
Bench
Morgan
Concepcion
Geronimo

1976
Bench
Morgan
Concepcion
Geronimo

1977
Bench
Morgan
Concepcion
Geronimo

1978
None

Cy Young Award Voting

1970 (10 received votes)
Merritt	4th place
Nolan	5th place
Granger	7th place

1971 (9 received votes)
None

1972 (10 received votes)
Nolan	5th place (tie)
Carroll	5th place (tie)

1973 (7 received votes)
Billingham	4th place
Norman	6th place

1974 (11 received votes)
Billingham	6th place
Gullett	7th place
Carroll	8th place

1975 (7 received votes)
Gullett	5th place

1976 (8 received votes)
Eastwick	5th place

1977 (6 received votes)
Seaver	3rd place

1978 (10 received votes)
None

National League (•) and Major League (••) Leaders

1970
Bench	45	home runs ••
Bench	148	RBIs ••
Rose	205	hits ••
Tolan	57	stolen bases ••
Granger	35	saves •

1971
Gullett	.727	winning % •

1972
Bench	40	home runs ••
Bench	125	RBIs ••
Morgan	122	runs ••
Rose	198	hits ••
Morgan	115	walks ••
Morgan	.419	on-base % •
Nolan	.750	winning % ••
Carroll	37	saves ••

1973
Rose	230	hits ••
Rose	.338	batting average •
Billingham	7	shutouts •

1974
Rose	110	runs ••
Rose	45	doubles ••
Bench	129	RBIs ••
Morgan	.430	on-base % •

1975
Rose	112	runs ••
Rose	47	doubles ••
Morgan	132	walks ••
Morgan	.471	on-base % ••
Gullett	.789	winning % ••
Eastwick	22	saves •

1976
Rose	130	runs ••
Rose	215	hits ••
Rose	42	doubles ••
Foster	121	RBIs ••
Morgan	.453	on-base % ••
Morgan	.576	slugging average ••
Eastwick	26	saves ••

1977
Foster	124	runs •
Foster	52	home runs ••
Foster	149	RBIs ••
Foster	.631	slugging average ••
Seaver *	7	shutouts ••

* includes record with Mets

1978
Rose	51	doubles ••
Foster	40	home runs •
Foster	120	RBIs •

References

The principal sources of information for this book came from interviews with players and club officials, and newspaper stories from 1967 to 1978. Interview subjects are credited in the acknowledgements section.

The primary newspaper source was the clip file of *The Cincinnati Enquirer* which included game accounts, news stories, feature articles and box scores. We also consulted *The Cincinnati Post* and *The Dayton Daily News* for exclusive stories and major news events regarding the Big Red Machine.

Another rich source of information on the era was a weekly newspaper first published in 1974 under the name *Pete Rose's Reds Alert*; it was later published under the names *Reds Alert* and then *Cincinnati Sports Alert*. *Sports Illustrated*, *Sport*, *Baseball Digest* and *The Sporting News* also proved to be valuable sources.

We made extensive use of Cincinnati Reds publications, including yearbooks, media guides and programs from the 1960s and 1970s, and audio and video recordings from 1970 to 1976.

The primary reference for baseball records and statistics was the fourth edition (1995) of *Total Baseball, The Official Encyclopedia of Major League Baseball*, edited by John Thorn and Pete Palmer. Other valuable reference works were *The Baseball Draft: The First 25 Years* (1990), a Baseball America Production, *The Baseball Encyclopedia* (eighth edition, 1990), published by Macmillan Publishing Company, and *The World Series* (1986), by Richard Cohen and David Neft.

Several books provided valuable information and context. In alpahabetical order, by title, they include: *Baseball's Ten Greatest Teams* (1982), by Donald Honig; *Beyond the Sixth Game* (1985), by Peter Gammons; *The Big Red Machine* (1976), by Bob Hertzel; *The Bill James Historical Baseball Abstract* (1985), by Bill James; *Branch Rickey's Little Blue Book* (1995), compiled by John J. Monteleone; *Catch You Later: The Autobiography of Johnny Bench* (1979), by Johnny Bench and William Brashler; *Cincinnati and the Big Red Machine* (1988), by Robert Harris "Hub" Walker; *The Cincinnati Game* (1988), by Lonnie Wheeler and John Baskin; *Cincinnati Seasons* (1987), by Earl Lawson; *Dollar Sign on the Muscle: The World of Baseball Scouting* (reprint edition, 1989), by Kevin Kerrane; *Five Seasons: A Baseball Companion* (1988), by Roger Angell; *Hustle* (1990), by Michael Y. Sokolove; *Joe Morgan: A Life in Baseball* (1993), by Joe Morgan and David Falkner; *Lords of the Realm: The Real History of Baseball* (1994), by John Helyar; *The Main Spark: Sparky Anderson and the Cincinnati Reds* (1978), by Sparky Anderson and Si Burick; *Men of the Machine* (1977 with 1978 update), by Ritter Collett; *October 1964* (1994), by David Halberstam; *Pete Rose* (1975), by Bob Rubin; *Pete Rose: 4192* (1985), by John Erardi; *The Pete Rose Story: An Autobiography* (1970), by Pete Rose; *Places Around the Bases: A Historic Tour of the Coors Field Neighborhood* (1995), by Diane Bakke and Jackie Davis; *The Politics of Glory* (1994), by Bill James; *The Relentless Reds* (1976), by Hal McCoy and Pete Alexis; *The Royal Reds* (1977), by Hal McCoy and Pete Alexis; *Sparky!* (1990), by Sparky Anderson with Dan Ewald; *Voices of the Game* (1987), by Curt Smith.

Subject Index

A's, Oakland
    1972 World Series, 138, 143-149, 151
    and Finley, Charlie, 139, 141, 151
    hair styles, 141
Aaron, Henry
    home run #714, 179-180
Alcala, Santo
    makes Reds, 236, 237, 238
    traded from Reds, 271
All-Star Game
    1970, 89-91
All-Star selections, 13, 200
Anderson, George "Sparky"
    1972 World Series blunder, 146-147
    1975 World Series (Game 6) maneuvering, 213-214
    1975 World Series (Game 6) reaction, 217
    1976 World Series prediction, 249
    batting order, 193, 195
    Captain Hook chart, 197
    Captain Hook nickname, 14, 197
    career statistics, 1953-1969, 79
    childhood, 64-67
    club rules and fines, 268
    clubhouse meetings, 129, 194, 196
    Dodger rivalry, 180-182
    evaluating players, 113
    fired by Reds, 285, 287-289
    and Grimsley, 167
    hired by Reds, 74-78
    hired by St. Louis Cardinals, 72
    hitting "streak", 281
    minor league manager, 64, 71-74
    Morgan trade, 118-119, 121
    Perez trade, 265-266
    pitching staff, 82, 84-85, 197-199
    playing career, 67-71
    rates Big Red Machine, 255-256
    Rose move to third base, 191-192
    Rose-Bench feud, 131
    San Diego coach, 74
    speed vs. power, 133
    spring training
        1970, 80-81
        1976, 231-232
        1978, 279
    starting lineup, 195
    support from Howsam, 107
    team chemistry, 126-127
    team rules, 124, 142
    temper, 72-74
    third-base dilemma, 189, 191
Armbrister, Ed
    Fisk collision, 209-210
    traded to Reds, 119
Astroturf, 14, 87, 89, 111
Bench, Johnny
    1970 MVP, 99
    1972 MVP, 130
    1972 playoff home run, 137
    1976 World Series (Game 4) home run, 258
    1976 World Series MVP, 258
    childhood, 29-31
    clubhouse meeting, 194
    defensive skills, 131-132
    injuries, 240, 284
    lung surgery, 136-137
    minor leagues, 32-35
    Perez-Bench home run duo, 266
    popularity, 130
    post-season heroics, summary, 257
    Rose feud, 130-131
    salary negotiations, 103, 154-155, 167
    scouts, 32
Bender, Sheldon "Chief"
    and Anderson, 72-74, 76, 78
    early career, 54-55
    farm system, 176, 178
    joins Reds, 53
    Rose move to third base, 192
    salary negotiations, 103-104, 168
    Tolan suspension, 159
Big Red Machine
    1976 statistics, 243, 245
    1977 salaries, 268
    batting order, 193-194
        1975–table, 195
        1976–table, 239
    bench strength, 240-241
    bullpen, 14, 197-199
    confidence and pride, 241-242
    decline, 262, 282
        chart, 285
        offensive production, 276, 284
        starting pitching, 271-272, 283-284
    dynasty team, 8-9, 14-15
    minor leagues, players in–chart, 36-37
    origin of name, 84
    pitching, 243
    pitching staff, 199
    place in history, 8-9, 13, 15, 289
    starting eight, 9, 11, 13-14, 195
        chart, 12
        projected 162-game record, 239

starting lineups, 241
    1975–table, 195
    1976–table, 239
starting pitching, 13-14, 196-200
team chemistry, 126, 264, 270-271, 275, 282-283

Billingham, Jack
    early career, 117
    Rose at third base, 193
    traded from Reds, 279
    traded to Reds, 118

Borbon, Pedro
    club barber, 167
    Major League debut, 85
    pitching signs, 199
    Rose-Harrelson fight, 161-162
    traded to Reds, 59

Bowen, Joe
    hired by Howsam, 54, 170-171

Bowen, Rex
    evaluating prospects, 173
    hired by Howsam, 54, 170-171

Brennaman, Marty
    1975 playoff broadcast, 203-204
    1976 playoff broadcast, 247
    1976 World Series broadcast, 258
    1975 clubhouse meeting, 194, 196
    comes to Reds, 169
    Rose move to third base, 193
    and Wagner, 169, 229-230

Carbo, Bernie
    1970 World Series, 96-97
    1975 World Series home run, 213-214
    sophomore "jinx", 124
    traded from Reds, 125

Carroll, Clay
    early career, 140
    relief record, 140
    traded from Reds, 236
    traded to Reds, 58

Concepcion, David
    1976 World Series, 258
    dryer episode, 237
    Hall of Fame candidate, 177
    injuries, 157
    and Kapstein, 267
    minor leagues, 178
    part-time starter, 125, 130
    salary negotiations, 267-268
    wins starting job, 155

Cy Young Award, 13

Dale, Francis "Frank"
    purchases Reds, 51
    hires Howsam, 52

Darcy, Pat
    1975 World Series (Game 6), 215-216
    Captain Hook, 196-198
    minor leagues, 176

DeWitt, William
    ownership of Reds, 49-50
    Robinson, Frank trade, 50
    selling of Reds, 51
    signs Shore, 106

Dodgers, Brooklyn
    dynasty team, 8, 9, 13, 255-256
    training ground for Anderson, 67-68, 70-71, 182

Dodgers, Los Angeles
    Lasorda, Tommy, 180, 182
    Reds-Dodgers rivalry, 180-183
    starting lineups, 1973-78, 182
    trade talks with Reds, 114

Driessen, Dan
    injury, 284
    Perez trade, factor in, 264-265
    scouted by Reds, 172
    third base, 155, 184

Dynasty teams
    Baltimore Orioles, 13
    Brooklyn Dodgers, 8-9, 13, 255-256
    chart, 10-11
    New York Yankees, 8-9, 13, 256
    ranking, 14

Eastwick, Rawly
    makes Reds, 191
    salary negotiations, 267
    traded from Reds, 274
    vetoes trade to Mets, 273

Evans, Dwight
    1975 World Series (Game 6) defense, 215

Fisk, Carlton
    1975 World Series (Game 6) home run, 216
    Armbrister collision, 209-210

Foster, George
    1972 playoffs, scores winning run, 138
    1975 World Series (Game 6) defense, 215
    1976 season, 238, 240
    1977 season statistics, 271
    becomes starter, 193
    minor leagues, 179
    sent to Indianapolis, 155
    traded to Reds, 109-110

Fryman, Woody
    leaves Reds, 275
    traded to Reds, 263

Geronimo, Cesar
    early career, 117
    injury, 284
    traded to Reds, 118-119

Gold Glove Award, 13

Griffey, Ken
    1976 batting title race, 243
    1976 World Series (Game 2) winning run, 252-253
    bats 2nd in lineup, 193-194
    minor leagues, 178, 179
    scouted by Reds, 173

Grimsley, Ross
    1972 playoff victory, 134
    hair style, 167
    traded from Reds, 165

Gullett, Don
　　Big Red Machine record, 197
　　free agency, 235
　　free agent, 262
　　hepatitis, 129
　　injuries 196, 249-250, 262
　　and Kapstein, 234-235
　　makes Reds, 82
　　salary negotiations, 168, 234-235
Hall of Fame, 13-14, 177
Howsam, Robert
　　1967 season, 57
　　1968 season, 58
　　1969 season, 59
　　1972 World Series, 151
　　1973 playoff riot, 163, 165
　　1975 World Championship, 221-222
　　1976 free-agent draft, 263
　　1976 World Championship, reaction, 262
　　1976 World Series (Game 2) weather, 251
　　1976 World Series security, 253
　　1977 free-agent draft, 276
　　agents, 234
　　American Football League, 47
　　Anderson firing, 288
　　Astroturf, 87, 89, 111
　　attendance records, 226-227
　　basketball, off-season, 102
　　Bears Stadium, 43
　　and Bristol, Dave, 52, 61
　　changes Reds' logo, 143
　　childhood, 40
　　Continental League, 47
　　Denver Bears, 43-44
　　evaluating players, 112-115
　　farm system, 176, 178
　　hires Anderson, 64, 75-77, 79
　　hires Bowen brothers, 170-171
　　joins Reds, 51-52
　　and Kapstein, 168, 234
　　labor issues, 233
　　1972 strike, 127, 129
　　arbitration, 168
　　free agency, 233, 262-263
　　marketing philosophy, 231
　　marriage and family, 41-42
　　minor league visits, 176, 178
　　motivational techniques, 179
　　organizes front office, 52-54
　　player's appearance, 141-143
　　promotions, 44, 56
　　"Reds-type" player, 174
　　resigns, 277-278
　　restocking a club, 83
　　and Rickey, Branch, 44-46
　　Riverfront Stadium, 86-87, 89, 111
　　Rose move to third base, 192
　　salary negotiations, 102-103, 155, 170
　　　　satire, 190
　　scouting, 171-173, 175
　　scouting department, 55, 170
　　speed vs. power, 133
　　St. Louis Cardinals, 47-48
　　Straight-A program, 231-232
　　ticket prices, 231
　　trades, 48, 57-59, 92, 102, 188, 277
　　　　chart, 1967-1969, 61
　　　　Foster trade, 107-109
　　　　Morgan trade, 110-116, 118-119, 121
　　　　Nelson, Roger trade, 154
　　　　Norman trade, 156
　　　　Perez trade, 264-265
　　　　Perez trade talks, 188
　　　　Seaver trade, 273
　　Vida Blue deal, 276-277
　　walkie-talkie controversy, 250
　　and Weiss, George, 46-47
　　Western League, 42-43, 53
Kapstein, Jerry
　　background, 234
　　and Bender, 168
　　and Concepcion, 267
　　and Gullett, 168, 234-235
　　and Howsam, 168, 234
　　and McEnaney, 267
　　and Perez, 168
　　shunned by Reds, 272
　　and Wagner, 168, 267
Katz, Reuven
　　1977 Rose negotiations, 269
　　1978 Rose negotiations, 285-286
　　and Rose, 104
King, Hal
　　1973 home run, 156-157
Kuhn, Bowie
　　1972 World Series, 149
　　1976 World Series (Game 2) weather, 251
　　Vida Blue deal, 277
Major League Baseball
　　1976 lockout, 235
　　free agency, 233, 262
　　labor issues, 84, 127, 129, 168, 233, 235
　　popularity of, 226
May, Lee
　　rookie year, 57
　　leadership qualities, 125
　　traded to Houston, 116, 118
McEnaney, Will
　　1975 World Series (Game 6), 214-215
　　1975 World Series (Game 7) final out, 220-221
　　major league debut, 201-202
　　minor leagues, 176, 178, 200-201
　　salary negotiations, 267
　　scouted by Reds, 172-173
　　signed by Reds, 173
　　traded from Reds, 263, 266
McIntire, Jim
　　1970 playoff broadcast, 94
McRae, Hal
　　1972 playoffs, 138
　　traded from Reds, 154
Merritt, Jim

injury, 91
traded from Reds, 125
traded to Reds, 59
twenty-game winner, 14, 91
Mets, New York
   1973 playoff riot, 163, 165
   1973 playoffs, 159-163, 165
   Harrelson, Bud-Rose fight, 161-162
Michaels, Al
   1972 playoff broadcast, 137-138
   leaves Reds, 169
   and Wagner, 229
Morgan, Joe
   1972 World Series (Game 7), aborted rally, 149-150
   1975 World Series (Game 7) winning hit, 220
   1976 MVP, 242
   bats 3rd in lineup, 193-194
   Bench's defense, 131-132
   injuries, 181, 194, 284
   offensive weapon, 242-243
   stolen base "tutor", 202-203
   team chemistry, 126-127
   traded to Reds, 114-119, 121
Most Valuable Player Award
   Bench, 1970, 99
   Bench, 1972, 130
   and dynasty teams, 12-13
   Morgan, 1976, 242
   Rose, 1973, 160
National League
   playoffs
      1970, 93-94
      1972, 132, 134-138
      1973, 159-163, 165
      1975, 202-203
      1976, 245-247
      saves vs. complete games–graph, 197
      stolen bases-home run–graph, 133
Nippert, Louis
   contract negotiations, satire, 190
   purchases Reds, 156
   Rose negotiations, 286
Nolan, Gary
   Big Red Machine record, 197
   injuries, 130, 179, 189, 271
   salary negotiations, 267
   traded from Reds, 274
Norman, Fred
   traded to Reds, 156
Orioles, Baltimore
   1970 World Series, 94, 96-99
   dynasty team, 96
Perez, Atanasio "Tony"
   1975 World Series (Game 7) home run, 217, 219
   1976 World Series (Game 2) winning hit, 252-253
   Bench-Perez home run duo, 266
   childhood, 24-25
   clubhouse leadership, 264, 270-271, 275, 282
   minor leagues, 25-29
   salary negotiations, 168, 235-236
   scouts, 25
   trade rumors, 188
   traded from Reds, 263-267
Phillies, Philadelphia
   1976 playoffs, 245-247
Pirates, Pittsburgh
   1970 playoffs, 93-94
   1972 playoffs, 132, 134-138
   1975 playoffs, 202-203
Rapp, Vernon
   and McEnaney, 200-201
   minor league manager, 200
Red Sox, Boston
   1975 lineup, 204, 206
   1975 World Series, 204, 206-217, 219-221
   Fenway Park, "Green Monster", 206
   history, 204
Reds, Cincinnati
   1967 season, 57
   1968 season, 58
   1969 season, 59
   1970 World Series, 94, 96-99
   1972 playoffs, 132, 134-138
   1972 World Series, 143-149, 151
   1973 playoffs, 159-163, 165
   1975 lineup questions, 189
   1975 playoffs, 202-203
   1975 World Series, 204, 206-217, 219-221
   1976 playoffs, 245-247
   1976 World Series, 248-259
   attendance, 226-227
   clinch 1975 division title, 202
   clinch 1976 division title, 242
   Dodger rivalry, 180-183
   draft chart, 1965-1969, 58
   evaluating players, 275-276
   failure to meet expectations, 184
   farm system, 176
      failure, 276
   gift shop, 232
   injuries, 105
   Japan trip, 287
   lack of bench production, 284-285
   logos, 143-144
   minor leagues, 200-201
   Morgan trade announced, 119, 121
   Parker, Dave as prospect, 174-175
   pitching problems, 91, 271-272, 274-276, 283-284
   pitching staff, 82, 84-85, 130, 197-199
   player's appearance, 141-143
   promotions, 231-232
   radio network, 229-230
   regional market, 228
   salaries, 1972-73, 128
   salary negotiations, 190, 267-268

scouting, 170-173, 175
speaker's bureau, 228
speed emphasis, 173-174
speed vs. power, 133
team chemistry, 132
third-base dilemma, 188
Venezuela trip, 127
vs. Dodgers in 1976, 238
win 1970 pennant, 94
win 1972 pennant, 138
win 1975 pennant, 204
win 1976 pennant, 247
winning percentage by month, 237
Riverfront Stadium
    characteristics, 111
    opening, 86-87, 89
    planning, 50
Robinson, Brooks
    1970 Series MVP, 99
Rose, Pete
    1973 MVP, 160
    1975 World Series (Game 6) reaction, 216-217
    1975 World Series (Game 7) baserunning, 217-218
    1975 World Series MVP, 220
    1976 lockout, 235
    3,000th hit, 280
    44-game hit streak, 280-282
    baserunning, 246-247
    Bench feud, 130-131
    childhood, 18-21
    Fosse, Ray, collision, 89-91
    free-agent, 286
    gambling rumors, 286
    Harrelson, Bud fight, 161-162
    hustle, 83
    minor leagues, 21-23
    named captain, 78
    salary negotiations, 104, 128, 155, 167, 190, 268-269
    scouts, 20-21
    signs with Phillies, 287
    team chemistry, 126
    third-base move, 191-193
Ruhl, Roger
    1972 playoffs, 136
    hired by Reds, 53-54
    marketing philosophy, 231
    Morgan trade, 121
    promotions, 232
Scherger, George
    early career, 68
    Rose move to third base, 193
Seaver, Tom
    1977 Reds record, 274
    1978 record, 283
    traded to Reds, 273
Shepard, Larry
    pitching staff, 84-85, 198-199
Shore, Ray
    1972 Series scouting report, 146
    1976 playoffs scouting report, 245-246
    1976 World Series scouting reports, 248-249
    advance scout, 106, 108
    Carroll, Clay, 58
    early career, 106
    evaluating players, 113
    Foster, 155
    Foster trade, 109-110
    Morgan trade, 115-116
    Nelson, Roger trade, 154
    role in trades, 106, 109
    scouting reports, 124
Simpson, Wayne
    drafted by Reds, 55
    early career, 93
    injury, 91
    traded from Reds, 125, 154
Starting Eights, Greatest
    chart, 12
    1927 Yankees, 12
    1929 Athletics, 12
    1938 Yankees, 12
    1955 Dodgers, 12
    1976 Reds, 12
Tolan, Bobby
    1972 World Series (Game 7) misplays, 148-149
    injuries, 102, 107, 111-112, 149
    suspension, 157-159
    traded to Reds, 59
Wagner, Richard
    agents, 234
    crowd control, 1972 playoffs, 138
    early career, 53
    enforcing club rules, 143
    fires Anderson, 285, 287-289
    hires Brennaman, 169
    joins Reds, 53
    and Kapstein, 168, 267
    market research, 230
    marketing the Reds, 227-232
    named president and GM, 277-278
    radio network, 229-230
    Rose negotiations, 269, 285-286
    salary negotiations, 168, 170, 267
Williams, William J.
    interviews Howsam, 51
World Series
    1970, 94, 96-99
    1972, 143-149, 151
    1975, 204, 206-217, 219-221
    1976, 247-259
Yankees, New York
    1976 lineup, 248
    1976 World Series, 247-258
    dynasty teams, 8-9, 13
    walkie-talkie controversy, 250
Zachry, Pat
    makes Reds, 236, 237, 238
    success against Dodgers, 238
    traded from Reds, 273

About the Authors

Big Red Dynasty is the third collaborative effort by Greg Rhodes and John Erardi. Despite this, they remain on good terms.

Their first book was *The First Boys of Summer: The 1869-70 Cincinnati Red Stockings*, published in 1994 on the 125th anniversary of the beginning of the professional game.

Their second book, *Crosley Field: The Illustrated History of a Classic Ballpark*, was published in 1995, on the 25th anniversary of the final game at Cincinnati's historic baseball field. *Crosley Field* was named one of the 10 best baseball books of 1995 by *Spitball* magazine.

Rhodes, a baseball historian, is a native of Richmond, Indiana, and holds an Ed.D. from the School of Education at Indiana University. He is a former teacher and author of curriculum materials. He has also written numerous articles and edited *Baseball in Cincinnati: From Wooden Fences to Astroturf*, a 1988 publication of the Cincinnati Historical Society. He lives in Cincinnati, with his wife, Sallie, son, Ben, and daughter, Kara. He considers the fifth game of the 1972 playoffs the finest baseball game he has ever seen.

Erardi, a sportswriter for *The Cincinnati Enquirer* since 1985, first began working for the paper in 1974 in the heart of the dynasty run of the Big Red Machine. He grew up in Syracuse, New York, and is an alumnus of the U.S. Naval Academy, Murray State University and Chase College of Law at Northern Kentucky University. He is author of *Pete Rose: 4,192* and several special sections for *The Enquirer*, including "Cincinnati and the Negro Leagues," which was named the best feature story in an Ohio newspaper in 1993 by the Associated Press. He is a three-time national award winner of the Associated Press Sports Editors (APSE). He lives in Crescent Springs, Kentucky, with his wife, Barb, and son, Christopher. He regards Tony Perez as the Most Valuable Red of the Big Red Machine era, and ranks Perez's two-run home run off Bill Lee in the seventh game of the 1975 World Series as the most important hit in Reds history.

To order additional copies of *Big Red Dynasty*, call 1-800-232-9900, or address inquiries to: Road West Publishing Company, 1908 Dexter Avenue, Cincinnati, OH 45206.